AMERICAN POLITICAL LEADERS
EDITED BY ALLAN NEVINS

RUTHERFORD B. HAYES
By H. J. Eckenrode

THOMAS B. REED
By William A. Robinson

JAMES A. GARFIELD
By Robert Granville Caldwell

JOHN G. CARLISLE
By James A. Barnes

In preparation

GROVER CLEVELAND
By Allan Nevins

CARL SCHURZ
By Claude M. Fuess

ANDREW JOHNSON
By St. George L. Sioussat

JOSEPH G. CANNON
By William Allen White

CHESTER A. ARTHUR
By George F. Howe

THEODORE ROOSEVELT
By Charles R. Lingley

JAMES G. BLAINE
By David S. Muzzey

ROBERT M. LaFOLLETTE
By Frederick C. Howe

SAMUEL J. TILDEN
By Alexander C. Flick

JOHN HAY
By Tyler Dennett

WILLIAM McKINLEY
By Geoffrey Parsons

GEORGE FRISBIE HOAR
By Frederick H. Gillett

WILLIAM JENNINGS BRYAN
By Henry Steele Commager

ULYSSES S. GRANT
By William B. Hesseltine

JAMES ABRAM GARFIELD AT THE AGE OF SIXTEEN

JAMES A. GARFIELD

Party Chieftain

By

ROBERT GRANVILLE CALDWELL

DODD, MEAD & COMPANY

New York   *1931*

PRINTED IN THE UNITED STATES OF AMERICA
BY THE VAIL-BALLOU PRESS, INC., BINGHAMTON, N. Y.

PREFACE

The career of James A. Garfield is perhaps more clearly than that of any other single individual a summary of the course of American political history from 1861 to 1881. Where can we find another statesman who, after taking an active share in the actual fighting in the field, came into Congress at a great crisis to bear his part in the determination of so many national questions? Reconstruction, the tariff, the greenbacks, the period of scandals, the contested election of 1876, the question of the election laws, are all topics in Garfield's life as they are in the history of the nation. Without minimizing inevitable mistakes and failures, for Garfield was very human, we shall find him growing through the years, gaining from the high office of the Presidency the added dignity and vision which a position as the chief executive has also given to other men, and at length becoming ennobled by a nation's sympathy.

Garfield had, like Jefferson, a genius for making friends, and naturally found also his enemies. The mere list of these, Hinsdale, Cox, Dana, Lincoln, Chase, Stanton, Butler, Sherman, Black, Thurman, and the rest makes his life especially worthy of consideration.

For his boyhood until the date when the Garfield papers begin, one still needs to depend on published lives, many of which, notably Bundy's, Riddle's, and above all Smith's, contain materials derived in part from Garfield or documents not now available. Then public documents become increasingly useful, and the later chapters can rest principally on contemporary materials in various collections. These are referred to in the bibliography.

The author desires to express his special obligations to Mr. James Garfield of Mentor, Ohio, for placing the papers of his distinguished father in the Library of Congress, where they will furnish an almost unexampled mine of information to future historians; to President Harry Garfield of Williams College for generous and unrestricted permission to use these papers; to Professor Robert M. McElroy of Oxford University for similar permission to use the Morton papers; to Dr. J. Franklin Jameson, Dr. T. P. Martin, and Dr. C. W. Garrison of the manuscripts division, Library of Congress, and to Mr. W. R. Leech of the New York Public Library, who have been most generous in their assistance. The Rev. A. Ellwood Corning of Newburgh brought to the author's attention materials which he would otherwise have overlooked. Above all, he is indebted to Professor Allan Nevins for important suggestions and assistance at every stage in the preparation of this biography and to his wife, Edith R. Caldwell, who has undertaken the laborious tasks of proofreading and the preparation of the index. His list of obligations would not be complete without the mention of a generous leave of absence for which he is indebted to the President and Board of Trustees of the Rice Institute and which made possible the completion of this biography at this time.

R. G. C.

New York
Aug. 1, 1931.

CONTENTS

CHAPTER   PAGE

I   ANCESTRY AND BOYHOOD   I

Garfield in 1880 and today—The Garfields and the Ballous—
Eliza Ballou and Abram Garfield—Birth—The Western Reserve
—Religious backgrounds—Boyhood experiences—The adventure
on the Ohio canal.

II   ACADEMY AND COLLEGE   17

An Academy in the fifties—Garfield at Geauga—The school
teacher—Conversion—A visit to Southern Ohio—The Western
Reserve Eclectic Institute—Books and friends—First love—Alexander Campbell—Lucretia Rudolph—Williams College—The influence of Mark Hopkins—College friends—Graduation.

III   THE EVANGELIST   39

Hiram College—The transition to evangelism—Garfield and
Dunshee—Engagement and marriage—The debate with John
Denton—Public lectures—"Saving boys for education"—Typical
sermons—A portrait of Garfield.

IV   THE POLITICIAN   51

The path to public office—The candidate for the legislature—
Views of old friends—Ohio in 1859—The political strategy of
the Republicans—William Dennison—Garfield in Louisville—
Secession—An early estimate of Lincoln—The militia—Garfield
defeated for a colonelcy—He enters the army.

V   THE SOLDIER   70

Garfield at Camp Chase—Recruiting a regiment—Colonel
Garfield of the Forty Second Ohio—Buell in Kentucky—Thomas
and Garfield—Buell's orders—Humphrey Marshall—The Campaign on the Big Sandy—The battle of Middle Creek—Conflicting reports—Garfield becomes a brigadier-general—His early
views of West Point men—Pittsburgh Landing—Corinth—The
Turchin trial—Return to Hiram.

VI   AN INTERLUDE IN WASHINGTON   90

The nineteenth congressional district in 1862—The nomination
for Congress—Garfield visits Washington—Criticisms of Lincoln
—Salmon P. Chase—The Emancipation Proclamation—Garfield
elected—Ambitions for an independent command—The trial of
Fitz-John Porter—Military studies.

VII   GARFIELD AND ROSECRANS   106

Garfield at the headquarters of Rosecrans—The friendship of
the two men—Chief of Staff—Garfield's admiration for his
commander—The Streight expedition—Rejected advice—The

vii

CONTENTS

Tullahoma campaign—Garfield's first criticism—Chattanooga—
Chickamauga—The mistaken order—Garfield's ride—General
Thomas—Renewed criticisms—Charles A. Dana—The broken
friendship.

VIII THE CONGRESSMAN 131
Washington in October 1863—Henry Winter Davis—Lincoln's
advice—A visit to Hiram—The military committee—Fellow congressmen—Significance of Garfield's safe district—Views of Lincoln in 1863—Lincoln's plan of reconstruction—Garfield favors
confiscation—Provisions for a national army—The reply to Long
—The Wade-Davis manifesto—Garfield on Lincoln, 1865, 1866,
1878.

IX RECONSTRUCTION 157
Three major problems—Johnson's plan—Garfield on negro
suffrage—Garfield and Cox—New members—Garfield and Johnson—"The States are only geographical divisions"—The Milligan case—Jeremiah Black—Garfield's dilemma—Garfield in
the campaign of 1866—Military governments—Impeachment of
Johnson—The controversy with General Hancock—The Clark
election case—Garfield's views of reconstruction in 1877 and 1879.

X WIDER INTERESTS 183
The home life of Garfield—An incident at Mentor—Garfield
and Education—Garfield as a lawyer—The Campbell will case
—Legal associates—The insurance cases—Garfield's early position on the tariff—The tariff problem in 1867 and 1872—Increasing orthodoxy—His position in 1880.

XI THE GREENBACKS AND THE BONDS 202
Congress and the Greenbacks—Garfield's consistency on this
subject—How the problem arose—Arguments for inflation—Garfield's argument in 1866—His demand for "honest money"—Garfield investigates "Black Friday"—Committee on Appropriations
—His opposition to the free coinage of silver—The Bland-
Allison act—The resumption of specie payments.

XII THE SCANDALS OF 1873 219
The Credit Mobilier charges—Oakes Ames—Garfield's sweeping denial—Effects of the charges in the campaign of 1872—The
conflicting testimony of Garfield and Ames—The Report of the
Poland committee—Newspaper criticisms—Garfield and the increase of salaries—The De Golyer pavement charges—Investigation by two committees—Garfield in the campaign of 1874—
The results of the attacks on Garfield.

XIII THE PARTY CHIEFTAIN 245
Garfield's decision on a Democratic offer—Garfield as a party
leader—His replies to Hill and to Lamar—The Belknap scandals
—Garfield in New Orleans—The Electoral Commission—The
Wormley Conference—Garfield as the spokesman of Hayes—
The Potter Committee—The election laws—"An attempted rev-
olution in congress"—Garfield's authorship of a veto message—

CHAPTER   PAGE

Renewed attacks on the election laws—Garfield taken at his
word—Election to the Senate—A summary of eighteen years in
the House.

XIV   THE CANDIDATE   278
Garfield and Sherman—Suggestions of the Presidency—The
plans of Wharton Barker—Garfield assumes command of anti-
Grant forces—His reply to Conkling—The speech for Sherman
—The nomination of Garfield—The letter of acceptance—A visit
to New York—The strategy of silence—The contest for Indiana
—Hancock's interview on the tariff—The effects of the Morey
letter—The hospitality of Mentor—Victory.

XV   THE PRESIDENT   312
A visit from Hayes—The choice of Blaine—The problem of
the Treasury—Sherman—Levi P. Morton—An ultimatum from
the West—Robert T. Lincoln—The reasons for Conkling's insistence—Conkling comes to Mentor—Disappointments—The
inauguration—The cabinet completed—Relations of Garfield
to cabinet members—Windom—Blaine—James—McVeagh—The
plague of office seekers—The Star Route frauds—The appointment of W. H. Robertson.

XVI   THE TRAGEDY   349
Garfield in the White House—The illness of Mrs. Garfield—
A visit to Elberon—Charles J. Guiteau—Attitude of the People
—The illness of Garfield—Mistakes of the doctors—The return
to Elberon—Death of Garfield—Blaine's eulogy—Personal qualities of Garfield—Garfield's mistakes—His achievements—His
place in history.

BIBLIOGRAPHY   365

INDEX   375

ILLUSTRATIONS

James Abram Garfield at the age of sixteen . . . . *Frontispiece*

FACING PAGE

Garfield's mother 44

Garfield's wife 44

The soldier 82

The Congressman 82

Plan of Chickamauga battle-field 114

Oakes Ames 226

Jeremiah S. Black 226

Every public question with an eye only to the public good . . . 234

Garfield as a presidential candidate 282

Forbidding the Banns 290

Major-General W. S. Hancock 298

William H. English 298

In line at last 304

The forged Morey letter . . . . *Following* 306

A genuine letter from General James A. Garfield . . . *Following* 306

"From the tow-path to the White House" 314

President Garfield and his Cabinet 322

The national barber shop. "Next!" 338

A humiliating spectacle 346

JAMES A. GARFIELD
PARTY CHIEFTAIN

THE election of James Abram Garfield of Ohio to the Presidency of the United States in the year 1880 and his tragic death the following year led to an unprecedented demand for biographies of the dead hero. Journalists, clergymen and college professors entered the field, and within two years, twelve lives had appeared. One of these, badly written and depending for its facts largely on the exuberant imagination of the author, was even published in London, and under the appealing title, "From Log Cabin to White House," was sold to thousands of Englishmen and in as many months had passed through seven editions. Another entitled "From the Towpath to the White House" was equally popular in America. But the Garfield legend had none of that persistent vitality which was already beginning to give to the name of Lincoln its unique position in American thought. The interest in Garfield disappeared almost as quickly as it had arisen. The first serious life was to be published more than forty years after the death of its subject, and though based on a thorough knowledge of the documents, had none of the great popular appeal which had carried the earlier books through their various editions.[1] In the years that lay between, and somewhat unjustly, Garfield had become dimly known, a minor and almost discredited figure in the history of his generation. An incident of his boyhood on the Ohio canal, a vague memory that his name was once connected with unpleasant scandals in a period which teemed with many, the picture of a massive figure falling under an assassin's bullet in the

[1] The chief source for the correspondence of Garfield is T. C. Smith's extremely full *Life and Letters of Garfield*, New Haven, 1925. A typical early biography is W. M. Thayer, *From Log Cabin to White House*, Seventh Edition, London, 1882.

old railroad station in Washington, had left a significant career almost as little known as that of his murderer, Guiteau.

And yet the instinctive interest of his own contemporaries in a warm and compelling personality was sound—not because his character was without a flaw or his career entirely unsullied, but because Garfield developed in pioneer conditions and lived through and helped to mold one of the most significant revolutions in American social and political life.

The poverty of the frontier, unlike that of the great industrial cities which were beginning to arise before the death of Garfield, was often a mere prelude to wealth and opportunity. In giving their homage to Lincoln and to Garfield, the Americans of the closing decades of the nineteenth century were looking back half wistfully to a period that was none the less ended because it was still within the memory of living men and paying lip service to a type of democracy in which the poorest was the potential equal of the wealthy and the well endowed. Hence the numerous biographies in which the poor canal boy was seen in command of armies, holding great crowds spellbound by his eloquence, moulding the policy of a nation, and reaching at last the post to which the names of Washington, Jefferson, Jackson and Lincoln had given so great prestige. Very soon the frontier had disappeared, the log cabin had ceased to be a potent talisman, wealth and early education were increasingly respected, and such careers as that of Garfield came to seem less real and vital. Only Lincoln's literary genius and his commanding position in a dramatic crisis had saved his great name from a similar neglect.

There were points of curious likeness between the early lives of Garfield and of Lincoln. But at the very outset there was a fundamental difference. Thomas Lincoln was undoubtedly typical of the first wave of settlement into the frontier. His restlessness, his frequent changes of abode, his failure to establish himself definitely on a given piece of land, his tendency to leave the institutional beginnings of church and school to his successors, his lack of knowledge of or interest in his ancestors were to be repeated many times in other lives on the first settled frontier. To this day, despite the immense interest of the subject, the student of Lincoln is greatly puzzled to establish the details of his heredity or birth.

The habits of the Garfields and the Ballous were quite different, and were equally typical of the second wave of settlement which in the Western Reserve of Ohio was just coming to a close when James Abram Garfield was born. They seldom arrived in a community until their predecessors were already abandoning their clearings in the forest; they always secured a modest piece of land in fee simple and remained at least one generation before new opportunities lured them further into the opening west; their children were often born in log cabins, but these were merely temporary and within the lifetime of the parents had given way to more substantial houses of frame or brick, built on the same site or at least in the same neighborhood; their neighbors came from the same towns in Massachusetts to New York, and from New York to Ohio, and were frequently kinsmen, married brothers and sisters, uncles and cousins; they built school houses on the corners of their farms, and boarded the visiting teachers; they organized meeting houses and churches and sometimes under strange new names perpetuated in the west the religious habits and ideals which were already passing away "back home" in Massachusetts; above all they never had the slightest doubt about their family history carefully preserved in the family Bible. There was none of that individualistic carelessness as to marriage certificates or dates or places of birth which help to puzzle the student of scores of biographies of settlers of the first wave.

Garfield knew perfectly well from his mother that he be-

longed to the ninth generation of American Garfields, that his
ancestor Edward Garfield had settled at Watertown, Massachusetts, as early as 1635, and that one of the Garfields had
fought in the Revolution. He also knew that on his mother's
side he was seventh in line from one Mathurin Ballou, who had
reached Rhode Island soon after the revocation of the edict
of Nantes in 1685.

It was especially characteristic of the religious development
of the country that while the New England Ballous under the
leadership of their distinguished relative, Hosea Ballou, were
seeking to reform religion in the name of Universalism and
under the inspiration of the rationalism of the early nineteenth
century, the Ohio Ballous, like thousands of their neighbors in
the west, were joining a new denomination, called "Campbellites" after its founder, who hoped to reunite all Christians by
turning from creeds and rational statements of Christianity to
the essential Puritan basis of the literal acceptance of divinely-
inspired scriptures. When Garfield went back to New England
to go to college, he was regarded as a strange product of the
new west because he called himself a follower of Alexander
Campbell. Actually the religious and social ideals of old New
England had continued to live among her children in the
Western Reserve when in many parts of Massachusetts they
had already been partially forgotten.

For, in many ways, the function of pioneer life in the west
was not to change but to preserve and perpetuate ideals and
forms of thought that would otherwise have yielded more
quickly to the hand of time. Thus, Garfield's friend and teacher,
Amelia Booth, was often called the Margaret Fuller of the
Western Reserve, but the two women certainly resembled each
other in very little save a common love of letters and the accident of sex. Miss Booth would have been deeply pained by
ideas which were the very commonplaces of the thought of

Margaret Fuller. At the same moment when Ralph Waldo Emerson was the foremost religious leader in the thought of New England, Alexander Campbell held an almost equally powerful position of leadership in the new west. But any reader of the writings of the two men will realize at once that Campbell was spiritually older than Emerson by at least a hundred years.

The Garfields and the Ballous, settled side by side in the woods of northern Ohio, did not push their study of their ancestors beyond the first who had settled in America early or late in the seventeenth century. Whether the first Garfield had been of Welsh or pure English stock was a problem that interested none of them until Garfield himself attempted to solve it on the occasion of his one brief visit to England in 1868. It was characteristic of the spirit of a new and less democratic generation that he should then think the problem important and take a boyish pride in finding some dim evidence of descent from crusading ancestors. But with all the characteristic pride in ancestry which later led to the creation of such societies as the Sons and Daughters of the Revolution, there was a curious scarcity of records of pre-American beginnings. The prejudices which had been engendered by two wars with England, and in many cases a wise forbearance, have kept most American families from pushing their researches too far across the waste of waters. A typical American family of the middle of the nineteenth century begins with a colonial ancestor as clearly as the human race begins with Adam. The Ballous took pride in their ancestor, the Huguenot, Mathurin. They knew much about his life in Rhode Island. But about what he had done or where he had lived in France, they knew little and cared less.

The Garfield men were tall and strong. Garfield's grandfather left a reputation as a wrestler, a sport which was greatly admired on the frontier; his father, like himself was almost six

feet tall and had the same genial manners which were to serve
the son so well in a career of politics. The Ballous, true to their
French extraction, were slight and dark. There was a tradition
in the family that the Ballous were more intellectually keen
than the Garfields, a tradition which seems to have little to
support it save the celebrity of the founder of Universalism.
But slightly educated as they were, both Eliza Ballou and her
mother, in bringing up in two successive generations of orphan
children, showed courage of a type which was fortunately common among the women of the frontier.

Eliza Ballou, Garfield's mother, and probably the strongest
personal influence in his life, was born in New Hampshire in
1801 in the same town as her celebrated relative, the Rev.
Hosea Ballou. When the little girl was eight years old, her
mother was left a widow, and to join certain relatives moved
to one of those outposts which, in her physical and spiritual con-
quest of the northwest, New England was beginning to establish in the wilderness. Worcester in Otsego County, New
York, was simply another New England village farther west.
It had been settled at the close of the Revolution by New England families. There the Ballous found the Garfields already
established on a small clearing, where they had been for two
generations since Solomon had come from Massachusetts in
1780. Solomon had been succeeded by Thomas, the father of
a boy who had been christened Abraham but who was called
Abram. While the Ballous were living in Worcester, or shortly
after, Thomas Garfield died and Abram, being left an orphan,
was bound out according to the practice of the times to a char-
itable settler. Mrs. Ballou was evidently very poor, and managed to make a living by weaving for her neighbors. Abram
Garfield and Eliza Ballou were friends and playmates. Abram
Garfield had been born in 1799 and was accordingly almost
two years older than his future wife.

To such a community as Worcester, New York, standing as it did on one of the highways to the lakes, the second war against England and its unexpectedly lucky conclusion brought again the dream of greater prosperity farther west which summoned the grandchildren just as the close of the Revolution had urged forward their grandfathers. At the end of the war, in which he had served, James Ballou, the uncle for whom James Abram Garfield was to be named, brought back to his mother a glowing picture of the fresh opportunities of the Ohio country, and early in 1815 the Ballous made the long and tedious journey to the neighborhood of Zanesville, Ohio. The trip which today could be made in twelve hours then took six weeks, from which we may infer that the means of locomotion was the common ox team of the pioneers.

The boy and girl friendship between Eliza Ballou and Abram Garfield evidently had more vitality than one might have expected. Four years after the Ballous had moved to Ohio, Abram had finished his period of service and followed his friends to Zanesville. In a few weeks, February 3, 1820, the boy of twenty and the girl of eighteen were married and made their way at once to the neighborhood of the little village of Cleveland, Ohio, in the region known as the Western Reserve, which was becoming still another outpost of advancing New England.

At a spot which today lies within the boundaries of a great city, but which was then in the wilderness, Abram Garfield "took up" a piece of land containing forty acres, fifteen in the bottom and the rest on the hill. On this farm the two young people built a log cabin and commenced the task of putting in their first crop. Since in her reminiscences to her son Mrs. Garfield afterwards said that they did not own a house of their own until 1829, their first piece of land must have been rented. The hardships of those first years were pathetic, of the kind which destroy some of the familiar glamour of the frontier.

By September the girl wife was shaking with the ague. Both she and her husband were sick all that fall, and she tells us as if it were quite a matter of course that they had fever regularly every fall. And the children came with almost unbroken regularity: Mehitabel (Hitty) in 1821; Thomas in 1822, the son who at the age of eleven was to prove a second father to the family; Mary in 1824. Then came a break.

The opening and the immense success of the Erie Canal gave a great impulse to similar enterprises throughout the west. The coming of the railroads which were to supplant the canals within ten years was naturally unforeseen, and Ohio planned a great system of waterways which was to join the waters of the lake with those of the river at the south. Accordingly, in 1826, Abram Garfield was tempted by the new opportunity, and, having built at a profit a small section of the canal in his own neighborhood, undertook a more ambitious venture in the southern part of the state. There in Tuscarawas County another child was born who died in infancy. A sudden rise in prices threw out all Abram Garfield's calculations, and in 1828 the Garfields were bankrupt and back in the neighborhood of Cleveland with their three children and the necessity of making a new start in life.

This time Abram Garfield went a little farther from the village of eleven hundred inhabitants which was just beginning to give some faint promise of its future growth. Deep in the woods, in Orange Township, on the Chagrin River, sixteen miles from Cleveland, and at a price of two and a half dollars an acre, for which he was largely in debt to the owner in Connecticut, Garfield bought eighty acres of land and arranged to have twenty immediately cleared. The only close neighbor was his half brother, Amos Boynton, the "Uncle Amos" of Garfield's boyhood, who had married Eliza Garfield's sister.

Within a few miles, in typical New England fashion, were other members of the large Garfield family. By neighboring springs the two families, the Garfields and the Boyntons, had soon built log cabins, and in one of these, the vestiges of which have long since disappeared, on the nineteenth of November, 1831, James Abram Garfield was born.

The country about was fertile, marvelously situated along a great lake, and it had the advantages of a homogeneous and vigorous population. For, unlike southern Ohio, Indiana, and Illinois, the Western Reserve was untroubled by cross currents from different sections, and the people tended to look on most questions, social, religious, and political, from essentially the same point of view; no part of the United States was quite so far from the South. Thus, when Garfield went to Bethany, West Virginia, to visit the college which had been founded by Alexander Campbell, he was making his first trip away from a familiar environment, and he writes as if he had come to a strange new world, much like John Adams on his first trip to Philadelphia. Unlike Hayes, who was educated at Kenyon at a time when the little college was largely attended by Southern men, and of course unlike Lincoln and Johnson, Garfield had little opportunity to understand the problem of the South until in a later period contact with Southern men in Congress had led him to revise to some extent his early feelings. From such failure to know and understand each other, due in large part to the accident of lines of transportation and movements of population, it is possible to explain in part the mistakes of secession on the part of the South and of Reconstruction on the part of the victorious North.

In following the career of Garfield, economic geography must be kept in mind in another aspect. The Western Reserve in which Garfield was born and spent his boyhood was a vastly different place from the region which first sent him to Congress, and that in turn was even more different from the one which he represented in the closing part of his long career.

The Western Reserve had been too close to the Indian country to be rapidly filled up. It had to wait two generations after southern Ohio, and even when the campaigns of 1812–13 had ended forever the dread potency of the names of Tecumseh and the Prophet, it did not come quite into its own until the opening of the Erie Canal and the building of the railroads had given access to wider markets and the sea. Hence with all its almost unequalled natural resources and the immense advantages of position, when the region once began to fill it developed with a speed almost unprecedented even in America. Garfield was born in a pioneer region which contained only one village of more than a thousand inhabitants. There were, of course, no railroads and his father had just helped to dig the first canal. At that time, the population numbered 100,000, a large number of whom had arrived in the last five years. But when Garfield entered Congress, the inhabitants were more than 350,000 and Cleveland was a city of 43,417. Finally in 1880, at the close of Garfield's career, the census showed more than half a million, Cleveland alone having grown to a city of 160,146; Youngstown and Akron were rising manufacturing towns. Manufactures and commerce were equally important with agriculture, and large fortunes were by no means uncommon. In studying the evolution of Garfield's views on such subjects as the tariff, we need to remember that the man never changed as fast as the region from which he came.

For the Garfields on the new farm, after the birth of their youngest son, things began to go much better. In after years, Mrs. Garfield remembered that they lived as well as their neighbors, for the crops were good and the food was abundant. The denomination founded by Alexander Campbell was growing rapidly throughout the west. The Garfields became interested in the new religion, and almost every Sunday attended services which were held either in private houses or in the school house. They resolved, as Mrs. Garfield put it, to lead a different life if they could find the right way. Early in 1833, first the husband and then the wife were immersed, and "from that time they were perfectly happy."

The new religion was not so different from other evangelical sects, Presbyterians, Methodists and Baptists, as the early converts believed, but Campbell and his followers thought that they had discovered again the lost simplicity of the Gospel and that they were at the beginning of a new reformation which was sure to unite the various branches of a divided Christianity. Accordingly, they called themselves Disciples or Christians. In their lack of regularly ordained preachers and in some of their ethical teachings, especially as to non-resistance, the Disciples were somewhat like the Quakers. For they took literally the injunction to leave unto Caesar the things that are Caesar's and looked on political remedies for social ills with a doubtful eye. On the other hand, in the insistence on the ceremonial importance of immersion and of the celebration of the Lord's supper they were more nearly akin to the Baptists. Their early preachers were like the circuit riders of the Methodists. From their interest in the study of the Bible they were led to emphasize education. Thus Alexander Campbell himself became the founder of a college at Bethany in what is now West Virginia, and in 1850 the Disciples of the Western Reserve established the Western Reserve Eclectic Institute, with which the life of Garfield was so closely connected and which became later Hiram College. Before the death of Campbell the new denomination had almost three quarters of a million members, but the high hopes of an early reunion of all Christians had already begun to disappear.

Abram Garfield was an attractive figure, tall, broad in the shoulders, generous and quick tempered. He could do as much hard work on the farm as two ordinary men, and still have enough energy left to talk politics or religion with his neighbors. Men came from miles around to wrestle with Abe Garfield, but his wife remembered with pride that he never met his match. A few weeks after his conversion a dangerous fire broke out in the neighboring woods. Garfield worked hard and saved his little clearing; but he had become overheated, and an illness followed that was not helped by the ministrations of the itinerant doctor. Pneumonia developed. Immediately before the end, the vigorous young man of thirty-four knew that he was dying. He got up and walked across the room, looked out at his oxen and called them by name, went back and sat down on the bed, and said "Eliza, I have brought you four young saplings into these woods. Take care of them." And he died sitting up against the head of his bed.[1]

The tradition of courage had come to her from her mother. Eliza Garfield would not "put the children out" among kind neighbors, as they urged her to do. The sale of fifty acres still left her with the central clearing of thirty acres. The neighbors were helpful, and especially good Uncle Amos Boynton, her sister's husband. Her older boy Thomas was not quite eleven, but he was a true Garfield, unusually strong and tall for his years. In even the hard first year the fence was finished and the crop tended until harvest, for Thomas was evidently taking the full responsibilities of a man. In the winters the widow added to the resources of the family by sewing for the shoemaker in exchange for shoes. She had a few sheep; and with her daughters, for Hitty was already twelve at the time of her father's death, carded the wool, wove the cloth, and made all the garments

---

[1] The death of Abram Garfield was described by Mrs. Garfield: J. A. Bundy, *Life of Garfield* (1880), p. 9.

that could be made of wool. The hardships of poverty did not touch the youngest child, who was not yet two years old when his father died; Mrs. Garfield never acknowledged that they were poor, for poverty was synonymous with laziness. After the fashion of the frontier Thomas served his mother until he was twenty-one, when he was free to make a home for himself in Michigan. The daughters married early, Hitty when she was barely sixteen and her younger sister Mary when she was twenty, and both went to live in the neighboring town of Solon.

The family made a surprisingly good living on their little farm of thirty acres; enough, after all, for one growing boy to cultivate. For Thomas did not go to school. Mrs. Garfield was a great Bible reader and strict with her children and they never failed to go to church on Sundays. But she made the house cheerful with her songs, for she knew all the hymns, and, what they liked better, the patriotic ballads which the war of 1812 had generally inspired.[1]

James had a quick mind, and, as was so common in such families, was selected for an education, with the hope no doubt that he might reach the high place of a teacher or even of a preacher. Textbooks were few, but they were thoroughly mastered. Webster's spelling book, Pike's arithmetic, Kirkham's

[1] The Garfield Papers, Library of Congress, include some interesting letters, containing boyhood reminiscences, from Thomas Garfield to his brother. See especially, Thomas Garfield to James A. Garfield, Feb. 9, 1854; April 15, 1854; Feb. 28, 1855; April 1, 1855; Feb. 4, 1856. One letter ends, "pleas excus bad spelling and writing and all mistakes you know that my education is very limited." At this time Thomas Garfield was established on a farm in Michigan. Garfield's mother wrote, Sept. 16, 1854, "Thomas has got as good a piece of land as ever lay out of doors. It is the best land I ever saw. If nothing happens he will be well off in a few years." But the land proved swampy and Thomas never prospered. More than once James helped him out of difficulties. The relations between James and his sister Mary seem to have been close, especially in the early years: Mary Garfield to James A. Garfield, Sept., 16, 1854. The letter mentioned above is one of the few from Garfield's mother.

grammar, the *English Reader*, Denham's arithmetic, were practically learned by heart. In declamations from the reader on Friday afternoon James excelled. For lighter reading he was limited to the few books which were to be found in the house or in those of the neighbors. By the time that he was fourteen he had read *Robinson Crusoe* many times and other books of the sea, now forgotten, had quickened his imagination. History was not studied in school, but Goodrich's *History of the United States,* with its emphasis on Revolutionary battles, had fallen into his hands and had been read so often that in manhood Garfield could quote it by the page, and an old copy of Josephus was almost as familiar as the Gospels.

After he was twelve or thirteen, the growing boy began to work in vacation times for wages, sometimes as much as twenty-five cents a day. The journal which he began to keep, and which is preserved in part in the pages of Smith, shows that he chopped wood, "planted for H. Brainerd," cradled wheat, and mowed in the hay field. His wages soon rose to fifty cents and even in a busy season to a dollar a day. Later on he was able to help at house raisings, learned something of carpentry, and once or twice before he was sixteen helped to load a boat with wood and even accompanied it to the rising town of Cleveland. In the winter he had plenty of time to go hunting in the dense woods which still separated the clearings. When he was fifteen, he spent several weeks away from home boiling "black salts" from the ashes of logs.

The first great turning point in the life of Garfield came in the summer of 1848, when at the age of seventeen he determined to go away from home and become a sailor. He went to Cleveland, bent on shipping as a hand before the mast. He boarded a vessel, found some drunken sailors, and a captain who drove him off with curses. Walking away partly disillusioned, but not wholly, he met a cousin whom he knew only by sight and who was running a canal boat. This cousin, Captain Amos Letcher, evidently a rough specimen, who little realised how eagerly his reminiscences would be sought in the eighties when men were writing books to be entitled "From the Towpath to the White House," offered Garfield a post as driver of the horses on the towpath; and, on the sixteenth of August, 1848, the boy who had left home to be a sailor was installed as part of the crew of the canal boat *Evening Star* which was taking a load of copper ore destined for Pittsburgh.

Ten days later, by way of Akron and Beaver, on the Ohio River, where they hired a steamer to tow them up stream, they reached the chief manufacturing city of the west. It was the first time that Garfield had been as much as twenty miles away from home. The new hand was looked on with suspicion and had the usual fights and narrow escapes from drowning which constituted an initiation into the life of the Ohio canal. But he had strength and courage, and by the time the *Evening Star* reached Beaver Garfield was accepted into the fraternity of boatmen. On Sunday the twenty-seventh, Garfield took a stroll and listened to two sermons in the street by men hired by the authorities of the town to preach to the public. The boat was loaded with coal for the return trip. Garfield had served his apprenticeship and was promoted to bowman, where his duties were to get the locks ready and to see that the boat got safely through. His wages of fourteen dollars a month seemed very generous.

At the end of the fourth trip, Garfield's canal experiment, of which less than ten days had been spent on the towpath of which his early biographers made so much, came to an abrupt conclusion. Early in October he was taken ill with fever and ague, and returned to be carefully nursed back to health in his mother's cabin.[1]

[1] T. C. Smith, *Life and Letters of Garfield*, Vol. I, pp. 20-26.

His mother had been unable to persuade him not to go. But she now pointed out again the advantages of an education. His mother and brother gave him the seventeen dollars that they had in the house and in the spring Garfield went away to attend Geauga Academy at Chester. His illness had proved to be a blessing in disguise. The role of the mother in the boy's life had come to an end. His future was now in the lap of the gods.

In later times, as Garfield looked back over the first seventeen years of his life, they did not have all the glamour that they came to have for so many others. "I lament sorely," he wrote to a friend, "that I was born to poverty and allowed to catch up any or no chance habits of mind, body, morals, and manners, and in this chaos of childhood seventeen years passed before I caught up any inspiration which was worthy of my manhood." All of which was natural, but not quite fair, surely, to Eliza Garfield or to his brother Thomas. The canal experience seemed also a danger escaped, rather than a real part of education.

But now in the spring of 1849 he was to commence the part of his life which he always remembered with satisfaction. At the time his only purpose was to go to school one term, until he had fully recovered his strength, and to postpone sailing until the autumn. In the last three years, while Garfield was growing to manhood, the country had passed through momentous changes. The armies of Scott had planted the flag of the country on the heights of Chapultepec. An imperial domain, for better or for worse, had been added to the limits of the republic. New issues had arisen which were to be only temporarily settled by the compromises of the next year. Gold had been discovered in California, and many boys no younger than Garfield were even then on their way to the gold fields. In the name of liberty, only one year before, the flag of revolt had been unfurled in many of the chief capitals of Europe. But these things had left untouched the imagination of the boy as they had that of the community in which he lived; for, in his journal, there is apparently no reference to the momentous changes of his own time. In the next decade, when Horace

17

Greeley's *Tribune* became the political bible of the Western Reserve, such a boyhood was to be no longer possible, even on the frontier. With the newspaper, life was to be marvelously secularised in the woods of America as it had once been in the days of the Renaissance. As it was, Garfield in one of his first debates at the academy defended the thesis, "That Christians have no right to participate in human governments." A strange preparation for statesmanship!

The neighborhood school teacher, a young man by the name of Bates, who afterwards became a celebrated preacher in the western country, had attended Geauga Academy for a term or two, and advised Garfield to choose that institution. The Disciples had as yet no convenient school of their own, and Geauga, founded in the neighboring county by Free Will Baptists, was fairly close in distance and not too far away in theology.

The academy was a neighborhood institution which developed with astonishing rapidity throughout Ohio in the forties and the fifties to meet the needs of secondary studies before education had come to be regarded as a proper function of the state, just as at an earlier stage the frontier had called forth the equally voluntary log school house for purposes of primary instruction. Each was essentially a frontier institution. The primary schools were already becoming the little red brick township schools under public control. But the academies continued to flourish until they disappeared under the increasing competition of the public high schools of the eighties and the nineties. By that time many had closed their doors, and others, like Hiram, grew into the little denominational colleges which still endure in spite of the newer growth of great private and State universities.

When through the growth of population the demand for secondary education in a county became sufficiently insistent, and when the roads were good enough to allow a certain amount

of travel through the woods, a group of seven or eight enterprising farmers, usually with children of their own to educate,
frequently though not always members of the same denomination and inspired by some far-seeing clergyman, organised
themselves as the Board of Trustees of this or that academy.
Some of the academies were entirely secular in outlook, but
these were few. A donation of a piece of land was secured at
some convenient village, with other gifts a building was erected,
and a principal was selected who was frequently joined by his
wife as a teacher of the more advanced subjects. The academy
was supported by the fees of the students, usually ten or
twelve dollars for a term of instruction in the so-called English
branches, advanced arithmetic, algebra, advanced grammar, and
rhetoric. Students who desired to add natural philosophy paid
slightly more, and those who commenced the classical course
in Latin or Greek paid as much as fifteen dollars for a term of
three months. The principal was allowed to hire the other
teachers whom he regarded as necessary for whatever wages he
had to pay, and made his living from the remaining profits of
the enterprise. In the heyday of the academy, there are cases
on record where a principalship was relatively profitable and
attracted men of ability and very good training. In making his
own school efficient, each principal was controlled in theory by
the trustees, but much more really by the necessities of competition with other academies in the same or adjoining counties.

As the academies began to decay, some were taken over and
others founded directly by religious denominations. But even
at the very beginning the religious influence and interest was
pronounced. In many cases the academy, the leading church of
the village, and the cemetery were to be found side by side. Instruction always commenced with a compulsory religious service at a very early hour, and the principal taught a course in the
English Bible or in the principles of moral philosophy. There

was none of that rigid organization which became so characteristic of the later high schools, and each student was allowed
to go as far as his ambitions or his more eager teachers could
carry him. It was not uncommon for an ambitious student to
study geometry, trigonometry, and advanced mathematics or to
read the Letters of Cicero or the orations of Demosthenes with
teachers who were themselves considering these subjects for
the first time, and quite without regard to the number of terms
that had been attended or without the careful mathematical calculations of credits which were to become so characteristic of the
next generation of American students. All this was of course
exceptional and possible only because the impulse was essentially voluntary and the number of advanced pupils was necessarily small.

Population was widely scattered and very few students were
residents of the same village where the academy was located.
Many, like Garfield, came at considerable sacrifice from dis-
tances of twenty miles or even more, at a time when in the
winter five miles on horseback or on foot made frequent returns to their own homes entirely impracticable. The course was
frequently interrupted by the necessity of making a living by
manual labor in the summer, and as a result the summer term
was given up and a long vacation became customary in American education. Many of the more advanced students, like Garfield, also made it a practice to spend a part of every winter
teaching in some neighborhood school, returning to the academy in the spring. The best work was done between two interruptions, in the autumn and the spring. The extracurricular
activities of a later day were represented by the singing school
in the evening and by the meetings of the literary society, with
orations, essays, declamations and debates on Friday afternoons.

Some of the larger academies, like Geauga at the time when
Garfield was there in 1849, had as many as two hundred and

fifty students and six or even seven teachers. But such an academy was unusually large, and even at Geauga the numbers given for Garfield's first year were probably not present at the same time. The academies were almost without exception co-educational. Sometimes the house of the principal was sufficiently elastic to give accommodation to a considerable number of students, frequently young women, and thus became the predecessor of the dormitory of the later college. But the majority of the students necessarily found rooms in the houses of the village. Some provided their own food and even cooked it themselves, subsisting on an unvaried diet of pork and fried mush. Others, like Garfield and two friends in his first term at Geauga, organised a club and had their meals cooked by the wife of the owner of the house in which they lived. After his first term Garfield, having supplemented his depleted funds by teaching school during the winter, was able to give up the anxieties of housekeeping, finding board at the price of a dollar and six cents a week. Why the six cents, does not appear upon the record. History and general literature were unrepresented in the curriculum, but Geauga had a typical library of one hundred and fifty volumes, which to boys like Garfield, coming from the limited resources of a clearing in the forest, helped to open new and untried fields of intellectual adventure.

A summer as a carpenter near home was followed by the fall term at the academy, and then Garfield began the second stage of his higher education as a school teacher in a district not far from his boyhood home, where the boy of eighteen was called "Jim Gaffil," in the vernacular of the region, and could not expect to be treated as a prophet in his own country. Such a school was often a contest for mastery between the older boys and the young master, and Garfield won his way through these unseemly tussles more by his strength than by intellectual attainments. "Nov. 13. Punished S. Herrington severely for disobeying and being saucy. He endeavored to fight me but he finally gave up and is now a good boy. . . . Nov. 29. School rather noisy. I hardly know what to do. I cannot whip a scholar for making a noise and talking will not do any good. Here is a dilemma. . . . Jan. 4. Compositions and declamations. A boy sixteen years old refused to obey me and was very saucy. I flogged him severely and told him to take his seat. He caught a billet of wood and came at me and we had a merry time." Such entries in Garfield's journal indicate that the thirteen dollars a month which he received for his services were well earned, though probably from an educational point of view they were all that the inexperienced young teacher was worth. The wonder is that in such schools boys and girls managed to learn anything.

But a fundamental characteristic of Garfield, even at this time, was a ready capacity to adjust himself to new situations. Indeed, he took the color of his environment with an ease which helps to explain in later years the astonishing transitions in his life. Teacher, preacher, soldier, congressman, lawyer, no one of these careers carried to the highest point of distinction, but each coming to seem reasonably natural—where in American biography can we find a more varied list? So it was with the early experiences in teaching, in which the master undoubtedly learned more than the scholars. In a short time the young teacher had gained the necessary mastery of one of the most difficult of the arts, and was able to dominate his scholars by the essential dignity and intellectual enthusiasm of his personality. After the first two months entries like those we have quoted suddenly vanish and do not reappear in Garfield's later adventures in teaching frontier schools. He knew his pupils individually, he evidently liked them, with characteristic conscientiousness he did not underestimate the essential importance or dignity of his task, and there is abundant testimony that many of his pupils came first to respect and finally almost to worship the tall, genial boy who was their teacher.

Early in March, 1850, the short term of school in District Number Two came to a close. A hundred persons were present in the afternoon. There were some regrets and some rejoicing. In the evening came the usual public exhibition, and the scholars were free, part to work and others to play in the woods, until they met again under a new and untried master in the next November. Like other school teachers of his time, Garfield never taught twice in the same district. Such was the educational system through which thousands of boys were passing whose college education was to be received on the battlefield of Gettysburg and before the entrenchments of Richmond and Atlanta.

A young man brought up as Garfield had been was almost sure to pass through two great emotional experiences, conversion and first love. In this respect Garfield was typical. Of course, Lincoln missed the first experience entirely and did not meet the second until a later period in his career, but then Lincoln was in many respects, as witness his marvelous sense of the music of words, quite exceptional; Garfield's career, on the contrary, is chiefly interesting just because it was typical of his times, quite like that of hundreds of other young men. His experiences were merely to be intensified by the warmth of an eager personality and in later years to be underscored by the astonishing adventure of the Presidency and by the deep red line of a dramatic death. So at eighteen, at the close of his first term of teaching, Garfield was converted.

The religion of Alexander Campbell, radiating from its center at Bethany, was in its third decade of evangelistic fervor, but had not lost the glamour of its early hopes. Through the Disciples of Christ the new reformation by the inherent simplicity of its teachings was to make a new and a better earth.

Conversion was not marked by the gloomy forebodings of a conviction of sin nor followed by the exuberant excitement of the redeemed which was to be found in the camp meetings of many sects on the frontier. It was a quiet acceptance of the new life, and was sealed, in the technical language of the day, by the symbolic ritual of immersion. A visiting preacher was holding meetings in a neighborhood school house, and on March 4, 1850, Garfield wrote that he "was buried with Christ in baptism and arose to walk in newness of life." To Garfield conversion was a great emotional experience. His journal for several months became eager, joyous, almost exuberant. The pious expressions with which it is filled are only saved from a disagreeable flavor of cant by their obvious sincerity. For the moment Garfield had accepted so completely the unique and unusual quality of the Campbellite gospel that he was unable to understand how others could continue to adhere to what seemed to him to be mere sects and denominations. For a time, and quite unconsciously, Garfield had become what in an older religion would have been a High Churchman.

On the American frontier the freedom of religion was often the freedom to divide, and contrary to a common impression did not always lead to religious toleration. The conflicts between forms of religion which a more secular age finds it peculiarly difficult to distinguish were sometimes bitter and acrimonious, and on more than one occasion led to actual persecution none the less real because its chief weapons were social ostracism rather than physical penalties. Eager new groups like the Disciples were closely united into brotherhoods by a consciousness of kind which also separated them from others like the Free Will Baptists. Religious groups sometimes lived side by side in the same community with only the slightest social contacts, and looking on one another with either hatred or contempt. In some villages in northern Ohio for a Presbyterian to marry a Methodist was almost as complete a social disgrace as it was later for a Republican to become a Democrat; for religion was taken as seriously in the fifties as politics were to be in the seventies and the eighties. Fortunately for his intellectual life, Garfield had a mind that was essentially critical, and after those first few months he began to develop with his Christianity a sense of humor and a tolerance to other interpretations of religion, which later as a politician and a Republican he did not live quite long enough to manifest so completely. In his attitude to other religions, the change through which Garfield passed was quite characteristic of a similar change which was general in the community in which he lived. The Americans of the next generation would never understand how seriously their fathers, even when all were Protestants, and evangelical Protestants at that, had taken the differences that separated them.

Garfield returned to the academy for two more terms, continuing his studies, Latin, algebra, and botany. But his religious zeal was quite too fresh and intense to make him comfortable in a Baptist school. A bitter quarrel broke out between the principal, who like himself had accepted the tenets of the Disciples, and the Trustees; and when in the fall of 1850, the principal was compelled to leave, Garfield was happy to shake the dust of Geauga from his feet. For almost a year his formal education was interrupted and Garfield devoted himself to his teaching. In the summer of 1851, the lad accompanied his mother on a visit to her relatives in southern Ohio. Except for his trip to Pittsburgh on the *Evening Star*, it was his first journey to a new community. But the critical spirit still persisted. He went on the train to Columbus, a marvelous adventure to a boy who was trying a means of locomotion then new and strange. He visited the legislature, but was disappointed with the members, who seemed coarse, hard-drinking men, entirely unfit to represent a great state. From Columbus he went to Zanesville, and then by skiff and steamer down the Muskingum River. Manners in southern Ohio were different from those to which he was accustomed. The people turned their work into play, and the frolics when the neighbors joined in husking, sawing, logging, or the other chief tasks of the farm seemed foolish to the stern spirit of the young Puritan. Going to hear a Methodist missionary, Garfield thought that he had done some good, but "that it had been adulterated with sectarianism." A German Catholic service seemed to him irreverent and insincere. He went to hear a woman preacher, and was reminded of the words of Paul. The manners of his young Ballou cousins lacked a proper seriousness. Garfield was in danger of becoming a prig.

In the autumn of 1851, the young Disciple entered the Western Reserve Eclectic Institute at Hiram, which in spite of its sonorous title was merely another academy of the later type which marked the transition to the denominational college. It had been opened a year before under Campbellite auspices, and was capable of giving training equivalent to the first two years of the college course of the times. It had the defect of all the academies in a lack of a properly trained faculty, as well as their merit in allowing an ambitious student to go as far and as fast as he was able.

Of this feature, the eager Garfield took complete advantage. After his first term, he was engaged as a teacher in the elementary branches and was no longer compelled to interrupt his residence to teach in some district school. The days of his chief hardships were now over. At first he taught three classes a day and later six; but in spite of his duties as a teacher he did a prodigious amount of work for himself. His day began with a class at five in the morning and every moment was carefully planned in advance until he went to bed at eleven. One sometimes wishes, that, like Lincoln, he had spent some time swapping stories and talking politics in the village grocery, but such wastes were not for him. In 1852, he wrote to a friend that he was ignorant of the issues of the Presidential campaign, and congratulated himself that he was just under the voting age, for he was disgusted with politicians who seemed to him to be engaged in wirepulling. Political discussions in the newspapers seemed low trash "unfit for refined feelings or kind hearts," as indeed much of it undoubtedly was. In the same year in debating the question, "Can war ever be justifiable under any circumstances?" he took the negative.

But while he turned from politics, he was living in a world of books. During his last year at Hiram, from the summer of 1853 to that of 1854, with his friend Almeda A. Booth as a voluntary fellow-student, Garfield read thoroughly and for the first time, the *Pastorals* of Virgil, six books of Homer's *Iliad*, Livy, Herodotus, Demosthenes' *On The Crown*, the *Germania* and *Agricola* of Tacitus, and a portion of Hesiod. During one term, two professors and two students met each evening to make an independent translation of the book of Romans. And all this for a half-trained youth, who was still in what we we would call the Sophomore year of college.

Garfield's chief recreations in these years were his friendships and his increasing activities as a public speaker. The friendships that he formed with Miss Booth, with Hinsdale, who became celebrated as a scholar and administrator, with Fuller, who afterward wrote useful reminiscences of this period, with Charles D. Wilber, the lame boy who accompanied him to Williams, were deep and lasting. His themes as a speaker were usually religious. Starting first as an occasional preacher, he was soon expected to deliver an address almost every Sunday. Such activities were encouraged by his denomination, which had at the time no regularly organised clergy, and depended for its preaching on the services of volunteers. Sometimes Garfield engaged in more ambitious debates. In one of these he challenged a spiritualist by the name of Treat who made some pretensions to scholarship and who had a considerable vogue, and in a warm debate vanquished his opponent by proving his total ignorance of Greek, an argument which certainly did not go very far into the merits of the question but which was entirely satisfactory to his admiring friends.

Such a life evidently had its spiritual dangers; and Garfield was among the first to realise that he needed a wider training. This decision was probably quickened by an experience which to many a boy would have seemed quite trivial, but to a nature as sensitive as Garfield's was at once bitter and probably wholesome. For over a year he had been paying marked attentions to the daughter of a prominent Disciple in the neighborhood of Orange. His journeys home from Hiram usually took him by the house of the young lady, and it is evident that both her family and probably the lady regarded the friendship in the light of an engagement. Suddenly it dawned on Garfield that he was not really in love at all, and he had to acknowledge to himself that he had been playing with a foolish and dangerous flirtation. After some natural hesitation he decided to write a letter and explain to the lady in question that he could only be a friend. The result was a bitter correspondence and much gossip; the friends of the injured lady told him in no uncertain language precisely what they thought of the conduct of the rising young preacher.[1]

[1] Henry Boynton, Garfield's cousin, wrote to him, June 7, 1855, describing the anger of the young lady's family: "We have been to Solyman's to make an evening visit. Mary was at home. She talked about you a little to Susan. Her mother told Susan that Mary's father told her not to give up the letters. She says there is enough in them to prove all they want. . . . The Hubbells are high-spirited folk." Another cousin, Philip Boynton, tried to overcome Garfield's hesitations as to

Garfield's vanity and self-confidence were severely shaken, as they were to be once again during the public scandals of 1873; and, in spite of the fact that the young man had nothing more to blame himself with than a selfish carelessness, he had the wholesome honesty to judge himself as severely as he would have judged any one else. The world which had seemed so bright and full of hope suddenly became very dark. He began even to doubt the reality of the emotions that had followed his conversion: "After all that I hear," he wrote, "there seems to be something within me, I cannot name it, that whispers fearful words into my heart. It tells me that I'm not honest, that this is all a pretense on my part—that there is no such thing as human sincerity or real honesty." We are to meet similar expressions after the crisis of the seventies, but even now Garfield was mellowed and softened by criticism, all the more because he had to acknowledge to himself that it was more than half just. Perhaps he had learned the fundamental truth of the ancient adage, "Judge not that ye be not judged!"

This experience probably hastened a decision to complete his college education in some new environment. The natural choice was Bethany, the college in Virginia of which Alexander Campbell was himself the President and the founder. So Garfield and his cousin, William Boynton, in the early summer of 1853, made their pilgrimage to sit at the feet of the leader of their denomination. Alexander Campbell was a very remarkable man, who deserves to be better known, and the two young men were not disappointed; they heard him preach, and were even invited to his house, where they participated in family prayers. When in his presence, Garfield later wrote, he felt the

matrimony: "You know that she will make a faithful, dutiful, honest, and superior wife, and although she is not what you would like in every particular, so is every other young lady in the world, and gentleman too! And bear in mind that our life is made up of a choice of evils." (Philip Boynton to James A. Garfield, June 28, 1854, Garfield *Papers*.)

shadow of a great man falling upon him and he was deeply impressed by the freshness, originality, and brilliance of his thought. He was not to be so deeply moved until two years later he heard Emerson. But though he could not acknowledge that he was disappointed in the great leader, the college itself was in its methods and standards not very different from Hiram; the politeness of the students seemed to him mere Southern dandyism; and he was deeply shocked by a general tendency to justify slavery. So his final decision was postponed for another year, and he came back to Hiram, more than partially disillusioned.

The delay was not wholly ungrateful, for he had already met and had begun to notice the charm of Lucretia Rudolph. She did not have the intellectual brilliance of his friend Amelia Booth, but Miss Booth was older, her first romance had been ended by the early death of her lover, and with Miss Booth, in spite of a boundless admiration, Garfield's relations were to remain entirely platonic, for Garfield and Amelia Booth were intellectual comrades, and nothing more. Here was something different. Lucretia Rudolph had been with Garfield at Geauga, where he had scarcely noticed the modest young girl, whose father, a man of prominence in the denomination, had been interested in the organisation of the new institution at Hiram. The acquaintance there deepened into friendship, and now each was sure that friendship had ripened into love. But remembering his very recent mistakes, Garfield was determined to move slowly in what in language which still retained a pious flavor he called "the sacred subject of matrimony." Time, which changes all things, might still make a change even in feelings which for the moment seemed so deep and abiding. Accordingly, the two young people agreed to wait before entering into a formal engagement.

In the meantime, Garfield, whose mind had greatly matured

in the past year, was carefully considering the choice of a college. He now saw what he would have stoutly denied a little while before that the Disciples were a denomination with peculiar views and distinctive characteristics. He wanted to get away from the provincialism of the Western Reserve and from the narrowness of a denominational college and he did not realise that in choosing New England he was selecting not a new strange country but his own motherland, and that in a New England College of the fifties he was sure to meet again the same fundamental views on both religion and politics that he was leaving back home. But he was wisely eager, as he put it, "to liberalize his mind," and "to spend some time in an atmosphere that is different," and in the same mood as when a boy when he left home to go on his great adventure on the canal, he now wrote to Yale, Brown, and Williams. Each of the three wrote back that he would need two years to graduate. But Garfield had heard that Yale was aristocratic; the letter from Professor Wayland at Brown seemed rigid and stern; and in the reply of President Mark Hopkins at Williams there was a single sentence in which Garfield rightly saw the kindly nature of the greatest college President of his times. For Dr. Hopkins had written, "We shall be glad to do what we can for you"; [1] and so Garfield who had read his Lowell lectures and who knew from Horace Mann of the attractive personality of the President of Williams, made his choice and embarked in what to him two or three years before would have seemed an impossible adventure, where, among the hills of western New England, he was to seek a wider and a deeper culture. A thoughtful student of the history of the country might well wish, in the light of the event, that in the fifties half the Southern boys had gone to college in New England, and that some of the boys from the Western Reserve

[1] Mark Hopkins to J. A. Garfield, June 7, 1854 (Garfield *Papers*).

and even from New England had been able to spend at least
one winter in the distant South; but by that time, of course, the
inevitable trend of great sectional influences in the nation was
quite too strong, and even a young man who, like Garfield,
reasoned against them was quite unable to control even in his
own career the mighty forces of a great historical destiny.

Having made his decision, with boyish eagerness, Garfield
only waited for the close of the academic year at Hiram and set
out at once, arriving at Williamstown early in July, 1854. Williams was a college of two hundred and fifty students to which
for the last eighteen years the influence of President Hopkins
had given a national reputation for thoroughness in scholarship,
for in spite of rigid theological conservatism, the President of
Williams knew how to use a curriculum still largely classical,
especially in the first two years, to train young men to think and
to think clearly for themselves. At Williams, the close relations which were possible in the American college of the fifties
between faculty and students was at once illustrated by Garfield's first experience. He called on the President and received
an impression of a powerful personality which the next two
years only served to deepen. The new student from the west
was surprised to learn that the academic year in an eastern
college did not end until late in August, and that with a very
short vacation of about three weeks, the new year began in
September. From the President, Garfield went to call on the
Professors of Latin, Greek, and Mathematics, by whom he was
examined orally in their respective subjects. On the strength of
these personal interviews, and in spite of some weakness in
mathematics, Garfield was admitted to the Junior class which
was to begin its studies two months later. In the fifties the complicated devices of modern methods of admission had evidently
not been invented, and the only care was to determine in the

simplest and most direct manner the state of preparation of the candidate.

Garfield's mistake as to the time table at Williams was on the whole fortunate, for he had two months in which to take the measure of his future classmates by attending classes without immediate responsibility for recitation. In this time he had mastered the difficulties in mathematics which his oral examination had revealed. With the spirit of emulation that was to be so marked a feature of his later career, Garfield had studied the qualities of his classmates, and wrote to one of his old friends that of the forty-two members of the class thirty-seven would stand behind him within two months, a promise that was amply fulfilled but that would scarcely have added to the personal popularity of the author, even in the fifties, had it been known. The commencement speaker for 1854 was no less a person than Ralph Waldo Emerson, and it was to the credit of the young Disciple that he did not allow any theological prejudice to obscure for a moment his appreciation of a mind of profound depth. All of his life Garfield could quote from that oration. Imagine the good fortune of a young man who within a year had come into fairly close contact with three of the most significant personalities in the America of his day, Alexander Campbell, Mark Hopkins, and Ralph Waldo Emerson! There was still time for a short visit to his Garfield relatives in Massachusetts, who received him with ready hospitality.

In September began those two years on which Garfield never ceased to look back with gratitude and affection. The program of the Junior year was unusually varied: Greek, Latin, mechanics, astronomy, political economy, chemistry, and German. The study of German, especially, opened to Garfield whole new worlds of thought, and as a result he published in the *Williams Quarterly* an essay on the life, letters and poetry of

Theodore Koerner. The teaching must have been unusually efficient, for in a surprisingly short time Garfield had acquired a ready knowledge of German both as a spoken and a written language. The senior year at Williams was devoted almost exclusively to various branches of philosophy, logic, metaphysics, theology, apologetics, the kind of a course which one would expect to find in a theological seminary. For this final year the forty-five members of the class came under the almost exclusive guidance of Mark Hopkins, whose chief interest was in training the members to think for themselves; and it was the significance of that last year that usually remained in the memories of Williams men. There was ample time for wide reading on his own account and for more intensive preparation for the series of comprehensive examinations, given first by the members of the faculty and then by a board of visiting examiners on the results of which the standing of the various members was finally to depend. At the end of these academic activities, Garfield stood second in a class of forty-five, and in the final exercises in 1856 was assigned the Metaphysical Oration.

In the meantime Garfield was winning his way as a leader of the students, one of whom, Silas P. Hubbel, has left a vivid picture of the early college life of the future President of the United States. When Garfield entered the Junior class in the fall of 1854 he brought with him from Ohio another student, Charles D. Wilber, who joined the class at the same time. Between the two young men there seemed to be a strong attachment; they roomed together in South College, and were regarded as college chums. Wilber unfortunately was lame, limping badly and requiring the help of crutches or a stout cane. They were always together, and Garfield's kindness to his crippled chum was very noticeable. The pair in their daily walks to and from the recitation rooms and about the college grounds excited the eager gaze and curiosity of their fellow-students, from their quaint and odd appearance and evident unfamiliarity with college ways and doings. The contrast in the appearance of the couple was very striking—Garfield of large frame, looming up six feet high, strong and healthy, and looking like a backwoodsman, and Wilber, with a pale, intellectual cast of countenance limping along beside him. Their position at first was a very isolated and peculiar one, made more so by a whisper that soon circulated among the students that they were Campbellites. Now, what that meant, or what tenets the sect held, nobody seemed to know, but it was supposed to mean something very awful; but the two young men continued the even tenor of their way, unmoved by the stares and criticisms of their companions, until after a time this feeling had passed away, and Garfield, by his successful attainments and straightforward manly course, commanded the respect and admiration of his class and of the whole college.[1]

By the middle of his first year at Williams, Garfield had made himself the leader of the non-fraternity men in college politics, and, using that position as a vantage ground, was chosen one of the editors of the *Williams Quarterly*, the chief student publication, and president of one of the two leading literary societies. Most of his contributions to the Quarterly were literary, and commonplace enough. His single political venture was a poem entitled "Sam" in which he satirized the tenets of the Know-Nothing party, but this was probably inspired at the time more by his contest with the secret fraternities to which the new party bore a certain outward resemblance than by any conscious interest in national politics. Garfield's commanding position among the students was largely due to his mature capacity as a debater in a period when the literary society was still in the east as in the west the chief form of student self-expression.

[1] S. P. Hubbell to J. A. Bundy, June 28, 1880. J. A. Bundy, *op. cit.*, p. 37.

At a time when the first function of the college was still regarded as the preparation of young men for the ministry, the religious life of such a college as Williams was naturally very prominent. Twice a day, morning and evening, the students gathered together for chapel, and on Sundays attended two preaching services, morning and afternoon, at the Congregational church at the head of Main Street, these regular services being supplemented by voluntary prayer-meetings, by a regular series of revival meetings in the winter, and by the classes on the shorter catechism under the direction of the President which were a prominent part of the curriculum of the final year. In addition to such activities Garfield joined the Mills Theological Society, of which he was made librarian, and where he soon found that his theological views were just different enough from those of his fellow-students to give him the zest of the arguments in which he always delighted without arousing inconvenient religious prejudices. In all this, it must be remembered that the majority of the students were frankly preparing for the ministry, so that these intense interests which today might make a student peculiar and separate him from his fellows were in the fifties merely an additional intellectual bond.

In all this there was no conscious break with his past. In his Junior year we find Garfield reading at the same time Byron's *Childe Harold*, which he found "a most sublime poem," and "the writings of Brother Campbell," each with unbounded admiration and without seeming to feel in the least that they belonged to different worlds. In his short vacations he showed his loyalty by finding Disciple communities in Vermont and especially at Poestenkill, a village near Troy, New York, where he preached to admiring audiences. As he was about to return to college on one of these occasions, he wrote to Lucretia Rudolph back in Ohio, that he had received not only twenty dollars in cash, but various presents, including four new shirts, two silk handkerchiefs, a satin stock, and a trunkful of cakes and apples. His two best friends were Mrs. Maria Learned and "Sister Rebecca Selick." As he read *Alton Locke* and Tennyson with this young lady, whom he admired frankly, one suspects that sometimes the memories of the quiet young girl who was waiting for him in Ohio were growing a little dim. But although on his single visit to Ohio during his college course he failed for several weeks to make any visit to Lucretia Rudolph, he wrote to her regularly and kept her closely informed of his new associations. At the end of his college course, both Lucretia Rudolph and Rebecca Selick, accompanied by their mutual friends the Fullers, were present to hear him speak and to see him graduate, all apparently on the best of terms.

Nor did he forget the powerful personality of his mother. One of his classmates afterwards told the story of the last class holiday. On the Fourth of July, the traditional "mountain day," the students were gathered about their camp fire in the evening, seven miles from college, on the summit of old "Greylock." Garfield, the recognised leader, took a copy of the New Testament from his pocket and said, "Boys, I am accustomed to read a chapter with my absent mother every night; shall I read aloud?" All assenting, he read the chapter his mother in Ohio was then reading, and called on a classmate to pray.[1] And the incident was perfectly typical of Garfield's complete lack of self-consciousness and of his instinct for the emotional and dramatic implications of a situation, qualities which were to become the chief sources of his undoubted appeal as one of the most powerful orators of his generation. We shall see the same man more than once again, in New York in 1865 and above all in Chicago during the nominating convention of 1880.

[1] E. N. Manley to J. A. Bundy, July 8, 1880: Bundy, *op. cit.*, p. 41.

College days were almost over. Garfield had started with some money that he had saved at Hiram, but he had borrowed five hundred dollars from an uncle, and kindly Mark Hopkins had helped him out with a small loan at commencement time. Now after some hesitation, he had decided to go back to Hiram, and all that was left was the "Metaphysical Oration," on no less a subject than "Matter and Spirit," which his friends had come so far to hear. Across the glamour of the years, Fuller was to remember that when Garfield reached his peroration and finally closed his speech, the church shook with applause and "dozens of bouquets were showered at his feet." But the strictly contemporary reporter of the Springfield *Republican* was evidently less deeply interested in the young man from Ohio, and recorded with heartless precision: "Mr. Garfield's Metaphysical Oration betrayed much thought and won three bouquets." It would not require a detective to say that one of them was Lucretia Rudolph's.

FRESH from college, and not yet twenty-five, as a teacher of Greek, Latin, and English grammar, Garfield came back to his old associations at the Eclectic Institute. Hiram was then a village, five miles from the nearest railroad, with fifty or sixty houses grouped around the ugly red brick building of the academy—not an inspiring prospect for an eager, ambitious young man in search of a career. The teacher in America in the fifties, even the college professor, was still essentially a drill master, with a schedule of six or even seven classes a day in which his chief function was to listen to stumbling translations or to even more stupid repetitions of the words of some pre-scribed textbook. The life of the professor as an investigator in science or in history or as a literary critic, the whole modern conception of creative scholarship, which two generations later was to give dignity and real importance to an academic life, was as yet undreamed of. Only an occasional individual of genius, and largely in spite of the college rather than by its organised aid, such a man as Joseph Henry at Princeton, or Silliman at Yale, or Mark Hopkins at Williams, was able to rise above his environment. Nor did Garfield have the patient curiosity which is the essential feature of the successful academic career. Eager, energetic, friendly, it is no wonder that he found Hiram flat, stale, and unprofitable. He had neither the training which would make him in any given subject one of the efficient men of his generation nor the conception of the essential dignity of an intellectual life which he would have needed to become a prophet of a new educational period.

Not that Garfield shirked his work. He taught his classes regularly; he even gave voluntary courses of lectures on grammar; and was soon recognised as the best teacher at Hiram. But it is no wonder that he was soon writing to his best friend, Fuller: "You and I know that teaching is not the work in which a man can live and grow. I am succeeding in the school here better than I had any reason to hope, yet my heart will never be satisfied to spend my life in teaching." For a young Disciple, trained as Garfield had been, with a commanding presence, a voice which under the shade trees could be heard easily and apparently without effort on the part of the speaker by crowds that sometimes at yearly meetings of the Disciples reached into the thousands, and a ready use of words, untroubled by the slightest limitation of self-consciousness, the sure path to prestige in the community and to leadership even in educational life was the work of the occasional preacher and the evangelist. In the next six years, before Garfield was much more than thirty, his career was to pass through astonishing outward changes. Where in American life can we find a man who was college president, state senator, major general in a great war, and a member of the national legislature within so brief a period? But each of these changes and all of them taken together are, to the social historian, not so much important as proofs of the versatility of one young man, as they are of the inherent possibilities of the career of a popular and successful evangelist in Ohio and especially the Western Reserve of Ohio in the closing years of the pregnant fifties. At first in the same technical sense as Dwight L. Moody, and later more like Gladstone, Roosevelt, or Bryan, Garfield was to remain throughout his life a preacher of righteousness, and was to find in that conception of his mission a potent source of political strength.

In the presidential campaign of 1880 the writers of campaign biographies were to minimize or to explain away a phase of Garfield's career which was at the beginning central and almost inevitable. Among the people of the interior towns of

Ohio it was considered a very great achievement to graduate
from an Eastern college; and accordingly Garfield was at once
received as a man of learning, his ideas on theological questions
being accepted by the lay members at least as the authoritative
exposition of spiritual truth. The stage was thus set for a use
of Garfield's abundant energies which made him well known to
an increasing circle of admirers. For the first five years he
preached somewhere every Sunday. Hinsdale afterward remembered that his stricter brethren found much fault with him
because he was not more denominational, but, wherever he
went, the people would turn out to hear Garfield preach. These
activities came to a climax in the fall of 1857 and the early
winter of 1858 when a great revival swept through all denominations. One of these occasions when three came forward
for baptism was described by one of his intimate friends. The
service, as so frequently, was out of doors. A large assembly
was gathered around a little lake and yet all were so hushed
that the slight murmur among the leaves could be distinctly
heard. Then Garfield's voice rose in terms so clear and me-
lodious, his thoughts so perfectly adapted to the occasion, that
his friends felt "as if they had been transplanted away from
earth to some tranquil, beautiful region of heaven." Is there
another politician in whose career such scenes have their place?
In the early winter, the movement reached Hiram. All other
engagements were postponed, and Garfield preached twenty-
seven times on successive days. At the last meeting seven students "came forward."

With the prestige of his college education, so rare even in
the academies of the west, and with an increasing fame as one
of the most eloquent of the preachers of his denomination, Garfield was sure of rapid advancement. Towards the close of Garfield's first year the presidency of Hiram became vacant
through the resignation of "Brother" Hayden, the clergyman

who had been the founder of the Institute. Apparently, the natural choice of a successor would have given the appointment to Professor Norman Dunshee, a sound classical scholar, who had been one of Garfield's teachers and a prominent member of the faculty from the beginning; but with the outside world, at least, Dunshee could not begin to compare in influence or importance with his pupil who had arrived fresh from Williams just eight months before. The trustees, and wisely as it seems, turned to Garfield, making him first chairman of the little faculty of five and shortly after giving him the formal title of president or principal. Such a choice could not fail to be a bitter blow to the disappointed Dunshee. The community in general had just become sharply divided on the subject of abolition, a political question on which at the time Dunshee's views were advanced and radical. Garfield for the first time and almost as a natural by-product of his evangelism, had participated in the presidential campaign in the fall of 1856 and had engaged in debates which had helped to swing the vote of northern Ohio to Frémont. But he had some conservative men on his Board of Trustees, and in the judgment of Dunshee he did not make Hiram such a center of abolition propaganda as Oberlin was already becoming. Dunshee, aflame with anti-slavery enthusiasm, openly criticised Garfield as a preacher who in his own college was not awake to the ethical implications of the one great moral and social question of his times. Garfield retorted by attacking Dunshee at the most sensitive point of his professional pride, calling Dunshee's teaching "wooden," which perhaps it was.

In a small faculty of five, the situation was of course impossible, and at the meeting of the Trustees in May, 1859, on the motion of Harmon Austin, Garfield's closest friend on the Board, and without the slightest warning, Dunshee was dismissed as a teacher at Hiram. As a result, and for the second time in his career, Garfield was subjected to serious criticism, and this time of a kind which left permanent and bitter memories. As soon as the Trustees were gone, Dunshee told his friends that the whole difficulty was a plot of Garfield's, and the dismissed teacher was regarded as another martyr to the cause of anti-slavery. Garfield replied that the move was made by the Trustees without plotting or connivance: "I did not directly counsel it and did not expect it." This statement was literally true, but scarcely candid, for Garfield's correspondence shows that during the winter he had kept his friends on the Board in close touch with the unpleasant situation. On April 7th, a full month before the dismissal of Dunshee, Garfield wrote a long letter to his closest friend, J. Harrison Rhodes, who had gone to Williams at the advice of Garfield and was about to graduate in the class of 1859, urging him to come back to Hiram and to unite an educational with a political career: "If you should do this, I think the Trustees would dispense with N. soon and your salary would be a fair one." As a matter of fact, Garfield's friend, Rhodes, was promptly given the position which had been vacated by Norman Dunshee.[1]

Rhodes was perhaps a better teacher than Dunshee, and the situation in the college was decidedly unpleasant. It was long before the ideas of academic security and freedom had been defined, and it would be unfair to judge the incident in the light of the more advanced ethics of a later time. Austin wrote, during the height of the controversy, that things had come to a strange pass if the Trustees did not have the right to select such teachers as in their judgment the interests of the school demanded. The Trustees took the full responsibility for the action. But the instincts of the members of the community who criticised the manner as much as the fact of Dunshee's dismissal

[1] Dunshee to Garfield, Nov. 13, 1855; Austin to Garfield, March 5, 1859; May 28, 1859; May 29, 1859; June 12, 1859. Garfield Papers.

were in line with a movement to add to the dignity and security of academic positions in America. Garfield's best friends might well have wished that he had boldly defended an action which he undoubtedly believed to be sound, and that he had assumed his share of the responsibility for the result. There were a few periods in Garfield's career when he told the truth, but not quite the whole truth. And this time, as once again, candor would have been evident wisdom as well.

But whatever one may think of the Dunshee incident, there was something infinitely attractive in the frankness with which Garfield treated Lucretia Rudolph and in the quiet confidence with which she waited for him to make up his mind. When, in 1856, Garfield returned to Hiram, the informal understanding between the two young people had already lasted two years, but Garfield was not ready to be married. There were, of course, the debts that it might take him two years to save money to pay; but there was also something deeper. For a time Garfield seems to have hesitated between the quiet strength of Lucretia Rudolph and the eager responsiveness of Rebecca Sellick. More than once he took advantage of a vacation to go back to Poesten-kill to visit the friends of his college years. After one of these visits he returned certain that if he married at all it must be with Lucretia Rudolph. He could not lose her, and begged her to give him time. The definite engagement took place in the spring of 1858. On a buggy ride to Ravenna to attend an examination for teachers, Garfield was accompanied by "Crete" Rudolph; they talked about their past lives for the last four years; and with regret for the past and mingled hope and fear for the future, they quietly resolved that they would "try life in union before many months." On November 11, 1858, at the home of Zeb Rudolph in Hiram, in the presence of a small group of friends, James Abram Garfield was married to Lucretia Ru-dolph. After so much thought and hesitation, what both young

GARFIELD'S WIFE

GARFIELD'S MOTHER

people had regarded as a dangerous experiment was infinitely successful, and from that time there was a beauty in the home life of Garfield which was more than once in sharp contrast with the bitter storms which were sure to play about the career of a rising politician. It was characteristic of the decreasing intensity of Garfield's purely denominational consciousness, that at his request the ceremony was performed not by a Disciple but by a Presbyterian, his friend and neighbor, President Hitchcock of the Western Reserve College at Hudson.

Immediately after his marriage, Garfield was given what he regarded at once as a remarkable opportunity to combine in a dramatic fashion his activities as an evangelist and a public teacher. At a time when the lyceum with its dignified lectures had a vogue in the older parts of America which is matched only by the moving pictures of our own day, the give and take of the public debate was even more popular in the newer regions of the west. In the west, throughout the leisurely winter months, the debate, as a form of public entertainment, was often the only rival of the dramatic criminal trial at the County Court House. Many of these debates were political, as witness the immense crowds that listened hour after hour in the same year to the contest between Lincoln and Douglas. But religion was only second to politics, and given two clever and well matched antagonists, debates on very serious subjects and of almost incredible length were followed day after day by the unflagging attention of large crowds. When one remembers that Darwin's *Origin of Species*, with its unconscious challenge to a new consideration of the borderland between science and religion, was not published until the following year (1859), the subject which in December, 1858, Garfield was called upon to debate in a region which less than two generations before had been unbroken forest, was in itself an eloquent proof of how completely some of the problems which the next generation was to con-

sider were already in the air. John Denton, a well-educated Eng-
lishman, proposed to maintain against all champions of religious
orthodoxy the following proposition: "Man, animals and
vegetables came into existence by the operation of the laws of
spontaneous generation and progressive development, and there
is no evidence that there was ever any exercise of direct creative
power on this planet." Here was a subject that was more significant than that of Garfield's boyish debate in 1852 on spiritual-
ism, nothing less than the age-long dispute between materialism
and idealism in a new and a concrete form, and an opponent
who was to be a more serious antagonist.

John Denton was thirty-seven years of age, a speaker whom
Garfield found rapid, elegant, and fiery, quick as a lightning
flash to seize a thought. At the time of his debate with Garfield,
he had already discussed the same subject more than forty times
with antagonists, many of whom were eloquent and some of
whom were eminent in church or state. Denton had acquired
many of the tricks and graces of the orator and knew how to
win his way with an audience.

Forewarned, Garfield had not despised his opponent and
had given the weeks just before the debate to careful preparation. Denton was the editor of a paper and had written a book,
so that Garfield was able to gain a fairly accurate idea of the
points which he was to be expected to meet. According to an
early biographer who is probably well informed, Garfield sent
one of his friends to listen to and to take notes on one of Denton's debates in a distant town, and with these notes before him
commenced a period of feverish activity, reading not deeply
but sufficiently for purposes of debate and taking notes on
books on geology, botany, zoölogy, and anthropology, a course
of reading which not only made him a dangerous antagonist,
but opened up to the classically trained young evangelist whole
new worlds of thought and adventure.

The debate, well advertised, took place in the little town of Chagrin Falls. A hall was hired which would hold a thousand people, and in the course of a series of speeches which lasted from Monday to Friday, the smallest audience almost filled the hall. Frequently it was crowded. On each of the five days there were two sessions, each of two hours, in which each speaker had two opportunities of half an hour each to meet the arguments of his opponent. Apart from Garfield's voluminous notes, these speeches do not seem to have been preserved, which is probably just as well, for such a debate could not be expected to settle anything finally. But we do know from orthodox criticisms that were made of Garfield that, as a result of his reading, he had the intellectual honesty and the debating wisdom to acknowledge at once his opponent's contention that the world had probably existed for millions of years, a point which seemed to him quite beside the central problem of the debate. In his final speech, Denton courteously acknowledged that Garfield was far the strongest antagonist whom he had met. One only hopes that similar courtesy was not habitual. But Garfield and his friends were immensely pleased; Garfield referred to the incident as the most important in his life; and one of his friends wrote that since the smoke of battle had partially cleared away, they were beginning to see more clearly the victory that had been gained. He had not met a man who would acknowledge that Denton had made good his position.[1] As the outstanding defender of religion against infidelity, Garfield had undoubtedly gained a host of friends, and the stage was almost set for the first step in his political advancement the next spring.

During the winter Garfield followed up his initial success by a series of lectures in various towns on the subject "Geology

[1] Garfield to Hinsdale, Jan. 10, 1859, Bundy, *op. cit.*, p. 50; Hinsdale, *Garfield and Education*, p. 80. The notes on the debates and numerous letters on the subject are in the Garfield *Papers*.

and Religion." He had come to feel that the battle of the evidences must now be fought on the field of the natural sciences. Partly for religious reasons, and also because he recognized the importance of science in education, he introduced a course in geology into the narrow curriculum of Hiram, and encouraged the formation of a Natural History Society. Similar steps in other places were soon to begin what was to be a veritable revolution in the methods and content of American higher education. There are also some hints that Garfield had learned from Denton, and from the time of the debate there was no longer to be the same tone of absolute finality in Garfield's religious and theological opinions. If so, the change which came to him, and which made the transition to the secular life of politics easy, was merely a single instance of another unconscious social process. Between the lines, one begins to feel that the Garfield of 1859 is a very different man from the young man who returned from the orthodox atmosphere of Williams. Perhaps the victory in the debate was after all not quite so bloodless or so sweeping as it had seemed.

During these busy years, with his seven classes a day, his Sunday sermons, his administrative duties and heavy correspondence, and his public addresses, the same attitude towards life which had given him success as an evangelist and the same personal qualities were long remembered by his students. One of them, who was afterwards to become the most distinguished President of Hiram, wrote that he called out the demonstrativeness and affections of men in a way that was almost unprecedented. When he put his great brotherly arm around a discouraged boy, poor, homesick, or blind to the way before him, the mists began to clear away from the youngster's vision and his heart grew strong. Another recalled that Garfield had a marvelous memory for names, and knew every boy in the school personally and joined freely in their sports on terms of equality.

In later reminiscences Garfield used almost the language of evangelism when he said that he had taken more solid comfort and received more moral recompense in after life from capturing young men for an education than from anything else in the world. During the past generation and as compared with the beginning of the century, there had been a marked decrease in the percentage of the population attending college. The college was finding it difficult to compete with the opening west as a few years later it was to meet the still more intense competition of a new industrial era. In accumulated resources, America was poor, and in view of undeveloped wealth America was very busy. The frontier parent, as was amply illustrated in the relations of Abraham Lincoln to his father, believed that he had a vested right to the services of his son during the productive years of the adolescent period. It was often difficult to persuade such a father that he ought to let a son go to school who was old enough to be a useful hand on a clearing where necessary labor, in the days of ax and hoe and cradle, was all too scarce. There was the concrete problem of the college President of the fifties to which Garfield referred when he spoke of "saving young men for an education," and with which, as all the reminiscences show, he was unusually well qualified to deal. Sometimes Garfield persuaded an obdurate father to leave the boy for one more term in Hiram by holding before his eyes the possibility of twelve dollars a month as a teacher in some district school during the next winter when the farm would be covered with ice and snow. But again and more frequently Garfield appealed to the deep religious feelings of his constituents. Accordingly, in these years one of Garfield's favorite sermons was on the parable of the talents, with the obvious analogy between the child without opportunities and the talent that was hid in a napkin.

In many of Garfield's sermons the same note of practical ethics was increasingly apparent.[1] The time when the colleges would be compelled to select their students was still very far away, and was to wait on a whole series of social and economic changes at the heart of American life.

When Garfield went to Williams in the summer of 1859 to deliver a so-called master's oration and to attend the graduation of Rhodes, he met Washington Gladden, a member of the graduating class who was later to become one of the most celebrated liberal clergymen of Ohio. Gladden remembered Garfield as a fine, strong young fellow with a ruddy face, a massive head, a cordial manner and an air of mastership: "Few who knew him in those days were surprised at his swift ascent to places of command." [2] It was in that same year that Garfield ceased to be primarily an evangelist and became a politician.

[1] For one of Garfield's published sermons, see B. A. Hinsdale, *Garfield and Education* (1882), p. 75. The Garfield *Papers, Public Addresses,* have two large volumes of sermons. Some of these are definitely evangelistic in tone. For example one concludes: "As these thoughts are now before you, let me ask you to choose the undying Jesus as your Friend and Helper. The hopes of the world are false . . . but the Christian shall never die." More frequently, the note is distinctly ethical in tone.

[2] Washington Gladden, *Recollections,* p. 76.

In the America of Garfield's day, and to some extent still, it was a dangerous thing to apply frankly for any office or position in church, state or school. The office was supposed to seek the man, even when his snares were carefully set to secure it without fail. To this tradition Garfield was astonishingly faithful, even, sometimes, to the extent of almost deceiving himself. So he prided himself that his first district school had been offered to him before he had applied for the position which he evidently desired, and also that the Trustees of Hiram had given him a Presidency without an application on his part. Once or twice Garfield tried to break with this tradition but usually with disastrous results. So he learned to abide by the rules of the game, to such an extent as to give to the changes in his life an unplanned and fortuitous appearance which they did not have in fact, and which would be frankly absent in a similar career in England or in France. And so it was now. The democracy of a pioneer America liked a coy servant and preferred to do its own wooing.

The first requisite for a successful political career was a wise, tactful, and influential friendship. Garfield had already found precisely such a friend in Harmon Austin of Ravenna, a member of his Board of Trustees at Hiram, who, like Mark Hanna or Colonel House at a later day, without personal political ambitions was essentially a king-maker. In a game so competitive as politics, such a friendship made it possible for Garfield to remain discreetly in the background until the right moment had come for an open declaration. Throughout his life Garfield found in Austin an almost ideal political manager.

By the spring of 1859 Garfield had fully decided to use his

51

growing prestige as a stepping stone to politics, an ambition which he had of course revealed to his friends. The district in which he lived consisted of the two neighboring counties of Summit and Portage and was about to select a senator to sit in the next state legislature. Summit was by this time almost safely Republican, but Portage, in which Hiram was located, was fairly closely divided between the members of the new party and the conservatives who were now grouped under the banner of the Democrats. Accordingly, the political leaders had wisely decided that the Republican candidate must come from Portage. For governor, the Republicans, sobered by the responsibilities of growing success, had decided on the relatively conservative William Dennison, a successful banker, as their candidate to succeed Governor Chase, who was coming to the close of his second term and who was now looking either to the national Senate or perhaps to the Presidency itself. In contrast with Chase, Dennison represented the alliance between idealism and business which was to characterise and insure the success of a very young party. Garfield attended the convention on August 26th, where he found himself confronted by three rivals from his own county; but his friendly manners, his effective eloquence, and especially his reputation for comparative conservatism on the great national issue of slavery or abolition, secured his selection as their candidate by the delegates of his own county, a choice which was promptly ratified by the nominating convention itself.

To many of Garfield's friends, and especially to his mother, who had long cherished what seemed to her the highest possible ambition, that her son should take his place as one of the great preachers of his time, a hope which his recent success as an evangelist had seemed completely to fulfill, the knowledge that he was to become a politician came as a bitter disappointment. To others Garfield's decision seemed almost treason to a higher calling.[1] In Garfield's own diary there was a hint that his conscience for the moment troubled him, and he comforted himself by writing that he had taken the fatal step at the instance of his friends and not his own; for he was not to shake off easily the habit of years in which the Christian and the politician were set in persistent hostility, and for a time he continued to half believe that his political life would be a mere interlude. Since he could not possibly make a living as a member of a state legislature, he retained the Presidency of Hiram, and with the consent of the Trustees merely turned over his administrative duties for the time of his necessary absence to his friend Rhodes, who for years kept him in close touch with the affairs of the college. But the eyes of his mother were not to be so easily deceived; she knew that the die was cast; and Garfield left her in tears as he plunged into the activities of the first campaign in which he was personally interested.

By his nomination in such a district his own election was almost assured, and the issues of the campaign turned to a large extent on considerations which transcended the limits of his district and even of his state. The results of the Kansas-Nebraska Act and their own quarrels had largely discredited the Democrats, but if the Republicans were to capture Ohio and to win the next Presidency, they would be unable to rely exclusively on the old free soil vote. They must commend themselves in the northern states which held the majority of the votes in the electoral college to thousands of former Whigs and Democrats who were opposed to the extension of slavery, but who were equally determined to act within the limits of constitutional legality. Thus one of Lincoln's chief objectives in his debates with Douglas and in the speeches of the next two years was to

---

[1] The first suggestion seems to have come from Austin who remained friendly to the experiment in politics: Austin to Garfield, June 12, 1859. For criticisms see Loos to Garfield, Aug. 23, 1859, and Hayden to Garfield, Oct. 6, 1859. (Garfield *Papers.*)

show that he was quite as conservative as Douglas. In Ohio, in the campaign in which Garfield was for the first time a candidate for office such considerations were obviously in the forefront. So Garfield as a conservative was preferred to his three opponents for reasons that were not dissimilar to those that led on a larger stage to the nomination of Lincoln over Seward the next year.

The State of Ohio was still predominantly agricultural. More than half its area was under cultivation, and the majority of its adult males were farmers, there being of this class two hundred and seventy-seven thousand owning farms which averaged ninety acres apiece. The agricultural products of the state were more than twice as great as were needed for the food of the people of the state. In 1860 the farmers exported nearly two million barrels of flour, over two and a half million bushels of wheat, three million bushels of other grains, and half a million barrels of pork. But manufactures were arising, and the value of the products of the factories of Ohio had doubled within a single decade. Cincinnati which had been founded almost within the memory of living men had already become a greater center for the manufacture of clothing than New York. And such municipal growth was now being matched in other towns and villages.

As a political and social community the state was still divided by a line which could be roughly traced along the course of the old national road through Zanesville to the west almost as clearly as the nation was divided by the imaginary boundary of Mason and Dixon. The southern part of the state had been settled very much earlier and had still the larger part of the wealth and population. It had been occupied, not exclusively, but to a sufficient extent to give a peculiar social and political atmosphere, by people who had originally come by the various gateways through which the Old Dominion had sent its surplus population to the growing west. In one war the region had been won for the nation by troops from Virginia and in another guarded by the friendly protection of Kentucky. On the south and east, Ohio was separated for more than four hundred miles from slave territory by the narrow boundary of its great river. Families not only had relatives on either side, but from the beginning, the rivers that flowed to the Ohio and that stream itself had been the chief means of communication, and the only convenient avenue for the export of surplus products. Cincinnati had become the Queen City of the West as the most convenient source of food and clothing for southern plantations. Even an interior town like Chillicothe on the Scioto had its connections with the South and a social atmosphere that had a distinct flavor of the old South.

As one passed north from the national road, the type of people changed, until in the Western Reserve one met again the institutions and ideals of New England. Except in counties like Holmes and Ashland which had been settled recently by German Mennonites and were therefore peculiar, northern Ohio had a remarkable political and social uniformity which separated it from the counties to the south. In this northern region, economic outlets and lines of communication also no longer looked to the south, but back by way of the canals and the great lakes to the markets of the east.

The policies of the state had naturally been dominated by the more populous and conservative south. But in the last two decades the north had gained in relative strength and had come, first to hold the balance of power and then to contend for the dominance of its own ideals. In the meantime the completion of great lines of railroads leading to the east were rapidly reducing the relative significance of the Ohio river. Every year even southern Ohio was exporting an increasing proportion of its wealth through the seaports of the Atlantic coast rather than

to New Orleans. These new lines of transportation blurred
ancient differences and prejudices between northern and southern Ohio at the same time that the canals and later north and
south railroads were bringing the people of the two sections into
ready communication with each other. Garfield as a boy had
gone to southern Ohio as to a strange new country. But such
differences though still visible were by 1859 by no means
equally vital. The national road as a social boundary was about
to disappear.

Such changes were, of course, revealed in the figures for successive elections. Back in 1840, Ohio like other western communities had thrown up its coon-skin caps and beaver hats alike
"for Tippecanoe and Tyler too." Van Buren had been left far behind, and the radical anti-slavery Birney had received a paltry
nine hundred votes, which the leaders of the two major parties
could afford to look on with a complacent smile. But in 1844,
when, true to her conservative Whig traditions, Ohio had voted
for Clay, Birney's vote had been multiplied by ten. Four years
later, in 1848, and again in 1852, the anti-slavery vote, first for
Van Buren and then for Hale, had passed thirty thousand and
held the balance of power sufficiently to swing the state by narrow majorities away from the Whigs and into the Democratic
column. Here was a force to be reckoned with, and making skillful use of his position the southern leader of anti-slavery, Salmon P. Chase, had been elected first to the Senate and then
twice to the governor's chair. In the four years of the Presidency
of Pierce, the swing in Ohio had been very definitely to the left.
In the first campaign in which Garfield, like many other young
men in northern Ohio, had taken an active interest, the Republicans had carried the state for Frémont with a surprising total
of 187,497 votes, but even then as the result of temporary discontent and by the division of the conservative votes between
Buchanan and Fillmore. The power of conservatism, especially

in southern Ohio, was still apparent, and the people had by no means accepted fully the positions of such leaders as Giddings in the Western Reserve or even of Governor Chase.

Now, in 1859, the Republicans under Dennison made a bid for the same kind of a victory in Ohio which under Lincoln they had vainly sought in Illinois one year before and which they were to win on a national scale in the vital election of 1860. In Garfield's district the general problem arose in concrete form. At Oberlin, the chief center of anti-slavery agitation, a mob had obstructed the enforcement of the national statute for the return of fugitive slaves, and the leaders in spite of much popular sympathy had been indicted and found guilty under the express terms of the hated measure. In the supreme court of the State, to which the case was carried, a Republican judge joined with the Democrats in upholding the constitutionality of the fugitive slave law. For this position, the Republican, Judge Swan, was of course bitterly assailed, but, at the beginning of a vigorous campaign Garfield came to his defense, announcing publicly that if Judge Swan were to follow the precedents of Federal and State courts, he could not have decided differently. The general Republican strategy was evidently sound. Dennison and a Republican legislature were elected, and in spite of his letter on the Swan decision, or possibly on account of it, Garfield carried his district and won his first election by a commanding majority of more than fourteen hundred votes in a total of nine thousand. He had made more than thirty speeches and had laid deep foundations for a political career.

Early in January, 1860, Garfield reached Columbus in time to participate in the inaugural ceremonies and to listen to an address by the new governor in which, perforce, Dennison insisted on his hostility to the extension of slavery, but recognized the deeper problem that lay behind it by advocating the colonization of the blacks in Central or South America, and promised faithful obedience to the constitutional obligations of Ohio to the slave-holding States. But during the period of the Ohio campaign, events had taken place on the distant Potomac that were to make such a policy of conciliation increasingly difficult; and, in Garfield's career, it was a coincidence of no small significance that he was elected a senator of the State of Ohio and that almost at the same moment John Brown of Ossawattomie was hanged. For passions had been aroused which it would take more than wise and conciliatory speeches with a definite old Whig flavor to allay; and Garfield's journal shows a conflict between his deep sympathy for the ideals of Brown and a desire to uphold the cause of orderly progress to which he had been committed early in his campaign and which was now summed up in the quiet inaugural of Governor Dennison.

With his eager appreciation of new experiences and without quite realising what a vital step they were in his education, Garfield greatly enjoyed his two years in the legislature. So many of the members of the Republican party were new to politics that a beginner like Garfield had an almost immediate opportunity for leadership which would have been absent to the follower of an older standard. Garfield called at once on the titular leader of his party, the outgoing governor, Chase, who received the young legislator with deference that Garfield had the humor to ascribe to Chase's persistent political ambitions. But he found in William Dennison a directness and simplicity that at once won Garfield's heart, and from the beginning the new governor could count on the hearty support of the senator from Hiram. Garfield was lucky enough to find a place to live in the home of the chairman of the State Committee of his party, where he was at once introduced into the intricacies of party politics and where he made friendships that were especially useful to him. In James Monroe, a professor at Oberlin, and in Jacob D. Cox, an older man from the district immediately to the east of his own, Garfield found kindred spirits. The three young men were soon inseparable, and there were few questions on which they did not vote alike. The newspapers were soon speaking of the three as a single unit in the leadership of the more radical element among the Republicans. In later years Monroe was to accept the reward of his political services as a consul at a South American port, but Cox and Garfield were both to ride the coming storm to positions of still higher leadership. Cox especially knew the intricacies of legislative procedure, and in a place where the emotional oratory of the evangelist was no longer useful, he proved to the younger man a specially capable mentor in parliamentary law of which in later days Garfield was to prove so proficient a master.

Having made his maiden speech in favor of State appropriation for school libraries, Garfield was confronted with his first critical decision in connection with a conservative measure which had been introduced to prohibit military expeditions like the one which had made famous the name of John Brown. After some hesitation Garfield decided to vote and to speak against the proposed bill. For a representative of the Western Reserve, where Brown was already gaining the name of a hero and a saint, such a decision was not surprising; but Garfield was still uncertain and voted with the evident hope that he might be left in a minority, and that the power of a conservative majority would prevent such scenes on the soil of Ohio as had occurred in Maryland. In spite of this decision, the conservatism which had marked his campaign was seen almost at once in his support of an invitation which Governor Dennison wished to extend to the united legislatures of the states of Kentucky and Tennessee then assembled at Louisville. The meeting was intended to serve as a symbol of the indivisible unity of the west and to allay the wild talk of secession which had been greatly stimulated by the exciting events of the last three months.

Having helped Dennison to carry this measure through the legislature Garfield was chosen to act as spokesman in presenting the invitation of Ohio to the assembled statesmen of her two sister States. The duty, for a young member in his first term, was a compliment, but not without its dangers, for everything that Garfield said in Louisville was sure to be read in the Western Reserve, where the atmosphere was to say the least decidedly different. In his speech to the assembled southern legislators, Garfield made the usual references to Clay and to Jackson as prophets of an indivisible Union; he expressed the belief that when the voice of the west was heard no note of disunion would appear in its utterance; as long as a single system of rivers carried the commerce of the west, the spokesman of Ohio refused to believe that any part of the region would support the movement to draw across the valley of the Mississippi an artificial boundary. Here was a geographical interpretation of the inherent unity of the continent and especially of the west, to which Garfield was to return in his speeches during the summer and in which he seems to have anticipated a theme that Lincoln later developed at length in his second message to Congress. What both Garfield and Lincoln forgot was that the binding power of the commerce of the Mississippi had been measurably weakened by new lines of railroad transportation which almost without exception now ran east and west instead of north and south.

Garfield's Louisville speech seems to have been well received, although the meeting of the legislatures of three western States proved to be a mere straw in the path of the advancing current of secession. But Garfield returned from Kentucky without any premonitions of the coming storm, and after the session of the legislature went back to Hiram to pick up again the broken threads of his ordinary life. Again, as he might have done in any less critical period, he was seen teaching his classes and preaching regularly on Sundays. During the summer his first child was born. But Garfield's new position as a politician appeared in the important part which he took in the state Republican convention and in his activity during the campaign which elected Lincoln to the Presidency. For Garfield saw at once that in Ohio, at least, Lincoln's only rival was Stephen A. Douglas. And without wasting his energy on Breckinridge or Bell, he devoted himself to proving that the idea of squatter sovereignty opened up more problems than it settled. In a speech at Ravenna, and throughout the campaign, Garfield, like Schurz and other Republican orators, brushed aside the solemn warnings of Douglas as mere political buncombe. The South could not afford to secede. Secession, at the worst, would be limited to a single state: "If there were one, would not the thirty-two remaining sisters throw their arms of affection around the erring one and bring her gently back again to the sacred circle of the home?" Illusory as they were soon to appear, there can be little doubt that such arguments were decisive of the election of 1860; hundreds of men voted for Lincoln who would have pondered long if they had realised the seriousness of the crisis. On November 6th, Garfield cast his vote for Lincoln and Hamlin and in the evening went to Ravenna to receive the returns. When, at midnight, he knew that the Republicans had elected their first President, Garfield "thanked God that the question had at last been met squarely and that the country had not been frightened into another compromise!"

When in January, 1861, Garfield returned to Columbus for the annual meeting of the legislature, the easy optimism of the previous year had been destroyed. South Carolina on December 20th had seceded, and it was now apparent that she would be followed at least by the States of the lower south. The middle south under the leadership of Virginia might yet be saved and schemes of conciliation were again in the air. But Garfield was not the man to join the cry of Horace Greeley to let the erring sisters depart in peace. On January 15th, Garfield wrote to Hinsdale: "Peaceable dissolution is utterly impossible. Indeed I cannot say that I would wish it possible. To make the concessions demanded by the South would be hypocritical and sinful; they would neither be obeyed nor respected. . . . All that is left us as a State, or say as a company of Northern States, is to arm and prepare to defend ourselves and the Federal Government. I believe the doom of slavery is drawing near." [1] So at the outset, Garfield saw the problems of the preservation of the Union and the destruction of slavery as merely two phases of a single movement. From that time on he never allowed himself to separate these two great desires. Perhaps more completely than any other Republican of his time, Garfield spoke at once with the voice of the west, to which the unity of the continent was an axiom, and, as a true son of the Western Reserve, with that of New England, where the hatred of slavery had risen to the heights of an almost religious fervor. So he was now writing, in language which is reminiscent of John Brown: "The sin of slavery is one of which it may be that without the shedding of blood there is no remission."

The conciliatory Garfield who had gone to Louisville the year before had now wholly disappeared. He opposed bitterly a movement to repeal the personal liberty law of the State, which was frankly intended to nullify the fugitive slave law; he sought in vain to prevent the appointment of delegates from Ohio to a peace congress which under the chairmanship of an ex-President was to seek a compromise between the two embittered sections; he introduced a bill to make the advocacy of secession treason against the State of Ohio, and to punish such treason with imprisonment for life. When this first essay in legislation was met with almost universal ridicule as an obvious evasion of constitutional safeguards that had been regarded as sacred, Garfield

[1] J. M. Bundy: *Life of Garfield,* p. 51.

was not discouraged and bided his time until the revolutionary incidents of war should establish new canons of constitutional interpretation.

In January, Garfield had felt that the hour of opportunity had come but not the man to ride upon the storm and to direct it. But when in February Lincoln visited Columbus, Garfield's estimate of the new leader was higher than it was to be at a later period, and so he wrote to Hinsdale: "Mr. Lincoln has come and gone. The rush of people to see him at every point on the route is astonishing. The reception here was plain and republican, but very impressive. He has been raising a respectable pair of dark brown whiskers, which decidely improve his looks, but no appendage can ever make him remarkable for beauty. On the whole I am greatly pleased with him. He clearly shows his want of culture, and the marks of western life; but there is no touch of affectation in him, and he has a peculiar power of impressing you that he is frank, direct and thoroughly honest. His remarkable good sense, simple and condensed style of expression, and evident marks of indomitable will, give me great hopes for the country." [1]

Such an estimate of Lincoln at this early period is in sharp contrast with that of other men like Seward, Chase, and Charles Francis Adams who failed completely to realise the strength of the new President. Garfield was now certain that after the period of weakness and cowardly imbecility under Buchanan the American people had found a strong and vigorous leader. His disappointment in Lincoln's first inaugural was proportionately great. For Garfield believed that it would be an economy of bloodshed to commence the new Administration with a ringing declaration of a purpose to defend the forts and to enforce the laws, and when in the first month of his term Lincoln seemed to pursue precisely the same policy of watchful waiting that had

[1] Bundy, *op. cit.*, p. 51.

characterised Buchanan, Garfield found the President unequal
to the heroic demands of the hour. Making an estimate of Lincoln's qualities which was initially just, Garfield was unable to
understand the delays that were made necessary by a changing
and confused Administration, an empty treasury, and an army
that was practically non-existent. He did not have the experience
needed to estimate at its true value the problem of Virginia and
the border States, and he became as unjust to Lincoln as he had
been to Buchanan, whose problems were not dissimilar. From
that time, Garfield was never an admirer of Lincoln; and in the
years to come, on such critical questions as the postponement
of emancipation in 1862, and reconstruction in 1864, we shall
find in Garfield one of the President's most severe critics.

During the fateful month of March, 1861, while Lincoln
in Washington was seeking for some wise solution of the difficulties in which he was placed, Garfield in Columbus was managing
the campaign of his friend Governor Dennison for the Senate
of the United States. Much to Garfield's disappointment, Dennison was defeated by a rising young politician, John Sherman
of Mansfield, with whose career Garfield was in later years to
have intimate contacts. This defeat quickened a half-formed
purpose to give up politics after all and to return to an educational career. Then on April 13th came the news that Fort
Sumter was under fire. After a few hours of excitement and
suspense, Ohio knew that Anderson had yielded to the inevitable and had surrendered. Garfield was delighted. On the
day when the news arrived he wrote that the incident at Sumter
was just what was needed to shake the government and people
from their lethargy and to prevent the nation from drifting
into disunion. War would come; but such a war would soon
make sharp the inevitable issue between slavery and freedom
and in the long run would redound to the good of humanity.
Such a letter, on April 14, 1861, had within it a remarkable

quality of far-sighted statesmanship. That very day, before any word had come from Washington, the Governor summoned Garfield and Cox in consultation, and the three men together decided to proceed to arm and equip the militia and to ask the legislature for authority to borrow a half million dollars for the purpose. The next day Lincoln issued his call for 75,000 militia to serve for three months, and within a few hours the untrained and unarmed regiments began to reach Columbus. Everybody was willing to save the nation if it could be done before harvest time, and the quota of Ohio was soon oversubscribed. But Garfield expected a long and sanguinary war, and he and his friend Cox were soon spending all their leisure time in reading military science and the campaigns of Napoleon and Wellington. In a few weeks Garfield felt that his attainments were such that he deserved a position as staff officer.

In the meantime, the young man from Hiram was coming to his own as a Republican leader in the Senate. Against Garfield's opposition, the conservative forces of conciliation were still strong enough to secure the ratification of the proposed Thirteenth Amendment which would reassure the South by removing slavery in the States from the reach of national action. On this question, the three friends from the Western Reserve were in a minority of eight, for the measure had been sponsored by Thomas Corwin, whose influence in Ohio was still potent, and had the reluctant approval of Lincoln. But the "Million Bill" for a State loan, of which Garfield was one of the authors, and which looked to war as much as the Corwin amendment looked to peace, was passed by an overwhelming vote on the same day, and Garfield was even able to carry through the Senate his bill defining treason, which one week before would undoubtedly have failed.

Everybody was in a state of feverish activity. The problem was not so much to raise the three months' militia as to secure a position within the narrow limits of the quota. The time would come when everybody would have a chance without such evident eagerness; but at the moment, competition was intense, and, according to time-honored custom, the officers were to be elected just as if they were running for some political office. Garfield went to Cleveland to see that the Western Reserve was "fairly represented"; and incidentally, for perhaps the only time in his political life, he became an active candidate for the colonelcy of one of the regiments. The campaign was full of personalities, Garfield accusing his rival, Erastus B. Tyler of Ravenna, of stooping to use "brandy and bargains" for the privilege of fighting the nation's battles, and the newspapers that supported Tyler being equally severe on Garfield. As a result of this bitter contest, Tyler was elected to the eagerly desired position by a vote of 580 to 243. With an army organised for the most part in such a way, the defeat of McDowell at Bull Run was certainly not surprising. As for Garfield, in his only serious reverse he had learned a lesson as to the ways of democracy that never needed to be repeated.

Garfield always believed that he would have won if it had not been for a trip to Indiana and Illinois, where he was sent at this time on a semi-diplomatic mission as the personal representative of the Governor of Ohio. He was to secure a loan of five thousand stands of arms from the Governor of Illinois and he was to persuade the troops of these western States to serve under a major-general from Ohio, George B. McClellan. Such a mission, in which Garfield was successful, throws a curious light on the element of State pride which even in a national crisis and in northern States was a necessary feature of the preparation for war. The element of sovereignty was evidently not a complete fiction in the American Union before the Civil War.

It was soon entirely apparent that the war could not be won

by trusting to militia enlisted for a brief period and carrying democratic principles to the length of serving under elected officers. Such an army was sure to be dissolved just at the moment when it might be expected to serve with reasonable efficiency. The Confederates had already begun to raise an army of volunteers to serve for a minimum of twelve months and had thus secured a stable military force that was in sharp contrast with the useless militia of the North. From the point of view of military critics, the ideal solution would have been a national army secured by draft or conscription and commanded by the distribution of the officers and soldiers of the regular army, who would have been of great service in training raw recruits. Contrary to a common impression, of the 1063 West Point men in the United States of 1861, more than three quarters adhered to the Union, and from these trained men officers might have been found for most of the higher positions. But, in the spring of 1861, the necessity for technical training was not sufficiently appreciated and most of these resources were overlooked. As it was, the Administration took a bold step in advance when on May 3d, 1861, and without waiting for any authorisation from Congress, it decided to follow the Confederate example and to commence raising an army of volunteers to serve for three years and to supplant the militia when their three months of service was ended. The officers, previously elected, were to be nominated and practically appointed by the governors of the various loyal states. Sometimes a governor found a retired West Point man, like McClellan or Grant or Sherman, and had the wisdom to appoint him to a responsible command. The result often was to carry the officer who had retired from the army to a higher position than could be readily attained by those who had continued to follow the profession of a soldier. But since the volunteer army was at first on paper, in selecting officers for mythical regiments it was entirely natural and perhaps almost necessary to turn in most cases to orators and popular local politicians whose influence in their home communities might be trusted to fill the ranks that they were later to lead into battle. Every one had an easy confidence that such men would soon acquire the necessary knowledge of tactics and strategy before the day of trial. The transition from politics to general-ship was thus made easy; the trained abilities of many West Point men were wasted; and politicians became over-night colonels and even generals. Some of these volunteer officers, like Garfield and Cox, became reasonably efficient, but not one was to attain a reputation of the highest distinction.[1]

Such considerations belong to the historian of a later epoch, and for the moment no one seems to have doubted that positions in the army should be assigned as spoils of office precisely as civil officers of government were appointed. In June, Governor Dennison, who had made Garfield's room-mate, Jacob D. Cox, a brigadier general, offered Garfield the position of lieutenant colonel of one of the new regiments. Whether any element of natural disappointment entered into the decision or not, Garfield decided not to enter the army at that time, and in the summer, while the first battles of the war were being fought and lost, Garfield paid a final pilgrimage to the home of Alexander Campbell where he found the college closed and the students dispersed. Campbell was loyal to the Union, but his son, wife, and daughter sympathised strongly with the South. The leader of Garfield's church looked old, and broken, and prophesied sadly that he would never see peace in this country again. The visit to Bethany was one of Garfield's last efforts to turn back the pages of his destiny. The call of the war was too strong. On

[1] General E. Upton, *Military Policy of the United States,* p. 236, discusses this question and proves the relative superiority of the north in trained West Point men.

August 14th, 1861, he decided to accept the post which in June
he had refused and going to the telegraph office sent a despatch
to the Governor to say that he was ready. A new stage in what
Henry Adams would have called the education of James Abram
Garfield was about to begin.

THE transition in Garfield's career was sudden but not more so than that of thousands of other young Americans in the same year. He was now an officer of a volunteer regiment that did not as yet exist. Accordingly, his own training must precede the enlistment of his soldiers. Going directly to Columbus, he reported at Camp Chase, where he was placed temporarily on the staff of one of the generals. Having no quarters assigned to him, he slept that night, his first in the army, on a pile of straw, and the next morning, after making the necessary purchases, he was able to put aside his civilian clothes and appear in the uniform of a soldier. His first duty was to read the correspondence of some forty prisoners who had been taken in the early campaigns in West Virginia, a task which fortunately required little military erudition; but in the meantime he was devoting himself to the Infantry Tactics, and first using blocks of wood to represent companies, officers, and non-commissioned officers, he was soon able to learn the art of command by practice in actual drill. After a few days, Garfield was entrusted with the oversight of the camp guard, assigning them their duties as sentinels and repeating over and over again the same little speech; once he even held trial and sentenced a sentinel to three days' imprisonment on bread and water for sleeping at his post. Within two weeks, Governor Dennison felt that his young protégé had advanced so rapidly that he deserved a promotion, and he became Colonel Garfield in command of the Forty-Second Ohio.

The regiment was as yet entirely mythical. About the middle of September, accompanied by the two officers next in rank, Garfield went to Hiram and began recruiting. Quoting freely from

Byron, and appealing to patriotism and college pride, Garfield addressed the students, and within two or three days he raised the first company, composed largely of the older boys at Hiram. In October Colonel Garfield had six companies and a "fine brass band," and he was greatly interested in securing a gift of regimental colors from the home folks at Hiram; but by that time the officers had done all that they could in the communities where they were personally known, and the remaining men came in slowly. There was no longer any eager rush to arms, such as had followed the news from Sumter. Many a young fellow who was asked to volunteer for three years had been sobered by the defeat at Bull Run, and thought long and carefully before he listened to the appeals of military evangelists. When he could, Garfield gained permission to speak at regular Sunday services in the churches where he had been heard so frequently on other topics, but especially in Ashland County he found the churches closed to such arguments by conscientious objections to military measures, and he was hard put to it to secure even an audience. But his training in recent years stood him in good stead; the war could be pictured as a great idealistic crusade, much as all wars have been described to their supporters, and on November 30th, Colonel Garfield found himself in command of a full regiment of a thousand men.

In controlling his soldiers, Garfield used at first the same appeals to honor that had been effective at Hiram, but he soon found that such methods did not reach the careless and the unruly; but though he was a stern disciplinarian, his soldiers recognised his capacity for inspiring leadership and their devotion to their colonel never waned. As so frequently in his career, Garfield's personality atoned for unavoidable ignorance. And it was well; for, barely had the last volunteers come in, when, on December 14th, the Forty-Second Ohio was summoned to active duty in the field.

The Union forces under McClellan in Virginia, Buell in Kentucky, and Halleck in the West, were engaged in a process of organization for which the events of the summer had shown the evident necessity. None of these commanders had any intention of moving forward on a large scale until spring. Buell's line stretched across southern Kentucky from the Mississippi to the Cumberlands; the State which had attempted to remain neutral could not be regarded as safely Southern or Northern in its sympathies and was likely to adhere at least nominally to the section that retained military control. With such considerations in mind and largely for political effect, the Confederates were even in the winter threatening at two points the eastern end of Buell's line. Humphrey Marshall, with a force estimated as between two and six thousand and actually of about three thousand soldiers had pushed through the mountains to the valley of the Big Sandy, a stream partially navigable which flowed north through Kentucky near to the Virginia boundary and emptied into the Ohio. Such an expedition, if given adequate support by the nominally hostile people of the mountains, might obviously drive a dangerous wedge between the forces in Kentucky and those to the east of them in western Virginia. Somewhat farther to the west, a much larger Confederate force under Zollicoffer and Crittenden was making another dangerous threat against Buell's long line. Buell decided to send General George H. Thomas against the larger force with a command of eight regiments, in an expedition that does not concern us here, but which proved to be eminently successful. To deal with Humphrey Marshall in the valley of the Big Sandy, and for reasons that do not appear, he selected the totally inexperienced and presumably unknown Colonel Garfield of Ohio.

The contrast between the two commanders chosen by Buell for independent and responsible expeditions could scarcely have been greater. Thomas was a Virginian, born in 1819 of a good family, but like seventy-eight percent of the West Point men of his generation, and in spite of such outstanding exceptions as Lee, Johnston, and others, kept true to the Union by the soldier's habit of obedience—quiet, almost taciturn, conservative, an experienced and well-established soldier, his hair already sprinkled with grey, who had made a name in the Mexican war and had fought Indians from the Seminoles of Florida to the Comanches of Texas, a West Point man through and through, standing high in the class of 1840, a class which gave to the war two other great commanders in Sherman and Ewell. And Garfield! Barely thirty, a preacher, a college professor, a politician, with a big booming voice and a jovial personality, a charming conversationalist essentially and always an orator, eager and certain of himself to the point of rashness, who had read "the campaigns of Wellington and Napoleon" the winter before, on the evenings after a day of debate in the legislature of Ohio, who had studied the Infantry Manual for as much as ten days in August, and who had been in command of a thousand men within the quiet precincts of Camp Chase, Columbus, Ohio, for just two weeks! The reasons for this strange choice, in the papers of Buell, or Secretary Chase, or Governor Dennison, may yet come to light. One thing only is quite certain; when Garfield appeared in Louisville to receive his orders, Buell had never seen him, and apparently had barely heard of him. But he liked and trusted him at once, and in the end both Garfield and Thomas accomplished what they had been sent to do.

After all, from the point of view of a generation which has learned to look on war as a difficult and technical business, the choice of Garfield was no stranger, even in an army where Sherman was idle, and Grant and Sheridan as yet unknown, than the similar selection of Banks, Patterson, Butler, Sigel, and Hunter for even more responsible commands. It proved to be a better choice than any of the others mentioned, and is only worth noticing because it was so typical of the methods of the early part of the war and of a day when the amateur with all his youth and eager hopefulness was still characteristic of the spirit of America.

Garfield called on Buell, whom he found direct, martial-spirited, with an air of decision which he liked. Buell outlined the problem, which was of course to drive Marshall back and to occupy the valley of the Big Sandy. Then, with an injunction to study the geography of the region for himself, he had the wisdom to leave to the younger man the satisfaction of planning his own campaign. That night at ten Garfield was back in his hotel armed with the necessary maps and census reports for the eastern counties of Kentucky, and, working feverishly and eagerly, with a single interruption at midnight to write a letter to his wife, he had by breakfast time a completed scheme to lay before his commander.

Garfield, who had never commanded as much as a company and had never heard a gun fired in battle, was to lead a brigade of four regiments, two from Ohio, including his own, and two from Kentucky, recently enlisted and so ill-trained that by comparison the boys from Hiram seemed to their commander like real veterans. Had they not been in camp since August? The little force of four regiments of infantry, of which the Kentucky regiments were at the time from a military point of view, merely a "well-disposed Union mob," was accompanied by six companies of Kentucky cavalry, under the command of an efficient leader, but tired and discouraged by the incessant labors to which in the uncertainty of the times that branch of the service had been exposed. Nominally, Garfield had well over four thousand men. Actually the force was reduced by desertions and the necessity of guarding supplies, and in the single battle of the little campaign he was able to bring on the field only about two thousand men. Fortunately, Buell was evidently well informed and the forces of the enemy proved to be almost exactly equal in numbers and perhaps inferior in training to his own.

The plan which Garfield worked out was to take the main part of his little army by way of the Ohio to the mouth of the Big Sandy, and then using that river for his supplies, to march south against Marshall while the Fortieth Ohio under Colonel Cranor came east from the neighborhood of Lexington against the rear of his enemies. It was a dangerous plan because either section of the divided army might be defeated in detail by a united enemy, and especially dangerous in rough mountain country where the two expeditions might never come together. But Buell decided to let the young student of the campaigns of Napoleon have his way, and with a few minor changes in detail, had Garfield's orders in precise soldierly language ready for him when he called in the evening. On December 20th, 1861, Garfield left Louisville, and three days later, the two sections of his little army, divided by the whole spread of eastern Kentucky, from Lexington to the Big Sandy, started towards their common objective.

That objective was Humphrey Marshall, whose instructions could not be so precise as those that Buell had given Garfield. Marshall was a West Point man, having graduated as early as 1832, but for many years he had been more celebrated as a politician and an orator than as a soldier. He had been a congressman and minister to China, and was still regarded as a man of great influence in Kentucky. Despite his corpulency, for he weighed two hundred and fifty pounds, he was expected to prove nimble enough to win the somewhat coy population of the mountains of Kentucky to the cause of the Confederacy. For some time Marshall had found the country unfriendly, and being expected to subsist his troops in a wild region sparsely settled and almost devoid of food, had been writing despatches

eloquent of his difficulties to the authorities in Richmond, who
had their hands quite full of other and more pressing affairs.
It was perhaps in view of the essentially human and political
problems that were involved that Garfield had been selected
as a foil for the redoubtable Marshall.

As Garfield advanced by muddy roads up the valley of the
Big Sandy, he had one of the persistent advantages which later
on the Mississippi and the James proved perhaps more than any
other single feature of geography decisive of the war. The river
on his left, dominated by northern steamers, gave him a safe
means of communication which could not be cut by the enemy
and which made him relatively independent of the scant supplies
of the poverty-stricken mountains. In another respect he had an
advantage that more frequently redounded to that of the South.
The population was on the whole friendly to the Union, and
Garfield, with commendable enterprise, was enabled to organise
a system of spies and scouts that not only gave him knowledge
of the movements of the enemy but which carried his orders to
the second part of his expedition. Garfield wrote that the return of the scout whom he had feared lost and who gave him
certainty that Cranor was coming brought him greater pleasure
than any other news which he had ever received. The country
was so rough that it was impossible to form a regiment in line
for lack of level ground, but Garfield took advantage of every
opportunity to drill his Ohio and especially his Kentucky troops,
and he soon had an esprit de corps which substantially lessened
the numbers of desertions. At a stream called Jenny's Creek, the
commander himself stood knee deep in the mud encouraging
his men to lay a log bridge. And that was only a single picture
of many which tended to endear the colonel to his men.

One of Cranor's messengers, announcing his approach, fell
into the hands of Marshall, and the Confederates marched from
Paintsville to attack Cranor in detail before he could be helped

by Garfield. Fortunately, Cranor changed the plan of the campaign and instead of continuing to a point to the south of Marshall, as had been planned, turned north and east, and on January 8th, the whole command was for the first time united. In view of the result, there seems to have been little advantage and a constant danger in the original division.

The Confederates were now known to be established at Middle Creek, a short distance from the little town of Prestonburg. The night of January 9, 1862, was spent by the Union forces under a drizzling rain and with no fires, a precaution that was made necessary by the nearness of the enemy. On the next day, January 10th, 1862, occurred the only battle in which Garfield was destined to command, and which therefore has a greater prominence in a biography than it would have in a general history of the war. Each commander reported that he had about two thousand men on the field, and as so often in early battles overestimated the forces of his adversary. Later Garfield was to develop an almost uncanny accuracy in counting his enemies, but such skill required experience.

As to the course of the battle itself, the incidents take a very different appearance, depending on which of the two eloquent commanders is followed as a guide. Both agree that the battle commenced with the approach of the Union skirmish line at eight, that the volleys were severe during four hours of the afternoon, and that Marshall withdrew at about four-thirty. As to the losses and the reasons for Marshall's retirement from the field there are wide differences in the two accounts. Garfield gives an impression of fighting at close quarters which is not borne out by an examination of the losses. As he watched the contest, he was sure that a thousand bullets came within a foot of him. They cut the trees, splintered a rock and cut a canteen which hung at his side. He recorded that he had never seen such terrific volleys, which was not strange since it was his first time under fire. The hill trembled under the recoil, and he was full of gratitude to the Hiram boys as he saw their loved banner sweep up the slope. As the enemy fell back over the crest, the college boys continued to fire even when many of them were faint from loss of blood. The next morning, after he visited the scene of carnage, he recorded that it was a terrible sight to see the dead rebels stretched on the hill in all shapes and positions. He told William Dean Howells that at the sight of these dead men whom other men had killed, something went out of him, the habit of a lifetime, that never came back again; the sense of the sacredness of life and the impossibility of destroying it.

Garfield reported officially that the Confederates carried off the majority of their wounded but left eighty-five dead upon the field, including three officers. Not to be outdone, Marshall calculated the losses which the Confederates inflicted on their enemies as 250 killed and 300 wounded. But making the assumption, usually safe, that each commander was well informed as to his own losses, and knew little of those of the enemy, the Official Records show that the Union losses were 3 killed and 18 wounded, while the Confederates reported 10 killed and 14 wounded. Those ten men were the ones whom Garfield saw stretched upon the hill "in all shapes and positions," and whom in the natural excitement of his first skirmish he so greatly magnified.[1]

In later years, with the experience of a great battle behind him, Garfield reached a very modest estimate of his first campaign. "It was a very rash and imprudent affair on my part," he told his friend Whitelaw Reid. "If I had been an officer of more experience I probably should not have made the attack.

[1] The two reports were written the same day. Garfield's, in *Official Records*, Ser. I, Vol. 7, pp. 30–32, may be compared with Marshall's *Official Records*, Ser. I, Vol. 7, pp. 46–50. Marshall wrote:—"The enemy were well whipped. . . . If I had had bread for my men . . . I should have renewed the action after night." See also W. D. Howells' *Years of My Youth*, (1917), pp. 204–207.

As it was, having gone into the army with the notion that fighting was our business, I didn't know any better." But Garfield could well afford the pleasure which his success brought to him; for even granting Marshall's entirely probable statement that he withdrew in good order, not on account of any charge by the Hiram boys, but because his food was failing, the fact remains that he did withdraw, retiring sixteen miles the next day and soon leaving the valley of the Big Sandy, and with it the whole mountain region of eastern Kentucky, in the exclusive control of his young rival. Garfield deserved the praise of Buell, who said that he had shown "the highest qualities of a soldier, perseverance and courage," and was especially pleased by the official congratulations of the commander-in-chief, General McClellan, on "his handsome achievement."

The army had reached a region in which family feuds and vendettas had become habitual through generations that had forgotten the origin of the quarrels. Having congratulated his troops on a victory over an enemy of "twice their numbers" who had left "scores of corpses" unburied on the field of battle, Garfield's first problem was to prevent his Kentucky soldiers from using the Union victory as an excuse for settling old feuds. One such soldier he was compelled to sentence to death for shooting a prisoner (a neighbor of his) in cold blood. But though the Union commander was able to reduce his own soldiers to discipline, and wrote that he had the confidence of the people of the valley, the wild and disturbed condition of the times allowed many murders, and persons who were hated were charged freely with Confederate sympathies and either killed or driven from their log cabins in the mountains.

Then as the snows began to melt and the rains to fall in torrents, the rise in the river made it difficult for the steamers to breast the swift and turbulent stream, and for a time supplies began to fall short. Late in January, going down the river, Gar-

field himself piloted a steamer which the official pilots refused
to conduct, and using the scant experience of his canal days,
brought it through in safety. Two weeks later the streets of
Piketon were under water and two steamboats were moored in
the principal thoroughfare. Tents were swept away and horses
drowned. Then the waters subsided and as the mud began to
dry, the inevitable camp diseases made their deadly appearance.
Very soon out of a small force four hundred were in the hospital
and sixty more were ready to go. To Garfield, the battle had
been a glorious adventure. But here was an enemy much more
grim and terrible. At first he used the same old methods. Two
Hiram boys came to him shaking with fever and in tears through
homesickness. They wanted to go home; but the colonel told
them that they must wrestle with sickness as a giant enemy. In
spite of such well-meant admonitions typhoid had its way and
within the month the two boys were dead.

Such an experience brought to the spirit of Garfield a
vindictive element which had at first been wholly absent and
that he was never completely to lose. He was angry when he
heard that Confederate prisoners were being well treated at
Camp Chase, and felt that the vengeance of an outraged law
should be brought to bear on those whom he called the cursed
villains who had instigated the rebellion. Before the summer
was over the blood of hundreds of the Eighteenth Brigade would
be calling from the ground for vengeance. Such a spirit, natural
and inevitable as it was, was soon to result in the ravaging of
the Shenandoah Valley and of Georgia, and even after the
close of the war were to make it impossible to follow the mild
philosophy of Lincoln's second inaugural. Garfield now believed
that the war would be soon over, but he hoped that the contest
for Union would last long enough to make it possible to strike
a blow against slavery and slave holders. With his intellect he

reasoned that a declaration of emancipation would at the moment be a mistake, but, in spite of logic, he was certain that on the chief moral issue of the war, General McClellan was weak, wicked, and conservative, and "the President nearly as bad."

Colonel Garfield deserved to be promoted. He had from the beginning been in actual and successful command of a brigade. But, in the conditions which then reigned in Washington, he secured recognition not through the orderly recommendation of superior officers who had praised his efficiency, but because his friends in Ohio, and especially his former landlord, W. T. Bascom, conducted a systematic campaign for his promotion much as if it had been a political office. Influential men signed a petition which they laid before that guardian angel of the interests of Ohio men, Secretary Salmon P. Chase, and Chase was soon able to record in his diary that at his personal request, Colonel Garfield had been made brigadier general. The new commission was dated back to the tenth of January, the day of the bloody exploit at Middle Creek. Garfield recorded that he "had never by word or written sentence made any approach to forwarding the movement or inviting it." The promotion was another of those surprises which with astonishing regularity mark out the stages of Garfield's progress.

Humphrey Marshall had retired to Pound Gap on the Virginia boundary, where in discouragement and with forces greatly reduced he watched for a new opportunity to win back the laurels that had faded at Middle Creek. Garfield led a small expedition against him, and on March 14th, outflanked the Confederate position by a clever movement, and after a few volleys in a blinding snow storm compelled another Confederate retreat. It was to be his last exploit as an independent commander, for when he returned to his headquarters on the Big Sandy, he received an order to leave Colonel Cranor in command and to report at Louisville. At that city he was instructed to reach Buell, whose army was then on its way to join Grant on the banks of the Tennessee for the proposed advance on Corinth.

Leaving his baggage in Louisville, Garfield overtook Buell at a point thirty miles south of Columbia, Tennessee, and on April 4th was at once assigned to the command of the Twentieth brigade, made up of two Ohio regiments, one from Michigan, and another from Indiana. Garfield's division commander was Major-General T. J. Wood, who like Col. Harker, the senior officer in his own brigade, was a graduate of West Point. To Garfield, the new situation in which he found himself a mere cog in a great machine of which the leading figures were trained soldiers, and where he was asked merely to obey orders without being consulted in the least as to problems of strategy which even on a small scale had given to war the interest of a peculiarly fascinating game of chess, was irritating to the last degree; nor can it be said that he ever adjusted himself to the necessary tedium of the duties of a brigade commander in a great army. The rough language which the professional soldiers had learned in army camps, interspersed on suitable provocation by occasional profanity, shocked Garfield to the point of exasperation; their insistence on military formalities seemed a mere display of petty tyranny; and above all, the willingness of the typical West Point man to fight the nation's battles without any of Garfield's growing eagerness to have the cause of the Union joined to the deeper problem of emancipation seemed to Garfield cold and heartless and to border on disloyalty. He could not appreciate the point of view of men like Wood and Sherman, who made the war a duty and not a crusade. In a larger sense the dislike of James A. Garfield for General Wood in particular and for West Point men in general was a mere expression of the necessary revolt of the individualism which had come from the frontier against the exaggerated organization which was imposed by military life.

THE CONGRESSMAN

THE SOLDIER

It is extremely probable that the initial dislike between Garfield and Wood and Harker was entirely mutual, and it cannot be said that the two West Point men softened their language for gentle ears. They were probably subjecting their new colleague from Hiram, Ohio, to a rough but wholesome initiation which they felt to be necessary for the good of his soul. In any case, after about a month Wood began to consult Garfield about the affairs of the division, much to the evident satisfaction of the latter, and, in the next year, when their positions had been substantially reversed by Garfield's advancement to Chief of Staff, the two officers became not only friendly, but even intimate companions. Garfield's dislike for professional soldiers continued, but was limited more and more to what he believed to be their usual attitude on the question of slavery, and was finally dissolved by his recognition of soldierly qualities and great services to the cause of the republic. When Garfield entered Congress, the regular army found in him a constant friend at court. But for the next few months there can be no doubt that he really hated the professional soldiers with a fierce hatred, and his attitude was important because it was so typical of a general feeling among the volunteers. As the war went on, the initial differences between the two types of officers were destroyed by experiences that gradually reduced all the officers who served through to the end to what was virtually a common type.

When on Thursday, April 4th, 1861, Garfield became the commander of a brigade in the Army of the Ohio, Buell was almost in sight of his objective. He had advanced rapidly, and a fundamental principle of strategy, inculcated by Napoleon in his maxims, seemed about to be violated with impunity. The Napoleonic axiom is that in effecting the concentration of troops, the point of concentration must be nearer to your own corps than to that of the enemy. Yet Halleck had selected Pittsburgh Landing, a point on the Tennessee only twenty-five miles from the

Confederate army at Corinth, and had ordered Buell to join
Grant by a march of more than a hundred miles from Nashville.
The Confederate commander, Albert Sidney Johnston, had
waited until the last moment, but on Sunday morning, April 6th,
taking advantage of this fundamental error in strategy and probably aided by a certain carelessness on the part of Grant, had
fallen with great fury on the Union positions in what was to
prove quite the bloodiest battle of the war. Grant's army was
driven back several miles and seemed on the point of being
destroyed before Buell could arrive from the other side of the
river. But the presence of Union gun boats in the river, the death
of the Confederate commander, and his own courage saved Grant
from what seemed a certain disaster, and the tide of battle had
already turned when Buell's first divisions reached the field. All
day Sunday and throughout the night, Garfield's men continued
their march, hearing plainly the roar of the guns across the
river. But when they reached the field early on Monday afternoon the battle was virtually over, and their only duty was to
engage in minor contests with the Confederates who were now,
under the command of Beauregard, falling back sullenly from
the field which they had barely failed to win.

Halleck now took command of the united armies of Buell
and Grant, having a force of a hundred thousand men to oppose
to less than half as many under Beauregard. But Halleck, and
for that matter the whole Union army including Garfield, believed that their enemies numbered one hundred and fifty thousand, an illusion which Beauregard used every possible means
to support. Halleck moved forward with great caution, erecting
breastworks as he advanced, and Garfield was chiefly engaged
in such undramatic tasks as building bridges and repairing roads.
When he had leisure he went to the picket lines, where he was
interested in watching the sharpshooters who hunted for each
other across the wheat fields with the eagerness and nonchalance

of boys on the hunt of squirrels. They would creep out behind stumps and trees and fire away at each other, laughing merrily as though it were a holiday sport. On May 19th, Halleck had reached a point three miles from his objective at Corinth, and while he built elaborate siege works that might have been worthy of Lesdiguières or Vauban, the pickets by common consent declared a truce, which the officers overlooked, and sometimes became so friendly that they would sit in the middle of the open fields for a neighborly chat. On May 30th a rumor, carefully nurtured by Beauregard, who desired a quiet opportunity to escape from a position where in case of siege he must lose his entire army, spread through the Union camp that the Confederates were about to attack. General Wood, who in the last month had come more and more to rely on the sagacity of Garfield, sent the latter forward to reconnoiter. Garfield returned at midnight satisfied as to the general correctness of the story.[1] The Union soldiers stood under arms expecting every moment the shock of attack; but when the pickets reached Corinth the next morning they found the Confederate positions abandoned. Halleck had gained a barren victory and the army of Beauregard was still intact. Garfield was bitter in his criticism of a policy of caution on the part of Halleck which had allowed a great opportunity to slip through his fingers.

Life in the camp in Corinth did not agree with Garfield and he was soon seriously ill with dysentery. Early in June, while he was still weak, the army of Buell was sent east towards Chattanooga along the railroad which ran parallel to the Confederate front. Garfield's men were soon scattered along a line of railroad laying rails which might be torn up in a single raid of Forest's cavalry and building bridges which would need to be built again and again. He felt instinctively that the true line for Northern advance ran north and south and not east and west,

[1] *Official Records,* Ser. I, Vol. X, pt. 1, p. 708.

and that no railroad could compare in value with the rivers where
the Northern advantage in steamships could not be dissipated by
the Southern advantage in efficient horsemen. The work which
he was doing might be done equally well or better by any officer
in his command. His bitterness and discontent increased as the
Union army passed through the rich fields of northern Alabama
and he saw the slaves at work raising harvests that were destined
to feed Confederate soldiers. Garfield was now certain that the
war would never end until the true enemies were recognised not
in those whom Seward had called misguided leaders, but rather
in the whole body of the Southern people who would need to
be conquered. And they could never be conquered until their
slaves were freed and their crops destroyed. "It may be a
philosophical question," he wrote to Hinsdale, "whether 11,-
000,000 of people can be subdued, but we need no longer disguise the fact that this is the thing to be done before there is
Union and peace." [1]

Many others were thinking the same thing, and it was evident that the contest would not long continue merely between
armies. The war was passing into a stage of ruthless bitterness,
which always comes sooner or later in every long war, but the
nature of which in the war between the North and South has
been touched very lightly by historians of a generation that was
trying, and trying wisely, to forget the past, and to carry out
Lincoln's dying behest to bind up the nation's wounds. Garfield was among the first to feel that a successful war cannot in
the very nature of the case be essentially humane. How far on
the path of realism had the young man travelled who had once
thought that no Christian man can be a soldier! Who only the
summer before had sat at the feet of Alexander Campbell and
had preached a sermon on the Beatitudes!

But Halleck and Buell, who had preached no sermons, were

[1] T. C. Smith, *op. cit.*, Vol. I, p. 237.

still determined that private property and civilian lives should be safe along the line of their invasion. Serious charges, some of them unspeakable, were brought against officers under the command of General O. M. Mitchell, who was to die so soon of the yellow fever in distant South Carolina, and whose campaign in northern Alabama Garfield regarded as unnecessarily ruthless. The most celebrated case was that of Col. J. B. Turchin, a Russian soldier of fortune who had found service in the American cavalry. The specific charge on which Turchin was convicted was of giving up Athens, Alabama, a town which contained many fine houses, to be pillaged by his soldiers.

On June 15th, 1862, Garfield was made president of the court-martial which was to try the first of these cases, an unpleasant duty which occupied the last six weeks of his service in Buell's army. He approached his task with mingled feelings, for even his worst enemies could not deny that at heart he was kindly, generous and humane. When the charges were first laid before him, he wrote that he could scarcely express his horror. But when Turchin came before the court, Garfield was struck by his attractive personality and manners; and when the Russian colonel defended himself by saying that he had merely tried to teach rebels that treason was a terrible crime, and especially when Turchin charged his superior officers with being willing to treat rebellion tenderly and gently, Garfield wrote that the accused man had won his heart and that he would always be proud to call him a friend. On the evidence presented, there was nothing else to do but to convict Turchin. The court-martial found him guilty of neglect of duty, conduct unbecoming a gentleman, and disobedience of orders, and sentenced him to be dismissed from the service of the United States. But though six members of the court appealed to Buell for clemency on the ground that Turchin was laboring under excitement when the houses were pillaged, Buell refused. The formal order for

Turchin's dismissal was promptly signed. But Turchin's threats of his arguments seem to have had their full effect. For the sentence was never carried out, and, instead of being cashiered, Turchin was made a brigadier general; and Garfield whose own vote in the court-martial has not been recorded, seems to have more than kept his promise to be a friend to Turchin. At least General Stanley, who is a none too friendly witness, is authority for the statement that in the next year the convicted officer, against his protest but by the direct and powerful influence of Garfield, was placed in command of the important division of cavalry which Turchin led in the battle of Chickamauga.[1]

The very slow and inglorious advance of Buell's army, which was moving east and not south, and an illness which after some improvement was followed by a relapse, brought to Garfield every day an increasing dislike for the unexciting duties of a brigade commander. Early in May his ever watchful Hiram friends had written that the political situation was favorable and that if he allowed his name to be brought before the Republican convention, he would be almost certain of an election to Congress. The Congress to be elected in 1862 would not assemble in regular session until December, 1863. Garfield calculated that the war would end in ten months, and he had the future to consider. Accordingly, on June 25th, he wrote to his political manager, Harmon Austin, that he would like to enter Congress. He could not afford to come before the convention and be defeated, but if success was reasonably certain, he would place himself "in the hands of his friends." In the language of politics, this meant that he was an active candidate. On July 30th he re-

[1] D. S. Stanley, *Personal Memoirs*, 1917, pp. 131, 135. Stanley hated Garfield, but, on this point is corroborated by Garfield's letters regarding Turchin given by T. C. Smith, *op. cit.*, Vol. I, pp. 228–229. For the documents in the Turchin case, see *Official Records,* Ser. I, Vol. 16, pt. 2, pp. 273–278. Turchin was dismissed from the army on Aug. 6, 1862 and received his commission as brigadier general, Sept. 1, 1862.

ceived his furlough and, weak and emaciated as he was, made
his way slowly back to Hiram where he arrived on August 6th.
At Louisville, an incident occurred which, trivial as it was,
strengthened his decision not to stay long in the army. An unguarded phrase in an interview gave the watchful reporters an
opportunity to guess the outcome of the Turchin trial which had
not yet been made public, and Garfield received from Buell
a sharp inquiry that amounted to a reprimand. When he again
took up the career of arms, it would be with the added prestige
and power of a congressman-elect.

As Austin and Rhodes had written, the political situation in the Nineteenth Congressional District was peculiarly favorable. For twenty years the congressman had been the celebrated Joshua R. Giddings, who had placed himself in the forefront of the radical anti-slavery movement at a time when abolitionists were still regarded with marked suspicion and who thus dramatised the most persistent emotion of his constituents. He had been returned so regularly that he had come to regard the seat as almost a vested right, when in 1858 some unfortunate arithmetical calculations in which Giddings' estimate of the distance to Washington, and consequently of the sum which was due him for mileage, proved to be at variance with the facts of geography. This incident not only weakened Giddings' professional position as a moral leader, but enabled his opponents to send John Hutchins as his successor to Washington. John Hutchins had now been congressman for two terms. But the district had become accustomed to striking personalities and, in that respect, Hutchins, though a good lawyer, could not begin to compare with the white-haired man who had borne with audacity and courage the brunt of so many battles in defense of his ideals.

Giddings was no longer a candidate, for he had secured in Montreal a consulship which he found entirely to his liking and where the old warrior was to spend in dignified retirement the remainder of his days. But his friends, especially in Ashtabula County, had neither forgotten nor forgiven the slight to their favorite son. Then, too, the boundaries of the district had recently been changed, and containing as it now did the five counties of Ashtabula, Trumbull, Mahoning, Geauga, and Portage, the proper occasion for a change seemed to have come.

Garfield's position was peculiarly strong. He had been compelled to leave to wise and loyal friends all the initial steps, and even now on his return from the army, he was sufficiently ill to wait discreetly in the background, being always available to deal promptly with emergencies as they arose. Thus, on August 12th, only six days after his return, when challenged to say what he would do about his command in the army if elected to Congress, he answered squarely: "In answer I have to say that should my fellow citizens choose me to represent them in the next Congress, I should still continue with my brigade in the field while I am needed there, unless the duties in the new Congress should sooner call me from it." And he added a characteristic sentence to the effect that the position was not of his own seeking and that he would only accept it if it were the spontaneous wish of his fellow citizens. The political sagacity of this answer to a dangerous question is at once apparent and strengthened still more Garfield's claims for the nomination.

When the convention met at Garrettsville on September 2, Garfield was the only one of five candidates who was not present in person to guard his interests. But the demand for his services was not sufficiently spontaneous to relieve his friends from vigorous efforts on his behalf; for it was at once evident that Congressman Hutchins had no intention of yielding his post without a struggle. On the first ballot, Garfield led Hutchins by a single vote, the others being divided almost equally among their three opponents; and, for seven ballots the contest was very close, with Hutchins ahead on the fourth. But as the minor candidates withdrew, Garfield gained strength, and on the eighth ballot was nominated by a vote of 78 to 71 for Hutchins. It is curious to consider that a change of just four votes would in all human probability have left Garfield in political obscurity from which only a miracle could have rescued him. As it was, with a nomination in his pocket which every one knew quite well

to be equivalent to an election, for only in his own county of
Portage was there any substantial opposition, the way was clear
for the high adventures that were to characterise the remaining
years of Garfield's life. Even in the army Garfield could now
speak with a degree of influence and authority that no exploit on
the Big Sandy could possible have given.

Garfield's constitution was naturally vigorous, and in the ela-
tion of his recent success, he was soon quite recovered; but he
had no intention of leading his brigade in Buell's army again if
he could help it. His friend Governor Dennison had advised
him to go to Washington, where, as the guest of Secretary Chase,
and close to the seats of the mighty, he might be assigned to a
division or perhaps attain the command of an independent expedition. So Garfield turned his face to the east, and on the
morning of September 19th, arrived in Washington.

For the next four months, Garfield lived in an atmosphere
that was seething with criticisms and intrigue. The capital was
full of congressmen, politicians, contractors, and ambitious soldiers who were seeking opportunities for personal advancement.
Opinion was divided between the friends of General McClellan
and his critics, among whom Garfield was soon numbered, who
were certain that he ought to be removed and who even suspected him of treason. On the political side there were those
who were opposed to emancipation and others who were equally
certain that such a proclamation was the sure pathway to victory.
As to Lincoln, the general opinion was that his heart was right,
but that he was totally lacking in strength of character or capacity to make a wise decision. Garfield's letters pictured the
President as a mere child in the hands of ambitious generals.
Again and again, in letters to his friends, Garfield reverts to
the same theme in which "criminal vacillation" and "timidity
of the Administration" are among the mildest of his phrases.
One of his letters, which under any other form of government

would have secured his instant ruin, was captured on its way
to a friend in the army and was published by the gleeful Confederates in the *Tennessee Vidette* for November 11: "I appreciate and feel all that you say about Generals Halleck, McClellan, and Buell. If the President only had the nerve, there would
be a rattling among the dry bones very soon. My heart cries
out, How long, Oh Lord, How long." Among the generals,
Garfield liked Hooker, with "his fighting blue eye," but his
favorites were Banks and Sigel. Banks he regarded "as one of
the ablest of our generals," whose abilities were not sufficiently
appreciated by the Administration, while with only a part of the
soldiers that McClellan would not use, Sigel, if he had a chance,
could strike a blow upon the rear and flank of Lee which might
go far to destroying the power of the Army of the James.

In many of these views, the inexperienced young soldier
from Ohio was merely taking the color of his environment and
echoing the opinions which he heard freely expressed at the
table of the Secretary of the Treasury. Salmon P. Chase, with
commanding figure and manners of great dignity and charm,
had made his house, over which Kate Chase presided with the
scepter that had recently fallen from the hands of such women
as Mrs. Roger Pryor and Mrs. Stephen A. Douglas, the social
center of the first Republican administration and the source of
witty criticisms of the harassed President. Chase had met Garfield at Akron during the campaign of 1859 and had seen the
young man again when he first came to Columbus in the next
year, and on Garfield's first day in Washington, invited him to
dinner. Garfield played a good game of chess, a recreation of
which Secretary Chase was inordinately fond. He not only could
talk well, but he had the eager curiosity which makes a good
listener, and the Secretary of the Treasury soon found in the
young congressman-elect an apt pupil in public finance. On a ride
from a visit to McClellan's army, Garfield told Chase about his

boyhood and his hopes of becoming a political leader in northern
Ohio, and Chase insisted that Garfield should come to his house
as a permanent guest.[1] Garfield, on his side, had an almost unbounded admiration for Secretary Chase as the strongest figure
in the Administration, and accepted the hospitality of the older
man with a deference that soon colored his own opinions. At
the house of Chase he had an opportunity to meet the politicians
who criticised the President and the soldiers who were equally
certain of the weakness and imbecility of the commander of the
army, Gen. George B. McClellan.

In one typical conversation Chase described the situation.
Holding up two fingers, he compared one to Halleck, well
trained and able but cold as a stone, the other to Stanton with
administrative ability but lacking in tact, and then between the
two Lincoln, with humor, tact, and honesty, but without either
the technical training or the administrative force to shake off
the shackles of West Point. And by these shackles Chase undoubtedly meant slavery and McClellan. Did he mean to suggest also, that not far away there was a hand, complete and
strong, uniting in a single personality the intellect of Halleck,
the driving power of Stanton, and the broad humanity of
Lincoln?

But after all the President's wise deliberation, the two
friends from Ohio did not have long to wait. Four days after the
battle of Antietam, on September 21st, 1862, Lincoln signed the
preliminary proclamation of emancipation. In October Garfield's old commander Buell was displaced, a step which Garfield hoped would lead to the removal of the other obnoxious
West Point men, Halleck and McClellan; and on November
7th he was partially satisfied when McClellan was replaced by

[1] The interest of Chase in Garfield, appears in his "Diary." *Amer. Hist. Asso.
Rep.*, 1903, Vol. I, pp. 92 and 97. See also Garfield to Chase, Jan. 14, 1863 (Chase
Papers, Library of Congress).

Burnside in command of the army of the Potomac. For the moment the radical Republicans were quieted and public criticisms of the policies of the Administration were left to Democrats and former Whigs.

Garfield was, of course, immensely pleased with the emancipation proclamation, which he prophesied would bring strength to Lincoln in all parts of the country except Kentucky. But even when Chase told him that the President had made the great decision on his own responsibility, that it had come as a surprise to the cabinet, and that it had the support of only two members, Stanton and himself, Garfield did not yet recognise the fundamental courage that lay behind the immense patience of Abraham Lincoln, and merely recorded the hope that before the time to put the policy into actual effect Lincoln might not yield to bad advice and change his mind. When in his message to Congress in December Lincoln made a tentative suggestion of gradual and compensated emancipation as an alternative to immediate abolition, Garfield's fears were strengthened, and the suggestion that it might be wise to postpone the final stages until the year 1900 seemed to Garfield "weak and absurd." When finally Lincoln's conciliatory and conservative alternative had been rejected both by slave holders and Republicans, and the definitive proclamation issued on January 1, 1863, he recorded a judgment that was by no means uncommon at the time that "a second-rate Illinois lawyer" had been the instrument to utter words that would mark an epoch in the history of the world.

The immediate political effects of the emancipation proclamation were not so satisfactory as Garfield had prophesied. The Democrats carried New York, and greatly strengthened their very weak position in Congress. But in the Western Reserve, as might easily be imagined, the new policy was immensely popular, and in October Garfield received the welcome though not unexpected news that without any campaign on his part, he had been elected to Congress over his Democratic opponent by a vote of almost two to one.[1]

In the meantime Chase had not forgotten the desire for a separate command that had brought his young friend to Washington. He took Garfield to call on the busy Stanton, who under other circumstances might have been brusque and abrupt enough. There were so many brilliant young men who wanted to win glory, and so few who were willing to serve in obscurity under other men! But when he was confronted by a powerful colleague with a future congressman in tow, even Stanton knew how to be polite. Garfield found the interview satisfactory, and seems to have missed the subtle irony of Stanton's remark that he feared it would be difficult to give him any place "that would save him from West Point." Again when Stanton, harassed, suggested that it would be easy to make Garfield a Major General but that others had to be consulted in organising independent campaigns in some convenient corner of the South, Garfield replied quite seriously that he wanted to earn his stars before he received them, and wrote to Rhodes with evident satisfaction that Stanton was willing to make him a Major General. Chase finally suggested that Garfield be sent with twenty thousand men to occupy confiscated rebel plantations in Florida and so make at least one Southern state permanently loyal. Stanton seemed to agree, subject to Halleck's approval, and without even suggesting to Garfield that twenty thousand men would be very useful in defeating Lee, allowed him to go to New York, where he was to see Eli Thayer, whose experience in organising emigrant aid societies for Kansas was to be used on this occasion. In New York, Garfield consulted not only Thayer, but Greeley, Beecher, and other leading men of the same type. But somehow the matter dragged out from week to week, and without being formally rejected, Halleck's approval

[1] *Tribune Almanac,* 1863; Garfield, 13, 288, and Wood, 6, 763.

had not been obtained. The incident did not strengthen Garfield's love for West Point men in general or Halleck in particular, but reading between the lines one gathers the impression that General Halleck was a more useful man in Secretary Stanton's organisation than the general public suspected.

Other schemes, only less fantastic than the Florida adventure, were taken up by Chase in the interest of Garfield. For a time it seemed likely that he would be sent to the valley of east Tennessee, a plan that was being urged with his usual zeal by the famous "Parson" Brownlow; but Stanton and Halleck at length consented to an independent expedition to South Carolina, to be under the command of General David Hunter, a severe critic of Lincoln's early negro policy, with whose general point of view Garfield was in complete sympathy. Garfield was to be second in command and was greatly pleased at the prospect of a dramatic stroke to capture the cradle of the Confederacy. The plans were complete and Garfield had even assembled his staff, when the whole scheme was postponed and finally abandoned on account of the virulence of yellow fever there.

Garfield's most intimate correspondents during this period were his old Hiram friends, Rhodes and Hinsdale. Rhodes was an admiring and sympathetic friend, but Hinsdale, whose mind was essentially clear and unsentimental, could on occasion be a severe critic and served more than once as an objective conscience. It was to the credit of Garfield that he recognised the deep loyalty of Hinsdale and accepted criticism without the slightest pettiness of spirit.

And so it was now. Hinsdale wrote in November that Garfield's long inactivity in Washington was beginning to hurt his reputation, and Garfield was evidently troubled by the justice of the warning. His ambitions did not agree with his own intellectual judgment, for Garfield had a clear mind, and he saw as well as any military critic today, that the true objective was the army of the enemy; and so he wrote to Hinsdale: "There is no hope of the republic unless we pulverize the great rebel armies. We may take small or large cities, girdle their country with expeditions and blockade—but there is no end till their armies are broken." [1] This was sound doctrine, that might well have emanated from Halleck himself, and whether or not Garfield applied it consciously to his late ambitions, we see him no longer waiting in the ante-chambers of Secretary Stanton. The victory for which all hoped would require not only courage but unselfishness.

On November 21st, 1862, Garfield was appointed to a court which was to try Major-General Fitz-John Porter on very serious charges. It was a case that was to remain before the American people for almost a quarter of a century, and though now forgotten, to attain a celebrity which made it in some respects similar to the Dreyfus affair. It is apparent that Garfield had no realization of the difficulty of the problem, for he wrote that "the case will keep us here a week or two." Actually the court was in session from November 27th until January 10th. When, many years later, in 1878, the case was reopened on account of the availability of new evidence, the final report, which completely exonerated Porter, was not handed down for more than a year. The story of the origin of this case is worth telling briefly.

The defeat of Pope in the closing days of August had caused general disappointment. Military critics today are agreed that the defeat was due primarily to the recall of McClellan's army from the James and to the impossible attempt to unite that army with Pope, who lay before the defenses of Washington. Since McClellan had to return by water, the result was to give the initiative to Lee, who occupied a favorable position between the two Union armies and could attack Pope long before McClellan could arrive. Since Lee was very much closer to each of the two

[1] T. C. Smith, *op. cit.*, Vol. I, p. 263.

Union armies in Virginia than they were to one another, the general strategy of this movement violated in Virginia the same fundamental Napoleonic axiom which at Pittsburgh Landing in April had already created so great a danger. By waiting until the last possible moment, like Albert Sidney Johnston before him, Lee had lost a part of his advantage; when he commenced his attack against Pope, the advance division of McClellan's army under Porter had landed and was within supporting distance. In his eagerness to cut Pope's lines of communication, Lee divided his own army, and for a time on August 28th Pope had an opportunity to overwhelm Lee's advance under Jackson before Longstreet could arrive. This opportunity was lost by mistakes on the part of subordinates, particularly McDowell and Sigel, and early on the morning of the 29th Longstreet had arrived, Lee's dangerous but brilliant movement had been completed, and the whole Confederate army with its back to the mountains lay on the flank and rear of Pope. The result was an overwhelming Union defeat second in completeness only to the one incurred on almost the same ground one year before. In his report, Pope blamed the loss of what had undoubtedly been a great opportunity on disobedience of orders, insubordination, and even treachery on the part of high officers of McClellan's army, and named specifically Major-General Fitz-John Porter, who was now placed on trial before a court under the presidency of General David Hunter.

In the heated atmosphere of the times, the air had been full of rumors, and for a time there had been talk of placing even General McClellan on trial for his life. But there was really not a particle of evidence of treason or even treachery; President Lincoln, with his usual instinctive coolness of judgment, had refused to give credence to the wild expressions of more heated minds, and in a great emergency, with Lee crossing into Maryland, had taken the responsibility of turning again to McClellan and placing him in command of the armies in the field. When the immediate danger was over, the same charges reappeared and were widely believed. Blame which might well have been distributed, and which belonged to Sigel, McDowell, Pope, Halleck, and Stanton, was now concentrated on a single individual. Fitz-John Porter was the intimate friend of McClellan, under whom he had rendered brilliant services during the Peninsular campaign. There was no question of his training or capacity as a soldier which might excuse the mistakes of an amateur. If he had failed it must be through treachery. From the beginning the trial of Porter assumed the character of a political inquisition, and as such it was followed with eager interest by the newspapers of all shades of opinion.

The public clamor which demanded the punishment of the guilty, the absence of essential documents, which were of course not yet available, and the composition of the court made a verdict which would stand the test of calm investigation absolutely impossible. In performing the unpleasant duty which was imposed upon him, Garfield's personal responsibility was only that of a single member of a court of nine officers. We may be sure that he was anxious to do his duty according to his lights, but it must be confessed that those lights were dim and his personal position peculiarly unfortunate. Without technical training of his own, he had become intimately acquainted with General McDowell, from whom he had gained impressions of the campaign quite unfavorable to the accused officer. If Porter were acquitted McDowell and Sigel would certainly be discredited. It was entirely natural for Garfield to lean on the judgment of distinguished officers whom he loved and trusted.

The only order received by General Porter from General Pope on the 29th was dated 4: 30 P. M., and read: "Your line of march brings you in on the enemy's right flank. I desire you to push forward into action at once on the enemy's flank, and if possible on his rear, keeping our right in communication with General Reynolds. The enemy is massed in the woods in front of us, but can be shelled out as soon as you engage their flank. . . . In case you are obliged to fall back, do so to your right and rear, so as to keep you in close communication with the right wing." [1] Porter received this order at 6: 30 P. M., but on account of the lateness of the hour and believing that he was not on the flank and rear of the enemy as Pope supposed, but face to face with the whole division of Longstreet who outnumbered his isolated troops by almost three to one, chose to regard the order as permissive rather than mandatory and failed to attack. This failure was the essential charge in the courtmartial in which Garfield participated.

The nature of the charges, the distinguished services of the accused, and the rank of many of the witnesses made the trial of Porter one of unusual interest. At the head of the table sat General Hunter, whose face, showing the marks of his sixty years, was in striking contrast with hair dyed coal black. He had a curious habit of shaking his head from time to time as he spoke, seeming to sling quick decisive words right and left. On either side were ranged the eight younger officers, all, of course, in the uniform of their rank. The prosecution was conducted by Joseph Holt, the Judge Advocate General, genial and pleasant, seeming to forget the immense power over life and liberty which he wielded during the war, but alert and never missing an opportunity to fasten his doom on the accused. For the defense, Porter was represented by the most celebrated lawyer of his generation, Reverdy Johnson of Maryland, whose huge face and strongly marked features, topped by bristling white hair, gave him the appearance of a battle-scarred old mastiff, all the more so when one noticed the eyes of which one was blind. His

[1] *Proceedings and Report of the Board of Army Officers in the case of Fitz-John Porter,* Vol. 2, p. 1706.

questions in defense of Porter had a searching fierceness which seemed to make more than one witness hesitate in his charges. The chief witness for the prosecution was General McDowell, whose clearness and evident sincerity made a deep impression on Garfield. Porter did not maintain that he had obeyed the order, but claimed that he was confronted with the whole right wing of Lee's army, and that the circumstances were so wholly different from those implied in the order that he was compelled to accept the alternative of retreat rather than attack.

The court found the defense of Porter, even when backed by all the eloquence of Reverdy Johnson, entirely unconvincing. He had been ordered to attack and had not done so. Porter said Longstreet had arrived, which Pope denied. The court preferred to believe Pope; for if Longstreet had arrived the justification of Porter's judgment would be beyond question. On January 6th, Garfield wrote a letter which was ominous for the accused: "Tomorrow we begin to review the evidence. Saturday, the defense of the accused will be read and that day or Monday we shall give sentence. . . ." By that sentence, foreshadowed even before the end of the trial, on the twenty-first of January Porter was cashiered and forever disqualified from holding any office of profit or trust under the government of the United States.

The years passed, and Porter had never ceased to ask for a vindication. His friends offered to bring proof that would be entirely convincing of the innocence of the convicted officer. As was natural enough in the circumstances of the times, a problem that should have been purely judicial had become an issue in politics, the Democrats for the most part defending Porter, and the Republicans continuing to insist on his certain guilt. Seven years after the trial, in 1869, Garfield wrote to Pope that no public act with which he had been connected was ever more clear to him than the righteousness of the findings of the court that convicted Fitz-John Porter.

At length, in 1878, President Hayes, whose party position was often far from orthodox, ordered a new and sweeping investigation, and the War Department appointed for the purpose a new Board of distinguished officers under the presidency of General Schofield. More than a year later, after considering testimony that filled two large volumes, the Board reported. General Longstreet had testified that his command of twenty-five thousand men was in front of the position occupied by Porter with nine thousand men and was ready to receive any attack after 11 A. M., and this testimony was borne out by contemporary orders and other documents.

The essential sentences of the new report were as follows: "If the 4:30 order had been promptly delivered a very grave responsibility would have devolved upon General Porter. The order was based upon conditions which were essentially erroneous and upon expectations which could not possibly be realised. . . . Such an attack, under such circumstances, would have been not only a great blunder, but, on the part of an intelligent officer, it would have been a great crime. . . . It is not possible that any court martial could have condemned such conduct if it had been correctly understood. On the contrary, that conduct was obedient, subordinate, faithful, and judicious." [1]

Seldom has a vindication been more complete; but to Garfield, who had so long and in such conspicuous places maintained the guilt of Porter, the decision of the Schofield board came as a very bitter blow. Originally his part in the decision had been minor and would not occupy a large place in his biography. Gradually, however, his position as a political chieftain had made it necessary to defend the court-martial of 1862, until its

[1] *Proceedings in the Case of Fitz-John Porter,* (1880), Vol. 2, pp. 1709, 1710.

findings had become an article of faith. He wrote in 1880 that
he was so stung by the decision of the Schofield board that he
found it difficult to speak his mind. Such influences were sufficient to prevent for another six years the Act of Congress that
would be necessary to remedy what had evidently been a great
wrong. Finally in 1886, almost a quarter of a century after the
original trial, and when most of the actors of the drama of 1862
were long in their graves, President Cleveland signed an act
by which Fitz-John Porter was reappointed to the army to rank
as Colonel from May 14th, 1861; and one likes to remember
that the old soldier lived to enjoy his lost honors until another
war had been won and the first years of the twentieth century
had brought forgetfulness.[1]

During the trial of Porter, Garfield had been studying strategy
and preparing himself for new opportunities when they should
arrive by commencing a translation of "The Secret Instructions
of Frederick II to his Inspector Generals." His intimate friendship with the well-trained McDowell gave him occasions to discuss the matters which he was considering in books, and tended
also to break down the prejudice against West Point which he
had brought with him to Washington. But it was high time for
him to escape from the intrigues and enervating criticisms of a
wartime capital to the more bracing atmosphere of service in
the field; and it was to the credit of Garfield's essential sanity,
that, when he asked for an appointment, it was to the army of
the Cumberland. He believed that in a great western army he
would find life and work, and that in the west the country
would finally be saved. At the suggestion of Stanton he asked
Chase for a letter of recommendation to General Rosecrans; he
hoped for a division but was willing to take his chances with a

[1] For a critical review of the case see Gen. Emory Upton, *Military Policy of
the United States,* Washington, 1907, pp. 341–345.

brigade; and, before the result of the trial had been announced, he set out for the west, where in some future battle he hoped to win the stars of a Major General which he might so easily have gained by intrigue.

AFTER a brief visit at Hiram and a slow and tiresome journey by rail and on horseback, Garfield, on January 25th, 1863, reached Murfreesboro, Tennessee, the headquarters of General W. S. Rosecrans, in command of the Army of the Cumberland. The relations between the two men who now met for the first time were for the next nine months to be peculiarly intimate, and no one would have suspected that the friendship which was being established would one day change to bitter hatred.

Rosecrans was at the height of his reputation. In early campaigns in West Virginia at the head of Ohio troops he had won a name as a strategist of ability, and, like Garfield, he had the confidence and support of Secretary Chase, from whom a letter of introduction was a document not to be neglected. His army on the last day of the old year had fought a bitter battle at Stone River, which if not decisive had at least been followed by the withdrawal of Bragg's army. The losses had been very heavy, and as a result there were two divisions without commanders. Rosecrans was also without a Chief of Staff, for General Gareschè who had held that important and intimately confidential post had been killed in the same engagement. Did Rosecrans have in Garfield, who had come to him with such significant introductions, the right man for a place in the very heart of his military family?

Outwardly testy and choleric, seldom troubling himself to put his opinions in a tactful form, seemingly impulsive, certainly warm-hearted in both his likes and dislikes, the idol of his officers and men, Rosecrans was in fact one of the most cautious of men, with a certain inertia of will which made him very slow in making up his mind or in taking any important step. Having once decided, however, he never doubted his judgment, and without turning back, placed all his cards on the correctness of an opinion which he had reached with infinite caution and pains. This type of personality, at once cautious and impulsive, in spite of logic, is by no means uncommon and is likely to win both enduring friendships and sometimes to arouse equally bitter hatreds. The qualities of Rosecrans are evident in his campaigns and appeared at once in his relations with James A. Garfield.

Garfield, on his side, was quite prepared to like Rosecrans, as was natural enough on the part of a young man seeking an opportunity within the gift of a distinguished officer of fifty-five. Many years later he was to record his impressions which appear also in contemporary letters: "There were men in our army," wrote Garfield, "who fought gallantly, simply because they believed it to be their duty to obey orders. . . . General Rosecrans was not a man of that sort. His opinions were all convictions. He was intensely right or intensely wrong, but never indifferent. . . . He looked upon rebellion as a crime which sapped the very foundations of the Union, and upon the leaders of the rebellion as personal criminals in the sight of God and man." [1] And when Rosecrans told Garfield that within three days of the receipt of the emancipation proclamation he had begun to put it into effect by the liberation of all the slaves within reach of his army, Garfield felt that here at last was a soldier whom, though trained at West Point, he could serve with energy and zeal. The very next morning after his introduction, Garfield wrote: "I am greatly pleased with some features of Gen. Rosecrans' character. He has that fine quality of having his mind made up on all the questions that concern his work. . . . In this he is perfectly unlike McClellan who rarely has a clear-cut decisive opinion and dares not trust it when he has." Evidently, Rosecrans knew the straight path to the heart

[1] B. A. Hinsdale, (Editor), *The Works of J. A. Garfield,* Vol. 1, pp. 479, 480.

of the critical young congressman from the Western Reserve!

Rosecrans, for his part, was not quite so sure. The position which he had to fill was very important. With his abundant energy, his clearness of literary expression, and above all his close political friendships, such a man as Garfield might be very useful indeed to the commander of the army of the Cumberland, but without personal loyalty and devotion, these same qualities might well make him a center of dangerous intrigues. So he determined to get acquainted. Much to the bewilderment of Garfield, he was first invited to the tent of the commander in chief, and when he hesitated he was ordered to come. Night after night, sometimes until two or three in the morning, the two men discussed all kinds of moral and theological questions. Rosecrans was a devoted Roman Catholic, probably the first whom the young Disciple had ever met in any intimate way; and in those evening sessions the younger man was compelled to argue the merits of individual freedom against the benefits of a religion of authority. Sometimes the question was the difference between profanity and blasphemy, for, like many professional soldiers at the time, Rosecrans regarded occasional profanity as an essentially useful art, but professed horror for blasphemy which he was careful not to use. Again the conversation reverted to politics, but it was obviously difficult to make a long matter of a subject on which both men agreed so heartily. All this time Garfield lived in the tent of Rosecrans. He was becoming restive and eager for duty. For his two favorite horses had arrived, and though an aunt had remarked drily when he joined the army that he would have to be tied on his horse, the old lady had done less than justice to his capacity to become a horseman. About three weeks after his arrival Rosecrans asked Garfield to become his most confidential officer and to accept a position as Chief of Staff. For a moment Garfield hesitated, wondering whether it would be wise to risk his own career on the success of one general, or as he put it "to take so much stock in one market," but any hesitation was but momentary, and the next day after the offer he wrote a letter to his friend Secretary Chase in which he described his new chief in most enthusiastic terms as "sound to the bone on the chief issues of the war," and prophesied that if the country would stand behind Rosecrans he would justify the highest expectations.

Many years later, when Rosecrans was an old man and Garfield was already mentioned as a presidential possibility, Rosecrans told the same story from his point of view: "Garfield was a member of my military family during the early part of the war. When he came to my headquarters I must confess that I had a prejudice against him, as I understood that he was a preacher who had gone into politics, and a man of that cast I was naturally opposed to. The more I saw of him the better I liked him, and finally I gave him his choice of a brigade or to become my Chief of Staff. He chose the latter. His views were large and he was possessed of a thoroughly comprehensive mind." [1]

Rosecrans might move slowly enough, but when he had made a decision he never did anything by halves. So now, having chosen Garfield, he not only asked his new Chief of Staff to perform the ordinary routine duties of his position, writing despatches, preparing reports, and the like, but he leaned on him as a confidential friend at all points, sought his advice on questions of personnel, initiated him closely into every detail of his proposed strategy, and sometimes allowed his new officer to prepare strategical combinations of his own and even to carry these out on a small scale. Thus in April, when he had been in his new position for about two months, Garfield, with the permission of Rosecrans, took up a plan that had been sug-

[1] J. M. Bundy: *Life of Garfield*, p. 63.

gested by an officer from Indiana. Two thousand men under
Colonel Streight were to move rapidly around the whole Confederate army, striking directly at the single line of railroad
which was Bragg's only means of communication with the
South. Streight was expected to destroy the railroad and to
burn the bridges, and when the news of his success arrived the
Union army was to move directly against the Confederates
who lay in a strong position along the Duck River, which with
precipitous banks runs east and west through southern Tennessee. Garfield took an eager interest in a plan that seemed to
have possibilities of brilliant success. Unfortunately there was
a shortage of horses and Streight was furnished with mules,
being instructed by Garfield to draw his supplies and to keep
his command well mounted from the country through which
he passed. The region was mountainous and thinly inhabited;
adequate supplies and horses were entirely unavailable, and
just when the anxious Garfield hoped that Streight had
reached the railroad, rumors arrived that his command had
been hunted down by the efficient cavalry under Forrest, and,
still ten miles from the railroad, broken down by loss of sleep
and exhaustion, had been compelled to surrender.[1]

During these months of waiting, while the two armies were
watching each other across the hills of middle Tennessee,
Rosecrans was reorganizing divisions that had been shattered
by the last bloody battle, establishing his lines of communication, and writing numerous despatches to Stanton, in which,
with growing irritation, he explained the necessity for an efficient force of cavalry and for arms to displace the hetero-
geneous and antiquated weapons that at the beginning of the
war were still in use. With these delays and demands Garfield
was at first in sympathy, and satisfied himself by organizing
an efficient secret service that soon made it possible for him to

[1] *Official Records,* Ser. I, Vol. 23, pt. 1, pp. 280–295.

give Rosecrans a surprisingly accurate account of the numbers and disposition of the enemy. His numerous despatches were always clear, and his life in the army gave to the style of Garfield a vigour and compactness that had formerly been lost in useless rhetoric.

In this period, Garfield's admiration for Rosecrans was unbounded. A group of Republicans was critical of what seemed to them Lincoln's lack of the qualities of a true leader. Accordingly, even as early as the spring of 1863, they began to canvass the country for another candidate for the presidency in the next year, and were beginning to consider the use of Rosecrans, whose views on the treatment of slavery were so much more advanced than Lincoln's. J. A. Gilmore appeared at the army headquarters as the agent of these critics, and as he told the story in later years, called on Garfield, who appeared to be greatly pleased and who said that if the country were canvassed from end to end, so fit a man could not be found. He advised Gilmore to visit Rosecrans, and to discuss the subject with him in direct business-like fashion. Rosecrans had the wisdom to reject such an overture. The story was afterward denied by one of Garfield's early biographers, but is certainly quite in line with views of the relative capacities of Lincoln and Rosecrans which, fantastic as they would seem today, were at the time held by more men than Garfield.[1]

For the success of Garfield in his new position it was of course important that he should be on good terms with the sixteen generals who, in command of brigades and divisions, were the immediate subordinates of Rosecrans, and in this he seems to have succeeded admirably. The close and confidential relations between Garfield and Rosecrans were certain to cause

[1] Compare J. A. Gilmore, *Personal Recollections,* p. 118, with A. G. Riddle, *Life of Garfield,* p. 69.

jealousy on the part of soldiers of longer training and experience, and the influence of Garfield on the decisions of the commander in chief were sure to be exaggerated. In later years, when Sheridan wrote his reminiscences, it was apparent that he disliked the new Chief of Staff, but the dislike may have been the result of later criticisms that Garfield passed on Sheridan's high-handed measures in Louisiana during the Reconstruction period, and if so is entirely creditable to Garfield. More specifically, General D. S. Stanley, the commander of the cavalry, blamed Garfield for saddling him with inefficient subordinates, one of them the Turchin of the trial of the year before, and remembered Garfield as a meddlesome politician who without military capacity was always interfering with the plans of better men. But if these criticisms were being made at the time, they did not come to the ears of Garfield. In contemporary documents we find Crittenden on one occasion and his old commander T. J. Wood on another protesting against advice that Garfield had given. Otherwise, Garfield seemed to have the confidence of the generals through whom he had to work, as he certainly did have the unbounded regard of Rosecrans.[1]

In later years, even during Garfield's lifetime, Whitelaw Reid, who wrote *Ohio in the War* under the inspiration of Garfield himself, exaggerated greatly the probable influence of the Chief of Staff on the strategy of Rosecrans, and the early biographers like Ridpath even went so far as to give Garfield complete credit for every plan that succeeded, while leaving to Rosecrans the blame for every failure. But while Garfield discussed the details of each campaign with his superior, and drafted the plans for each advance, serving Rosecrans with

[1] For criticisms of Garfield see P. H. Sheridan, *Personal Memoirs*, Vol. I, pp. 200, 201; and D. S. Stanley, *Personal Memoirs*, 1917, pp. 130–135.

loyalty and ability, there is abundant evidence that Garfield's enemies and friends alike entirely over-estimated the degree of his influence.

In the first place, the strategy of Rosecrans continued to follow the same general lines by which his reputation had already been securely established. And while Garfield undoubtedly had influence in matters of detail, there is certainty that his advice was rejected on at least two important occasions. The three corps commanders under Rosecrans were McCook, Crittenden, and Thomas. Garfield advised Rosecrans to replace the first two, whose politics he disliked as much as he distrusted their capacity, and to find new corps commanders in Buell and McDowell. But, whether wisely or unwisely, Rosecrans used his own judgment and continued his organisation unchanged. Again on June 8th, Rosecrans, who was under great pressure from Stanton to commence an immediate advance, sought the advice of his various generals on the wisdom of such a step. All, including such men as Thomas, Granger, Sheridan and others, coincided in Rosecrans' own opinion that the time had not yet come. On June 12th Garfield wrote a very able opinion showing accurate knowledge of the size of Bragg's army and standing alone in advising an immediate attack on the Confederate position. Garfield argued that the Union army with an effective force of more than sixty-five thousand could defeat Bragg with a little more than forty thousand, figures which proved to be accurate, and thus gain the rich and abundant harvests of Tennessee. But Rosecrans waited twelve days longer until he felt that he was ready. In a brilliant campaign, highly praised for the accurate timing of its various moves, he made a feint at the strong Confederate front along the Duck River, and then by a sweeping movement to the east captured the mountain passes, threatened the railroad base at Tullahoma, and with negligible losses compelled Bragg to withdraw to the south bank of the Tennessee. Early in July the Union army was in control of the whole region north of the river.

The campaign had been a complete success. The report of Rosecrans as to the services of Garfield was generous and fair: "All my staff merited my warm approbation for ability, zeal and devotion to duty; but I am sure they will not consider it invidious if I especially mention Brigadier General Garfield, ever active, prudent and sagacious. I feel indebted to him for both counsel and assistance in the administration of this army. He possesses the instincts and energy of a great commander."

Again, as in June, Garfield thought that the Union army should press on in pursuit of the Confederates across the river, even at the risk of a general battle; once more he was overruled; for Rosecrans, with a more accurate knowledge of the difficulties of the country, realised the dangers and insisted on securing the single railroad which was his only line of communications before embarking in new adventures. Accordingly he waited for another six weeks and did not begin the next stage of his campaign until after the middle of August. This time, too, Rosecrans sent to the irritated Stanton insistent and none too tactful demands for more cavalry, with which in spite of the object lesson of the Streight expedition Garfield no longer sympathised. In this period a change took place in the relations of the two men which became the basis of future charges against the character of Garfield.

When these charges were made in the New York *Sun* by C. A. Dana in 1874 and 1879, and when in the latter year they came to the attention of Rosecrans, then an old man in retirement in California, they gave the impression that from the beginning Garfield posed as a friend while merely a spy in the service of Chase, and that he was using a confidential

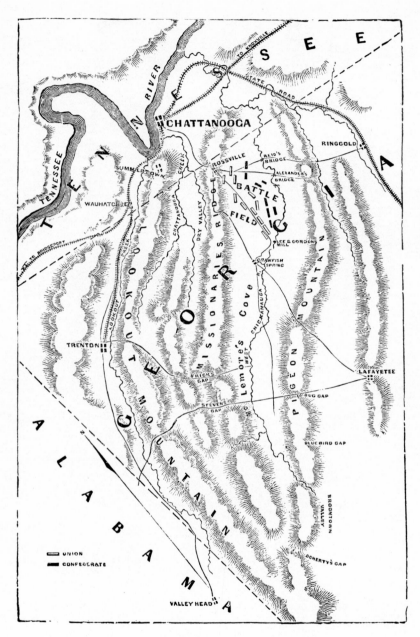

PLAN OF CHICKAMAUGA BATTLE-FIELD

position not only to ruin a man who trusted him but also to promote his own ambitions.[1]

But up to the period which we have now reached, the evidence is quite the other way. The critical attitude which was apparent during Garfield's residence in Washington had now quite disappeared, and in his most intimate private letters he had spoken in high praise not only of Rosecrans, but of others like Stanley and Wood who were not always his friends. As to Chase, his correspondence had been quite desultory. He had waited almost two months after being made Chief of Staff before reporting that appointment to the very man whose recommendation had done so much to bring it about. In that letter he had spoken in the most optimistic terms of the condition of the army and of its prospects of success. The next letter was written in May, when the news of the results of the Streight expedition had not yet been received. Garfield said that he "was in favor of striking, striking, and striking again until we break them." But there was no hint of criticism of Rosecrans or of displeasure with his strategy. On June 12th he had given advice which, as we have seen, was disregarded. But Garfield made no parade of his disappointment, participating in the Tullahoma campaign with energy and great ability, for which in his report of July 24th Rosecrans gave him full credit. Up to that point his record for loyalty to the man with whom he stood in such confidential relations was certainly beyond criticism.[2]

Having completed his report, two days later, on July 26th, Rosecrans sent General Rousseau to Washington to insist on cavalry which he still felt to be essential to the safety of his army before another advance. On the next day, July 27th, Garfield, who must have known of Rousseau's mission, wrote

[1] Editorial, *N. Y. Sun,* Sept. 25, 1874: "It Was Garfield Himself."
[2] Garfield to Chase, Feb. 15, 1863; May 5, 1863; May 9, 1863. Chase Papers.

to Chase a confidential letter in which he dissociated himself entirely from the pleas of his commander and for the first time brought to the attention of the Administration serious charges against Rosecrans. This is the letter of which Dana had probably heard vague rumors when he made his attacks on Garfield in 1874 and 1879, although the letter was not published until it was given to the world by the private secretary of Chase in 1882 after the death of Garfield.[1]

In this letter, Garfield told Chase, seemingly for the first time, of his rejected report of June 12th. He maintained that if his advice had been followed while the weather was still good, Bragg would have been destroyed. The Tullahoma campaign had ended on July 3d, and Rosecrans should have commenced a new advance not later than the 18th, at which date his communications from Nashville were fully reëstablished. Since that date he had constantly urged an immediate advance, and was in complete accord with the views of the War Department at Washington on that subject. Thus far the General had been singularly disinclined to grasp the situation with a strong hand, and to make the advantage his own. And then Garfield concluded: "I write this with more sorrow than I can tell you, for I love every bone in his body, and next to my desire to see the Rebellion blasted is my anxiety to see him blessed. But even the breadth of my love is not sufficient to cover this almost fatal delay. My personal relations with General Rosecrans are all that I could desire. Officially I share his counsels and responsibilities, even more than I desire; but I beg you to know that this delay is against my judgment and every wish."

Either at this time or later, for the date is difficult to determine, Chase seems to have shown this letter to Blair, Stanton, and perhaps other members of the Cabinet; and granting

[1] New York *Sun,* June 10, 1882; B. A. Hinsdale (Editor), *Works of Garfield,* Vol. I, p. 772.

the complete sincerity of Garfield's reasons for writing it, there can be no doubt that it was not calculated to promote the plans of Rosecrans or to increase the prestige of the commander of the army of the Cumberland. In any case, when Rousseau returned from his mission he reported to Rosecrans, who was of course in profound ignorance of Garfield's letter, that he was satisfied that his official destruction was but a question of time and opportunity, and quoted Stanton as saying "that he would be damned if he would give Rosecrans another man." [1]

When on August 16 Rosecrans was again ready to advance, he knew quite well that Washington expected him not only to drive Bragg out of Chattanooga but to fight and win a battle in which the prize would be no less than the destruction of the Confederate army. For the first ten days Garfield was confined to his tent by illness and was unable to take the active part which had characterised his services during the Tullahoma campaign.

Chattanooga lies at the head of a valley, flanked on the west by the commanding heights of Lookout Mountain and on the east by Missionary Ridge. The mountains and the valleys reach like long fingers toward the south, and were crossed, at the period of which we write, by only occasional roads. The railroad, which was of course Bragg's line of communications, runs for a short distance to the east, and then turns south to Atlanta.

Again, Rosecrans made his dispositions with the skill that had characterised his campaign at the end of June. Making a feint at the main Confederate position in Chattanooga, he crossed the Tennessee to the west, and with his army in three divisions to take advantage of the scanty roads, he pushed east in such a way as to threaten to outflank and besiege Bragg in the little town which he occupied at the bend of the river. But

[1] J. D. McCabe, *Life of Garfield*, p. 95; Whitelaw Reid, *Ohio in the War*, Vol. I, pp. 336, 337.

Bragg had no intention of making Chattanooga another Vicks-
burg, with Rosecrans in position to cut off the reinforcements
which he was daily expecting from Lee's army. On September
9th the northern section of the Union army found Chattanooga abandoned, and occupied that position without firing a
shot.

Up to that point, in the judgment of military critics, the
movements of Rosecrans had been skillful. In the light of the
result, and in view of the approach of Longstreet, who would
give Bragg an actual numerical superiority, Rosecrans should
now have kept his army well in hand in the neighborhood of
Chattanooga and waited for reinforcements. But a telegram
from Halleck gave the impression that Bragg was to reinforce
Lee, and Rosecrans had no inkling of the reverse policy which
had been adopted. His caution had been the subject of bitter
criticisms, and Garfield was eager for pursuit. Accordingly,
much to the delight of Garfield, a pleasure which appears
clearly in contemporary letters, Rosecrans decided to cross the
next ridge at once and to strike by three divergent roads for
the railroad. The result of this fanlike movement was to bring
the three divisions into the next valley at points more than
fifty miles apart. And, just as Garfield earned praise for his
part in the Tullahoma campaign, he now deserves his share of
the blame for a movement which came so close to wrecking the
central Union army in the west.[1]

Bragg was, of course, not in flight along the line of the railroad, as both Rosecrans and Garfield supposed, but had merely
retreated beyond the next range of hills, where he had his army
well in hand and was waiting the expected reinforcements
under Longstreet. The country was a tangled wilderness,
rough and broken, with only an occasional clearing to open the

[1] Gen. W. F. Smith in *Mil. Hist. Soc. Mass.*, Vol. VIII, p. 153.

sombre reaches of the forest. In the absence of sufficient cavalry to protect his wagon trains in the rear and also to serve as eyes to the Union commander, the whole Confederate army found itself able to lie concealed within a few miles from the advancing soldiers of Rosecrans. On September 11th, the Union forces under Negley came on overwhelming resistance and were driven back, and though Garfield still wrote confidently of continued advance, Rosecrans realised at once that it was a matter of life and death to bring his scattered divisions together before Thomas or Crittenden should feel the whole weight of the Confederate attack.

Fortunately for Rosecrans, Longstreet had to come by an almost incredibly long detour, and though hourly expected had not yet arrived. Bragg did not feel strong enough for an immediate attack. With feverish eagerness, McCook, who lay the farthest to the south, now turned north, and, in spite of an unnecessary march due to a misunderstanding of his road, on the seventeenth his tired men came into touch with the rest of the Union forces. Even now, with his whole army concentrated with its back to Missionary Ridge, Rosecrans was in a dangerous position. For his left wing was more than ten miles to the south of Chattanooga. Throughout the battle that was to follow Rosecrans was haunted by the fear that the Confederates might strike north and cut in behind his left wing. His problem was thus to edge north along the hills and to secure his base before he should feel the weight of the attack which was now quite sure to come. The loss of the battle of Chickamauga, apart from individual mistakes, was evidently due to the weakness of a position in which the northern end of the Union army was left hanging in the air. The result was to make it impossible to withstand a frontal attack with the confidence that would have been necessary to bring victory. And the whole situation was in turn due to the initial strategy that had carried the Union army too far south of the base at Chattanooga.

By the morning of the 18th of September, Bragg had been reinforced until he had 69,000 men against 65,000 under Rosecrans. And though 4,000 more men were due to arrive the next day, Bragg could not afford to delay. For in another day, Rosecrans would occupy the chief gap through the Ridge at Rossville, and with his army along the crest and his back to his supplies at Chattanooga would again be in a strong defensive position. There he could await in safety the reinforcements under Hooker, who was on his way through Ohio and Kentucky to strengthen the Army of the Cumberland.

Accordingly, by the evening of the 18th, the massing of the Confederate forces showed that Bragg was at last ready to attack. For the reasons that we have indicated, Rosecrans was thinking all the time of his endangered left, and now that McCook had arrived from the south, he sent his central division under Thomas behind the stationary Crittenden. All night long the soldiers of Thomas marched to the north to the position that they must reach if they were to cover the vital gap in the hills at Rossville. At nine-thirty the next morning, while the soldiers had barely arrived and many of them were without rest, the storm broke. The battle was accordingly fought with Thomas to the left, Crittenden in the center, and McCook on the right. Of these soldiers, those of McCook had been moving for days and Thomas had marched all night to reach the positions that would protect the vital roads. All that day, as the battle surged back and forth through the forest, Rosecrans and Garfield were stationed at a log cabin which belonged to the widow Glenn, unable to follow the battle except through the knowledge that came to them from the clouds of dust and the crash of firearms. The war correspondents gave a vivid picture of the commander pacing restlessly up and down before the house, while Garfield sat at a table writing despatches which Rosecrans dictated, pausing in his labors to reassure the widow and her children who had remained in a house that was so soon to be the very center of a great battle.

When night came, after fighting of the greatest bitterness, the Union lines were still unbroken, and Rosecrans was able to telegraph Stanton: "By the blessing of Providence the defeat of the enemy will be total tomorrow." But the dangers of the situation were quite too apparent to allow over-confidence, and at midnight he wrote to his generals: "Widow Glenn's 11:45 P. M. The line of battle for tomorrow is your present line. . . . You will defend your position with the utmost stubbornness. In case our army should be overwhelmed it will retire on Rossville and Chattanooga. Send your trains back to the latter place."

At dawn Rosecrans and Garfield were on horseback, inspecting their lines. Just as Rosecrans had every reason to fear, the Confederate attack commenced on the exposed left wing, and the problem of the Union commander was to send reinforcements to the left without creating a gap in the center of his lines. But his orders were obeyed slowly, one commander became confused and marched his soldiers to a position where they were quite useless, and as Thomas still asked for reinforcements, other troops were ordered from the center to the left, their places being occupied by divisions from the right. This complex series of movements took place in the face of the enemy and in country so dense that its blindness can only be appreciated by one who stands today in woods which after the passage of many decades still remain thick and gloomy and impassable.

Until 11 A. M., the Union army, as it had the day before, seemed likely to maintain its position unbroken. At that time an officer reported to Rosecrans that there was a gap in the line almost in the center of his army. Since troops had been ordered from that very position to the left, Rosecrans and Garfield accepted without a question the mistaken report. Rosecrans ordered Wood, the next general to the right, to "Close up on Reynolds as fast as possible and support him." Curiously enough, this fatal order that decided the result of the battle, was one of the few not written by Garfield in person. Colonel Starling, to whom the order was handed for transmission, hesitated, evidently not believing that there was any gap to be filled at the point indicated. But Garfield called out that the object of the order "was that General Wood should occupy the vacancy made by the removal of Brannan's division, Brannan having been ordered to Thomas' left." Starling rode away, General Wood thought he had no alternative but to obey, and finding no gap, moved away from his position in the line and marched behind the next division to the left, where he was, of course, unable to be of service. The result of a mistaken report and of a hasty order was thus to create an unnecessary gap. The mistake was Rosecrans'; and Garfield can only be blamed for falling in with his commander's judgment and failing to take advantage of Starling's hesitation to correct a blunder. The early biographers of Garfield made much of the fact that he did not write the fatal order, but in view of the sworn statement of Colonel Starling that Garfield agreed with its purport, that contention seems quite beside the point. The whole incident revealed a weakness in the relations of Garfield and Rosecrans. It is an axiom of executive organization that the initiative should come from the commander, the caution from the self-effacing adviser. This relation was here precisely reversed. So when in the heat of battle Rosecrans lost his caution, he found in Garfield eager energy, but not the cool and quiet judgment that alone could prevent so great an error.

Whether the Confederates were about to attack the center anyhow, or whether Longstreet with quick eye saw the gap, is a question on which the evidence is not decisive, and which of course belongs to the biography of the Confederate general. In any case, Wood was scarcely gone to his new position behind the lines of Brannan when in a resistless tide, and with a yell which became the subject of future tales at the camp fires of the veterans of the war, the rebel soldiers poured through, aiming straight at the headquarters of the Union general and involving both the center and the right of the army of the North in hopeless and inextricable confusion. The unfriendly C. A. Dana has left a vivid picture of Rosecrans counting his beads and muttering prayers as the Confederate line advanced. But there is no doubt that both Rosecrans and Garfield waited, trying to rally the broken divisions until all hope of victory in that part of the field was gone, and then were carried back with the broken rabble that had been the proud center of the Union army. The Dry Valley road led the commander and his chief adviser to Rossville, in front of which the lines of Thomas and Granger alone were now left to meet the overwhelming power of the whole Confederate attack.

From Rossville Rosecrans continued to his base at Chattanooga, while Garfield turned sharply to the right, and by a road that took him close to the Confederate position, accompanied by a single staff officer, rode the gauntlet back to the headquarters of Thomas. In later years, the story of the incident at Rossville became the subject of very different versions on the part of Garfield's friends and those of Rosecrans. According to one account, Garfield asked to go. According to the other Rosecrans, knowing that his own duty was in the rear where new lines must be prepared, sent Garfield. But like so many controversies about lost battles, this one from the standpoint of Garfield's life seems unimportant. It is clear that neither man at the moment knew whether or not the Union left was still intact. Both saw the need for definite information, and Garfield at least, whether at his own suggestion, as seems more probable in the light of the personalities of the two men, or by Rosecrans' orders, rode away to join Thomas, still eager and hopeful and counting yet on a victory that might even now be snatched from the jaws of defeat. Garfield was young; Rosecrans was for the moment many years older than he had been that morning.

Garfield's ride to the Union left was to become a legend, second only in the political campaigns of future years to the boyhood incident on the Ohio canal. The ride was undoubtedly very dangerous; but in that respect not more so than hundreds of other rides made by devoted staff officers on that and many another field of battle. It became important chiefly because Garfield escaped those dangers; and it is only fair to say that though he lived, he did not live to tell the story, for he never made half as much of this adventure as others insisted on making for him.

From that time Garfield was the eyes of the commander, and his reports were clear and vigorous. But Garfield carried no orders to the battlefield, and there are no indications that he had any important influence on the later movements of the army. Thomas fought well, very well indeed, and when he retreated to Rossville, he was accepting, against the advice of Garfield, permission accorded him by Rosecrans with which his own judgment coincided. Again at Rossville, Garfield wanted Rosecrans to return and to make that position the one for defense. But once more he was over-ruled, and it was Thomas who decided to retire behind the fortifications of

Chattanooga. Tradition was entirely unfair to Rosecrans in blaming him for a retreat which was due to Thomas. In the firm will of Thomas, Garfield had found his match; and he respected Thomas, who had put him in his place, as he never had Rosecrans, who had leaned sometimes too heavily on his judgment.[1]

The Union army which had been pursuing Bragg with hopes so high was now besieged within its lines at Chattanooga, where Jefferson Davis on a visit to Bragg looked down on the tents of his enemies from the commanding heights of Lookout Mountain. But though Rosecrans' recent mistakes both in strategy and tactics had at the time met with the complete approval of his Chief of Staff, the old-time confidence between the two men was no longer there, and it was natural enough that Garfield should be a mouthpiece for many of the criticisms that through the correspondence of Stanton's emissary, C. A. Dana, were reaching the War Department and preparing the way for a change in the high command. There can be no doubt that Garfield no longer regarded Rosecrans as fit to command the army and that he felt it his duty, in spite of his position, to bring his advice to bear where it would do the most good.

Thus on September 30th, Dana reported that Garfield, Wood, and Opdyke had spontaneously waited on him to represent the state of feeling in the army. "I learn also confidentially from these officers and others," reported Dana, "that the soldiers have lost their attachment for General Rosecrans since he failed them in battle." And Dana made this remark a text for a definite recommendation that Thomas should be appointed in his place. Again on October 12th, Dana reported that the commanding position on Lookout Mountain had been yielded

---

[1] After Garfield joined Thomas, he wrote three important despatches dated on the day of the battle, 3:45 P. M., 8:40 P. M., and the next morning, 7:45 A. M. In these his relations to Thomas can be traced. *Official Records,* Vol. XXX, pt. 1, pp. 141, 144, and 146.

by Rosecrans against the protests of Garfield and Granger. Rosecrans "pettishly rejected all their arguments." This is information that seems to have come from the officers in question. About the same time Garfield talked to Henry Villard, who represented the influential New York *Tribune* and in that capacity might be regarded as holding power not second to that of Dana. "General Garfield," Villard reported, "knowing that he was safe with me, took me freely into his confidence. He told me how fully convinced he was that his chief was making a mortal mistake in going to Chattanooga, how he tried to dissuade him from it, and how relieved he was to be permitted to rejoin Thomas." From Garfield Villard also learned of his dramatic ride, and was told about the foolish abandonment of Lookout Mountain, much as the story was given at the same time to Dana.

About this time Garfield talked to Rosecrans as to the coming session of Congress, asking him whether in his opinion he could honorably give up his position in the army for a political career. Rosecrans did not then and was not for many years to know of the criticisms which were being directed against him, but he must have felt something of the strained atmosphere. At least he made no effort to persuade Garfield to remain in his present position. Referring to Garfield's new opportunity, he said: "I not only thought he could accept it with honor, but I deemed it to be his duty to do so." On October 10th, Rosecrans in a general order in which he spoke in praise of his subordinate relieved Garfield from his duties as Chief of Staff. At the same time he was preparing his report of the recent campaign in which he again wrote generously of Garfield's services. On October 15th, as a special messenger from Rosecrans, bearing this report and other despatches, Garfield started from Chattanooga for Washington.

In Louisville Garfield was summoned to see Secretary Stanton, who was in the city. Many years later, Garfield reported to Rosecrans that in that interview he stoutly defended Rosecrans. But the impression left on Stanton at the time was quite the reverse. For, on October 21st, Stanton telegraphed the War Department: "Generals Garfield and Steedman are here on their way home. Their representations of the incidents of the battle of Chickamauga more than confirm the worst that has reached us as to the conduct of the commanding General and the great credit that is due to General Thomas." In Cincinnati, Garfield met his old friend, General J. D. Cox. The two men sat late into the night talking over the army experiences of Garfield which had now come to an end. Garfield told Cox that his liking for Rosecrans amounted to a warm personal affection. But both men were convinced that Rosecrans, with all his fertility, lacked the steadiness which would make him a safe leader for a great army.[1]

The decision to remove Rosecrans had virtually been reached as early as October 3d, and the chief factor in that removal was the influence of the reports to Stanton by the Assistant Secretary of War, C. A. Dana. But there can be no doubt that beginning with the delay in July, Garfield had lost confidence in his commander, and that in a series of incidents commencing with his letter to Chase of July 27th and culminating in his Louisville interview with Stanton, he had used his influence to secure the removal of General Rosecrans. The ethical dilemma was by no means simple. On the one hand were his confidential relations, and a friendship which was undoubtedly deep and sincere, and which in later years Garfield was to prove on more than one occasion. On the other hand was a sense of public duty founded on reasons which had great weight. Garfield tried to solve the problem by doing what he

[1] For Garfield's criticisms of Rosecrans, see: *Official Records*, Vol, XXX, pt. 1, pp. 202, 204, 215; Vol. XXXI, pt. 1, p. 684; H. Villard, *Memoirs*, Vol. II, p. 185; J. D. Cox, *Military Reminiscences*, Vol. II, pp. 9–11.

felt to be his public duty without sacrificing a friendship that
he deeply valued, or injuring the susceptibilities of a man to
whom he was personally under the greatest of obligations.
That Garfield was wholly wrong would be difficult to assert.
It would have perhaps been sounder for Garfield to have resigned first as Chief of Staff, and then criticised Rosecrans when
he felt it to be his duty to do so. But Rosecrans would have
been removed, and Garfield would have remained his friend,
if it had not been for the journalistic instincts of Charles A.
Dana and the New York *Sun*.[1]

For some years the friendly relations between the two men
who had been in a great emergency so close to one another remained outwardly unbroken. In 1864, when Garfield had been
in Congress only a few weeks, he devoted one of his first
speeches to the defense of the record and the services of his
commander. Again in 1870 Garfield was called upon to deliver a eulogy on the career of Thomas, a task which he performed with such delicacy and restraint that he was able to
give full praise to Thomas without implying at any point any
criticism of Rosecrans. And Rosecrans, who was becoming restive and suspicious through the publication of unjust accounts
of the campaign in which his attitude was compared unfa-
vorably to that of Thomas and of Garfield, was deeply grateful. Again in 1879, when Rosecrans was nominated for
Governor of Ohio on the Democratic ticket and declined, Garfield used the occasion to praise Rosecrans in a public speech.

The charges made by Dana required considerable effrontery
on his part, for Dana rather than Garfield had been the chief
cause of the removal of Rosecrans. But the volumes of the
Official Records that contained Dana's secret and bitter criti-

[1] For Dana's charges see:—New York *Sun*, Sept. 26, 1874; Nov. 26, 1879;
March 8, 1882; June 10, 1882. These charges are discussed at length by T. C.
Smith, *Life and Letters of Garfield*, Vol. II, pp. 845–885, where the conclusions
reached are somewhat at variance with those given below.

cisms were not published until 1890. In the meantime, in 1874 and again in 1879, Dana published an account of the removal which placed the blame, from the point of view of Rosecrans and his friends, on a letter that Garfield had written to Chase. In 1874 these charges do not seem to have come to the attention of Rosecrans, who was engaged in mining ventures in California. But when they were repeated in the latter year, Rosecrans wrote to Garfield, who answered that charges from Dana, "or any other liar," that he had been untrue to his friendship with Rosecrans did not have a particle of truth.

In spite of the inaccuracies of detail, however, Garfield must have seen at once that there was enough substantial truth in Dana's story to make any more specific denial impossible. For at any moment his letter to Chase of July 27th, 1863, might be published, as indeed it was two years later. His embarrassment appears quite clearly in the wording of his denial. When, during the summer, campaign biographies of Garfield appeared written by correspondents like Bundy who had visited Mentor and had presumably the assistance of Garfield himself, and when these biographies praised Garfield's ride in terms that were far from complimentary to the steadiness and courage of Rosecrans, the old soldier was deeply offended.

During the Presidential campaign, Rosecrans, in California, took an active part against Garfield, and when he was charged with inconsistency and confronted with his own high praise in 1863, replied "that seventeen years is a long time, and many a splendid young man in less time has descended from honor to infamy." After the election, Rosecrans wrote to Garfield apologising for his conduct, saying that he had been irritated by what he regarded as the lies of the recent biographies, and asking for a renewal of the old friendship. But Garfield was now implacable, and on December 31, 1880, the President-elect replied in cold and formal terms that the statements made by Rosecrans during the campaign were an insuperable barrier to the restoration of the old relations.[1] The attempt to reconcile public duty and private friendship had failed. From that time, in the growing list of memoirs of the Civil War, the friends of Garfield and those of Rosecrans were to belong to different schools. Around each name conflicting legends grew apace.

[1] Garfield to Rosecrans, Dec. 31, 1880 (Garfield *Papers*).

LATE in October, 1863, a full year after his election to Congress, Garfield reached Washington. The border States, including Maryland, had not been included in the emancipation proclamation of the previous January; but public opinion was moving with great rapidity in favor of a measure that only a year before would have seemed very radical, and Garfield was invited by Secretary Chase to accompany him to Baltimore and to address a huge mass meeting in the interests of abolition in Maryland by State action. As a result Garfield became acquainted with Henry Winter Davis, once conservative, but now an enemy of the Blairs and a leader in the radical opposition to President Lincoln. Davis, whose career was to run so short a course, had soon won the eager admiration of the young soldier with whom he was to take his seat in the coming Congress. The friendship with Davis was to help to determine Garfield's position in the curious three-cornered contest of the next two years.

On his return to Washington, Garfield presented his report to Stanton, and had a number of interviews with Halleck and Lincoln in which he was able to explain with vividness the military situation in the west. About this time he was given his commission as Major General of Volunteers to date from September 19th, the day of Chickamauga, an honor that he could now accept. For a moment he considered resigning his post in Congress and even at the last minute continuing his career as a soldier. But Lincoln, whom he consulted, advised him just as Rosecrans had done. The resignation of Garfield would leave the Republicans without one needed vote. His experience would be of great value in the framing of necessary

military legislation. It is probable that Lincoln, who was often
a shrewd judge of men, recognised even more clearly than Garfield the true field for the display of his ambitions and talents.
Was it possible, as seems to be indicated by the frequency with
which similar advice was given to other men, for example
Schurz, Schenck, and Blair, that Lincoln accepted with some
relief the resignations of civilians who had held high command?
By this time it was clear to Lincoln, who had made his mistakes,
that the day of the professional soldier had come. Lincoln's
advice was strengthened by the promise of Stanton to keep his
place for him in the army whenever he decided to return; and
with this assurance, two days before the meeting of the Thirty-
eighth Congress, James A. Garfield became again a private
citizen.

In the meantime Garfield had found time for a short visit
to Hiram, where he lived for the first time in the house which
he had bought in 1862, and which was to remain for many
years the center of his family life. In that house on October
11th his first son had been born, named for two old friends,
Harry Augustus Garfield, the son who was one day to become
the President of his own old college at Williams. But the visit
was saddened by the sudden illness and death of the first child,
a daughter not yet two years old, who died in the week that the
father had to return to take his seat in Congress. Garfield had
been married five years, and his family life had been limited
to a few brief weeks.

In Washington there were the usual wartime rumors of an
outbreak on the part of Southern sympathisers to prevent the
meeting of the new Congress and at the Republican caucus the
members were advised to report armed; but these rumors
proved to be without foundation, and on December 7th the
House was organised without difficulty by the selection of
Schuyler Colfax of Indiana as speaker. Garfield was at once

assigned to the military committee, of which the chairman was General Robert Schenck, an experienced Congressman also from Ohio and who like Garfield now resigned from the army to resume a political career. A few years later, Schenck was to be defeated for Congress and consoled by the appointment of American minister to the Court of Saint James's, where his knowledge of draw poker, an American game on which he had written a treatise, and his advertisements of doubtful mining ventures were not to add luster to the position that had been held by so many eminent Americans, including three generations of the Adams family. But whatever one might say of General Schenck as a diplomat, Garfield found in him an experienced, able congressman, who knew well the House rules. Schenck was a generous chairman and a good friend. He invited the inexperienced young congressman to live in the same boarding house, which soon became the center of military discussions; he placed Garfield almost at once in charge of the chief bill which originated in his committee, and when Garfield became involved in the intricate confusion of the rules, steered his young friend to a successful outcome. Garfield had already had some experience in Columbus, and within a short time he needed help from no one.

The acknowledged master of the house was Thaddeus Stevens of Pennsylvania, who at the age of seventy-one, as Chairman of the all-powerful Committee of Ways and Means, which was responsible for financial measures, was at the height of his power. Bitter, sometimes unscrupulous, a master of invective against which few debaters liked to stand a second time, there was yet in Thaddeus Stevens a certain vein of idealism that had shown itself first in his support of a system of free public schools for his own state and that made him to the end a representative of a waning conception of democracy. More, perhaps than any other member of the house, Stevens hated the old South because he conceived it as essentially aristocratic in spirit. Even now he was eager to make the war result in a social as well as a political revolution. But the conservative tradition in America, supported by two successive Presidents, Abraham Lincoln and Andrew Johnson, was to prove too strong; and, although his power in the House of Representatives was to remain unmatched until his death in 1868, the victories of Stevens were to be in the long run essentially temporary and illusory.

Next to Stevens the most powerful figure was the Speaker, Schuyler Colfax of Indiana, who came from a reasonably safe Republican district that had sent him regularly to Congress since 1855. At the age of forty, Colfax was already a veteran, with a career before him which would make him Vice President and that might have led even higher if it had not been wrecked by the scandals of 1873. Among other powerful veterans, from whom Garfield was to learn much, were J. S. Morrill of Vermont, the author of the first Republican tariff bill; H. L. Dawes of Massachusetts, Chairman of the Committee on Elections; and Henry Winter Davis of Maryland and General Robert Schenck of Ohio, whom we have already noticed.

On the Democratic side, the leaders, whose function for many years was to be chiefly negative and critical, were first Samuel S. Cox, then of Ohio and later of New York, whose popular sobriquet of "Sunset" was an indication of oratorical ability, but whose capacity for witty debate was only second to that of Stevens himself. "Gentleman George" Pendleton of Cincinnati was to make himself the leader of the section of the Democrats that desired monetary inflation and as such to cross swords more than once with Garfield. With their love of nicknames, the newspapers called D. W. Voorhees of Indiana the "Tall Sycamore of the Wabash." He was to prove a sharp critic of Reconstruction measures, while his colleague, W. S. Holman, specialising on appropriation bills, was winning for himself a name as the "Watch Dog of the Treasury." The list of leading Democrats included Fernando Wood of New York, backed by the power of the Tammany organization, whose point of view on financial questions was often conservative and out of touch with other elements of the party. James Brooks, also of New York, was an effective debater, whose career was closed by his unfortunate contact with the Credit Mobilier scandals.

Among the new members who like Garfield were to win their spurs were W. D. Kelley, whose belief in high protective tariffs was a religion and whose speeches on his favorite subject won for him the name of "Pig Iron Kelley." Also from Pennsylvania, and with views on protection that followed the orthodox pattern of that state and brought him into later conflict with the low tariff position of his Democratic colleagues, winning his way to leadership in spite of a rough tongue and a sharp temper, was the future speaker of the house, Samuel J. Randall. But the newcomer whose arrival meant the most to Garfield was James G. Blaine of Maine. In later years, Garfield and Blaine were first rivals for the power which fell from the hand of Stevens, and then in a great crisis friends and intimate companions. Roscoe Conkling of New York, with whom Blaine and Garfield were to quarrel bitterly, had been in Congress but was not to return to the House until 1865. The relations of these three young men, Blaine, Garfield, and Conkling, each at this time in his early thirties, were one day to become one of the central themes in the history of American politics.[1]

By a familiar feature of the American Constitution, the Congress of which James A. Garfield became a member at so interesting a moment in the war had been, as we have seen, elected in the autumn of 1862 and was only now beginning its

[1] See Johnson Brigham, "Blaine, Conkling, and Garfield," *passim*.

activities in December of the following year. For Garfield there had even been time between the election and the assembly for a whole career in a new position in the army. Now most of the members were within a few months of contests that would be necessary to new nominations and new elections. In the Northern States, which were at the time, of course, the only ones represented, about half the districts were close and the issue between the parties was doubtful. In the rest one of the two parties was clearly dominant, in the majority of cases the Republican, and the sitting member had only one contest for his nomination and not two, for his nomination first and then for his election. The members who had serious double contests had their interests centered quite as much in politics back home as in the affairs of the legislative session.

There were doubtless able men in this Congress as in others whose names are now quite forgotten. But as one examines the list of congressmen who attained prominence and affected the policy of the nation, it is at once apparent that the members from districts that were not close had a great advantage. They alone could devote themselves with comfort to the intricate details of their committees. They could give adequate attention to the careful preparation for debate. While others were fighting for their lives they could speak outside of their own districts and on wider themes and thus attain national reputations. Above all, with reasonable certainty of reëlection they needed only to wait to attain the seniority which, granted adequate ability and industry, would make their influence effective. For them entrance into Congress was a career. The members from the doubtful districts, on the other hand, were from the beginning necessarily troubled about many things. As the session drew to a close they were perforce compelled to leave the management of important measures to their more fortunate colleagues. Sooner or later in the kaleidoscope of politics, and it was often sooner, they were almost certain to fall by the way-side, and unless rewarded by some convenient diplomatic post, were apt to be forgotten. For them Congress was an episode.

In this respect Garfield was from the beginning peculiarly fortunate. He came from a district where the only possible problem was that of his nomination and whose political sta-bility was even greater than that of many districts in the "solid South" of the next generation. The district had for thirty-six years been represented by two men, Elisha Whittlesey and Joshua R. Giddings, and in the case of Garfield it was to main-tain the tradition of choosing the same man for an average period of eighteen years. Every two years, Garfield was nomi-nated, often by acclamation, always by large majorities, and was then elected by majorities that ranged from two to three to one. Only twice in eighteen years did he have a serious con-test for the nomination, and only once, in 1874, and that under conditions entirely exceptional, was his election over a Demo-cratic opponent open to the slightest doubt. Garfield's habits of study, his industry and capacity for hard work, his debating skill and instinctive realization of the spirit of the House marked him for a position of leadership; but it is doubtful whether he would today be remembered as one of the two or three most significant parliamentary leaders of his generation if he had not come from the nineteenth congressional district of Ohio, or from another substantially like it. His strategic ad-vantage was increased by the fact that he not only came from a safe district, but from a safe district in a large and at that time politically doubtful State. Such a man was sure to com-mand increasing respect, which in turn would add, and add justly, to his prestige at home. He could even afford the dan-gerous political luxury of thinking for himself. In any case, Blaine, who entered Congress at the same time, testified later that though Garfield was at the time with a single exception

the youngest member of the House, within sixty days he had
been picked out for a position of influence and authority.

In the first Congress, Garfield made the mistake of speaking
too often. His army experience had been useful, but the generation that had admired rhetoric sprinkled with classical allu-
sions was gone, and Garfield had not yet learned the full value
of rhetorical restraint. Accordingly, he was for a time in danger
of losing his audience before they were fairly won. But the
young congressman had abundant capacity for constructive self-
criticism and was able to learn from his own mistakes. He had
the debater's instinct for the weak points in the armor of an
adversary, and the orator's sense for dramatic opportunities
that on one occasion carried his words beyond the halls of
Congress. By the end of that first session the House knew that
it had a future leader and the nineteenth district took pride in
a congressman who with greater intellectual vigour than
Joshua R. Giddings or Ben Wade had something of the same
capacity of these older leaders to make his personality vivid
and compelling.

In the period after the war, when Lincoln was dead and rising rapidly to heroic proportions, the campaign orators liked
to believe that during the war all the Republicans stood shoulder to shoulder with the great President in the measures necessary for success and all Democrats in sharp opposition. From
this point of view, of which the classical exposition is Blaine's
"Twenty Years of Congress," the contest between the President and Congress began after the death of Lincoln and was
due almost exclusively to the malignity of Andrew Johnson.
But firmly as this tradition was to be established, it is of course
false, as any examination of contemporary documents at once
reveals. Even in the previous Congress Lincoln had not had
more than one or two outspoken supporters, and the situation

in the Thirty-eighth Congress of which Garfield was a member
was substantially the same. The life of the legend tends completely to conceal the essential theme of legislative history in
the closing years of the war. For the contest between the President and Congress had been clearly foreshadowed in the last
Congress, and was to commence sharply with Lincoln's annual
message and his proclamation of December 8th, 1863, in which
he announced definitely his so-called Louisiana plan of reconstruction. From that time the contest between two departments
of government and between two ideals of reconstruction, only
kept in abeyance for a few months by the remoteness of the
issues and the necessities of a political contest in the midst of
war, went on without a break to the dramatic culmination in the
attempted impeachment of Andrew Johnson. All this is abundantly illustrated in the career of James A. Garfield, as it might
be with equal ease in the lives of other men.

Lincoln's popularity among the masses of the northern people and in the ranks of the army was already very great; but
curiously enough, among the politicians of Washington criticism was more common than praise and the President stood
between two fires. On the one hand were the extreme Democrats, like Alexander Long of Cincinnati, who believed that the
game was not worth the candle and that the war should be
ended by negotiation even at the cost of a recognition of the
Confederate States of America. On the other hand were the
Republican leaders in Congress who still desired to continue a
system of volunteering, and who yet criticised Lincoln's conduct of the war as weak. Lincoln's suspension of the writ of
habeas corpus by which the prisons were filled with political
offenders, his postponement of emancipation, his evident
doubts about the wisdom of negro suffrage, his failure to
recommend a policy of confiscation that would place the landed
property of the South in the hands of Union men, both negro

and white, all caused criticism; and this now came to a climax
when he announced his desire to keep reconstruction in his own
hands and to return the various States to self-government at the
earliest possible time.

By Lincoln's plan, when ten percent or more of the voters
under the old State laws should be willing to take an oath to
support the Constitution of the United States and to obey the
emancipation policy as long as it was not declared unconstitutional, he would be willing to entrust the future of the South
to these voters. Granting that the actual admission of members
to Congress was quite beyond his power, before the end of his
term, three States, Louisiana, Arkansas, and Tennessee had
been reorganised substantially on the basis suggested in the
first message to which Garfield listened. For the moment, the
problem not being really pressing, the congressional leaders
bided their time, but in private conversations and intimate letters they made it quite clear that they had no intention of leaving the problem of reconstruction either to Lincoln or to any
other President, especially when his announced plan seemed to
them to endanger what in the political cant of the day was so
often called "the legitimate fruits of victory." In December of
1863, that victory was still far enough away.

Gradual and compensated emancipation in 1862! The return
of political privileges and the security of the property of par-
doned rebels in 1863! Such a policy, from the point of view of
Garfield and his friends was weakness and imbecility. It would
make impossible the social and economic changes in the conquered South on which the safety of the Union would depend.
When Garfield on the 28th of January, 1864, delivered his
first important speech in the House, he was evidently thinking
of the plan that he had once considered of leading twenty thousand men to make Florida forever loyal to the Union. That
speech was on the confiscation of rebel property and in support

of a bill that had been introduced by J. F. Wilson of Iowa in direct challenge to the doctrines that had been enunciated by President Lincoln.

Congress on July 17, 1862, had passed a so-called confiscation bill. But Lincoln had been able to insist, by the threat of a veto, that confiscation of real estate should not "be construed to work forfeiture of the real estate of the offender beyond his natural life." After emancipation, real estate was the only important form of property in the South. To confiscate plantations temporarily was obviously useless; and the result, as Lincoln had no doubt wisely foreseen when the law was passed and signed, was to leave the policy of confiscation a dead letter. With the President's pardoning power always available and in view of the mild policy of reconstruction that he had now announced, there was every reason to believe that southern property in case of victory would continue to belong to the same persons as before. The negro and the Union man would still be under the necessity of acquiring land by some more laborious process.

In the debate on Wilson's bill, S. S. Cox had pointed out on January 14th, as Lincoln had done in July, that confiscation of real estate as a punishment for treason was definitely prohibited by one of the limitations of Article III of the Constitution. Whatever one might think of a measure which would repeat the policy that had once been pursued towards Tories in the Revolution, the thing could not be done legally. This argument was seemingly unanswerable. But Garfield's speech is important, although its arguments could not have continued to command his respect, because it is one of the clearest expressions of the bitterness which many men at the moment felt for the policy of the President.

Garfield met the objections of Cox and Lincoln by citing the example of the English revolution: "The people said, We will have a king, but not James. . . . The throne was vacant and their king was unworthy to fill it. The British nation cut through the entanglement of words, and filled it with a man of their choice." Was this an illustration, or a threat? "When the government of the United States declared the country in a state of war, the rebel states came under the laws of war. By their acts of rebellion they swept away every vestige of their civil and political rights under the Constitution of the United States." Having dealt in this cavalier fashion with the difficult constitutional objection, Garfield came to the concrete purposes of confiscation of plantations: "I hold it as a settled truth that the leaders of this rebellion can never live in peace in this republic. . . . This is true of every State over which the desolating tide of war has swept. If you would not inaugurate an exterminating warfare to continue while you and I and our children and our children's children live, set it down at once that the leaders of this rebellion must be executed or banished from the republic. They must follow the fate of the Tories of the Revolution." And then Garfield meets squarely the recommendations made by the President six weeks before: "We can hold the insurgent States in military subjection half a century if need be, until they are purged of their poison and stand up clean before the country. They must come back with clean hands if they come at all. I hope to see in all those States the men who have fought and suffered for the truth, tilling the fields on which they pitched their tents. . . . Let no weak sentiments of misplaced sympathy deter us from inaugurating a measure which will cleanse our nation and make it a fit home of freedom and of glorious manhood." [1]

On February 5th, the House passed the confiscation measure. The Senate took no action, and though confiscation was

[1] *Cong. Globe,* 38th. Cong., 1st Session, pp. 403–405.

more than once thereafter a theme of Garfield and was advocated for many years by Stevens, this was the end of all serious attempts to legislate further upon the confiscation of the property of rebels for the punishment of treason. Twice within a year the checks and balances of the Constitution as represented first by the President and then by the Senate had given the American people time in a moment of passion to think twice before they took through the majority of their representatives a step that must have been costly and, whether for good or evil, difficult to retrace.

By his initial speech, Congressman Garfield had thus placed himself on the extreme left and in opposition to President Lincoln. His position, however mistaken and constitutionally unsound, had been frank and bold to the point of temerity, and no one could ever say that he had carried water on both shoulders.

Early in the session Garfield received a visit from his old friend, General J. D. Cox, and arranged a little dinner, at which beside his host, Cox met General Schenck and Henry Winter Davis, all of them playing leading roles in the House of Representatives. In describing the dinner, Cox wrote: "We four were alone, and it was a rare opportunity for me to hear unrestrained discussion of everything in public affairs." Davis let loose in a witty and scathing denunciation of Lincoln and all his ways. Of all his epithets, "baboon" was one of the mildest. The soldier, fresh from the army and accustomed to "hurrah for Lincoln, as the rebels shouted for Davis," was shocked. "General Schenck did not appear to differ greatly from Davis." Garfield treated the outburst as a sort of extravaganza, and in his position as host, met these sallies with jovial laughter and prodded Davis to fresh explosions by shafts of wit. "It was a strange and not altogether exhilarating experience for me," wrote Cox, "but I had afterwards to learn that the be-littling view of Lincoln was the common one among the public men in Washington." [1]

However bitterly in private and in public Garfield opposed Lincoln's plans for reconstruction as foreshadowed in his annual message and however doubtful he might be of the President's ability, his own experience at the front had made entirely clear the necessity of vigorous measures to fill the depleted numbers in the army. On this subject he was willing to give the Administration full support and even to go beyond the recommendations of the President. The enrollment act of March 3d, 1862, had not been a sincere measure of conscription, an idea which continued to the end to be very unpopular even in communities like the Western Reserve that were fully committed to the prosecution of the war. The chief reliance was still to be volunteering, encouraged by national bounties, which were in turn supplemented by various local bounties to fill the necessary quotas. Only in case a community failed to provide its proper number of volunteers under any call was the President authorised to resort to a compulsory process. But even then the list of exemptions was very long and included thirteen various classes of citizens. A person who had been enrolled and drafted and who had not found some plausible reason for exemption might even then furnish a substitute, if he could persuade or hire someone to go in his place, or if he had money enough and the worst came to worst, might pay a commutation of three hundred dollars and thus avoid actual service. The evils that had resulted had created a public scandal. The bounties encouraged bold and unscrupulous men after enlisting to desert and then under new names in other communities to receive still other bounties that sometimes reached a total of thousands of dollars. But quite apart from this new crime of

[1] J. D. Cox, *Military Reminiscences of the Civil War*, 1900, Vol. II, p. 396.

bounty jumping, the system could be attacked because it did not bring in the needed soldiers.

At one stage in the draft, as Garfield pointed out, 290,000 names had been drawn from the wheel. Of these 73,000 were exempted on account of disability, and 74,000 for other reasons under the terms of the law; 41,000 had enough money to pay commutation; 24,000 furnished substitutes, of whom a large number immediately deserted; and 11,000 went to the field. The remainder were excused as having been improperly enrolled.[1]

Such figures were eloquent. From his strong position on the military committee, placed by a generous chairman in charge of the first military bill of the session, a dangerous measure that Schenck was probably willing to leave to the young member from the district so much safer than his own, Garfield saw from the beginning that three things must be done: the bounties that caused a ruinous drain on the Treasury must be abandoned; the list of exemptions must be reduced; and the undemocratic and entirely indefensible commutation privilege must be destroyed. But not even he was bold enough to learn at once that all differences between the volunteers and the drafted men must be given up. Only in the World War had public opinion advanced to the point of rejecting entirely the volunteer system, which by its very nature placed a stigma on the drafted man and made him eager to avoid service if he could.

Everybody agreed that the system of bounties, for lack of money if for no other reason, must go. But when in January Garfield pressed for immediate action he was voted down, standing with Grinnell of Iowa in a minority of two; and even after the repeal of national bounties, the various local communities continued the same system in rivalry with one another to the end. Garfield's military bill, his first legislative

[1] *Cong. Globe,* 38th Cong., 1st Sess., pp. 528–534 (Feb. 8, 1864).

venture, reducing the number of reasons for exemption, was passed by the House on February 14th. And then came the tug of war; for every one knew that the heart of the old system was the commutation clause which drew a sharp distinction between the drafted man with three hundred dollars and the one without. In support of commutation powerful forces were arrayed.

After the opening of the campaign in May, the tale of losses from the armies in the field and especially from the Wilderness of Virginia was appalling. Lincoln appeared in person before the military committee and told them what he did not dare to tell the House, that without more soldiers the war could not be won. As Garfield afterward remembered the scene, the President was warned by the Republican members that to give up commutation was to make almost certain his own defeat for reëlection. Lincoln drew himself up to his full height and replied that he could afford defeat but that the country could not. If they would give him the soldiers, the war could be won before the end of his term.

On June 25th, 1864, in support of the policy of Lincoln, Garfield delivered one of the most powerful and effective speeches of his career. All superfluous rhetoric was now abandoned and Garfield spoke with directness and simplicity to the heart of a living issue: "Gentlemen doubt what the people will say and how they will feel. I have learned that the people are braver than their representatives . . . I know that the people whom I represent have united their destiny with the destiny of the Union, and will share its fortunes whatever betide it. I have not asked them, but I believe they will respond cheerfully to this measure." No other speech was delivered at this important session of Congress that reveals more clearly the will to victory which accounts more than any other single factor for the outcome of a long and often doubtful struggle.

At the very end of the session the desired repeal of commutation was passed, but accompanied by an unfortunate amendment introduced by Garfield on July 1st, that was to be the source of great injustice. By this amendment, volunteers in Southern States might by a legal fiction be credited to the quota of some Northern State, thus reducing its own obligations under the draft. The result was an unseemly scramble for soldiers, especially among the mountaineers of Tennessee and the recently emancipated negroes, a contest in which the State with the most unscrupulous agents and the most powerful political affiliations was obviously sure to win. Apart from this amendment, Garfield had made a fine record in which, often at the risk of popularity, he had given adequate support to the effective maintenance of a national army.

To the Democrats the position of the President and the sharp division on many questions between him and the leaders of Congress furnished an opportunity both from a partisan and a patriotic point of view. But though some measures of obvious justice, like the repeal of the commutation clause, were carried by the aid of Democratic votes against powerful Republican opposition, at this time as so often afterward, the Democrats were divided and had no clear-headed leader of the type of Douglas who might have seen that the constitutional position of the President, especially on the already looming problem of reconstruction, was really their own. So more often than not, they contented themselves with futile and obstructive criticisms, and occasionally one of their members on what may be called the extreme right was allowed to commit the party to indefensible positions and so to play into the hands of the group to which Garfield at the time belonged.

Such a member was Alexander Long of Cincinnati. He was a respectable and conservative gentleman of the old school, and if the war were to lead to the confiscation and the social revolution that Garfield had described he preferred immediate recognition of the Southern Confederacy. And so in the course of extended remarks, Mr. Long inquired: "Can the Union be restored by war? I answer most unhesitatingly and deliberately: No, never. War is final and eternal separation. My first and highest ground against its further prosecution is that it is wrong. It is a violation of the Constitution and of the fundamental principles on which this Union was founded. My second objection is, that as a policy it is not reconstructive, but destructive, and will if continued result speedily in the destruction of the government and the loss of civil liberty, to both the North and the South, and it ought therefore immediately to cease."

It was a dramatic opportunity of the first order and on April 8th, 1864, in a speech full of burning invective, but through which ran a vein of serious argument, Garfield took full advantage of the occasion. In his constitutional argument with S. S. Cox, Garfield had not added to his reputation, but all that was forgotten in his reply to Long. The scene was described by the newspapers, and thus early in a Congressional career, Garfield attracted the attention of the nation.[1]

In his opening sentence, raising his left arm to its full length, for Garfield was left-handed, he called on the sergeant-at-arms to place a white flag of truce in the aisle between him and his antagonist. Only so could he discuss such a proposition as the House had just heard: "And that proposition comes—God forgive and pity my beloved State!—it comes from a citizen of the honored and loyal Commonwealth of Ohio." From in-

---

[1] *Cong. Globe,* 38th Cong., 1st Sess., pp. 1503–1505: For the effect of the reply to Long see Whitelaw Reid, *Ohio in the War,* Vol. I, p. 758. The expulsion of Long was proposed, but after a bitter debate was changed to censure: *Globe,* p. 1634.

vective, Garfield passed to his main theme. In sharp contrast with the views that he had stated in January, he now argued from the historical illustration of the Scottish border that a successful war might lead at length to peace. But if the Confederacy were recognised where would the boundaries be drawn between the North and South? How long would peace endure between two rival and independent republics? Grant that the war was leading to a new constitutional system: "I would take all the old sanctions of law and the Constitution and fling them to the winds, if necessary, rather than let the nation be broken in pieces and its people destroyed with endless ruin."

Precisely there was also the heart of Garfield's feeling that Lincoln, who kept looking back to the old Union, with its constitutional safeguards, was weak and unworthy. Could such a man ride the whirlwind and direct the storm? Was there another to take his place?

The controversy between Salmon P. Chase and the Blairs, represented in the cabinet by the Postmaster General, Montgomery Blair, was growing increasingly bitter. General Frank Blair entered Congress, much as Garfield himself had done, with a promise that his place in the army should be kept open for him. In April Blair resigned his place in the legislature to take command of an army corps in the west, devoting his final speech to a bitter attack on the conduct of the Treasury Department, and even suggesting the presence of official corruption. Garfield came to the defense of Chase and was placed in charge of an investigation of the alleged frauds and immoralities on the part of Treasury officials. As usual in such cases, the report written by Garfield completely exonerated the Department from the charges which had been made, while the minority of the committee considered them at least partially proven. Garfield believed that Blair had been sent to Congress by Lincoln to attack a member of his own Cabinet, and wrote that the

"President is bound hand and foot by the Blairs and they are dragging him and the country down into the chasm."

When on February 22d, the Pomeroy circular appeared, placing Chase in active candidacy for the Presidency, Garfield found himself in a difficult position. For, friendly as he was to Chase, Garfield felt that the people wanted the reëlection of Lincoln, and that a movement in any other direction would not only be a failure but would tend to disturb and embarrass the friends of the Union. Garfield made no secret of his preference for Chase, but by the end of April he was certain "first, that Mr. Lincoln will be nominated—second, that he will be defeated and a Copperhead elected. I don't know a dozen men who believe it can be otherwise." Accordingly Garfield kept aloof from the Cleveland convention that on May 31st nominated John C. Frémont for the Presidency, even though the criticisms of the President in the radical platform were the very ones which he himself was making; and on June 7th he was even persuaded to attend, though with reluctance, the Baltimore convention of the Union party that by a unanimous vote placed in nomination Abraham Lincoln of Illinois and Andrew Johnson of Tennessee for the positions of President and Vice President of the United States.

In sharp contrast with the Cleveland platform, the one introduced at Baltimore by Lincoln's campaign manager, Henry J. Raymond, the editor of the New York *Times*, shrewdly omitted any reference to the rising problem of reconstruction, which every one recognised as the chief issue between the two groups in the party. But on their return to Washington, the leaders of Congress had no intention of leaving their own position in doubt. Should States in the South reorganised by Lincoln's plan be recognised? On June 13th, 1864, Garfield took a leading part, introducing a resolution to the effect that no such state should be eligible to cast its votes for President or

Vice-President without the previous consent of both houses of Congress. But when a Democrat quietly inquired what the effect of such a resolution might be on the candidacy of Andrew Johnson of Tennessee, Blaine saw the danger, and at once moved to lay the resolution on the table. With the unanimous help of Democratic votes, Blaine's motion was carried by a vote of 104 to 33. The defeated minority included Thaddeus Stevens, Henry Winter Davis, and James A. Garfield. Checked for the moment by the curious dilemma regarding Tennessee, the leaders of Congress contented themselves by passing on the last day of the session a reconstruction law in which, among other things, the reorganization of any State was made to depend on the consent of Congress.

The new plan was so mild that if Lincoln had guessed what was to happen two years later, he might well have signed it. But Lincoln saw in the claim of absolute control by Congress, a purpose to discourage the prompt measures of reconstruction which he had already inaugurated, and which he believed to be calculated to shorten the duration of the war. Accordingly, he not only refused to sign the bill, but issued a proclamation in which his willingness to accept the law as a mere alternative to his own plan was a further challenge to leaders who maintained the absolute supremacy of Congressional authority.

The issue was sharply drawn and if Congress had been in session the contest must have begun with the greatest bitterness at once. As it was, the two leading opponents of the President, in the New York *Tribune* for August 5th, published a vitriolic attack on the motives of the President signed by Senator Ben Wade and by Representative Henry Winter Davis.[1] In view of Garfield's frank acceptance of its doctrines, the language of the manifesto is essential to an understanding of his position at this time: "The President by preventing this bill from be-

[1] N. Y. *Tribune,* Aug. 5, 1864.

coming a law, holds the electoral votes of the rebel states at
the dictation of his personal ambition. . . . If electors for
President be allowed to be chosen in either of those states, a
sinister light will be cast on the motives which induced the
President to hold for naught the will of Congress rather than
his government in Louisiana and Arkansas. . . . A more
studied outrage on the legislative authority of the people has
never been perpetrated. . . . The President has greatly presumed on the forbearance which the supporters of his administration have so long practiced, in view of the arduous conflict in
which we are all engaged. . . . But he must understand that
our support is of a cause and not of a man; that the authority
of Congress is paramount and must be respected; that the whole
body of Union men in Congress will not submit to be impeached
by him of rash and unconstitutional legislation. . . . Let them
consider the remedy for these usurpations and having found it
fearlessly execute it."

But the authors of the document had not estimated correctly
the hold of Lincoln on the voters of the party, and the very
bitterness of the threats caused a general protest. Since Wade
was his neighbor and Davis his intimate friend, Garfield was
charged with a part in the authorship of the document; and
when the Congressional nominating convention met at Warren
on August 23d, a committee was appointed to invite Garfield
to address the meeting. When he appeared the chairman informed him of the charges that had been made against him,
and demanded an explanation. It was a crisis in Garfield's career,
for it was apparent that his nomination depended on his ability
to meet the issue with which he was confronted. Garfield accepted the challenge with complete frankness. He had not
written the paper, and he regretted the necessity for its appearance. He had made no factious opposition to the nomination of
Abraham Lincoln at Baltimore. But Lincoln was not his first

choice for the Presidency; Garfield had criticised his policy, of which he disapproved; and unless he could be nominated with perfect freedom to express his views of public issues, he did not desire the nomination. The convention had passed resolutions condemning Wade and Davis, but they were swept off their feet by the evident courage of their representative, and with the curious inconsistency that sometimes moves popular assemblies they nominated amid cheers and by acclamation the congressman who had just accepted his share in the views they disliked. The nomination of Garfield in such circumstances was a striking proof of the devotion of the West to its own deep-seated individualism.

At the time of the Wade-Davis manifesto and the Warren convention, many shrewd political observers, including Raymond and Lincoln himself, expected Republican defeat and the election of George B. McClellan. But in the next few days two incidents took place to unite and reanimate what had seemed a hopelessly divided party: Sherman entered Atlanta; and on September 21st, Frémont withdrew from the contest. His own district being entirely secure, Garfield took an active part in the general campaign, making more than sixty speeches and invading Holmes County and other centers of Democratic strength. In October he was elected to Congress for the second time by a vote of 18,086 to 6,315. Before the election both Chase and Montgomery Blair had left the Cabinet and after Chase became Chief Justice his relations with Garfield were to become less intimate.

It was now time for congressmen to return to Washington. During the short session which was about to begin, and entirely true to his function as critic and tribune of the people of which he had spoken at Warren, Garfield made a thoughtful and important address in favor of a movement to bring Cabinet members into Congress where they could be questioned and

in the fashion of parliamentary types of government kept subordinate to the legislature. Similarly, the military committee
of which he was a member performed a useful function in
making an examination of prisons in which civilians without
due process of law or a knowledge of the charges against them
were kept incarcerated by military authority. On January 18th,
1865, he made a speech in which he joined with Henry Winter
Davis in attacking the policy of military imprisonments as both
illegal and unnecessary, a speech which brought Garfield to the
favorable attention of no less a lawyer than Jeremiah S. Black,
and of which we shall hear again. Curiously enough, neither
Davis nor Garfield seemed at the time to realise that the reconstruction policy to which both were now so fully committed
would one day, and that soon, involve them in a hopeless
dilemma between their sincere hatred for military government
and the necessities of the system that they desired to impose on
the South.

On the morning of April 15th, 1865, the news of the assassination of Lincoln reached Garfield in New York, where he
had gone on a business trip.[1] There were men who had
criticised Lincoln the day before, who now admired him; but
Garfield did not so stultify himself. According to a tradition
which was well established during the lifetime of Garfield and
which is probably authentic, a great crowd gathered that evening in Wall Street in front of the Exchange Building. The
atmosphere was tense with emotion and ugly threats against
the New York *World*, a Democratic newspaper, could be heard.
Other speakers had failed to quiet the swirling masses, when in
the dim light Garfield's bulky figure was seen in the balcony
and his clear voice rang out over the crowd: "Fellow-citizens: Clouds and darkness are around about Him! His pavilion
is dark waters and thick clouds of the skies! Justice and judg-

---

[1] Garfield to Black, April 19, 1865 (Black *Papers,* Library of Congress).

ment are the establishment of his throne! Mercy and truth shall go before his face! Fellow-citizens: God reigns, and the Government at Washington still lives!" That was all; and it is at once apparent that this first speech on the death of Lincoln is quite as significant for what it did not contain as for what it did.

One year later, the anniversary of the death of Lincoln arrived, and Congress had forgotten to make any provision for its celebration. The news reached Schuyler Colfax, a few minutes before the House was to assemble, that the executive departments had been closed in honor of the day by President Johnson. It would never do to let Johnson capitalise the Lincoln tradition, and the speaker asked Garfield, without preparation, to make the necessary motion for adjournment. Garfield's position was peculiar, for he was to speak at once to the country and in the presence of many men to whom his views of the abilities of Abraham Lincoln were well known. This task Garfield accomplished with admirable restraint: "Mr. Speaker, I desire to move that this house do now adjourn. . . . The last five years have been marked by wonderful developments of individual character. . . . But greatest among all these developments were the character and fame of Abraham Lincoln, whose loss the Nation still deplores." Garfield had passed over the very thin ice, and the rest of the speech could be devoted to the usual account of the wickedness of treason and slavery. In the quaint language of the *Globe*, "The motion was unanimously agreed to; and thereupon, at fifteen minutes after twelve o'clock, the house adjourned." [1]

Finally, on February 12th, 1878, almost thirteen years after the death of Lincoln; when the Congressional plan of reconstruction had been fully tried, in the administration of Hayes by whom two years before it had been virtually abandoned by

[1] *Cong. Globe,* 39th Cong., 1st Sess., pp. 1952, 1953.

a return to the very principles that Lincoln had suggested so long ago; when time had brought knowledge and softened asperities, in accepting for the national Capitol Carpenter's well-known painting of the signing of the emancipation proclamation, Garfield was called upon to deliver the only full-length oration on the career of Lincoln that has been preserved in his *Works*. In speaking of Lincoln he said: "Gifted with an insight and a foresight which the ancients would have called divination, he saw, in the midst of darkness and obscurity the logic of events, and forecast the result. From the first, in his own quaint, original way, without ostentation or offense to his associates, he was pilot and commander of his administration. He was one of the few great rulers whose wisdom increased with his power, whose spirit grew gentler and tenderer as his triumphs were multiplied." Across the years, "the second-rate Illinois lawyer" of 1862 had at length come to his own.

DURING the years that followed the war, three major issues
were the central themes of political debate: the reconstruction
of the defeated South; the policy of high tariffs which had been
one of the by-products of the war; and the demand for monetary
inflation, at first through the further issue of legal tender paper
money, the so-called greenbacks, and later by the free coinage
of silver. On each of these problems which arose side by side
and required immediate solution, James A. Garfield, already
recognised as one of the leaders of the dominant party in the
House, was compelled to take his stand, and since other questions were either temporary in their interest or else too new to
command the attention of the nation, it is on the basis of his attitude to these three problems that the capacity of a congressman
of the seventies for wise statesmanship must finally be judged.
On each of these questions at the beginning there were sharp
differences of opinion within the same party, but the first almost
from the outset became an issue between the Democrats and
the Republicans, and on the other two before the close of Garfield's congressional career the dominant position of the parties
had become sharply differentiated. In two cases, Garfield in
the grip of a party system was compelled to yield at least a part
of his convictions, his views on the tariff placing him for a time
on the blacklist of powerful interests that controlled his party
and preventing him to the end from attaining the chairmanship
of the committee on Ways and Means which was always the
goal of his ambitions; as to the third question, however, that
of monetary policy, Garfield made himself from the beginning a consistent advocate of the gold standard against all forms
of monetary inflation, and at the close of his career had the

satisfaction of bringing party associates whose own views had often been doubtful to the position that he had advocated without wavering from the first. On other questions that in a later day were to become important, Garfield expressed opinions: woman suffrage, prohibition, the income tax, the national control of railroads, educational reforms; but only the last two were rising above the horizons of political consciousness in the lifetime of the representative from the nineteenth congressional district of Ohio.

The problem of reconstruction was, as we have seen, a direct inheritance from the administration of Lincoln. Indeed, the most radical leaders of Congress welcomed the accession of Johnson with a confidence that appears clearly in the reminiscences of George W. Julian. Ben Wade was frank in his delight, and exclaimed, "Johnson, we have faith in you," a sentiment with which Garfield undoubtedly agreed. And it is apparent that so long as the steps were taken that he regarded as necessary to safeguard the interests of Union men and negroes, Garfield had not been long enough a member of Congress to care greatly whether those measures were adopted on the initiative of Congress or the President. But with all of Johnson's dislike of the wealthy leaders of the rebellion, Wade and others had entirely misconceived the essential conservatism of the President's position, as became at once apparent when on May 29th, 1865, during the long recess of Congress that would last until December, Johnson issued his proclamations in which he committed himself to almost exactly the same method of reconstruction that had already been foreshadowed by Lincoln. The basis of the suffrage in the South should remain essentially unchanged; the voters who should take an oath of allegiance to the Constitution would be allowed to frame new State constitutions and to establish governments which were required by the President to adopt the Thirteenth Amendment abolishing slavery and to repudiate the Confederate debts. Some classes of voters were, indeed, reserved from general amnesty but even these were granted individual pardons; the conditions imposed by the President were accepted if not cheerfully at least readily; and by the time Congress met, the process was virtually complete and the majority of the States had even elected Congressmen and Senators, most of whom, naturally enough, had very lately worn the Confederate grey, and were ready to seek admission in the Thirty-ninth Congress.

Face to face with the realities of an economic revolution some of the recently reorganised States, notably Mississippi and Louisiana, passed laws that compelled the continued labor of the negroes and that seemed to look toward peonage as a transition from the plantation system; and whatever might have been the necessity for such laws from the local point of view, they evidently constituted, in the light of the struggle that was bound to follow, a serious tactical mistake. But long before any Southern State had had time to make any mistakes and before President Johnson had made any tactless speech of the kind for which he was afterward so severely blamed, it was apparent that the Presidential plan would not be accepted without a severe struggle which Johnson could only have avoided by yielding his fundamental position. It is difficult to see how Lincoln could have escaped the same contest, although it is, of course, possible that with his greater popular prestige and the advantage of actual election to his office Lincoln might have won a victory where Johnson finally failed.

That at the close of a long and bitter war, the South should have been allowed to enter Congress, and at that with increased strength, and hold the balance of power between northern parties—the agricultural South, with a well-known dislike of high protective tariffs, of the kind that the war had produced—the non-commercial South containing no owners of five-twenty bonds and therefore all too likely to find some easy way of paying the national debts—the South in the very year of Appomattox already represented by Confederate brigadiers —would have been a miracle of magnanimity without parallel in the history of civil wars. Hence, however wise in the light of the result Johnson's patient and careful efforts may now seem, from the beginning the three major problems that we have mentioned, the problem of the negro, the one of the tariff, and the one of the money and the bonds, were inextricably bound together.[1]

Leaving aside all questions of theory, beside the solution that the President had adopted two others were available. The South might for a term of years be kept under military government, without dangerous rights of self-governing statehood. This was essentially the plan that had once appealed to Garfield and of which the leading sponsor at this time was Thaddeus Stevens of Pennsylvania. As an alternative, the basis of suffrage might be changed by the temporary disfranchisement of leading whites and especially by the enfranchisement of the negro, who out of gratitude and under national protection might be expected to vote the right ticket. It was of this last plan, which became in the long run, of course, the one actually adopted, that, as early as July 4, 1865 and many months before any personal issues had arisen with Andrew Johnson, James A. Garfield was to become one of the earliest prophets.

President Johnson's evident desire for a free hand had given congressmen, including James A. Garfield, a long vacation, and that too in an odd year when they had no need to fight for their political lives. Accordingly Garfield had more time at home than had fallen to his lot for a long time. It was the year of a State campaign, and on July 4th, Garfield delivered an oration at Ravenna in which he discussed boldly the problem of

[1] On this point see H. K. Beale, *The Critical Year.*

negro suffrage, on which at the time sentiment even in the north was far from favorable. In characteristic fashion he recognised the difficulties of the solution for the southern problem that he was advocating: "Is it safe," he asked his audience, "to admit to the elective franchise the great mass of ignorant and degraded blacks, so lately slaves? . . . I am fully persuaded that some degree of intelligence and culture should be required as a qualification for the right of suffrage." In spite of this preference, however, he had come to feel that the ballot must be given to the negro to permit his own protection against injustice. And then Garfield came to his central point, one which few politicians would have recognised with equal candor: "By the Constitution only three fifths of the slaves were counted in forming the basis of representation. The proclamation of emancipation adds the other two fifths, which at the next census will be more than two millions. If the negro be denied the franchise, and the size of the House of Representatives remain as now, we shall have fifteen additional members of Congress from the States lately in rebellion, without the addition of a single citizen to their population, and we shall have fifteen less in the loyal States. . . . Such an unjust and unequal distribution of power would breed perpetual mischief." [1]

In spite of political necessities, however, the Republicans of Ohio were unwilling for the moment to follow Garfield's lead. His old friend General J. D. Cox, who was the candidate for governor, much to Garfield's disgust came out in flat opposition to granting suffrage to the negro race; and in spite of the warmth of his personal friendship, Garfield was pleased when a sprained ankle gave him a reason for withdrawing from the campaign; but Cox had evidently interpreted correctly the prevailing opinion in the State and was victorious by more than the usual Republican majority. As to the course of Congress,

[1] Hinsdale, *Works of Garfield*, Vol. I, p. 91.

Garfield wrote in July that the Southern States should be held under military rule "until there is a voting population that can be trusted with power." In October he asked Chase a question that foreshadowed the very tactics that were later to be followed with complete success: "If we shall not be able to maintain the fight on the suffrage question alone, should we not make a preliminary resistance to immediate restoration and thus gain time?" Thus, as far as Garfield was concerned, it is evident that long before the meeting of Congress and quite apart from the results in the South, Johnson and his plan were in for a very determined fight.

The Republican leaders were back in Washington in good time to concert common measures. Of the members of the House whom Garfield now met for the first time and with whom his life was to have close connections, two of the most interesting were Roscoe Conkling of New York, of whom we shall hear again, and a new congressman from Ohio, Rutherford B. Hayes. What Garfield thought of Hayes does not appear, though in later years he was to express his views more than once, but Hayes found Garfield "a smooth, pleasant, ruddy man, not very strong," a judgment from which he never receded. The caucus under the leadership of Stevens resolved not to recognise the new governments in the South, and Garfield, who had had some needless anxiety on this score, praised the decision which made certain that the fruits of victory would not be thrown away.

The President's message, able and moderate in tone, showed at once the wide difference between his views and those of Garfield and other leaders. Johnson desired to leave the South to itself and to allow it to make its own mistakes; the more radical leaders of Congress wanted to establish in the South a new political and perhaps a new social order and were willing if necessary to resort to military force. With his greater realism, such a man as Stevens saw at once that the conflict was irrepressible, that the issues cut too deep to admit of compromise, and that one or the other must give up an essential conviction. But Garfield kept hoping that the President might be won to the congressional position. So he wrote to Hinsdale on December 11, 1865: "We appear to have a very robust House, and indications thus far show it to be a very sound one. The message is much better than we expected, and I have hoped that we shall be able to work with the President. He sent for me day before yesterday, and we had a free conversation. I gave him the views of the earnest men North as I understand them, and we tried to look over the whole field of the difficulties before. . . . I think we should assume that he is with us, treat him kindly, without suspicion, and go on in a firm, calmly considered course, leaving him to make the breach with the party if any is made." [1]

For two months Garfield listened in silence to speeches in which Congressional leaders, in characteristic American fashion, made elaborate theories that would allow them to deal with the South without changing the constitutional rights of other parts of the republic. Were the Southern States "conquered provinces," as Thaddeus Stevens believed? Or had they committed suicide by rebellion, as Sumner argued? Or had they merely forfeited their constitutional rights to self-government, without losing statehood? In his only elaborate discussion of the theory of reconstruction, on February 1, 1866, Garfield brushed aside all these elaborate distinctions, which after all led to the same practical conclusion, by adopting a naïve and thoroughgoing nationalism that would have made even Marshall and Webster turn over in their graves and that might have done credit to Theodore Roosevelt himself. There are clear indications that at this time Garfield had not read the

[1] J. M. Bundy, *Life of Garfield,* p. 76.

great judicial decisions in which the delicate structure of the federal system had been defined, and he shows none of the intimate acquaintance with the positions of the *Federalist* that appears in later years; but Garfield's nationalism had at least the attractive quality of applying without distinction to Ohio as well as to Georgia and Alabama, and his position was accordingly fairer than either Sumner's or Stevens'. In Garfield's view, the States of the American Union are "only geographical divisions . . . endowed by the people of the United States with the rights of local self-government." To all Constitutional scruples as to a radical reconstruction policy, Garfield opposed what seemed to him "the unanswerable proposition that this is a nation." [1]

Garfield having adopted a position that assimilated the Constitution to the essential simplicity of that of Great Britain or France, and that even a casual reading of the Tenth Amendment must greatly have disturbed, purely technical legal difficulties at once disappeared. The personal rights of the negro might be safeguarded by using the phrase in the Fifth Amendment that prohibited any deprivation of life, liberty and property without due process of law, and if by chance further authority were required, it could be found in the arrangement by which "the citizens of each State are entitled to all privileges and immunities of citizens in the several states." Under these provisions Garfield felt that Congress could and should enter within the limits of the individual State to protect all persons against injustice. At only one point did he acknowledge the necessity for a further amendment, and that was in the matter of negro suffrage. On that point he said: "If I cannot today get all I desire, I will try again tomorrow, securing all that can be obtained today. But so long as I have any voice or vote

[1] Hinsdale, *Works of Garfield*, Vol. I, pp. 95–117.

here, it shall aid in giving the suffrage to every citizen qualified by intelligence to exercise it."

Curiously enough, having made a proposition whose radicalism from the legal point of view, at least, could scarcely be surpassed, Garfield thought that he had furnished a basis for compromise. "In my speech," he wrote to Hinsdale, "I tried to take ground for both him (Johnson) and Congress to stand on." But this optimism was short-lived, for a few days later, on February 19th, Johnson vetoed the first of the Congressional measures, the Freedmen's Bureau Bill, which took the negro problem from the States and placed it under national authority, on constitutional grounds that were a world away from those that had been expressed by Garfield. In March, on narrow technical grounds, with a single vote to spare, the Senate unseated Senator John P. Stockton of New Jersey and from that time the radicals had the two-thirds majority that they needed to carry over the veto of the President first the Civil Rights Bill, the second law in American history to win its way through after a veto, then the Freedmen's Bureau Bill, and finally near the close of the session to adopt the Fourteenth Amendment, which now became the basis of the Congressional appeal to the country against the policy of President Johnson in the important election of 1866. Although, as we have seen, Garfield had recognised no necessity for an amendment and had believed that the Congressional program might be accomplished just as well by simple statute, he was of course found voting with the majority, and he undoubtedly deserved fully what his friend Whitelaw Reid intended as the highest praise: "He is not factious; and without ever surrendering his independence of judgment, he is still reckoned among the most trusty of the Radical majority."

Of that independence of judgment he was to give striking

proof when on March 6, 1866, scarcely more than a month after he had defined so fully his theory of reconstruction, he presented before the Supreme Court of the United States his argument in the case of *ex parte Milligan*, the first and to the end the most important of Garfield's legal adventures.

Years before, when Garfield was still President at Hiram, he had commenced the study of law, and, under the easy regulations of that time, soon after he had entered the legislature of Ohio, he had been admitted to the bar. He had always considered the possibility of becoming a practicing lawyer, but the war had come and then Congress, and he had never received a brief. Back in the fifties, Jeremiah S. Black, already recognised as a leader of the bar in Pennsylvania, and later celebrated as Attorney General in Buchanan's cabinet and a supporter of a vigorous policy against secession, had sent a son to the little college in Ohio of which Garfield was a member of the faculty. This son, Chauncey Black, had become involved in a boyish scrape and through the instrumentality of Garfield had been expelled. When Garfield came to Washington, he found the young man established as a lawyer; but Black cherished no hard feelings, recognised the justice of his treatment and, tending to regard the whole matter as a huge joke, renewed his old friendship with Garfield, and introduced him to his father, who by that time was one of the three or four most celebrated lawyers in America, especially interested in the cases on the borderland between politics and law which became so numerous in the early years of the reconstruction period. David D. Field, the most learned lawyer of his generation and the author of the New York codes, Robert J. Walker, equally celebrated as a politician and a lawyer, and Jeremiah S. Black became the brains of the legal contest of the Democrats against reconstruction, and in the next decade there were few great cases with which one or more of this celebrated triumvirate were not found before the Supreme Court pleading the rights of their clients against the Attorney General of the United States.

Jeremiah Black came from York, Pennsylvania, but he was frequently in Washington on legal business, and the two men soon became close friends and, in spite of differences in years and in political views, even boon companions, a friendship that remained close and unbroken to the end of their days. Black was a gentleman of the old school, a brilliant conversationalist, with the wide interests that a day of close specialization has made so rare. Garfield was undoubtedly the best-read man in the House of Representatives, deeply interested in English history, in literature and poetry (he read Lucretius and Horace in the original for amusement on the train), and in the contest between the old theology and the newer concepts of science. Both men had boundless curiosity; and each had to have some one to talk to. So we find the great lawyer and the congressman sitting up on one occasion to a late hour to discuss the relative position of Byron and Wordsworth and again to read and to admire in their literary quality the parables of Jesus. Through Black, Garfield was introduced to the practice of law, making his first plea before the Supreme Court in the most celebrated case of the times, and continuing to accept occasional appointments of the same kind.

It all happened in this way. In January, 1865, Garfield, at the time a critic of the policies of Lincoln, had, as we have seen, become interested in the fate of the numerous political prisoners in the Old Capitol and Carroll prisons at Washington. Garfield found more than one case of serious injustice and became a bitter opponent of the wisdom or necessity of what was called martial law. Before the close of the session, he had joined Henry Winter Davis, at that time his most admired friend, in attaching to an appropriation bill a rider to the effect that "no person shall be tried by court-martial or military commission in any state or territory where the courts of the United States are open, except persons actually mustered or commissioned or appointed in the military or naval service of the United States, or rebel enemies charged with being spies." [1] Davis and Garfield felt so strongly on this point that when the Senate refused to concur, they preferred to allow the bill to fail rather than to recede from the position that they had taken. At that time only the shrewdest men, like Thaddeus Stevens on the one hand and Jeremiah Black on the other, saw clearly the intimate practical connection between radical reconstruction and military arrests. For the moment Davis and Garfield could favor one and oppose the other, and it must be confessed that the logic of their position was certainly no weaker than that of Lincoln, whose attitude on both questions was the precise reverse of their own. Radical reconstruction would require soldiers and military arrests, but this was a position that Garfield was not yet required to meet.

In the meantime, in October, 1864, a case had arisen in Indiana in which Jeremiah Black was to take a very deep interest. L. P. Milligan, W. A. Bowles, and Stephen Horsey, penniless Southern sympathisers, otherwise unknown to fame, had been arrested by the soldiers, tried by a military commission, and on rather vague charges of "disloyal practices," had been condemned to death, a sentence which had been commuted by President Lincoln to imprisonment for life and which Milligan and the others were then serving in the penitentiary at Columbus. The case had first aroused the interest of J. P. McDonald of Indiana, and he had enlisted the services of such celebrated lawyers as Black and Field.

When Garfield was invited to join the case, the truth or falsity of the original charges was not at stake, but merely the deeper question as to the right of a military commission to

[1] *Cong. Globe,* 38th Cong., 2d Sess., pp. 318–320.

try and condemn civilians in a region where the ordinary civil courts were open. There was not a cent to be earned, for the defendants had no money, but it was evidently an opportunity for a young lawyer in celebrated company to win for himself almost at a bound an enviable reputation. Black and Field were obviously quite capable of presenting to the Court the technical arguments, but Black had admired Garfield's position in Congress. Here was a soldier, a Republican, a close friend of the Chief Justice of the United States, who would evidently be very useful to the defendants in removing from their counsel the possible stigma of partisanship; the issues were quite as much political as legal, and Black was undoubtedly not adverse to driving a logical wedge into the heart of the radical position. He asked Garfield whether he would be willing to make to the court the same argument that he had already made in Congress. But he was entirely fair: "Young man," he warned Garfield, "you know it is a perilous thing for a young Republican in Congress to say that, and I don't want you to injure yourself." There was in Garfield, however, a vein of the knight errant, and he replied that he believed in English liberty and English law and he would take the risk. The decision was one of the most creditable in his career, for the defense of Southern sympathisers was not popular in the Western Reserve, and the criticisms came just as the shrewd Black had prophesied.[1]

Garfield's argument, on the constitutional side was not strong, for, as he recognised himself, his education in American constitutional history had been almost entirely neglected and this deficiency was still to be made up by his later reading; but the chief task that had been assigned to the youngest member of the group of lawyers for the defense was to bring out the English precedents, and this task Garfield accomplished

[1] Garfield to Black, Mar. 11, 1865; April 19, 1865 (Black Papers); T. C. Smith, *op. cit.*, Vol. II, 842–847.

creditably, showing a surprising knowledge of the history of the English law and proving that he had worked hard on his first case. Garfield argued that military law applies only to soldiers and sailors; that martial law is not law but the negation of law; and that civilians have a legal right to the ordinary process of the courts. In his conclusion he made a prophecy that was to come true: "Your decision will mark an era in American history. The just and final settlement of this great question will take a high place among the achievements which have immortalized this decade. It will establish forever this truth, of inestimable value to us and to mankind, that a republic can wield the vast enginery of war without breaking down the safeguards of liberty; can suppress insurrection, and put down rebellion, however formidable, without destroying the bulwarks of law."

The case of the government was presented by the Attorney General, James Speed, who was assisted by another civilian general, Benjamin F. Butler, with whom Garfield was to have more than one contest, and by Henry Stanbery, whose position was later to be changed in new circumstances. The court speaking through Mr. Justice Davis approved the position of the defense and freed the prisoners, and though Chief Justice Chase in an assenting opinion sought to save some part of the power of military commissions, a blow at the system had been dealt that was immediately recognised by radical newspapers that were soon demanding the reorganization and even the abolition of the powers of the Supreme Court.

Garfield soon found his own position as one "of the most trusty of the Radical majority" endangered by the bad political company in which he had helped to fight and win the case of *ex parte Milligan*. The contest that was just beginning between the friends of the President and the radical leaders was the most intense and bitter that had ever been known; for the

first time in a non-presidential year both parties held conventions, two on each side, and also for the first time the President
of the United States was seen on the stump pleading with the
people for the election of a Congress that would save the
governments organised the year before in the South. Garfield
found it especially necessary to prove that he had not gone
over to the Democrats, as some of his enemies were saying,
and so his speeches in the campaign had a quality that contrasted strangely with his plea to the court only five months
before. Thus, at Warren, Ohio, on September 1, 1866, the
friend of Jeremiah Black plead for reëlection by the following
course of reasoning: "In the Democratic party is enrolled every
man who led a Rebel army or voluntarily carried a Rebel
musket; every man who resisted the draft, who called the
Union soldiers 'Lincoln's hirelings,' 'negro worshippers,' or
any other vile name. Booth, Wirz, Harold and Payne were
Democrats. Every Rebel guerilla and jayhawker, every man
who ran to Canada to avoid the draft, every bounty jumper,
every deserter, every cowardly sneak that ran from danger
and disgraced his flag, every man who loves slavery and hates
liberty, every man who helped massacre loyal negroes at Fort
Pillow, or loyal whites at New Orleans, every Knight of the
Golden Circle, every incendiary who helped burn Northern
steamboats and Northern hotels, and every villain, of whatever
name or crime, who loves power more than justice, slavery
more than freedom, is a Democrat and an indorser of Andrew
Johnson." [1] The worst of it is that such arguments were undoubtedly effective, and that to a large extent on such a basis
a cause for which serious political and economic considerations
might have been adduced was fought and won. Garfield, as a
matter of course, carried his own district by a vote of 18,362
to 7,376, and the radical majority in the next Congress was

[1] B. A. Hinsdale (Editor): *Works of Garfield*, Vol. I, p. 241.

such as to reduce the few conservative Republicans of the type of Henry J. Raymond and the Democrats like James E. English to hopeless impotence and against which the veto power of the President himself might struggle in vain. Andrew Johnson had laid his case before the American people and the people had decided against him; they had never made a more momentous decision.

From the point of view of statesmanship a great opportunity was now thrown away by Congress as it had previously been by President Johnson. Lincoln, Johnson, and even Garfield in his first speech on the subject in 1865, had advocated impartial suffrage rather than universal suffrage. If in the reorganization of the South the white voters had not been disfranchised and if the negroes had been granted a gradual and qualified suffrage based on an impartial educational test, such a policy would have had the support of many conservative southern men including Wade Hampton and L. Q. C. Lamar; under such a system, entirely consistent with democratic principles, the reconstruction period would not have been remembered as one of unparalleled anarchy and corruption. But Johnson had been prevented from insisting on such a policy by constitutional principles which made him unwilling to interfere more than necessary with the political structure of the Southern states; and Congress was now carried by the immediate political advantages to be gained into radical measures which many of those who voted for them did not really approve. As early as 1865, Thaddeus Stevens had argued that the universal suffrage of the negro and the disfranchisement of the whites were both essential to any hope for continued Republican supremacy in the South. Such a policy, made possible by the unexpected completeness of the victory that had been won, was now substituted for the carefully guarded impartial suffrage that Garfield had once desired. To the negro, who might have earned complete citizenship by a process of gradual political education, the results were to be peculiarly calamitous.

There are many indications that Garfield recognised these dangers at the time as clearly as they can be seen with the passing of the years, and that he approached the measures which were finally adopted only with the greatest reluctance. Thus he wrote to Hinsdale, on January 1, 1867: "In reference to reconstruction I feel that if the Southern States should adopt the constitutional amendment within a reasonable time, we are literally bound to admit them to representation; if they reject it, then I am in favor of striking for impartial suffrage, though I see that such a course is beset with grave dangers." And again: "I wish the South would accept the constitutional amendment soon and in good temper. Perhaps they will." As Garfield explained his position to his most intimate friend, he was trying to do two things: "to dare to be a radical and not a fool, which, if I may judge by the exhibitions around me, is a matter of no small difficulty." [1]

The difficulties were indeed insuperable. Party lines had never been drawn so sharply and the powerful majority was in no mood to listen to objections from one of its own members, nor was Garfield the man to stand against the storm. So finally, on February 8, 1867, with misgivings that arose from the position that he had taken so daringly in *ex parte Milligan*, less than a year before, and that he was now compelled to abandon, Garfield gave his assent to the bill for the division of the South into military districts and which was the first step in the congressional program. Even now, he comforted himself in the belief that the evils that he foresaw would be merely temporary, and the benefits perpetual: "Now, sir," he said, "as a temporary measure, I give my support to this military bill, properly restricted. It is severe. It was written with a steel pen

[1] J. A. Bundy, *Life of Garfield*, p. 77.

made out of a bayonet; and bayonets have done us good service hitherto. All I ask is that Congress shall place civil governments before these people of the Rebel States, and a cordon of bayonets behind them." From that time, Garfield gave an increasing share of his attention to financial problems; on reconstruction he spoke seldom and briefly; but he was found voting regularly with the majority for the various bills that were adopted to complete the program in the South and for the companion measures, like the Tenure of Office Act, which were designed to restrict the powers of the President of the United States.

When the most extreme members of Congress first proposed the impeachment of Andrew Johnson, Garfield could not be persuaded that the President was guilty of high crimes and misdemeanors within the meaning of the Constitution, and voted against the proposed policy; and when the resolution of impeachment finally passed the House, Garfield was among the small number of Republicans who were absent from their seats. But a few days later he accepted the attack on Johnson as his own, and about the same time went almost out of his way to prove his party regularity and his complete conversion to the views of the majority.[1] Garfield's contest with General W. S. Hancock was to gain added significance when twelve years later Garfield and Hancock became the rival candidates for the Presidency.

In March 1867, soon after the passage of the reconstruction law, General P. H. Sheridan, the noted cavalry leader, was placed in command of the district that had a few days before constituted the States of Louisiana and Texas. At two points, the relations of the new military power to the previous civil governments and the extent to which white men were to be disfranchised and prevented from serving on juries, the first

[1] *Cong. Globe*, 40 Cong., 2d Sess., pp. 1560, 1561.

reconstruction law was not entirely clear. According to Attorney General Stanbery, the civil governments, though provisional, might be allowed to continue in practical control, and the disfranchising provisions might be limited to previous office holders. But Sheridan was in complete sympathy with the radical point of view, and interpreted the doubtful law in the severest terms. He found, he said in his official report, that the civil officers had been Confederate soldiers or sympathisers with the rebellion, and were in his judgment "substantially aliens." Accordingly, he removed all these officers, beginning with the two governors, and including judges, sheriffs, and policemen, and even required a stringent test oath of jurors which few respectable men were able to take and that left the courts quite disorganised and unable to perform their ordinary functions.

The policy of Sheridan was of course very distasteful to the President as well as to the people of Louisiana and Texas, and Johnson, who had not yet lost his authority over the army, removed Sheridan and placed W. S. Hancock, whose views were known to be conservative, in command as his successor. The appointment of Hancock had a definite political significance; he was undoubtedly in close touch with Robert J. Walker and probably with Jeremiah Black before he left Washington, and his first proclamation, issued on his arrival in New Orleans on November 29th, was not only an implied criticism of the policy of his predecessor, but indicated a general point of view that might be made to undermine even at this late day the whole congressional position: "The general commanding," Hancock announced, "is pleased to learn that peace and quiet reign in his department. It will be his purpose to preserve this condition of things. As a means to this great end, he regards the maintenance of the civil authorities in the faithful execution of the laws as the most efficient under existing circumstances. . . . The right of trial by jury, the habeas corpus, the liberty of the press, the freedom of speech, and the natural rights of persons and the rights of property must be preserved."

The various reactions to Hancock's "General Orders No. 40," as this celebrated document was called, were curiously different. Jeremiah Black was in the midst of a law case, but the moment that he read Hancock's proclamation, he sat down at once to congratulate him, as he had congratulated Garfield for similar sentiments just three years before—so much had happened in the meantime! To Black, Hancock's conduct seemed "patriotic and noble," and his words were "a distinct recognition of the principles of American liberty." The anger of the congressional leaders was proportionately great and was not reduced by the fact that the author of the proclamation was a distinguished Union general whose services especially at Gettysburg had been of the most important character. Curiously enough, the burden of a reply fell to the congressman whose plea in *ex parte Milligan,* less than two years before, seemed to breathe so many of the same sentiments that were now made the basis of an actual experiment in the South.

At a later time, the practical results of Hancock's mild policy in removing soldiers from the polls, leaving the composition of juries to the judgment of the courts, refusing to close newspaper officers, and the like, were a subject of bitter controversy between Hancock and his enemies. But when, on January 17, 1868, Garfield rose to attack Hancock, there was no evidence that he might be used to point out the mistakes of the military commander of the Fifth District. Garfield described Hancock as "an otherwise meritorious officer, who bears honorable scars earned in battle for the Union." This officer had been drawn into the course of madness that had characterised the conduct of the President. But the indictment which followed this introduction seems today across the years surprisingly unconvincing. What had Hancock done? "We see him issuing a general order, in which he declares that the civil power should not give way before the military. . . . It is not for him to say which should be first, the civil or the military authority in that Rebel community. . . . With such a combination against us, does any one suppose that we can take one step backward— much less, that we will permit an officer of our army to fling back in our faces his contempt of the law, and tell us what policy shall be adopted?"

To give further point to his warning, Garfield, chairman of the military committee, introduced a bill reducing the number of major generals in the army. Since Hancock was the newest member on the list he would be the first to go; but too many people still remembered Hancock's services and too many approved his principles to make the measure either popular or safe. Hinsdale wrote to Garfield in evident disapproval and Garfield himself was troubled regarding the justice or wisdom of his course: "You were surprised that I introduced the Hancock bill," he wrote to Hinsdale; "so was I; but the orders and proclamations which he had been issuing were of so insubordinate a character as to endanger the whole work of reconstruction in Louisiana." Then Garfield describes with curious frankness the motives that had led him to propose the Hancock bill: "We must show that our refusal to impeach the President did not arise either from want of courage, nor from any purpose to abandon our work of reconstruction on the basis of universal freedom. With these views I introduced the Hancock bill, not so much for the purpose of passing it as to show him how completely he was in our hands. . . . I could readily have carried the bill through, but preferred to let it hang suspended."

Garfield thought that his threat would have "the desired effect" and he was right; for the President was first shorn of his powers and then impeached by the House. Every one expected him to be convicted; and Hancock soon saw that he could do little to avert the doom that had been pronounced. About this time he wrote to a friend: "I hope to be relieved here soon. The President is no longer able to protect me; so that I may expect one humiliation after another until I am forced to resign. I am prepared for any event; nothing can intimidate me from doing what I believe to be honest and right." After a sharp interchange of letters with Governor Pease of Texas, who had been appointed to his place by Sheridan, an argument of which Hancock seems to have had considerably the better, on February 27th, 1868, at his own request, Hancock was relieved from his command and was soon ordered by Grant to the innocuous distance of the Dakotas. One of the first acts of the administration of President Grant was the reappointment of Sheridan to his previous command, where he tended to confirm the President in his increasing radicalism and where the severity of his course later won the outspoken condemnation of even Garfield himself. In the strategy of his attack on Hancock, Congressman Garfield had won a victory which he found later to be almost too complete.[1]

After the virtual removal of Hancock, there are many signs that Garfield became increasingly doubtful of the wisdom of the policy in the adoption of which he had played a leading part. In Congress he spoke seldom of reconstruction, and at home there was no longer the appearance of certainty that had characterised his remarks in the decisive campaign of 1866. More than once he was placed clearly on the defensive and there were numerous indications that the tide of northern

[1] For the Hancock incident see, F. E. Goodrich, *Life of Hancock* (1886), pp. 231–300; C. W. Ramsdell, *Reconstruction in Texas,* p. 120; Republican Campaign Handbook (1880), pp. 191–195; *Works of Garfield* Vol. I, pp. 261–263; The important letter to Hinsdale is printed by J. M. Bundy, *Life of Garfield,* p. 183, but otherwise the Hancock incident is omitted from lives of Garfield, including that by T. C. Smith.

sentiment was beginning to turn. Thus in 1868, when Garfield was making a speech at Orwell, Ohio, a venerable Democrat in the center of the audience, who had been listening attentively, asked the speaker if he proposed to adopt constitutional amendments by the bayonet. To which Garfield replied: "We propose this, my friend. If you persist in forming Ku Klux Klans in the South to murder Union men, white or black, we propose to use the bayonet." With which reply, that seemed so completely to beg the question, the orator turned rapidly aside to consider the currency and the tariff. Was it possible that the unnamed old man had discovered a peculiarly disagreeable subject for discussion? [1] In any case, by 1871 Garfield had returned to the position which he had occupied five years earlier in his argument before the Supreme Court and though he voted for the enforcement acts of that year did so with evident reluctance and after making an extended argument against the wisdom of martial law in the South. In the next year, the solid party alignment was finally broken. In 1870, the House of Representatives had considered four contested election cases, and in all four the dominant party had unseated the Democrat and seated the Republican. But in 1872, with the House still Republican, two Republican congressmen from the South were expelled and their places given to the Democratic contenders.

The most notable case was that of William Thomas Clark, formerly Chief of Staff to Sherman and now, under a new name, William Tecumseh Clark, the leader of the Galveston negroes. Greeley had taken an active interest in the case and had pointed out in the *Tribune* that Clark had been defeated on the face of the returns, but had been sent to Congress by the certificate of the Republican governor of Texas, who had conveniently overlooked a number of ballot boxes where the votes favored Clark's opponent. General Clark made an almost

[1] B. A. Hinsdale, *Works of Garfield*, Vol. I, p. 397.

tearful plea, in which he argued his high services to the Republic and pressed a point that was undoubtedly correct, that his expulsion from Congress would be the beginning of the end of Republican domination in Texas. Garfield, who had made a close study of the case, replied from the majority with evident weariness that the time had come when the votes cast rather than the political consequences must determine an election to the House, and then joined with the Democrats in voting the expulsion of the first carpetbag representative from the South. Clark was of course at once rewarded by a suitable appointment in the Treasury Department, but the prophecy that he had made was amply fulfilled. One by one, the various Southern States returned to almost exactly the same type of control that had been in 1866 the point of departure for the strange experiment of reconstruction.[1]

In the Presidential campaign of 1872 Garfield supported Grant against Greeley, who strangely enough was now the Democratic candidate; but without enthusiasm, for he had written confidentially "that Grant was not fit to be nominated, and Greeley not fit to be elected." As to reconstruction Garfield limited himself to pointing out, with obvious justice, that however corrupt the carpetbag governments had been and whatever mistakes had been made, Horace Greeley as much as any man in the United States was responsible for those errors and that the editor of the New York *Tribune* could not at this late date turn them to his own political advantage. From the point of view of the nation the old issue was no longer vital or dominant.

By 1877, Garfield, whose sympathetic mind so often mirrored the changing views of the community in which he lived, was able to look at the problems of the reconstruction period with the detachment of historical perspective. The war, he

[1] See article, W. T. Clark, *Dictionary of American Biography*.

said, had disturbed the established order of society, awakened a reckless spirit of speculation, and greatly multiplied the temptations of evil. These evils had been increased by the disfranchisement of the Southern whites, which threw the Southern States for a time into the hands "of political adventurers, many of whom used their brief hold on power for personal ends, and thus brought disgrace upon the national legislature." The enlarged sphere of national legislation "so mingled public duties and private interests that it was not easy to draw the line between them." All of which was almost exactly what Andrew Johnson had foreseen ten years before! [1]

Extremes meet. In 1879, the enterprising editor of the *North American Review* conducted a symposium on the results of negro suffrage: "Ought the negro to be disfranchised? Ought he to have been enfranchised?" These questions were considered by eight leading Americans, J. G. Blaine, L. Q. C. Lamar, Wade Hampton, Alexander H. Stephens, Montgomery Blair, Thomas A. Hendricks, Wendell Phillips, and James A. Garfield. Some of the answers were vague and non-committal; Montgomery Blair, who had been a member of Lincoln's Cabinet, was the only one of the eight to declare flatly that the results had been pernicious and that the negro was incapable of forming independent political judgments; the answers of the two Republicans, Blaine and Garfield, were curiously alike and almost apologetic in tone. Garfield said, "Possibly a plan of granting the suffrage gradually as the negro became more intelligent would have been wiser; but the practical difficulties of such a plan would have been very great." Of the northern men, only Wendell Phillips, who lived far enough away from the problem he was discussing, now occupied in unchanged conviction what had once been the very axiom of the radical position: "The South owes to negro labor and to legislation

[1] J. A. Garfield, "A Century of Congress," *Atlantic Monthly*, July, 1877.

under negro rule all the prosperity she now enjoys. . . . The negro is the nation's ally in an enemy country." To Phillips the great mistakes of the reconstruction period had been the failure to disfranchise the whites for a longer period and the spirit of weak hesitation that had prevented the confiscation of the plantations. But the most optimistic prophecies of the political future of the negro race, prophecies that have been only partially fulfilled, came from two representatives of what may be called the new South, Wade Hampton of South Carolina and especially L. Q. C. Lamar of Georgia. Lamar said: "I am of the opinion that to make the negro a free citizen it was necessary first to take him from his master. Then it became necessary to take him from the party which claimed his vote as absolutely as his master had claimed his labor. The next step will be to take him as a class from either party and allow him to differ and divide just as white men do." But the very fact that this question could be discussed with cool detachment in the pages of the *Atlantic Monthly* and the *North American Review* was in itself an indication of the rise of new and more pressing problems.[1]

[1] *North American Review* (1879) : Vol. 128, pp. 225 ff.

GARFIELD's family was growing. The death of his daughter in 1863 and the birth of his first son were followed by the coming of other children: a son, James Rudolph, in 1865, who was later to become Secretary of the Interior under Roosevelt; two years later a daughter, Mary; then in 1870 another son who was named for Garfield's friend of 1862, Irvin McDowell; Abram Garfield, who was to become an architect; and one other son who died in infancy. The Garfields continued to make their home in Hiram, where Garfield took an active interest in the old college of which he was now a trustee and of which his closest friend, B. A. Hinsdale, was President. Once a year the family made the long trip to Washington, where, in 1869, for a sum of ten thousand dollars, they acquired a second home. In 1876, when the boundaries of the district were changed in such a way as to leave out his old county of Portage, Garfield bought a farm on the outskirts of Cleveland, where, at Mentor, he remodelled the house in which he lived in the closing days of his life.

Like other public men, especially in the seventies, Garfield found that his private life was everybody's business. Thus when he built his house in Washington, he was compelled to explain that it was not a mansion. But other charges could only be met with silence. Once, in 1864, a disappointed constituent circulated a story of the profligacy of Garfield's life in Washington and described him as a drunkard; and even as late as 1879 Mrs. Garfield came across gossip to the effect that she was soon to seek a divorce; but all such stories are clearly disproved by the letters of Garfield to his wife as well as by the reminiscences of the men of his time, all of whom give the impression of a warm-hearted, friendly personality, intensely attached to the members of his family.[1]

William Dean Howells, whose father was an editorial supporter of Garfield, was among the many young men who retained a vivid impression of the private life of the Garfields. One picture is characteristic: "As we were sitting with the Garfield family on the veranda that overlooked their lawn, I was beginning to speak of the famous poets I knew," for young Howells was fresh from Boston and full of his experiences. Garfield interrupted him with, "Just a minute!" He ran down the grassy space first to one fence and then to the other, and waved an arm of invitation to the neighbors who were also sitting on their back porches. "Come over here," he shouted, "he's telling about Holmes, and Longfellow, and Lowell, and Whittier." At Garfield's bidding dim forms began to climb the fences and to appear on the hospitable veranda. When all were seated, Howells went on "while the whippoorwills whirred and whistled and the hours drew towards midnight." In the rapt attention of Garfield and his neighbors Howells read a tribute to the great renowns that he was chanting so eagerly.[2]

Living in a little college town, the friend of Hinsdale, who was a remarkable educator, and to the end of his days the admiring pupil of Mark Hopkins, a man of Garfield's training and keen intellectual curiosity found it impossible not to retain his old interest in the educational changes of his time. At Hiram, to which he contributed time, money, and eager sympathy, he used his influence in securing a wider curriculum, including modern languages, history, government, and science; but he had small sympathy for the desire to place purely practical courses in the colleges. Thus, in 1873, in connection with

---

[1] This subject has been examined with care by T. C. Smith, *Life and Letters of Garfield*, Vol. II, pp. 931–936. The entries in Garfield's *Journal*, especially during Mrs. Garfield's illness in May, 1881, sustain this conclusion.

[2] W. D. Howells, *Years of My Youth*, p. 205.

the movement to found agricultural colleges, he wrote: "I do not believe in a college to educate men for the profession of farming. A liberal education almost always draws men away from the profession of farming. But schools of science and general technology are valuable." The later development of so-called agricultural colleges has proved the wisdom of the distinction that Garfield was making.

When Garfield was president of the alumni of Williams, he made a speech in reply to the position of those who were urging the great importance of new buildings and equipment: "No words of mine," he said, "shall in any way detract from the importance of everything that has been urged; but I am not willing that this discussion should close without mention of the value of a true teacher. Give me a log hut, with only a simple bench, Mark Hopkins on one end and I on the other, and you may have all the buildings, apparatus and libraries without him." [1]

In spite of criticism of his conservative position, Garfield saw one of the chief dangers in American education and returned more than once to the same theme, as when he wrote: "So long as Williams College can offer salaries which will command and retain the very best teaching talent in the country, she will offer a far greater attraction to thoughtful and ambitious students than any splendor of her architecture or richness of her cabinets and libraries." At the commencement of 1872, President Hopkins was succeeded by P. A. Chadbourne, who was expected to inaugurate a businesslike administration. Garfield addressed the new President in the presence of the old: "We will not ask you," he said, "to bend the bow of Ulysses. Let it here remain unbent forever as the sacred symbol and trophy of victories achieved. But we do expect you to confront the future with its new and difficult problems in a

[1] B. A. Hinsdale, *President Garfield and Education,* p. 43.

spirit conservative to save all the garnered wisdom which experience has purchased, and courageous to adopt and lead all true reforms." This speech may account for a certain coolness which one can detect in the endorsement of Garfield that Chadbourne furnished to the campaign biographies of 1880.

In Congress, Garfield soon became convinced that legislation was based largely on prejudice and proceeded by trial and error chiefly because the government did not take the trouble to gather the essential facts. Accordingly, in 1866, at the suggestion of the National Association of School Superintendents, Garfield introduced a bill to create a department or bureau of education in the national government. In spite of active opposition, largely from those who feared interference with the systems of the various States, the bill passed with a small appropriation for the maintenance of the department. When the reports of the first commissioner, the celebrated Henry Barnard, proved to be not only voluminous and difficult to understand but revealed appalling conditions in many States which had lived in the fond belief that their educational systems were really adequate, the result was a storm of ridicule and criticism; and the Bureau and the commissioner were continued only through the influence of Congressman Garfield. Surely, few agencies of the government have done more good at so small a cost! Again, in 1869, Garfield was made chairman of a special committee on the census. Garfield soon became convinced that the old system of taking the census through the United States' marshals was intended merely to add to the number of political plums and was wasteful and inefficient. He urged that the census should be broadened into a great fact-gathering agency, providing the social, commercial, and economic information on which legislation might be based, and for that purpose he wanted to create a special group of trained individuals to collect the desired information. The elaborate bill that he prepared failed in the Senate, and the census of 1870 was taken in the same old way. But ten years later many of Garfield's suggestions were accepted; and he deserves to be known as the father of the modern census. Similarly, Garfield gave constant support to the scientific activities of the national government, especially to the Smithsonian Institution at Washington and to the work of the Coast and Geodetic Survey. In all these respects, the nationalism and the scientific curiosity of Garfield made it possible for him to render efficient service to the development of knowledge.

Garfield's introduction to the law in the case of *ex parte Milligan* had not been fruitless. The friendship with Judge Black continued and almost every year Garfield was counsel in one or two important cases.[1] The most interesting of the early cases was one that involved the validity of the will of no less a person than Garfield's old friend, Alexander Campbell. The case came to trial in 1868 in the little town of Wellsburg, West Virginia. The founder of the Disciples of Christ had died the year before leaving to his children by his second wife a surprisingly large estate estimated at more than a quarter of a million dollars. In his closing years Campbell had been subject to hallucinations, one of which was that he had actually made a journey to Palestine. This and other harmless vagaries of the same general kind made it possible for the children by the first wife to contest the will challenging the competency of the testator. The problem at issue was the definition of the common law term competency; but apart from its legal interest, Black's choice of Garfield as leading counsel in the case was characteristically shrewd; Garfield could plead with special effectiveness when he seemed to be defending the mental soundness of his own old master.

[1] Black *Papers,* Library of Congress, 1865–1876. For early contacts see Garfield to Black, March 11, 1865; April 19, 1865; July 11, 1865.

Garfield wrote to Hinsdale with evident pleasure: "The trial occupied ten days, and Judge Black left me at the end of the second day. Young Richardson, of Wheeling, was my only assistant, and he was sick part of the time. There were sixty-eight witnesses, and the lawyers on the other side spoke over eight hours. I had the closing speech, and reviewed the testimony and opposing speeches. I spoke six hours and a half. The will and codicil were sustained. I suppose it may not be immodest for me to say to you that I think I have never done a more creditable piece of intellectual work than on that trial." [1] The fee of thirty-five hundred dollars seemed to Garfield generous; and from that time he continued to earn a substantial and steady income from his growing practice.

At first, Garfield was usually associated with Jeremiah Black; but, with a growing reputation, cases began to come in which he was retained independently; and, in 1874, his colleague in a very important insurance litigation was no less a man than Judge Benjamin R. Curtis of Boston, who had been a member of the Supreme Court. Garfield felt that he had acquitted himself reasonably well. He spoke for an hour and was followed for a like period by the distinguished judge, whose calm, judicial tone won the hearty admiration of his colleague. The court was equally divided on the question at issue, and when the case was heard again two years later, Curtis was dead, and Garfield was joined by the almost equally celebrated Senator Matt H. Carpenter of Wisconsin, whose great reputation at the bar was won at the expense of an equal standing as a working member of the Senate. In Garfield's last significant case, involving the ownership of a railroad and coming to trial in 1877 in Mobile, one of Garfield's colleagues was John A. Campbell of Alabama, the one member of the Supreme Court who at the time of secession had resigned to follow the fortunes

[1] J. A. Bundy, *Life of Garfield*, p. 184.

of the Confederacy. The law, unlike politics, in Garfield's case, made strange bed fellows.

Of all Garfield's legal arguments, that in the Milligan case and those in which he appeared as the attorney of the New York Life Insurance Company were the only ones that were deemed by his friend and editor, B. A. Hinsdale, as worthy of inclusion among his published works; and the selection was probably just. In the earlier case Garfield was dealing with the constitutional and moral problem that was at the basis of reconstruction, while in the second the stakes involved were enormous and an adverse decision might easily have led to the destruction of one or more of the important insurance companies. At the outbreak of the war, these companies had a large number of clients in the seceded States. As a result, cases arose which differed greatly in detail: some of the insured persons were Union sympathisers; others, and a majority, of course, were friendly to the Confederacy or even soldiers in the Confederate army. Sometimes the premiums which had been paid regularly until 1861 were tendered after the outbreak of war to the local agents, who refused to receive them because non-intercourse laws made it impossible to transmit them to New York; again, the premiums were allowed to lapse. Now, either directly or through their heirs, for many had, of course, died, these insured persons claimed the right to tender the overdue premiums and to continue the policies. What had been the effect of the war on these policies? Garfield was retained to argue the position that they were void.

The leading case was that of Dr. Samuel Bond of Memphis, who had been insured in 1854 and had paid his premiums regularly until 1861, when the premium had been tendered and refused by the local agent of the company. Dr. Bond was a non-combatant, had taken no part in the rebellion, and had died in 1862. His heirs now sought to collect the amount of the policy. In this case, which presented the important issues in their most extreme form, Garfield argued that all persons who continued to reside in the limits of the Confederacy were from the legal point of view public enemies; and that it was to the highest degree contrary to public policy for a company in the loyal States to continue to insure and be interested in the lives of public enemies. If such contracts had been kept alive, they would have added to the resources of the enemy. The Civil War was not an insurrection but a great public war "as though it had been waged between England and the United States." If the insurance companies were required to keep alive their contracts, the result would be to strike a staggering blow to those that had had a large Southern membership before the war. The court, in 1876, sustained this contention and held that the heirs could only recover the equitable value of the premiums already paid. The policy, as such, was void.

Garfield was equally successful in a large majority of the cases in which he was engaged; but he soon found that the law is a jealous mistress. He worked feverishly on a given case and never appeared without what seemed to be adequate preparation. But the case might take a new turn, the court might ask a technical question, and the lawyer would find himself without reserves of knowledge on which to draw; and, at such times, Garfield was always his own most severe critic. When in 1871 he became Chairman of the Committee of Appropriations, the most laborious of all the committees of the House, responsible for an immense mass of financial details that he must study and digest, the time for legal problems was increasingly slender, and Garfield began to realize that he must make a choice. He could not be both a great parliamentary leader and a great lawyer; although he continued to believe that the law was the career for which he was best fitted, he was soon completely absorbed in the activities of legislation and politics; and after

1877 his practice was virtually abandoned. In spite of his successes, the law, like teaching, evangelism, and the army, was to remain in Garfield's life merely a brilliant episode and not the central theme.[1]

The period of the war had seen an extraordinary number of financial measures, many of them expected to be temporary in character and raising problems of readjustment which next to the central question of reconstruction were the chief themes of legislative history during the years when James A. Garfield was a congressman. A huge national debt had been accumulated; the dangerous expedient of an inconvertible paper currency had been adopted; a system of national banks had been substituted for the previous uncontrolled state banks; an enormous system of heavy internal taxes had been made necessary by rapidly mounting costs; and, above all, duties on imports that exceeded the fondest hopes of the most extreme protectionist had unexpectedly arisen from the confusion of hasty legislation.

Garfield saw at once that problems of this kind would soon furnish more real opportunities for statesmanship than any that could arise after the war in the military committee, and accordingly in 1865 he was transferred at his own request to the Committee on Ways and Means that had as its chief task the question of the tariff, a subject in which he had become deeply interested through the influence of David A. Wells, the very

---

[1] The chief cases in which Garfield was counsel were, *ex parte Milligan*, 4 Wallace, 2; *In re Bennet vs. Hunter*, 9 Wallace 326; *Brooke and Barrington vs. Phillips Bros.*, 68 Penn. State 130; *U. S. vs. 100 Barrels distilled spirits*, 14 Wallace 44; *Putnam vs. Day*, 22 Wallace 60; *Hoffman vs. John Hancock Life Insurance Company*, 92 U. S. 161; *N. Y. Life Insurance Company vs. Statham*, 93 U. S. 24; *Newton vs. Mahoning County*, 100 U. S. 548; and *Duncan vs. Mobile and Ohio R. R. Co.*, 8 Fed. Cases 19. For Garfield's career as a lawyer see J. A. Bundy, *Life of Garfield*, pp. 170–187; T. C. Smith, *Life and Letters of Garfield*, Vol. II, pp. 821–844; and the arguments of Garfield in his *Works*, Vol. I, pp. 140–183; Vol. II, pp. 140–175.

able commissioner of the revenue and the chief authority on the fiscal and commercial policy of the United States. When Garfield joined the committee, there was very little free trade sentiment as such—even Wells was still an advocate of reform and reduction and had not yet become an avowed free trader; but it was generally assumed that when other war taxes were reduced or abolished the import duties would also be diminished; and with this position, Garfield, who came from the West and from a district in which agricultural interests were still predominant, was of course heartily in sympathy. For ten years after the war the majority of the members of both houses of Congress, sometimes a very large majority, was ostensibly committed to the policy of tariff reduction; but the internal taxes which had furnished if not the reason at least the excuse for the high duties were repealed one after the other, the income tax was abandoned, prices dropped until a moderate tariff of twenty-eight dollars a ton on steel rails worth a hundred dollars or more had become prohibitive when rails in England were manufactured for thirty dollars; and yet each year saw almost no decrease anywhere and definite increases here and there, especially in copper, wool, woolens, and refined sugar, until by the close of Garfield's life a temporary system had come to be generally recognised, at least by the members of the dominant party and also by many of their political opponents, as the permanent basis of the most prohibitive system that the world had known since the final abandonment of the mercantile philosophy. Such a result is an extraordinary illustration of the patient sagacity of the leaders of the protective movement, of whom the most notable was Mr. John L. Hayes, the Secretary of the Wool Manufacturers and for many years the efficient leader in one of the most powerful lobbies in Washington, who were able by playing one local interest against another to win an astonishing victory for a coherent and well-organised minority against a doubtful and divided majority. In this current, almost unconsciously, Congressman Garfield was caught; and, like many others both in and out of Congress, was carried from a position close to free trade in 1866 to almost complete partisan orthodoxy at the time of his campaign in 1880. The change in Garfield and in many others was of course only the natural result of the industrial revolution, so greatly hastened by the tariff itself, which turned the agricultural America of the period before the war into the industrial America that already in the eighties was beginning to loom above the economic horizon.

Like other public men, Garfield at the end of his career liked to think that his position on the tariff had not changed. But consider the story. The question arose first in 1866 when so many other taxes of the war period were being reduced; Garfield, as usual, prepared himself for the rising problem by an extensive course of reading in the history and philosophy of tariff systems, and as a result he wrote to Austin: "I am in favor of protection as a temporary measure and to secure us against foreign control, but I look forward to the constant tendency toward Free Trade which one article after another will reach as its manufacture becomes fully established." From the point of view of Kelley, Greeley, Dawes, and even Blaine, scarcely the whole-hearted position of a defender of protective systems! And in the same year he made an elaborate speech in which among other things he said: "I am for that free trade that can be achieved only through protection." How often was this sentence to be quoted against him by the iron men of the Mahoning Valley!—the men of whom Garfield was to write in 1870, that they wanted a representative "that they can own and carry around in their pantaloons pocket."

The crisis in the modern tariff history of the United States came in 1867, and Garfield spoke and voted in entire consistency with the position that he had already announced. David A. Wells had made a careful study of the whole tariff system that had resulted from the war, and had prepared a plan that lowered the duties on raw materials, either reduced those on manufactured articles or left them unchanged, and dealt drastically with the special favors and strange classifications which gave advantages to the individual with slight benefits to industry. A bill, moderately protectionist in tone, had been prepared by Wells and had passed the Senate by a vote of 27 to 10, but though it had the support of a large revisionist majority in the House, the friends of the existing system were able to invoke a technical rule that required a two-thirds majority for its consideration. Garfield supported the reduction of the tariff with great earnestness, and appealed to his party associates to vote so as to make up the two-thirds majority necessary for consideration, telling them that later they might "make their record" by voting against the bill. But in spite of Garfield's pleas, the friends of high duties were watchful and the vote of 106 for the bill to 64 against fell short of Garfield's hopes. In the judgment of the chief authority on the history of the tariff: "had the bill of 1867 been passed, the character of recent tariff legislation might have been very different. A beginning would have been made in looking at the tariff from a sober point of view, and in reducing duties that were clearly pernicious. The growing habit of looking on the war rates as a permanent system might have been checked, and the attempts at tariff reform in subsequent years would have found stronger support and met with less successful opposition." [1] After that time, so favorable an opportunity for reform was to wait many years.

Garfield's position on the tariff was undoubtedly a factor in

---

[1] F. W. Taussig, *Tariff History of the United States,* fifth edition, p. 177. For Garfield's connection with this bill see *Cong. Globe,* 1866–7, pp. 1657–1658.

the refusal of Speakers Colfax and Blaine to appoint him to the chairmanship of the Committee on Ways and Means, the one position in Congress that he really desired. In 1867 he was passed over for Dawes of Massachusetts, whose views were of course entirely satisfactory to the powerful woolen interests; and though Garfield held in succession important positions as chairman of the Committee on Military Affairs, then of that on Banking and Currency, and finally for four years of the almost equally important committee on Appropriations, as long as the Republicans held their majority in the House, he failed to regain the position that he had held for two years in his second Congress.

In the meantime, without general revision that might have aroused dangerous questions, the trend, schedule by schedule, was definitely upwards. Thus, in 1869, as a result of the opening of the copper mines in the Lake Superior region, a heavy duty was placed on copper, which had previously been low, and the curious result of the unexampled natural resources in the copper of the United States was to make the price to the American consumer distinctly higher than that paid in countries which had no mines and received their imports from America. In 1870, especially, Garfield was to find that the ways of the tariff reformer are hard: other congressmen were entirely willing to let him vote for a bill that reduced the duty on pig iron, the only important product of his district, from nine dollars to seven dollars a ton, but turned a deaf ear to his pleas for corresponding reductions in steel rails and other articles in which his constituents were interested as consumers. The results of Garfield's vote were a storm of criticism in Mahoning County; his enemies even talked of running for Congress so redoubtable an opponent as old Ben Wade, whose views on the tariff were sure to be more orthodox, but were prevented by the refusal of Wade himself to become a candidate against his neighbor; and Garfield's embarrassment with the "iron men" was soon relieved by a change that before the next election placed the Mahoning Valley in another district. In his campaign for reëlection Garfield argued that the tariff was not a test of party orthodoxy; that there were high tariff men in each party; and announced, rather sadly, the conclusion to which recent events in his own district had led him: "It is also manifest that the question has assumed a local rather than a national aspect." The truth of this remark is entirely apparent to any student of American tariffs; but when Hancock said almost exactly the same thing ten years later he was to meet a storm of ridicule.

In 1872, five years after the failure of Wells' plan of reform and two years after Garfield's courageous stand on the locally momentous question of pig iron, the eternal problem again arose. In spite of the abolition of almost all other forms of national taxation and the constant reduction of the public debt, the import duties were so high that there was a dangerous surplus in the Treasury. William McKinley's interesting plan of raising duties to so high a point that the revenues would be actually reduced had not yet been discovered, and it was entirely apparent that the next war taxes to be reduced would have to be those on imports. Both houses of Congress had large Republican majorities; but it was a year of agrarian depression and discontent and the members from the agricultural districts in the West were ready to join the Democrats in another effort for revision. Any detailed examination of the schedules of the existing tariff, such as was desired by Garfield and other reformers, might obviously open wide breaches in the citadel of high protection. Accordingly, against the short-sighted opposition of extreme protectionists like "Pig Iron" Kelley of Pennsylvania, but under the leadership of Mr. John L. Hayes, who was not a member of Congress, but who probably had more actual power than any single member, and with the able assistance of the chairman of the Committee on Ways and Means, Henry L. Dawes of Massachusetts, a plan was matured and carried through both houses of Congress that surpassed in strategic shrewdness almost any other single scheme of a decade that was by no means barren in such devices. It seems not too much to say that the plan of 1872, in spite of the farmers and the convinced reformers, saved the policy of high protection until a new generation could be convinced of its wisdom. Briefly, the plan called for the abolition of the duties on tea and coffee, purely revenue measures, which brought in a large income without any industrial effects one way or the other; the relative position of protective duties were left unchanged by the adoption of a flat horizontal reduction of ten percent all along the line without any regard to the duties that were exorbitant and those that were already moderate enough. The advantages of horizontal reduction from the point of view of those members of Congress who desired to save the system of war duties as the basis for the future were soon apparent. For the depression of 1873, together with the abolition of the convenient duties on tea and coffee, soon diminished the revenues to such a point that an increase was as clearly necessary in 1875 as a reduction had been in 1872. Accordingly in the latter year Mr. Dawes had merely to move for the repeal of his own horizontal reduction of three years before, and the duties on iron, steel, copper, marble, wool, and above all woolens were back exactly where they had been, with added security in the fact that the revenue duties on tea and coffee had been destroyed.[1]

Garfield was of course not blind to the implications of the seemingly innocent steps that were being taken. He was bit-

1 J. L. Hayes in *Bulletin of the Wool Manufacturers,* Vol. III, pp. 283–290, and Taussig, *Tariff History,* pp. 180–192. Dawes was among the opponents of the tea and coffee reduction, but was the author of the ten-percent idea.

terly opposed to the abolition of the duties on tea and coffee: "It makes me almost sick," he wrote, "to see the folly of those who claim to be reformers. They throw away twenty millions of revenue at a blow without touching an outrage in the system." Garfield's point of view was still that of the farmers and consumers of his district, who felt that revenue duties like those on tea and coffee caused them to pay a tax on the articles imported, while the protective duties like those on steel rails established taxes not only in favor of the government for foreign rails imported, but also in favor of domestic producers who were enabled to sell at a higher price behind a tariff wall. But party lines were now beginning to crystallize on the tariff question and the point of view of many districts, including his own, was beginning to change with growing investments in manufacturing. Accordingly, Garfield accepted the ten-percent horizontal cut, though without enthusiasm, writing: "The new tariff is a short step in the right direction. It must be followed by more hereafter when public sentiment works up to it."

Garfield's hopes for further tariff revision in 1872 were probably sincere, but that year, nevertheless, marked a turning point in his attitude, which seems to appear clearly in both the record of his votes on tariff changes and in the speeches which he made on the subject. This transition may have been due to the fact that his relations with Wells from whom he had gained much of his enthusiasm for reform were no longer so close; for Wells felt that he had been badly treated by the Grant Administration and had gone over to the opposition where he was now a thoroughgoing advocate of free trade. Then, too, the Republicans as a party had come to be recognised as the friends and defenders of a tariff which few leaders now remembered as a once temporary and almost accidental series of war measures, while most of the reformers like Wells were now Democrats, a situation that had by no means existed at the beginning. Garfield was always a good party man, as he showed when he supported Lincoln in 1864 and Grant eight years later, and, especially after he became the recognised leader of the Republican minority in the House, his views and votes on tariff questions became increasingly orthodox. Thus he no longer spoke of protection as a temporary step to ultimate free trade, but though he still fell short of the prohibitive ideals of Kelley and the Pennsylvania school, he began to emphasise the necessity for a tariff that would equalise the cost of production at home and abroad, and he seems to have begun to recognise in the protective system a permanent part of the economic structure of the country. More than once he voted for sharp increases in a tariff that had once seemed quite too high. Thus he supported the existing rates on steel rails and secured an increase in the duty on refined sugar greatly desired by the refiners of Philadelphia; and the repeal of the ten-percent reduction of 1872 was passed in 1875 by a very narrow majority which included James A. Garfield.

The corner had been turned; for by yielding a little, or at least seeming to yield, the tariff system as a whole had been saved and even strengthened. Only once again was there a real danger of serious reduction, and that came in 1878 when the Democrats were in control of the House and when Garfield was at last a member of the Committee on Ways and Means, of which Fernando Wood of New York was the chairman. Republican floor leader as he was, Garfield coöperated with Wood in the preparation of a bill that without going to the limits of free trade reduced greatly the duties on various classes of manufactured articles. If it had not been for the compelling consideration of his party position, there are indications that Garfield was half tempted to support a bill that in many of its provisions met with his approval. "I am distressed," he wrote, "by the curious state of conflict in my own mind upon the

various phases of it. To be an extreme man is doubtless comfortable. It is painful to see too many sides of a subject." But
when the bill came before the House, on June 4th, 1878, he
made a speech in which he opposed its reductions as dangerous,
and took ground that was entirely satisfactory to the defenders
of the existing tariff. He argued that low duties would tend
to limit the country entirely to agricultural pursuits and make
it dependent on foreign nations for all its chief manufactured
articles, and he no longer seemed to anticipate a time when the
manufacturers of America might be able to compete on equal
terms with those of other countries. "Let it be remembered," he
said, "that twenty-two percent of all the laboring people of
this country are artisans engaged in manufactures. Their culture has been fostered by our tariff laws. . . . To them the
country owes the splendor of the position it holds before the
world more than to any other equal number of our citizens."
On Garfield's motion to strike out the enacting clause and thus,
of course, to kill the bill, the Republicans were joined by
enough Democrats to defeat the chief measure of a Democratic
House. The Wood bill, the last serious effort during Garfield's
lifetime to repeal the provisions of the war tariffs of 1862 and
1864, was defeated by a vote of 134 to 121.

During the presidential campaign of 1880, *The Iron and
Steel Bulletin,* one of the leading protectionist journals in the
United States, made a careful examination of Garfield's record
on the tariff and gave to him what it considered the highest
praise: "It is both just and proper that we should state that the
protectionists of the country, who have kept watch over tariff
legislation during the past twenty years, and who have assisted
to shape and maintain the present tariff, are perfectly satisfied
with his tariff votes and speeches. They and all other protectionists have indeed abundant reason to be thankful to him for
valuable assistance rendered to the cause of industry when it

was in serious peril from free trade attacks." And this summary, in spite of his early views on tariff reform, did the
candidate no more than justice.[1]

[1] In 1879 Garfield wrote open letters to prove that his tariff position had become
orthodox: Garfield to Wayland, Oct. 27, 1879; Garfield to Beer, Dec. 15, 1879.
Garfield Papers. Similarly in 1880, he objected to Allison as a cabinet member
because Allison was not sufficiently friendly to the tariff. (*Journal,* Dec. 13, 1880.)

OF all subjects of legislation in the seventies, the one on which the average Congressman most dearly loved, as Garfield once remarked, "to make a weathercock of himself," was that of the currency. Three times within a decade, the same House passed measures of inflation or the reverse by huge majorities and then turned right around and by an almost equally large vote within a few months and on the same set of facts assumed exactly the opposite position. The most striking illustration of this congressional peculiarity, as we shall see, was the fact that the final resolution of January 18th, 1875, which paved the way for the resumption of specie payments was adopted by exactly the same persons who within eight months had voted with equal zeal a bill for the further issue of paper money. And the vagaries of the majority were of course greatly multiplied in the case of individuals.[1] There were not more than a dozen members of the House whose position on this question had any appearance of consistency; and it is greatly to Garfield's credit that he was one of them.

It was well enough for a Senator, elected by a legislature and for a long period of six years, to be consistent; but no wonder that the House was as nervous as a cat. The average Congressman reached Washington, usually within a few short months of a contest for reëlection, and was confronted at once with one of the most complex questions of economics, about which he knew practically nothing and his constituents back home even less, but a subject that was full of dynamite, and could be made to appear the basis of the welfare of every person in his district,

[1] Garfield *Journal,* Feb. 22, 1879; Garfield to Hinsdale, Dec. 15, 1876, J. A. Bundy, *op. cit.,* p. 100.

about which the conflict of passions soon darkened understanding. As a representative of the people, he might keep his ear tightly glued to the ground, as it was doubtless his duty to do, but the result was often a confused and inarticulate murmur, from newspapers and in letters, that only added to bewilderment. And more than once when he had voted he was to find that he had guessed wrongly what had seemed so clear a trend of sentiment on greenbacks, on five-twenty bonds, and on the free and unlimited coinage of silver at the ratio of sixteen to one. As to Reconstruction, the solution was comparatively easy, for here was a great question on which the welfare of the party seemed to be at stake and in which the chief beneficiaries of enlightened legislation virtually lived in a foreign country; the tariff also was simple, and the point of view of a Congressman followed a regular curve. For he was left in no doubt whatsoever as to the wishes of the iron men, or the wool men, or the sugar men of his district, as the case might be, and as to the consumers they were usually unfurnished with a lobby and most of them, of course, lived in somebody else's district. But on the greenbacks he had to make up his mind for himself either without any help at all, or often with quite too much. The historical curve of his opinions was thus necessarily broken.

As to leadership, consider Garfield's congressional career in connection with each of the three great historical questions of his times, Reconstruction, the tariff, the financial system of the nation, and turn it in any light; and on the first two great problems we find a man who is chiefly important as a symbol, by whose views we can measure the intensity of the struggles that went on; but the most partial biographer would be hard put to it to maintain that we have here one of the positive directing forces that really determined the outcome. For on each of these questions, Garfield was compelled to yield either a part of his convictions or else his position as a partisan leader. So he him-

self did not either win or lose, and with all his intellectual keen-
ness, with occasional flashes of the inspiration of the statesman
in his speeches, these were contests in which he often seems to
be a spectator rather than a participant.

As to Reconstruction, compare Garfield with Thaddeus
Stevens or Charles Sumner or Benjamin F. Butler on the one
hand or Allen G. Thurman or Reverdy Johnson or Andrew
Johnson on the other and the difference is at once apparent.
Similarly the story of the tariff must finally be told in the careers of such men as Stevens of Pennsylvania, Dawes of Massachusetts, McKinley of Ohio, merely to consider a few of the
leaders on one side, and not in that of James A. Garfield. But
the course of financial legislation of immense moment in the
history of his times is essentially different. Here was a question
to which Garfield gave the most early and careful attention and
regarding which he developed deep convictions to which he was
able to convert many who were originally doubtful and half-
hearted. Fifteen years after Garfield's death, the presidential
election of 1896 was won by the use of the very arguments that
before many an audience Garfield had already made familiar;
and the passage of the gold act of 1900 was the end of a long
struggle, in the early stages of which James A. Garfield had
done more than any other single individual to select the
weapons and to point the path to final victory. It is not too
much to say that on the other two questions, Garfield came to
agree or at least to vote with the Republican party; on financial
legislation, however, substantially during his lifetime, and de-
cisively after, the Republican party and the nation at length
came to accept a position which had been stated with perfect
clearness by James A. Garfield from the beginning. Here or
nowhere was his statesmanship.

Like everything else, it all began in 1865; and, though the
superficial problems changed, the essential issue was to remain

the same through the contests of the next thirty-five years. At the close of the war the public debt of the United States had reached a figure of two and a half billion dollars, more than the total expenses of the government from the beginning until the Civil War. The most important item in this debt was in the form of the so-called five-twenty bonds, reaching a total of $1,500,000,000, bearing interest at six percent payable in gold and with the principal redeemable at various times from five to twenty years. According to the letter of the contract, the principal was to be paid in "lawful money." In ordinary times this expression would have been entirely free from ambiguity; but, like other modern wars, that between the North and the South had led to the issue of unsecured paper money to the amount of $400,000,000, the so-called greenbacks, which had been made a legal tender for the payment of private debts. This paper, which was of course the fundamental currency of the nation, had become so seriously depreciated that at one time in 1864 it had been quoted below forty cents on the dollar and even after the close of the war was worth less than seventy cents in terms of gold. From the point of view of profits and of business, the war years in the North had been full of feverish activity and great apparent prosperity, and there were those who believed that this prosperity was due not to the unusual demands of a nation that was in the market for every conceivable commodity from wool to rifles, but to the cheapness and evident abundance of paper money.

The arguments for inflation took many different forms, but in the final analysis they appealed to two different convictions. In the first place, the issue of more paper money would raise the prices of many articles, especially agricultural commodities, increase profits and promote prosperity; conversely, the payment and cancellation of the paper would reduce prices, cause wages to shrink, and bring unemployment and hard times. In the second place, the return to a gold basis, or, to be more exact, to a hard money basis, for the issue between gold and silver had not yet arisen, would add unjustly to the difficulties of paying debts and would fall with crushing weight on every debtor. And at this point, there was a supreme example ready at hand, for towering above all the little debtors, the most important debtor of all was the government of the United States. When the debts had been created, and especially when the five-twenty bonds had been issued, the government had received "lawful money," which had often been worth only forty, fifty, or sixty cents on the dollar. The government had paid the interest faithfully in gold, as it had promised. Why should it now go beyond the letter of its agreement to return in gold what it had received in paper? The same argument applied to every debtor in the country, from the great railroad corporation to the farmer with a mortgage on his fields, whose load would be lightened by the further issue of paper money as much as it would be increased by the cancellation of existing issues. Consider the well known fact that the great majority of the bonds had naturally fallen into the hands of eastern capitalists, that great quantities were held in European countries, and that Garfield came from an agricultural community greatly interested in the price of wheat, and it is at once apparent that he had set himself a difficult task in combating these and similar financial heresies.

The problem that confronted the United States in 1865, was of course exactly the same that came to many countries after a greater struggle in 1918. Should the currency be established at the same old level as it was in England, or at a lower level as in France? Should the war debts, especially to America, be paid at a discount or in full? During the sixties and the seventies, after a long and bitter struggle, America was able to pay the debts in gold in full and to reëstablish the currency on the basis of the gold dollar, partly on account of the unexampled riches

of its untouched natural resources and partly because a portion
of the war debt was really repudiated, namely, the whole of the
obligations of the late Confederate States of America. But
although it could be done, as perhaps it cannot be done in
Europe today, it was by no means certain that it would be done;
and James A. Garfield is chiefly important as a historical figure
because of the leading part that he bore in the House of Representatives and before the public in promoting the reëstablish-
ment of the currency on the only basis that he regarded as sound
and free from dangers. It is more than doubtful whether Garfield and those who agreed with him could have won the victory they did if the debts had been between governments as in
1918 and not between a government and private individuals as
in 1865. But the importance of his position is not diminished
by the fact that to this very day the ethical and the economic
implications of many of his arguments are still the subject of
serious debate.

In the first flush of victory and with the country riding high
on what seemed a tide of rising prosperity, it was at first generally assumed that the debts would be paid in gold and that the
greenbacks would be retired. Thus on the 18th of December,
1865, the House by an overwhelming vote of 144 to 6 passed a
resolution favoring the contraction of the currency with a view
to an early resumption of specie payments. But the feverish
industrial activity of the war period was already beginning to
decline, and when a bill was introduced from the Committee on
Ways and Means, of which Garfield was a member, authorizing
Hugh McCulloch, the Secretary of the Treasury, to exchange
bonds for the greenbacks and to retire them at his discretion,
the opposition under the leadership of Thaddeus Stevens was
already strong.

On March 16th, 1866, Garfield made his first speech on
the question, coming to the defence of the endangered measure

and taking ground from which he never receded. He showed familiarity with the experience of England in returning to specie payments after the Napoleonic wars and, without blinking the necessary sacrifices that were involved, advocated a similar policy for the United States: "The gentleman from Pennsylvania," Garfield told the House, "tells us he is in favor of returning to specie payments when it can be done without disturbing or deranging the business of the country. If he waits for that it can never be done. It cannot be done without first contracting the currency and producing a temporary stringency in the money market. If we have not the nerve to do that, if we have not the patriotism to suffer that temporary inconvenience, we must go on in the swift road to financial disaster and ultimate national bankruptcy." Again on March 19th, Garfield challenged the position of another powerful member of his own party, W. D. Kelley, also from Pennsylvania, who outdid Stevens by advocating the payment of maturing obligations by the further issue of paper money. Garfield, on the other hand, urged a little period of suffering and then a free time: "For one I am unwilling that my name shall be linked to the fate of a paper currency. I believe that any party which commits itself to paper money will go down amid the general disaster, covered with the curses of a ruined people."

The result of this first debate was a compromise adopted on April 12th, 1866, by which the desired authority was given to the Secretary of the Treasury, but with limitations which restricted him as to the amounts of the greenbacks that he might retire in any given month. Curiously enough in all the debates of the period, no one seems to have thought of the compromise by which some European currencies, notably that of France, have been stabilized, namely that of redeeming the paper at some fixed figure, say seventy or eighty cents in gold. The result is that in the arguments of the sixties and seventies the issue was always sharp between unredeemed paper on the one hand and dollars equivalent to gold on the other. In the first contest, Garfield and his friends had evidently won a substantial victory.

For a few months after the adoption of the act of 1866, Congress was quite too busy with its struggle with the President to consider financial problems; but prices, especially of agricultural products, continued to decline, and early in 1868 the popular demand for inflation led to a sharp reversal of the policy of retiring the paper money. On January 23, 1868, after Secretary McCulloch had retired and cancelled $44,000,000 of the greenbacks, Congress put a stop to further measures of contraction, and bills were introduced looking to the payment of the national debt in "lawful money" and even to the taxation of the interest of the bonds, which from the point of view of the holder would of course amount to a partial reduction of the value of the principal. In the important debates of that year, Garfield's chief antagonists were Thaddeus Stevens, now broken by the infirmities of age and coming close to the end of an astonishing career, but fighting always for each of the three great objectives of his life, the punishment of the South, the increase of the tariff, and the expansion of the currency; Benjamin F. Butler of Massachusetts; and John A. Logan of Illinois, who had made himself the special advocate of the taxation of the income of the bondholders. Ready as Garfield was on occasion to vote with these powerful leaders when it came to problems of the tariff or the impeachment of the President, here was an issue on which his mind was clear and on which his convictions were left in no doubt.

On May 15th, 1868, Garfield delivered a carefully prepared speech on the subject of the currency.[1] Garfield's position required courage, for the Ohio Republicans had already adopted

[1] *Cong. Globe,* 40th Cong., 2d Sess., pp. 2480–2487.

a plank favoring the payment of the bonds in greenbacks and he stood alone among the Congressmen from his State and almost alone among the representatives of the Mississippi Valley, and the Republican national convention had not yet adopted the plank which, five days later and largely through the influence of Carl Schurz, was to commit the party to the payment of the national debt in gold. Garfield had gone over his arguments with his friends David A. Wells and Hugh McCulloch. On a subject on which few persons had definite convictions he delivered one of the few speeches of the session that probably changed votes; his argument received the high praise of Godkin in the *Nation,* for the first time made Garfield a national figure, and through the influence of John Bright led in England to the election of Garfield to the honorary membership of the Cobden club. He showed fairly conclusively that the apparent prosperity of the war years had been due to the unhealthy stimulation of wasteful consumption and not to the issue of legal-tender paper money; that a period of inflation falls with special weight on the workers whose wages do not rise in proportion to other prices; that gold and silver are relatively elastic since the quantity of the two metals through the effects of importations tends to rise and fall in answer to the demands of business; but that the issue of paper money has no possible relationship to the needs of the country and creates a constant atmosphere of uncertainty and speculation. In his conclusion Garfield advocated the return to specie payments by redeeming the greenbacks, beginning at 130, and gradually increasing the price in gold until the two currencies were of equal value. He did not deny that a period of deflation would cause hardships among debtors, just as the inflation of the war years had reduced the property of creditors; but he regarded such losses as unavoidable, and made a strong point by showing that the average life of private debts in the United States was only two years, so that the loss to a debtor who would be required to pay his debts in a money of greater value would not be heavy. These arguments had much wisdom, but they were of the kind to appeal to bankers and bondholders, especially in the Eastern cities, rather than to the farmers in the West. As for the South, its special economic point of view, thanks to the policy of Reconstruction, did not for the moment need to be taken into account.

The debate continued throughout the summer. On July 15th Garfield had a sharp clash with Logan and Butler on the question of a tax of ten percent on the interest of the bonds, pointing out that such a step, singling out the bonds for special taxation, would be ruinous to the credit of the country in the immense refunding operations that were constantly necessary and would cost in higher rates of interest far more than it would yield in revenue. Again, on July 23rd, Garfield rose to make a reply to Stevens who had challenged the villainy, as he called it, of those who wanted to pay the five-twenty bonds in coin. Garfield had been mentioned by name; but though his answer was temperate he quoted the record mercilessly to show that Stevens himself had virtually promised to pay in gold when the bonds were issued, and that he could not now honestly go back on his word. But in spite of the declarations of the national platform, it was with the greatest difficulty that further meaures of inflation were prevented; and Garfield's specific plan for a prompt return to specie payments had no chance of serious consideration.

Before the close of the year Thaddeus Stevens was dead and the forces of inflation had lost their most powerful leader, but the problem on which East and West were sharply divided had only been postponed and not settled. In 1869 the new Speaker of the House, James G. Blaine of Maine, refused as Colfax had done to make Garfield chairman of the Commit-

tee on Ways and Means, but placed him in the chairmanship of
the almost equally important Committee on Banking and Currency, where he soon had a unique opportunity to illustrate in
a concrete way the dangers of speculation that were inherent in
a paper currency. During the winter of 1868-1869, the immediate danger of inflation seemed to have passed and the price
of gold in greenbacks, which had stood at 145, had dropped to
130, the lowest point that had been reached since the beginning
of the contest. During the summer, slowly at first, and in September with increasing speed, the price of gold which was required by every legitimate merchant for the payments of duties on imports, and of course the consequent depreciation of
greenbacks, had gone on at an accelerating speed. On the famous "Black Friday," September 24th, 1869, gold reached 162
and little was to be had at any price. The government then in-
tervened, selling the gold in the Treasury; the price dropped
in fifteen minutes from 160 to 133; and, in the words of one
of the witnesses, half of Wall Street was involved in ruin, as
the other half would soon have been had the Secretary of the
Treasury withheld his famous telegrams ordering the sale of the
chief stock in the country.

Even without the use of a single name, the story was impressive enough, and showed that here again, as in the case
of tariff rates, was a constant opportunity to use the machinery
of government to enrich some individuals at the expense of
others. But rumors did not stop with figures, and when Congress met, the story was current that the great and ruinous
rise in the price of gold had been due to the manipulations of
two entirely unscrupulous and notorious gamblers and specu-
lators, Jay Gould and "Jim" Fisk of New York, whose effort
to corner gold had led them to use even the influence of the
President of the United States and the members of his family.
The investigation of these stories was assigned to the Commit-

tee on Banking, of which James A. Garfield was the chairman.

Garfield went quietly to New York, where he made a close study of the methods of the gold room, and found out just what witnesses to call. His committee then took voluminous testimony, which Garfield summed up in a report that remains to this day a masterpiece of judicial exposition. Garfield's report on the Gold Panic has been followed by all future historians, and his conclusions have been challenged at no vital point. In the story that he told, the Chairman of the Committee exonerated the President of the United States from all guilty knowledge of the hidden purposes of Gould and Fisk. But the plain unvarnished tale itself revealed a degree of moral obtuseness on the part of Grant and of trickery and ruthless treachery to their own friends on the part of Gould and Fisk, which proved to the country more clearly than many pages of argument would have done the need for fundamental reforms in the existing monetary system.

There was no single word of useless rhetoric, no attempt to point a moral or to adorn a tale, but through the intricacies of a voluminous story Garfield showed how Gould and Fisk had laid their plot, how they had not hesitated to entertain Grant in public to give the impression that they had control of him, how they had bribed newspapers to publish propaganda against the government sale of gold, how they had paid a large sum to A. R. Corbin, the brother-in-law of Grant, to get him to use his influence in the same direction, and finally when they had received intimations that the suspicions of the President were at length aroused and that he was likely to order the sale of gold, how Gould at least and perhaps Fisk also, for the testimony on that point was not conclusive, had withdrawn from the corner just in time to leave the ruinous losses to friends who had trusted them. Garfield minced no words and called Gould "the guilty plotter of all these criminal proceedings," a phrase that, as we shall see, did not prevent Garfield from applying to Gould in 1880 to help finance his Presidential campaign. But the strangest part of the story is that the President summoned Garfield to the White House, where he expressed himself "under a good many obligations to me for the management of the Gold Panic investigation." But if Grant were sincerely grateful under such circumstances, he must have failed completely to measure at its real value the effect of the whole incident on his own historical reputation.[1] From the patriotic point of view, however, the thanks of the President were fully earned, for Garfield was never to perform a more important public service.

For the next few years, the problem of inflation remained in abeyance. In the presidential campaign of 1872, both major parties denounced repudiation of any part of the public debt and recommended a return to specie payments, but the question was still dangerous and there was a general tendency to let sleeping dogs lie; and, in the meantime, the business of the country continued to be done as before in depreciated paper. Then, after the lull, came the disastrous economic depression of 1873, followed by the usual efforts to find legislative panaceas for widespread distress. One plan was to increase appropriations in order to promote prosperity by making jobs for men who were without employment. Garfield, with his usual conservatism, wrote that "it is no part of the business of government to find employment for people." He was now Chairman of the Committee on Appropriations and in this position he was able to secure measures of economy rather than of extravagance as a remedy for hard times. But prices were now so low and times so hard that the demand for a further issue of greenbacks seemed irresistible. In March, 1874, by an over-

---

[1] "Gold Panic Investigation," *House Reports,* No. 31, 41st Congress, 2nd Sess.; T. C. Smith, *Life and Letters of Garfield,* Vol. I, pp. 450, 451.

whelming vote of 168 to 77 and without debate, a measure was passed that Garfield called the most dangerous and fatal legislation that he had known during his service in the House. The more conservative Senate passed, by a narrow majority of five, the Inflation Bill, which provided for an issue of greenbacks to the amount of $44,000,000. Garfield knew well the temper of the House and saw that serious opposition was useless, but he called at once on Grant and urged him strongly to veto the bill. Grant was in a difficult position, for some of his closest friends, especially Benjamin F. Butler, were identified with the policy of inflation, but he accepted the advice of Garfield who was delighted and wrote to Hinsdale that he was inclined to forgive all the President's mistakes for the service that he then rendered to the nation.[1] But the pressure was so great that even Garfield was compelled to accept a compromise by which the amount of the greenbacks was finally fixed at $382,000,000, where they remained for many years.

The elections of 1874 resulted in a great victory for the Democrats. Many Republican Congressmen were defeated, and in the so-called "lame duck" session of Congress that followed their defeat, in January, 1875, many Congressmen who had recently voted for sharp inflation, now evidently feeling that they might as well be hanged for a sheep as a goat, and desiring to bring themselves into harmony with the views of the President, reversed their position and promised a return to specie payments on January 1st, 1879. It is a curious circumstance that a measure whose value is now generally acknowledged was passed by defeated Congressmen which at the moment at least could not have been carried by a Congress with an actual mandate from their masters, the American people. From that time on, Garfield's efforts were chiefly directed during the administration of President Hayes to prevent the repeal of this

[1] Garfield to Hinsdale, April 23, 1874. Garfield Papers.

promise and to assist Hayes and Sherman to fulfill the arrangement at the time stated.

In the meantime the old issue was entering a new phase, with an increasing demand for the free coinage of silver dollars, worth at the time about eighty cents in gold. In spite of the popularity of this form of inflation throughout the West, and especially in Ohio, Garfield stood again almost alone among Western members in challenging the movement as one intended primarily to scale down the private and the public debts of the United States, which he estimated as about five billions, by a discount of twenty percent. Hard times and low prices continued, and once in 1876 and again in 1877 free silver bills were passed by large majorities in the House only to meet with the conservative opposition of the Senate. But in 1878, against the opposition of Garfield and over the veto of President Hayes, a compromise, the so-called Bland-Allison Silver Act, was passed, that took a long step towards free silver by requiring the coinage of not less than two million or more than four million dollars in silver every month. With that compromise the forces in favor of a larger coinage were compelled to rest content until the whole question was reopened a decade later.

However much Garfield might tend to look on other questions from the point of view of party advantage, careful study had made his opposition to all forms of inflation firm and consistent. On this subject, even when the odds seemed to be against him, he retained something of the fire of a crusading spirit that had been so marked a feature of his early career when the safety of the Union had been at stake, and though the topics were seemingly dry and prosaic enough, his speeches more than once rose to heights of enduring eloquence. But even as late as the beginning of 1878 Garfield looked to the outcome with no great hopefulness, writing in his diary: "I am fighting for financial honor against the majority of my own party and

State—and I grow weary of the contest. If it were one of logic, reason, and sense I could enjoy it; but it is a fight of interest against honor—the brute force of votes against knowledge." [1] But the end was closer than Garfield had dared to hope, and the congressional elections of 1878 marked the last great struggle over the problems of inflation during Garfield's career. A new organization, the Greenback party, that had polled a comparatively small vote in the presidential election of 1876, was now able to capitalize the forces of discontent that had been strengthened by the poverty and unemployment that followed the great panic of 1873. The leaders of the party now united the demand for greenbacks and free silver, thus recognising the two movements as phases of the same thing; but their interests were far wider than the limits of the merely financial policies that had given birth to their organisation. In their speeches the members of the party, by their demand for an eight-hour day for labor, for the regulation of railroads, and for the destruction of the special privileges of corporations, especially the national banks, foreshadowed some of the most insistent problems of the next generation. For a time it seemed likely that the congressmen of the new party would be able to hold the balance of power, and Garfield, who was now recognised as one of the leading advocates of a gold standard, entered the lists, speaking in many places beyond the limits of his own district. On September 10th, 1878, before a huge audience in Faneuil Hall in Boston, he delivered one of the most important speeches of his career on the subject which he was among the first to denominate "Honest Money." Again he argued, as he had for the last twelve years, that laborers had a greater interest in a stable monetary medium than any other members of the community and took the position that the best thing that the government could do to promote the return of

[1] Garfield *Journal*, Jan. 7, 1878.

prosperity was to destroy any impediments to the healthy business of the country. The new House contained 149 Democrats, 136 Republicans, and only 9 members of the new party. But ideas of monetary inflation were sectional and not partisan. The rash greenback and free silver ideas commanded a substantial majority, and only the conservatism of the Senate again prevented the reversal of the monetary policy that had been foreshadowed and promised in 1875. President Hayes and Secretary Sherman continued to make preparations for the redemption of greenbacks in gold, a plan in which they were greatly aided by good crops and the gradual improvement of business conditions. The resumption of specie payments on the first of January of 1879 was successfully accomplished and a long contest which involved the most serious political and economic consequences came to an end with a victory for the arguments and forces with which no individual had been more closely connected than James A. Garfield of Ohio.[1]

[1] Garfield's chief addresses on the monetary problem, with careful introductions by his editor, B. A. Hinsdale, may be found in his *Works*, Vol. I, 35–42; 183–202; 284–322; 327–364; 439–443; 543–593; Vol. II, 175–185; 246–274; 329–353; 490–529; 586–609. These are only his formal speeches on the insistent problem which remained throughout the central interest of his career.

GARFIELD spent the summer of 1872 in Montana, where he had undertaken a mission to the dissatisfied Indians of that region. He returned in September in the midst of the presidential campaign to find his name, with those of other prominent members of Congress, involved in serious charges against his integrity as a public servant.[1]

In the period immediately following the war, the building of railroads had been encouraged by great public gifts of land and money both from the national government and from the individual localities through which the railroad passed. These gifts, which were certainly necessary to secure the rapid development of the country, might have been justified if these enterprises had been recognised at once as essentially public in their nature, and if there had been adequate supervision of the expenditure of funds of which the railroads were essentially trustees to the nation. But the gifts had been made and were generally wasted in such a scandalous fashion as to leave the railroads themselves loaded with debts, often mere streaks of rust across the prairies. In the meantime the public wealth that should have served as a fund against adversity had for the most part passed into the hands of private individuals.

Among other less creditable enterprises, one of the chief beneficiaries of this policy had been the Union Pacific Railroad, whose completion in 1869 had been the cause of great national satisfaction. The gifts to this important road had been typical and had included twenty sections of land to the mile,

---

[1] Garfield *Journal,* Aug. and Sept., 1872. Garfield writes (Sept. 9, 1872): "The political campaign has been waged with unparalleled bitterness and acrimony during the 30 days I have been absent. I see my own name dragged into some story which I do not understand, but see only referred to in the newspapers."

in itself an imperial domain, loans of public funds varying from
$16,000 a mile in the plains to $48,000 in the mountainous
regions, and numerous gifts and favors from individual communities, the various loans being so poorly secured as to amount
in fact to outright gifts.

During the period of the war, in spite of the immense potential wealth that had been assigned to the enterprise, the
actual building of the road had languished. But by 1867 it
was apparent that the road had wealth sufficient to complete
the building and to leave a very large surplus in its treasury.
At that time, as the public had come to suspect by 1872, seven
leading directors of the Company worked out an ingenious
scheme for robbing the public and the road of all this surplus
wealth. Under the leadership of Oakes Ames, a capitalist and
congressman from Massachusetts, T. C. Durant, and Henry S.
McComb, these seven stockholders of the Union Pacific road
gained control of a corporation known as the Credit Mobilier
Company of America and, in their double capacity, made a contract virtually with themselves by which the Credit Mobilier
should build the remaining 667 miles of the Union Pacific at
a cost ranging from $42,000 a mile to $96,000. The total
bill was $47,925,000; the profits were estimated at about
twenty millions, paid virtually by the American public and to
a large extent actually from the public treasury; and the result,
as was doubtless intended, was to change the railroad that was
being finished from a wealthy public corporation into a debtor
staggering under an almost impossible load.

These various contracts, in which Oakes Ames was the inter-
mediary, were signed on August 16, 1867, and October 15, 1867.
The Union Pacific Railroad had received almost everything
that it could desire from the government and was one of the
few roads that at the time was not in the market for additional
favors, but since Congress was paying the bills, there was evi-

dent danger of unfriendly legislation or at least of an investigation. As an indication of this danger, Congress had barely
assembled when on December 9, 1867, C. C. Washburne of
Wisconsin introduced a proposal, which at the time seemed
radical, for the public regulation of railway rates. Such a movement was likely to gain headway, especially among the Western
members who came from a region where the farmers were
already restive under the increasing burdens of the new indus-
trialism.

On account of the valuable contracts to which we have referred, the stocks of the Credit Mobilier Company were worth
many times their par value of one hundred dollars a share.
But in view of the danger of hostile action, a block of shares
to be sold at par to influential men was assigned to T. C. Durant,
to Oakes Ames, and apparently to Henry S. McComb. Ames
was entrusted with the distribution of these favors among Congressmen of his acquaintance. McComb seems to have become
dissatisfied with the number of these shares that had been assigned to Ames for use among his friends, and in reply to a
letter from McComb, Ames wrote on January 30, 1868, to
defend his use of the shares: "You do not understand by your
letter what I have done, and am to do with my sales of stock.
. . . You would not want me to offer less than 1,000 m. to
any one. We allow Durant to place 58,000 to some three or
four of his friends, or keep it himself. I have used this where
it will produce the most good to us I think. In view of King's
letter and Washburne's move here, I go in for making our
bond dividend in full. We can do it with perfect safety." A
few days later Ames furnished to the still suspicious McComb
a list that purported to be that of the Congressmen to whom he
had either given the shares or to whom he intended to give
them. This memorandum dated February 1, 1868, was as follows: "Blaine, of Maine, 3000; Patterson, of New Hampshire,

2000; Wilson, Massachusetts, 2000; Painter, reporter for In-
quirer, 3000; S. Colfax, Speaker, 2000; Elliott, Massachusetts, 3000; Dawes, Massachusetts, 2000; Boutwell, Massachusetts, 2000; Bingham and Garfield, Ohio; Scofield and
Kelley, Pennsylvania." McComb still suspected Ames of keeping some of these shares for himself and soon after the beginning of the transactions referred to, retained no less a person
than Jeremiah S. Black to bring pressure on Ames to secure
an accounting and if necessary to bring suit against Ames.[1]
Black pointed out that the publication of the letters and the
list in the hands of McComb would bring ruin to many reputations, including that of Ames himself, and urged Ames to
compromise the suit in the interests of secrecy. And even when
Ames refused, the matter was still kept quiet for some time.
But in 1872, in the midst of the Presidential campaign, Mc-
Comb seems to have made his threats good. In any case, the
letters and the list fell into the hands of Charles A. Dana,
who with his usual journalistic sagacity at once saw their importance and published these incriminating documents in the
New York *Sun*.[2]

The publication of the above list naturally created a great
sensation, for the names included those of the retiring Vice-
President of the United States, of the candidate on the Republican ticket for the same office, and of some of the most
influential congressmen and chairmen of committees. But most
of the congressmen mentioned at once published indignant and
sweeping denials of all knowledge of or connection with the
schemes of the Credit Mobilier Company of America. Among
the most complete of the various denials was that of Garfield,
who authorised the following interview published in the Cin-

[1] McComb to Black, Aug. 19, 1868; Aug. 27, 1868, Black Papers (Library of
Congress).
[2] New York *Sun*, September 4, 1872.

cinnati *Commercial* for September 16, 1872: "General Garfield, who has just arrived here from the Indian country, has today had the first opportunity of seeing the charges connecting his name with receiving shares of the Credit Mobilier from Oakes Ames. He authorises the statement that he never subscribed for a single share of the stock, and that he never received or saw a share of it. When the company was first formed, George Francis Train, then active in it, came to Washington and exhibited a list of subscribers, of leading capitalists and some members of Congress, to the stock of the company. The subscription was described as a popular one of one thousand dollars cash. Train urged General Garfield to subscribe on two occasions, and each time he declined. Subsequently he was again informed that the list was nearly completed, but that a chance remained for him to subscribe, when he again declined, and to this day has not subscribed for or received any share of stock or bond of the company."

These denials were generally accepted at their face value by the American people and tended, if anything, to react against the interests of Horace Greeley who was running on a reform platform as the joint candidate of the Independent Republicans and the Democrats.[1] It is perhaps creditable to the fairness of the public that they have always been extremely slow to accept charges of this kind against the party in power and that even when such charges have proved later to be at least partially justified, as in the cases of the elections of 1832, of 1872, and of 1924, the immediate effect has usually been unfavorable to those who made them. At least in 1872, the charge of corruption did not prove to be a winning card; when Congress met in December after the election, Garfield reported to his friend, Hinsdale: "We are in a singular condition here

---

[1] Garfield wrote (*Journal,* Nov. 4, 1872): "To many men this campaign has been a choice of evils and in some respects it has been so to me."

in Congress. There is virtually no opposition to the Republican party. The Democracy are stunned, perhaps killed by their late defeat, and there seems to be no limit to the power of the dominant party. If to its great strength it shall add, as I fear, arrogance and recklessness, it will break in two before the next administration goes far."

There, as far as the Credit Mobilier charges were concerned, the matter might well have rested if it had not been for the fact that one of the names mentioned had been that of James G. Blaine of Maine, occupying the dominant position of Speaker of the House, and one of the few in the list, perhaps the only one, who was entirely innocent of any connection whatsoever with the Credit Mobilier Company. Blaine was not only free from blame, but with what seemed a great career at stake, he could not afford to allow the recent charges to rest without further notice, and after consulting Garfield and other leading members of the party, on December 2nd at the beginning of the session he left the Speaker's chair and moved the appointment of a special committee to investigate the Credit Mobilier charges. The House accepted the motion without dissent, and an able committee that commanded the confidence of the country was appointed, consisting of Luke P. Poland of Vermont, chairman, with N. P. Banks of Massachusetts, and George W. McCrary of Iowa, Republicans, and W. E. Niblack of Indiana and W. M. Merrick of Maryland, Democrats, as the other members.

The investigations of the committee soon showed that in the contracts with the Union Pacific Railroad, the leading members of the Credit Mobilier Company had defrauded both the public and minority stockholders of large sums, and these matters were referred to another committee for special investigation. Among other individuals involved, the testimony showed conclusively that Blaine had had nothing to do with the enterprise; Dawes had subscribed and had never made the slightest secret of a fact that he still regarded as creditable to his business sagacity; the retiring Vice-President, Schuyler Colfax, over whom, of course, the committee had no jurisdiction, had subscribed, had received dividends, and had undoubtedly made false statements regarding the whole matter. The case of Garfield was one of the most puzzling, and although the chief facts are now apparent they involve evidence that was not at the time presented completely to the committee.[1]

Passing over the testimony as to other individuals, consider the evidence as to Congressman James A. Garfield. The chief witness was naturally Oakes Ames, whose testimony as to Garfield was first presented on December 17, 1872. In a prepared statement on that date, Ames testified as follows: "In the early part of 1868 our prospects were very flattering, and I was compelled in distributing the few shares I could get, to disappoint many. But I used them in a way that I thought most advantageous in spreading our influence everywhere." Among others, Ames mentioned Garfield: "I agreed to get ten shares of stock for him and hold it until he could pay for it. He never did pay for it or receive it." On cross-examination, pressed as to the matter of dividends, Ames testified: "He had some money from me once, some three or four hundred dollars, and called it a loan."

In his testimony on January 14th, Garfield gave an account of the whole affair that was in substantial agreement with the testimony of Ames, but that expanded and modified in important respects his Cincinnati interview of the previous September. In that interview, it will be remembered that Garfield had said that he had received an offer which he had repeatedly de-

---

[1] The *Credit Mobilier Report* is in *House Reports,* No. 77, 42nd Cong., 3rd Sess. As to Garfield, see pp. 5, 6, 20, 21, 28, 40, 91, 92, 128–131, 136, 180, 181, 223, 228, 303, 353–361, 450, 451, 471.

clined. Now it appeared that he had received an offer of stock, which he had held in abeyance for some time, at least a year, and had then declined. As Garfield put it to one of his friends, he had "held an option on the stock, but had not agreed to take it." He had known nothing as to the sources of the unusual dividends that were promised. On one occasion, whose date was not mentioned, Garfield had received a loan of three hundred dollars from Ames, which he had afterward repaid. Asked by Chairman Poland whether there was any connection between that loan and the offer of stock, Garfield replied that there was none except as to the time of payment: "Mr. Ames stated to me that if I concluded to subscribe to the Credit Mobilier stock I could allow the loan to remain until the payment on that was adjusted." The testimony as to the length of time that the two transactions were left open was vague and inconclusive.

For his part, Garfield now evidently felt that he had made a clean breast of the whole miserable business, and confided to his diary: "At 11 o'clock, went before the Credit Mobilier investigating committee and made a statement of what I know concerning the company. I am too proud to confess to any but my own intimate friends how deeply this whole matter has grieved me. While I did nothing in regard to it that can be construed into any act of impropriety (much less of corruption), I have still said from the start that the shadow of the cursed thing would cling to my name for many years. I believe that my statement was regarded as clear and conclusive." [1]

This last sentence, however, proved to be quite too optimistic, for, recalled on January 22nd, Ames came again before

---

[1] Garfield *Journal*, Jan. 14th, 1873. In contrast with many of the others implicated, Garfield showed good judgment in making no further statements during the session of Congress; and in the summer, when he published his so-called "Review of the Transactions of the Credit Mobilier Company," he found that the interest in the matter was already beginning to abate.

JEREMIAH S. BLACK

OAKES AMES

the committee armed with a memorandum book. From this it appeared that by June 19, 1868, the dividends on ten shares of stock were sufficient to pay for the full par value of the stock, one thousand dollars, and to leave $329 due to Garfield provided he was the owner of the stock at that time. Ames testified that he had given Garfield $329 about that time. On January 29th, the committee discovered a check of Ames dated June 22, 1868, for cash on the Sergeant at Arms for the sum of $329. Ames had initialled other checks to show their disposition. This one had no initials: but Ames testified that in his judgment it was the one by which the dividend that Garfield called a loan had been paid.

It is apparent from this review that as between Garfield and Ames there were only two substantial differences. Had Garfield in January, 1868, subscribed to stock of which he had become a legal owner, or had he merely received an option which he was later free to accept or reject as circumstances might warrant? On or about June 22, 1868, had he received a dividend of $329 or a loan of $300? In a transaction as vague and unbusinesslike as this, these discrepancies may well have been due to honest differences of purpose between the two men at the time and of memory afterwards. What Garfield regarded as an indefinite option, Ames, better accustomed to the ways of business, must have thought to be a purchase or a gift; what Garfield remembered as a loan from Ames, to Ames seemed a payment of a balance on dividends already due. In any case, in their report the committee was doubtless impressed by the fact that there was no memorandum, receipt, or even a definite memory as to the time, place, manner or circumstances in which the loan had been made or repaid. On the other hand, the theory of a dividend was borne out by the memorandum and by the check on the Sergeant at Arms, and while neither document was conclusive, they reported to the

House that Garfield had agreed to take ten shares of the stock for which he had not paid, and that he had later received $329 by a check on the Sergeant at Arms for the balance due him from dividends after the stock had been paid for. Since there was no particle of evidence that Garfield had knowledge of the sources of the profits of the company or of the purposes of Ames in distributing the stock, the committee merely reported the facts and recommended no punishment in his case. To one who examines the records again, the judicial fairness of the Poland committee in the case of James A. Garfield seems today entirely convincing.[1]

On one point at least, the testimony of Ames and Garfield, was entirely consistent. Garfield had never redeemed his option and never received a certificate of ownership. This point evidently puzzled the committee and did not become clear until Garfield himself later published letters from his friends.

In the spring of 1868, Garfield was evidently worried about either the wisdom or the propriety of his investment, for he consulted a banker friend, J. P. Robison of Cleveland, who promised to look into the matter for him, but later changed his mind and advised against the investment. Perhaps, for the reason was not given, the very size of the profits aroused the suspicions of a conservative business man. Late in 1869 or early

[1] The editor of Garfield's letters, T. C. Smith, Vol. II, p. 543, makes the issue between Ames and Garfield sharp, and speaks of the members of the committee as men who "had just publicly declared him guilty of lying or perjury." But the committee in its report made no such charge; and the points on which the two men differed are more easily explained as natural differences of memory on a vague transaction. Both men give one the impression of reluctant witnesses, neither of whom would willingly perjure himself. Garfield's only comment on the report of the Poland committee was: "Feb. 18, 1873. Listened to the report of Mr. Poland in regard to Credit Mobilier. The report produced a profound sensation and was listened to with silence and painful interest. . . . I am not satisfied with some of the statements of the committee in reference to my case; but with Ames' memorandum and testimony before them, they probably thought they were doing right." Garfield *Journal*.

in 1870, Garfield told his most intimate friend Hinsdale about Ames's offer, and again he seems to have been suspicious and troubled. About the same time, some two years after the original offer, Jeremiah S. Black, who as counsel for McComb was in close touch with the secrets of the promoters, warned Garfield of the dangers and evident impropriety of such an investment. Soon after his conversation with Black, Garfield, according to his testimony, which is entirely borne out by the fact that he was never on the books of the company as a stockholder, went to Ames and told him that he would have nothing further to do with the stock. But Ames continued to regard him as the actual owner of the stock, entitled to further dividends whenever he desired them; and he was probably entirely unable to understand the reasons that had led to Garfield's attempted withdrawal.[1]

Black's testimony in 1873 as to the motives of Garfield was quite in line with the report of the Poland committee: "He had not the slightest suspicion that he was to be taken into a ring organised for the purpose of defrauding the public; nor did he know that the stock was in any manner connected with anything which came or could come within the legislative jurisdiction of Congress." When Black told Garfield his amazing story of corruption he testified, "That all this was to him a perfectly new revelation I am as sure as I can be of such a

[1] The letter of Jeremiah S. Black, dated February 15, 1873, was published by Garfield in his "Review of the Transactions of the Credit Mobilier Company," Washington, May, 1873. It fixes the time of Garfield's refusal of Ames' offer at a period late in 1869 or early in 1870. But Garfield had apparently overlooked earlier opportunities to inform himself as to the character of the company. Thus as early as March 20, 1868, C. C. Washburne had made a bitter attack on the Credit Mobilier Company, and in the debate that followed Garfield was apparently present. Again in November, the official report of the Secretary of the Interior had estimated the profits of the company in building the Union Pacific Railroad at about $17,750,000, a figure that in itself might well have put Garfield on his guard. At various times in 1869 the nature of the scheme was again exposed. See *Cong. Globe,* 43rd Cong., 3rd Session, Pt. 3, pp. 1820, 1821.

fact, or of any fact which is capable of being proved only by moral circumstances." But Garfield now realized what he must already have suspected that for two years he had been playing with fire. Thus he wrote to Hinsdale somewhat later: "It is fortunate that I never fully concluded to accept the offer made me; but it grieves me greatly to have been negotiating with a man who had so little sense of truth and honor as to use his proposals for a purpose in a way now apparent to me."

Garfield's first mistake led him into a second. Any man dislikes to acknowledge even to himself that he has been a fool. So, when the charges were first made, instead of making a clean breast of a natural mistake, which in the long run would have been not only the best but also the safest course, Garfield dictated his quite misleading interview with the Cincinnati *Commercial*, and even in his sworn testimony before the Poland committee, while he told the truth, certainly failed to tell the whole truth, clearly evading an answer to certain vital questions and thus giving the impression of worse faults than those of which he was guilty. Garfield's own explanation, in his "Review of the Transactions of the Credit Mobilier Company," that he failed to tell more of the truth for fear of injuring his party and fellow members of Congress, is in itself an eloquent proof of the ethical confusion of a time in which loyalty to party could be regarded as an adequate defence against serious charges.

On February 18, 1873, the report of the Poland committee which left so many honorable reputations threadbare was listened to in tense silence by the House. The finding of the committee was unanimous, but it recommended action only in the cases of Oakes Ames of Massachusetts and James Brooks of New York. A resolution for the expulsion of these two members accompanied the report, but after a debate of ten days and by a close vote of 115 to 110 was changed into a vote of censure. The watchful reporters noticed that, while the vote was being taken, Brooks sat reading and Oakes Ames leaned his head on his hands and watched the proceedings intently. On the desk in front of him was an elegant bouquet sent by some sympathising friend. The penalty was undoubtedly severe enough; for both men went home broken and aged. Within a month and before the publication of Garfield's defence Ames was dead, soon to be followed by Brooks. There was a strong feeling in the House that the vote of censure ought to be extended to include Kelley and Garfield, regarding both of whom the report of the committee was similar. A motion to censure Kelley and Garfield was divided and the vote taken on Kelley's case first. Upon this motion Garfield voted no; and it failing, the proposition to censure him was not acted on further.[1]

In the meantime a storm of indignant criticism raged in the newspapers quite without regard to party affiliations. One of the mildest of the editorials was in the New York *Times*, which said on February 19, 1873: "Messrs. Kelley and Garfield present a most distressing figure. Their participation in the Credit Mobilier affair is complicated by the most unfortunate contradictions in testimony." On the same day the New York *Tribune* summed up the findings of the committee as follows: "James A. Garfield of Ohio had ten shares; never paid a dollar; received $329, which after the investigation began, he was anxious to have considered as a loan from Mr. Oakes Ames to himself. Well, the wickedness of all of it is that these men betrayed the trust of the people, deceived their constitutents, and by

[1] Chairman Poland was compelled to defend the committee against a charge of using Ames and Brooks as scapegoats. Ames, as the leading agent in all the transactions, and Brooks, who was a government director of the Union Pacific Railroad, were presumed to have guilty knowledge, and were convicted of bribery. As to the others, Poland said: "We say we did not find it established as against any of those gentlemen." *Cong. Globe,* Feb. 25, 1873.

evasions and falsehoods confessed the transactions to be disgraceful." The point of view of the Portland *Advertiser* was widely endorsed: "That Oakes Ames and Brooks deserve all the censure the committee put on them but very few will deny, or that they deserve expulsion; but the position the report takes on the cases of others who are implicated will excite severe criticism all over the country, among those who wish to see the politics of our nation freed from dishonesty and corruption. If they thought they were engaging in an honest transaction they were the most idiotic set of men that ever attained such high positions. If they had the intelligence they have always had the credit of possessing they must have known that the object of Ames in dealing thus generously with them was to influence their official actions; and further, they must have known that the concern was formed for the express purpose of fleecing the road and indirectly the government. Their foolish prevarications in regard to their connection with the road, during last summer's campaign, tends to show that their knowledge of the Credit Mobilier was more accurate than they were willing to own." In February, Garfield's personal enemy in the House, Benjamin F. Butler, had turned to him with the sneer, "De mortuis nihil sine bonum," and this sentiment found an echo in the Utica *Herald* for February 25, 1873, which exclaimed: "For heaven's sake let us bury our dead out of sight, that they may not offend the public nostrils."

The very violence of the attack soon caused a reaction; men who had known James A. Garfield all their lives did not believe that he had been guilty of more than an indiscretion; the tragic death of Ames caused a feeling of pity; the Credit Mobilier proved to be a mere seven days' wonder; and even as early as the middle of March, when Garfield returned to

Ohio, he found that public attention had been diverted to a new topic that voters were able to understand much better than they did the intricacies of high finance. The newspapers were discussing the so-called "Salary Grab of 1873." Fortunately for Garfield, it was an off year in which he did not have to contest his seat; for, although his position on this question had been open and above-board and capable of complete justification, the public anger regarding the recent increase of congressional salaries, an entirely legal and perhaps even a wise measure, for the moment far outdistanced the fast waning interest in the Credit Mobilier affair of 1868. The sudden subsidence of all interest in a question that had seemed only three weeks before worthy of bitter anger, and the almost immediate substitution of a wholly different topic, throw a strange light on the ways of democracy. Quite unfairly, Garfield, who was the chairman of the Committee on Appropriations, was made the center of this new and much more dangerous attack.

On February 24, 1873, Benjamin F. Butler introduced an amendment to the General Appropriation Bill, of which Garfield was of course in charge, increasing the salaries of Congressmen by fifty percent, twenty-five hundred dollars a year, and making the increase retroactive to the beginning of the existing Congress whose term was almost completed. Garfield opposed the amendment, taking the position that such an increase should only be adopted as part of a general revision of government salaries, and that in its special application to Congressmen it would be the inevitable subject of just criticism. Four days later, however, the amendment was adopted by a close vote of 100 to 97, and, being accepted by the Senate, became a part of a bill which was referred to a conference committee. The House members were Butler, the author of the proposal, Randall of Pennsylvania, a strong Democratic supporter of the proposed increase, and Garfield; while the

Senate was represented by Morrill, Carpenter, and Bayard, all
of whom favored the salary increase. In committee Garfield
again proposed the elimination of the objectionable feature of
the bill, but was voted down five to one. Garfield then moved
to deduct from the increased salaries all that had been received
as mileage and his proposal was accepted. Believing that it
was the best he could do, Garfield signed the report of the
conference committee and voted for the whole bill when it
came before the House on the final night of the session. An
opponent asked Garfield "how much plunder" would be taken
from the Treasury; to which half-humorous query, Garfield
replied that the cost for the present Congress would be one
and a quarter millions and after that a yearly outlay of three
quarters of a million, but said that he did not consider these
appropriations plunder unless the members of the House did
not regard themselves as deserving the increase. The last of
the twelve great appropriation bills for the safety of which
Garfield was responsible and which were necessary to the running of the government was passed at 1:30 A. M. on the night
of March 3, 1873, and the House thereupon adjourned.[1]

The friends of the measure could point out previous precedents for just such an increase, notably in 1856, when a retroactive increase of 150% had passed unnoticed. The salaries of
Congressmen when compared with the rising cost of living were
undoubtedly low; and recent events had given point to the
argument that it was in the public interest to have Congressmen
paid enough to live on in Washington. If an increase were to be
made it was perhaps unfortunate, but it was none the less inevitable that such an increase should be voted by Congress itself.
At the most, the issue was debatable, a question of expediency

---

[1] Garfield *Journal,* Feb. 28, 1873; Mar. 2, 1873; *Cong. Globe,* 42nd Cong., 3rd
Sess., pp. 1677, 2180, 2181. The leaders of the opposition were E. A. Hibbard of
New Hampshire and W. E. Niblack of Indiana, who objected especially to the
back pay feature: *Cong. Globe,* p. 2101.

EVERY PUBLIC QUESTION WITH AN EYE ONLY TO THE PUBLIC GOOD

JUSTICE (*to the Saints of the Press*): "Let him that has not betrayed the trust of the People, and is without stain, cast the first stone."

(The Credit Mobilier affair from the pencil of Thomas Nast, *Harper's Weekly*, March 15, 1873. The figures on the right are well known editors. The supposed culprits are on the left. Garfield stands against the pillar in the background.)

rather than of honesty, and Garfield's own position was peculiarly strong. He had openly and repeatedly opposed the increase and had only voted for the increased pay when he had to
choose between the fate of a bill whose failure would require an
extra session of Congress and the position that he had taken on
salaries. But after the various scandals that had so recently come
to light, the public was restive and suspicious; an agricultural depression, the harbinger of the great panic of 1873, had already begun; and many a farmer who had difficulty in paying the interest
on his mortgage looked on the increase of the salaries of Congressmen with almost passionate dislike. No precedents could
ever give propriety to the retroactive features of a bill that paid
salaries for two years of work that had already been done. Newspapers that had supported Garfield through all the charges of the
Credit Mobilier period now turned against him. Even his best
friends acknowledged that if he had been running for reëlection
he would have been defeated on that issue alone.

As soon as Garfield realized the bitterness of the feelings
that had been aroused, he returned his share of the retroactive
increase to the Treasury and published an open letter to his
constituents that today seems complete and satisfactory, though
for the moment it did little more than to check slightly the
violence of the storm. One after another, conventions in three
counties in Garfield's district passed resolutions of censure. In
May the Republican State convention referred to the Credit
Moblier and the salary incidents with equal disapproval; and
in the campaign for the governorship that followed in the fall,
Garfield for the first time in many years was definitely snubbed
and overlooked in the choice of speakers.[1] Other congressmen
had been compelled to defend themselves against the same
criticisms, and when the House met after the long summer vaca-

[1] Garfield *Journal,* Mar. 15, 1873; March 21, 1873; April 2, 1873; April 3, 1873;
Sept. 2, 1873.

tion, men who had cheerfully supported the increase when it had been made in March almost fell over one another to prepare measures for its immediate repeal. In a few hours as many as twenty-five bills were introduced for that purpose, and almost alone, Alexander H. Stephens, the former Vice-President of the Confederacy, raised his thin form on his crutches to defend the original measure as just, constitutional, and proper and to point out the indecency of a hasty repeal in the face of criticism. Garfield sympathised with some of the arguments of the famous Georgian, but in advocating a repeal that was almost immediately passed, he was acting in perfect consistency with the position he had held from the beginning. For Garfield the whole incident was perhaps fortunate, for he could debate the salary increase with any one and without the slightest need for reservations or apologies.[1]

As if to prove that troubles never come singly, Garfield had scarcely weathered two storms when he was compelled to meet other criticisms of the same general character. These charges were in reference to his connection with the De Golyer paving contract.

In February, 1871, the city of Washington was placed under a new government with a governor and council appointed by the President and a House of Delegates elected by the people. Public improvements were directed by a Board of Public Works to be appointed by the governor. To the very powerful office of governor President Grant appointed a personal friend in whom he had boundless confidence, Alexander R. Shepherd, a plumber of the city who was known to have remarkable energy and enterprise. Under the direction of Shepherd, who was soon

[1] J. A. Garfield, "Letter to the Republican Voters of the Nineteenth District," Hiram, Ohio, April 21, 1873, printed in full in R. H. Conwell, *Life of Garfield* (1881), pp. 306–317.

generally known as "Boss" Shepherd, the Board of Public Works initiated a scheme of general improvements which changed Washington as if by magic from an ill-paved, ill-lighted, unattractive city to one that was a model of regularity and cleanliness. But these changes were produced at an expense that left the city saddled with a large public debt, and increasing rumors of corruption and extravagance soon led, in 1874, to an investigation by a joint committee of the two Houses. The committee found enough evidence to warrant a change of the government to a simpler and more autocratic form under which the affairs of the district were assigned to three commissioners who continued to administer its affairs. Shepherd retired from his brief kingdom to engage in mining in Mexico, leaving behind enemies who called him a thief and friends who defended him as the founder of modern Washington.

Among other matters connected with the Shepherd régime on which the joint committee under the chairmanship of Senator Allison of Iowa took voluminous testimony was the awarding of contracts involving new pavements costing the city $4,500,-000 and the individual property owners $1,500,000 more. The very size of these contracts aroused suspicion and other indications of extravagance and corruption were by no means absent. One of the companies competing for these contracts was the De Golyer-McClelland Company of Chicago, interested in a patented wood pavement and seeking a contract for 200,000 yards at a price of $3.50 a yard, a total contract of $700,000. The evidence showed that through their agent, G. R. Chittenden, the company assigned the presentation of their argument before the Board of Public Works to a Cleveland attorney, later a Congressman, Richard C. Parsons, who was given a direct fee of $6,000 and was promised $10,000 more contingent on the success of his efforts. On March 13, 1874, Parsons testified that being called away by another case after the presentation of his argument, but before the contract had been awarded, he asked Garfield to take charge of the case for him and later paid Garfield $5,000 for his services.[1] The De Golyer pavement seems to have had some merits; the fees of $16,000 to Parsons and Garfield, standing alone, might have seemed large but not exorbitant, and would have aroused no special attention if other testimony had not shown that the company also spent an additional $72,000 distributed among persons who might be supposed to have influence with the Board before it secured the contract. Garfield was not called to testify, and the committee in its report made no criticism of his conduct; but in March, Garfield's connection with the paving contract became the subject of severe criticism in various newspapers, notably the influential Chicago *Tribune*, the argument being that his services were not legal but political and that his appointment was due to his position as Chairman of the Appropriations Committee. If the company was willing to spend as much as one-seventh of the total proceeds just to secure the contract, the inference was almost unavoidable that the contract itself was not favorable to the taxpayers of Washington and the connection of a leading congressman with the case might well seem at least an unfortunate precedent.[2]

This was the state of the matter at the opening of Garfield's

[1] The Report of the Allison-Wilson Committee on the District of Columbia is in *Senate Reports,* No. 453, 43rd Cong., 1st Sess., where the testimony of Parsons may be found in Vol. II, p. 1075.

[2] An entry in Garfield's *Journal* for Dec. 9th, 1872, shows that while the Board of Public Works did not receive the money for pavements directly from Congress, it was interested in appropriations: "In committee heard the Board of Public Works and General Babcock and before the close of the meeting, Committee voted, with one dissent, to reimburse the Board of Public Works to the amount of one and a quarter millions. This will no doubt be furiously assailed in the House." (Garfield Papers). It seems that this situation might well have suggested a danger and even an impropriety to the Chairman of the Committee on Appropriations in serving as an attorney before the Board.

campaign for renomination and reëlection. He had been so long accustomed to a unanimous nomination and an easy election that he was unable to understand the fact that in 1874 he had to fight for his political life; and he was even considering a trip to Europe, where he expected to meet his expenses by the sale of oil lands, when he was recalled to Hiram and his district by the urgent representations of close friends, especially Harmon Austin, who had so long served as his efficient political manager. Garfield was especially surprised to find that in a bitter campaign the De Golyer pavement matter had become the central theme of discussion, almost to the exclusion of the older questions of the Credit Mobilier Company and even of the "salary grab." In his speeches Garfield was able to show that the money for pavements did not depend on national appropriations, but was subject to the control of a local legislature. He had entered the case as an attorney, had studied the patents that were involved, and had prepared a brief describing the advantages of the De Golyer pavement. He felt that he had earned his fee, and could not understand how anything in the whole transaction could be made the basis of attack.

Garfield's defence was evidently satisfactory to a majority of his constituents, for in August he was renominated by a vote of 100 to 34, and in October, during one of the most severe panics that the country had known and in a year in which the Democrats gained the control of the House that they were destined to retain unbroken for the next six years, Garfield was reëlected by a small but secure majority against two opponents. As James Ford Rhodes has remarked, he had won his case before intelligent juries. But the margin was narrow, for a majority of almost eleven thousand in 1872 was now reduced to less than three thousand. It was especially significant that the district gave its usual majority to the Republican candidate for Secretary of

State over his Democratic opponent. More than ever it was peculiarly fortunate that James A. Garfield came from the Nineteenth Congressional District of Ohio.[1]

No one can read the contemporary letters and speeches of Garfield at this time without feeling that he had entered into the service of the De Golyer Company without a sense of danger, just as he might have accepted a retainer from any client who had no stake in the government. His surprise at the charges, his indignation at having his name connected with possible bribery, his eagerness to show that he had worked hard and had earned his fee were all quite too convincing to be feigned. But the danger, as the event was to show, had been present none the less, and was to bring to Garfield humiliation only less than that of the Credit Mobilier affair. In the long run the result of the discussion was to help to create new and sterner

[1] The charges against Garfield had undoubtedly reduced his popularity. The official records in the Office of the Secretary of State of Ohio give the following figures: In 1872, Garfield, R., 19189; Sutliff, D., 8254; in 1874, Garfield, 12591; Woods, 6245; Hurlburt, 3427. The vote for Secretary of State in the same years was: 1872, Wikoff, R., 19202; Wiley, D., 8313; in 1874, Wikoff, 15483; Bell, 6824.

In Garfield's campaign for reëlection the most notable incidents were an elaborate speech at Warren, Sept. 19, 1874, in which he discussed the various charges against him (*Republican Campaign Documents*, 1880, No. 7), and the circulation of a special edition of the New York *Sun*, Sept. 26, 1874, with 13 columns devoted to a bitter attack on Garfield. In the closing days of the campaign Garfield had the aid of Senator John Sherman who at Warren, on October 10, paid a generous tribute to his character and services (John Sherman, *Recollections*, Vol. I, p. 479). The motives behind Dana's attacks are discussed by T. C. Smith (*op. cit.,*) Vol. I, pp. 575, 576.

The case against Garfield may be followed in the New York *Sun* which published the following articles and editorials: Sept. 19, 1874, "Opposition to Garfield"; Sept. 24, 1874, "The Truth on Garfield"; Sept. 25, 1874, "It Was Garfield Himself"; Sept. 26, 1874 (Extra), "Mr. Garfield's Congressional Record," discussing Garfield's connection with "the Sanborn Contracts, the Credit Mobilier Corruption, the Back-Pay and Salary Steal, The Five Thousand Dollar Steal, the Washington Ring, the Landaulets, the Indian Ring, the Poland Gag Law, and the Contingent Expenses of the House of Representatives"; Oct. 3, 1874, "Letting Up on Garfield"; and Oct. 8, 1874, "Garfield's Pavement Job." For friendly discussion during the campaign see Cleveland *Leader*, Sept. 7, 1874; Sept. 16, 1874; Sept. 22, 1874; Oct. 14, 1874.

standards of professional conduct for eminent public officials.

Three years after the test before "the intelligent jury" of which we have spoken, the topic of the De Golyer contract was again the subject of investigation before a congressional committee, this time not so friendly as the one that in 1874 had been headed by Allison and Wilson. In 1876 the House, now Democratic, appointed a committee of which the chairman was J. M. Glover of Missouri, with the special function of investigating the machinations of the so-called "Washington Real Estate Pool." Among other things discovered by the Glover committee, was some new evidence as to the activities of George R. Chittenden in 1872 in securing the paving contract for the De Golyer Company. Of a series of telegrams and letters that passed between Chittenden and one of the partners in the firm, the most important, dated at the Arlington, Washington, May 30, 1872, read as follows: "Tuesday afternoon, Parsons arrived. We shall get 100 and how much more is problematical. The influence of Gen. Garfield has been secured by yesterday's, last night's, and today's labors. He holds the purse strings of the United States, is chairman of the Committee on Appropriations, and the strongest man in Congress and with our friends; —my demand is today no less than 100,000 yards more, 200,000 in all. The connection is complete. I can hardly realize that we have Gen. Garfield with us. It is a rare success and very gratifying, as all the appropriations for the District must come through him." This letter at least indicated that the agent, Chittenden, was willing to make it appear to his employers that Garfield was in a position to grant favors which as a matter of fact did not fall within the jurisdiction of his committee. Other evidence tended to minimize the actual importance of Garfield's legal services. For it appeared that the Board of Public Works had given no consideration to the brief which Garfield had prepared. He had not appeared at all before the Board and had only mentioned the matter of the De Golyer contract once and that casually to Governor Shepherd, who was shown fairly conclusively to have the actual determination of the whole matter.[1]

On March 1, 1877, Garfield appeared voluntarily before the committee, described again his employment by Parsons and his own services to the company, much as he had done three years before, and denied so positively that he had any inkling of the corrupt purposes of Chittenden that the denial carried conviction even with the unfriendly chairman of the committee who volunteered the statement that the committee had no direct evidence to show that Garfield had been at all aware of what was going on behind the scenes.

The whole experience had undoubtedly proved mortifying and humiliating to Garfield and he looked back on his connection with the De Golyer Company with frank regret. Thus, referring to the purposes of Chittenden as revealed in his letter and to the testimony of C. E. Jenkins, one of the partners in the firm, to the same effect, Garfield made the following statement to the committee: "Now, I will say frankly to the committee that, if I had known or imagined that there was an intent such as this witness insinuates, on the part of anybody that my employment by a brother lawyer to prepare a brief on a perfectly legitimate question—a question of the relative merits of certain lawful patents—had any connection whatever, or any supposed connection in the mind of any man, with any public duties, I certainly would have taken no such engagement."

For some reason that is not apparent, the voluminous testimony before the Glover committee was not published at the

[1] The testimony before the Glover committee referring to Garfield may be found in A. G. Riddle, *Life of Garfield* (1880), pp. 268–275, and in *Democratic Political Manual* (1880), p. 199. For unfriendly comment, see N. Y. *Independent*, July 30, 1880.

time and aroused little public interest until later, when, in the
campaign of 1880, the Chittenden letter was made the basis of
new attacks on Garfield on the part first of the Chicago *Times*
and later of the New York *Independent* and other papers. In
the meantime the old charges of the bitter campaign of 1874
ceased to be subjects of discussion in Garfield's district and the
figures show that as early as 1876 and later in 1878 he was
again the hero of his constituents and the unrivaled leader of
his party.[1]

For a time in the summer of 1874 when Garfield had been
under especially severe fire, a movement had been initiated in
the House to displace him from his important position as chairman of the Committee on Appropriations, a step that seems to
have been seriously considered by Blaine as possibly necessary
to the welfare of the party. But Garfield's reëlection at a time
when so many Republicans lost their seats brought him back to
the meeting of the short session of Congress with increased
power and prestige. When the Committees were announced
Garfield was, of course, in his old place. In the next year, when
as the result of the elections of 1874 the House came into Democratic hands for the first time since the Civil War, Garfield
was placed on the Committee on Ways and Means, a position
which in days of Republican ascendancy he had so long desired, and in the following year when Blaine, his only possible
rival, accepted an election to the Senate, James A. Garfield became the acknowledged leader of the Republican minority in
the House of Representatives. Strangely enough, largely
through the unbroken solidarity of his district, his own mis-
fortunes and those of his party had changed defeat into victory

[1] The figures in the office of Secretary of State of Ohio for Garfield's last two
elections are as follows: In 1876, Garfield, 17,166; Hubbard, 7,553; in 1878,
Garfield, 20,012; Casement, 11,349. The vote in the same years for Secretary of
State, was, 1876, Barnes, 21,760; Bell, 10,106; 1878, Barnes, 16,911; Paige, 7,571.

and had made Garfield one of the most powerful figures in American politics. If he lived, there was little doubt that the man whose political death had been described with such brutal directness in 1873 was at the beginning and not the end of a still more brilliant career.

A PARTY lives largely on its memories; and Garfield's success in this field was due to the fact that he did not underestimate the importance of this idea. For a moment in 1872 he had hesitated in his party allegiance. The incident of the gold panic and "Black Friday" had weakened his confidence in the Republican Administration and the abrupt dismissal of his close friend, J. D. Cox, from his position as Secretary of the Interior in Grant's Cabinet because he was unable to support a certain peculiarly scandalous demand on the Treasury known as the "McGarrahan Claim" had still further alienated his sympathy. Garfield expressed admiration for the platform of the Independent Republicans in their stand for reform, and on the tariff his own moderate position had subjected him to suspicion and humiliation from party leaders. Accordingly, when the Democrats in the legislature of Ohio offered to make him their candidate for the Senate and to elect him with the aid of dissatisfied Republicans, Garfield was certainly tempted. Even when the offer had been declined and the matter was settled Garfield looked back on his decision with some regret. Thus, on January 11, 1872, he wrote to Hinsdale: "The Senatorship went as I expected it would. I may say to you, however, that the Democrats tendered to me their unanimous vote, and enough Republicans to elect with the help of the Democrats expressed themselves willing to bolt from the caucus nomination. It was, I confess, some temptation with some risk. A position obtained in that way would have been an independent one. But, on the whole, though the Democrats did not demand any conditions, I felt I would be considered as placed under obligations and therefore declined. What say you, was it wise or otherwise?" [1]

The decision that Garfield thus announced was unquestionably one of the two or three most important in his life. The possibilities and the danger of an independent position in politics such as had once been assumed by John Quincy Adams and of which David Davis and Carl Schurz among his immediate contemporaries were exponents had been definitely rejected and Garfield had chosen to work within the limits of the American party system. From this position, once taken, he never wavered. In the campaign of 1872, as we have seen, he supported the regular ticket largely on the ground of the great services that the Republican party had undoubtedly rendered to the country. Later, the storm through which he passed in 1874 proved to him more forcibly than anything else could have done the necessity for a powerful organization behind the individual. And though, as a party leader, he seemed to Blaine even after his death to have missed the commanding position of Douglas or of Clay because too often he gave consideration to the arguments of his opponents, Garfield was from that time a party man, sometimes seeking to change the views of his party associates, but always in the long run voting for the measures which the majority of the party demanded. And in the end, as we shall see, he had his reward.

Neither James A. Garfield nor for that matter any other political figure of his times was responsible for the characteristic qualities of the American party system. But under that system he must play his part; and for five years after 1875 when the Democrats came into their long lease of power in the House of Representatives and when Garfield yielded perforce to his Democratic rival and critic, W. S. Holman, the position of chairman of the Committee on Appropriations which he had held for the last four years of the Grant administration and where he had

[1] Garfield to Hinsdale, Jan. 11, 1872, J. M. Bundy, *op. cit.*, p. 207.

been in effective control of the expenditures of a great nation, Garfield became less a legislator and essentially a party chieftain. From that time he was again as in his youth, playing a more intricate game of chess in which his objectives were the capture of Democratic pawns and if possible the checkmating of a Democratic king. Both results were finally accomplished when in 1880 the Republicans gained again the control of all departments of the government that they had lost in part in the landslides of 1874. No one could have foreseen that Garfield himself was to be the chief personal beneficiary, as he was one of the two or three leading architects, of this result.

In 1875, with a Presidential election only a year away, both parties were intensely interested in American political history; but while the Democrats were anxious to concentrate on the last ten years and to talk about carpetbag governments, about Sanborn contracts, about the dishonesty and corruption of high officials of government during the Grant régime, the Republicans were equally anxious to go further back to the time when their party was young and when it had been justly called the party of the Union. To Blaine and to his successor Garfield, it seemed clear that, if the light could be concentrated at the right place, success which the recent elections had made at least doubtful might yet be snatched from the jaws of defeat. Hence the lurid eloquence of "the era of the bloody shirt" which Garfield inaugurated in his reply to Hill and used again in answer to the more astute L. Q. C. Lamar. So important did these two speeches seem at the time, however cold they may leave us now, that even as late as 1880 one campaign biographer devoted a full third of his space to these minor incidents in a significant career; and both speeches were deemed worthy of a place in Garfield's published works to the exclusion of others that today might seem more pertinent.

One of the first acts of the now victorious Democrats was to introduce a general amnesty bill, relieving former Confederates from the disabilities defined in the Fourteenth Amendment. On January 10th, 1876, in a bitter speech obviously intended to trap the new Southern members into unguarded statements that could be used against the Democrats, Blaine moved to make a long list of exceptions, mentioning especially Jefferson Davis by name. The plot had the desired effect, for B. H. Hill of Georgia answered with equal bitterness. If Jefferson Davis had been guilty of a crime, then so too had every Southern man who had fought under the stars and bars; and if he was unworthy of citizenship, no other Southern man could claim a higher right. Two days later, Garfield rose to make the principal reply. He expressed regret at the course of the debate, but opposed amnesty, not because Jefferson Davis had been the President of the Confederate States of America, but because while he was President he was responsible for the suffering of the Union prisoners at Andersonville. These sufferings Garfield proceeded to describe in vivid language but with the artistic quality of dramatic restraint. Garfield's attempt to place the whole blame for Andersonville on the shoulders of one man may not have had any permanent historical value, but it aroused deep feelings that many hoped had been forgotten, and, quoted generally by the newspapers and paraphrased by political speakers, it undoubtedly proved one of the most effective campaign documents of its time. It was at once apparent that the amnesty bill was dead, for many a Northern Democrat would hesitate to vote for a measure with which a now hated name was so closely connected. Garfield himself was not deceived by the apparent success of his speech, and he remarked sadly that a single address on which he had spent but a few hours in preparation had brought him more letters of praise than the laborious weeks and months that he had given to perfecting the budget of the nation as chairman of the House Committee on Appropriations.[1]

In March, 1876, the long list of scandals that had been the central theme of the Grant Administration came to a climax when the Secretary of War, W. W. Belknap, was charged with bribery and was allowed by the President to resign to prevent the more disagreeable alternative of certain impeachment. Garfield felt that this incident would be the last straw, and for the moment he gave up any hope of Republican victory in the Presidential campaign that was just about to begin. With what he called the "horror of the Belknap scandal" weighing on his spirits, he made a trip through New England, where he was agreeably surprised to find that the people were greatly interested in Jefferson Davis and his possible connection with Andersonville and not at all in Belknap, or the sufferings of Indians in the West under corrupt officers. All this Garfield ascribed, and no doubt correctly, to the sound strategy that had made of the revived memories of the war a useful sedative against present ills.[2] The great contest had aroused feelings that would not disappear during the generation that had lived through it.

The debate that had been commenced in January was continued in the summer. Congress remained in session, and on August 3rd, 1876, L. Q. C. Lamar of Mississippi, in a speech that had been carefully prepared and that was obviously intended as a campaign document, made an attack on the recent policies of the Republican party which even the most convinced partisans at once acknowledged to be peculiarly dangerous. Lamar was in a strong position, for he was generally recognized as one of the most moderate of the Southern leaders; more than

[1] For Garfield's reply to Hill, see *Cong. Record*, 44th Cong., 1st Sess., pp. 382–389. For letters of congratulation, see Garfield Papers, Letters Received, 1876, *passim*.

[2] Garfield, *Journal*, March 15–April 15, 1876.

once he had gone so far as to advocate negro suffrage as a necessary concomitant of freedom; and in 1874, he had taken his political life in his hands by delivering a highly dramatic eulogy on the dead Sumner. Now he touched lightly on the other scandals that had been accumulating, and devoted the heart of his speech to an almost unanswerable indictment of the practical effects of the famous Reconstruction policy, showing how the South had been cheated and swindled by carpetbag governments maintained by Federal soldiers. In all this Lamar avoided the slightest show of sectionalism, such as had marred Hill's speech of January, and assumed throughout that the cause of honest government was the cause of the whole reunited nation, North as well as South.

The Republicans turned at once to Garfield, who though taken by surprise, rose instantly to make the expected reply. A fortunate adjournment gave him one night for preparation, and on the next morning he made his answer. He had no intention, he said, to shield the Republican party from criticism; it had stumbled and blundered; it had had bad men in it. But it had been the party of the Union when many Democrats had been fighting for secession and it had given freedom to the negro when most Democrats were still friends of slavery. The Democrats had been the party of obstruction and could not be trusted with the destinies of the nation.

It is at once apparent, that, as so often happens in debate, the points made by the two speakers never met, for Garfield talked about one decade while Lamar was describing another. But Garfield had the advantage of rousing memories of a period that was even more vital to many Northern men than the present itself. Letters of congratulation flowed in, as had happened in January, and Garfield's reply to Lamar was printed in huge editions to care for an increasing demand.[1]

[1] For this incident see *Cong. Record*, 44th Cong., 1st Sess., pp. 5178–5185; E.

The two speeches taken together might well make a patriot weep; for while the Democratic leader had proved by one set of facts that the Republicans were not fit to govern, the Republican by another had shown that the Democrats were at least no better. And on that basis the case went to the jury.

The rival candidates were Rutherford B. Hayes of Ohio and Samuel J. Tilden of New York, each satisfactory to the reform element within his party. As so frequently happens in American Presidential elections, the results to the country were perhaps not likely to be widely different whichever of the two parties was successful; but the contest was none the less intense and at times even bitter. Garfield had now nothing to fear in his own district, where the prominence that he had won in his replies to Hill and to Lamar completely overshadowed the personal criticisms that he had met two years before. Accordingly he took a very active part in the general campaign. On election night, Garfield knew well enough that the result would be very close, and as the returns came in toward morning it was soon apparent that the Democrats would again control the next House of Representatives, that they had a clear majority in the popular vote for President, and that on the face of the electoral vote, they had elected their first President since the war.

Thus, two days after the election Garfield wrote to his old friend Fuller: "I spoke almost every day till the election; but it now appears that we are defeated by the combined power of rebellion, Catholicism, and whiskey, a trinity very hard to conquer. What the future of our country will be, no one can tell. The only safety we can rely on lies in the closeness of the vote, both on the Presidency and the House of Representatives. . . . If we had carried the House of Representatives, it was almost certain that I should have been elected Speaker. But of course

Mayes, *Life of L. Q. C. Lamar*, p. 288; and T. C. Smith, *Life and Letters of Garfield*, Vol. I, 607–610.

that has gone down in the general wreck." [1] A letter that furnishes an interesting precedent for the ill-starred remarks of the Reverend Dr. Burchard, eight years later!

With 185 electoral votes needed to elect, Tilden had 184 without dispute, and had apparently carried the three Southern States of Louisiana, South Carolina and Florida, which would, of course, give him a commanding lead. One vote in Oregon was also in doubt on technical grounds. No wonder that Garfield and other leading Republicans were despondent, for Hayes would need every vote that was in the least doubtful to win, where a single vote would suffice for Tilden. But these three Southern states, under the control of carpetbag governments, had so-called Returning Boards, with the right to canvass the returns, and when others were ready to despair, it occurred to the Secretary of the Republican National Committee, the astute W. E. Chandler, that if these Southern boards could be stiffened to do what he regarded as their clear duty, the day might yet be won and the country saved from the dread calamity of a Democratic Administration. Accordingly on November 10th, three days after the election and the day after his despairing letter to Fuller, Garfield received the following telegram: "I would be gratified if you would go to New Orleans to remain until the vote of Louisiana is counted. Governor Kellogg requests that reliable witnesses be sent to see that the canvass of the vote is a fair one. Answer U. S. Grant." [2] Four days later Garfield was in the Crescent city, a member of a group of politicians, Republican and Democratic, for the Democratic National Committee had taken similar steps, which the newspapers described as the "Visiting Statesmen."

In spite of the study that has been given to the question it is not probable that any one will ever know just how Louisiana

[1] C. E. Fuller, *Reminiscences of Garfield* (1887), p. 423.
[2] Garfield, *Journal,* Nov. 10, 1876.

would have voted in 1876 under normal conditions. The evidence, even when fully discounted, shows that there had been extensive frauds and instances of repeating on the Republican side and numerous cases where negroes were prevented from voting by intimidation and other illegal devices on the part of the Democrats. But the Returning Board was interested only in the latter cases, and there can be no question that the steps that they took to change a majority of six thousand for Tilden into one of two thousand for Hayes were dictated entirely by partisan considerations.[1] In the successful strategy as well as the detailed tactics of this astonishing result, Garfield bore a very prominent part.

Garfield made no pretence of approaching the problem in the impartial or judicial spirit. Thus on the morning after his arrival in New Orleans, and before, of course, he had had any opportunity to examine any evidence, we find him writing, "I do not see the outcome of the work here; but I believe that a fair count of the lawful vote of this State will give it to Hayes." [2] At all points the members of the Board were evidently inclined to follow the lead of the experienced politicians from the North who had come to assist them. The first problem was to provide a reasonable theory on which to work. The Democrats suggested that the vote actually cast should be counted. This would of course add to Tilden's already large majority, for it would eliminate fraudulent ballots, leaving the others untouched. In the letter given above, Garfield had already outlined the Republican position as finally dictated by Stanley Matthews to the Board:—"that not the votes actually cast but the votes legally cast, were the object and aim of the law." At the first sight the

---

[1] The chief authority on this question is P. L. Haworth, *The Hayes-Tilden Disputed Election of 1876.* The leading document is the Report of the Potter Committee, 1879, House Exec. Docs., 45th Cong., 3rd Sess., No. 140. See also H. J. Eckenrode, *Rutherford B. Hayes: Statesman of Reunion.*

[2] T. C. Smith, *Life and Letters of Garfield,* Vol I, p. 616.

intent of this proposition was not quite clear, but as interpreted in practice, it allowed the Board to throw out the vote of whole parishes, whenever in any such parish there was evidence of intimidation or illegal practices.

The parishes actually considered with special care were naturally enough those in which the Tilden majority had been especially heavy. The hearings of the Board were attended by five visiting Democrats and five Republicans, who were in theory mere witnesses to report to the President and the country. Actually, the functions of the Republicans were more significant; for the disputed parishes were divided among them, one of the most important, West Feliciana, being assigned to Garfield, who examined some forty-nine witnesses, and though he had to acknowledge that much of the testimony was hearsay, found, as he expected, enough evidence to warrant the cancellation of the whole vote of the parish. The briefs prepared by the visiting statesmen were then followed by the submissive Board. The final result was to give the vote of Louisiana to the Republicans by a small but entirely satisfactory plurality.

The year before, when the same Board had acted with equal effectiveness to count in a Republican legislature, Garfield had publicly called them a "graceless set of scamps." But after a series of dinners and other social contacts, Garfield reported that his opinion of the members of the Board was much higher than when he came, and in the end he joined, though somewhat reluctantly, in the report written by John Sherman that not only announced the result to the President but praised in the highest terms the integrity and the courage of the members of the Returning Board. The qualities of the members were too well known to make this last touch quite credible; and when he was taken to task for this unnecessary step by his watchful mentor Hinsdale, Garfield acknowledged that it went beyond his own judgment. To his wife he wrote somewhat naïvely: "I have no doubt I run the risk of being called a partisan for the position I shall take." [1]

The methods used in other doubtful States, though not quite so thorough, led to the same result, so that when Garfield reached Washington, the whole vote of Louisiana, Florida, South Carolina, and Oregon had been added to the Republican column, and it now stood Hayes, 185, Tilden 184. From that time, Garfield was inclined to let well enough alone and was opposed to any compromise that might endanger the result. In recent years, Congress had repeatedly rejected the electoral votes of various States, and in 1865 had gone so far as to adopt the Twenty-second Joint rule by which the vote of any State to which either of the two houses objected was to be rejected. The original purpose had been obviously to allow either house of a Congress then safely Republican to reject a vote that might imply recognition of some Southern State. The situation had now changed, for with the House Democratic, the certain rejection of at least one State would lead to the election of Tilden.

Garfield now argued, and no doubt correctly, that such a rule is only binding on a single Congress and does not become a permanent rule of action. He held that the counting of the electoral votes is a mere ministerial duty, placed by the Constitution in the hands of the Vice-President or in his absence in that of the President of the Senate; that the function of Congress is merely to assist at a solemn ceremony in the character of witnesses; that the vote should be counted precisely as it

[1] T. C. Smith, *op. cit.*, Vol. I, p. 618. When they were later examined by the Potter Committee some of the witnesses examined by Garfield broke down under cross-examination and retracted their previous statements. Since most of them were uneducated field hands, their credibility is almost impossible to determine. But there can be little doubt that Garfield was sincerely convinced of the truth of their stories. Garfield's activities in New Orleans, social and political, may be followed in detail in his *Journal*, Nov. 15, 1876, to Dec. 2, 1876.

came from the Governor of each State; and that any examination of the vote by Congress would throw every close election into inevitable dispute. For his position, Garfield cited the early precedents, established by those close to the adoption of the Constitution against those recently used which he showed to be full of grave dangers. It was a very able address and on the whole convincing. What Garfield overlooked, or at least did not mention, was the fact that if it was dangerous to examine and perhaps to reject the electoral vote of a State, it was also dangerous, as recent history had abundantly proved, to place in the hands of partisan Returning Boards, even when ably advised, the right to examine and to reject the returns from parishes and other sections of States in such a way as to throw the validity of the whole vote into serious doubt. If Garfield had argued in New Orleans as he now did so convincingly in Washington, his reputation for statesmanship in a great crisis would have been beyond the possibility of challenge. But his party position would have been correspondingly weaker.[1]

The Democrats were naturally highly incensed by what they regarded as the theft of three Southern States, and there was some wild talk of revolutionary measures to prevent the counting of the vote and later the inauguration of Hayes. But Garfield refused to believe in the seriousness of the crisis and adhered throughout to his original idea that if the Republicans would insist on the counting of the vote by O. E. Ferry of Michigan, at that time the President of the Senate, the whole dispute would end in bluster and talk. In that position he was strengthened by the attitude of the business interests of the country which were naturally anxious for a peaceful and prompt

---

[1] Garfield's speeches on the problem of the contested election are in *Cong. Record,* 44th Cong., 2nd Sess., pp. 146, 378–381, 674–677, 968, 970. As to Conkling's position Garfield wrote: "Conkling has had some doubts concerning the electoral count, but will probably give the benefit of his doubts to his party." (Garfield *Journal,* Dec. 29, 1876.)

solution; and, as compared with other plans that were suggested, Garfield's certainly had the advantage of simplicity.

The attitude of Hayes to the South, due at least in part to his education in Kenyon at a time when the little college in Ohio was largely attended by Southern students and strengthened by boyhood visits to a famous plantation in the South and by his lifelong friendship with Judge Bryan of Galveston, was known to be mild and had already been foreshadowed in his letter of acceptance.[1] Indeed this attitude had already brought to Hayes the dislike of certain carpetbag and stalwart representatives, notably the influential Senator Dorsey of Arkansas. Accordingly, Garfield shrewdly suspected from the beginning that in applying a policy that would make certain the election of Hayes he might count at least on the benevolent neutrality of certain Southern Democrats who were much more likely to be more deeply concerned about their own local and insistent problems than about mere party success. Thus, as early as December 13th, before the contest had fairly begun, we find Garfield writing to Hayes: "Let me say I do not think anybody should be the custodian of your policy, or have any power to commit or embarrass you in any way, but it would be a great help if, in some discreet way, those Southern men who are dissatisfied with Tilden and his more violent followers could know that the South was going to be treated with kind consideration by you." [2]

With the electoral votes on the face of the returns now safely for Hayes, with a Republican President in control of the army, it was soon apparent to many Democrats that their only real chance of success lay in some form of compromise. In this position they were joined by influential Republican Senators, notably Roscoe Conkling of New York, who regarded the crisis

[1] "The Bryan-Hayes Correspondence," *Southwestern Historical Quarterly,* 1926.
[2] Garfield to Hayes, Dec. 13, 1876. Garfield Papers.

with more misgivings than Garfield and who were perhaps luke-
warm in their support of Hayes himself. The result was the
creation of the Electoral Commission, to be made up of five
Senators, five Representatives, and five members of the Supreme Court, with virtual power to decide the issues at stake.
This device, as all other compromises, Garfield considered unnecessary, unconstitutional, and dangerous. Thus he wrote: "It
appears to me not only a surrender of a certainty for an uncertainty but it seems to me a cowardly mortgaging of the safety
of the future to secure an escape from a present danger. I doubt
whether we shall ever have another Presidential election by the
people in the old sense if this bill becomes law."

In his attitude of bitter opposition Garfield was able to lead
two-thirds of his Republican colleagues in the House. Accordingly, when against his will the bill was passed by the combination of Democrats and Stalwarts to which we have referred and
when the Electoral Commission was actually created, Garfield
was confronted by a difficult personal decision. Should he accept membership in a body which he regarded as unconstitutional, especially when he was so fully committed to all the
questions at issue as to preclude the slightest appearance of
judicial impartiality? His old friend Jeremiah Black called on
him and told him that to take the necessary oath of office in the
circumstances would be not only unethical but politically unwise; and, though Black was a Democrat, his personal affection
for Garfield was sufficiently evident to give his advice great
weight. But, though Garfield hesitated, he finally decided that
his duty to the party required him to serve and to do what he
could to insure the election of Hayes.

In the heated partisan atmosphere of the times, the unexpected resignation of Judge Davis, an independent in politics,
and the appointment of a Republican, Judge J. P. Bradley, as

the fifteenth member of the Commission with a casting vote among his seven Democratic and seven Republican colleagues, virtually decided the result. But for a time the views of Bradley were unknown, and the numerous speeches by counsel and then by the members of the commission itself in the doubtful Florida and Louisiana cases were evidently intended to influence the only member of the Commission whose decision could be regarded as in the least in doubt.

Though probably no assembly in American history has listened to so many able speeches in so short a length of time, most of these on each side were as alike as two peas. In opposing any examination of the returns, the Republicans were necessarily led into a States' Rights position that often sounded strangely in the mouths of men who had lately uttered different sentiments. This incongruity Garfield evidently recognized. Thus, in his opinion in the Louisiana case, in which he was especially interested, Garfield said: "I am no champion of State sovereignty, as that doctrine has sometimes been taught in our political history. But there are rights so clearly and so exclusively conferred upon the States, that to invade them is to break up the solid foundations of our institutions; and if one act can be more sovereign than another it may fairly be said that the most sovereign act that a state of this Union can perform is the act of choosing the men who shall cast its vote for President and Vice-President." A comparison of these remarks with others to which we have previously referred proves conclusively that in politics, if anywhere, circumstances alter cases.

By common consent, Bradley was allowed to deliver the last opinion. In each of the leading cases, his remarks for the first ten minutes left his final opinion in doubt, but when he reached the sentences in which he accepted fully what had now become the orthodox Republican position, there was an audible sigh of relief in the crowded room which indicated the tenseness of emotional anxiety with which his words had been awaited.[1]

When the vote had been cast, the time remaining until the necessary adjournment of Congress was very short and there was still a possibility that dissatisfied Democrats might prevent the completion of the count by a process of filibustering. In these circumstances, Garfield returned to the device that he had already advocated in his letter to Hayes in December and, on February 26th, by invitation of Stanley Matthews of Ohio, who was justly regarded as the personal representative of Hayes, he consented to appear in company with other leading Republicans at a conference with a group of Southern Democrats under the leadership of Henry Watterson. In this meeting, which came to be known as the "Wormley Conference," Matthews definitely promised that Hayes would recognize a Democratic government in Louisiana and would abstain from all prosecutions under the election laws. Garfield did not go quite so far, but he did state that "he had no doubt that the new Administration would deal justly and generously with the South." These assurances the Southern men evidently regarded as satisfactory, for they abstained from dangerous obstructive tactics.[2]

It is by no means certain that the engagements of the Wormley Conference were necessary; for the Democratic Speaker, Randall, though an eager partisan of Tilden, showed every indication of abiding in a sportsmanlike way by the bargain that had been involved in the creation of the Electoral Commission, and now that the Democrats had played their best card and lost, he used the powers of his position to prevent filibustering. The policy indicated would in all probability have been followed by Hayes in any case; but the Southern Congressmen had used the

[1] Proceedings of the Electoral Commission, *Cong. Rec.*, 44th Cong., 2nd Sess., Pt. 4. For Garfield's speech quoted above see page 242.
[2] T. C. Smith, *op. cit.*, Vol. I, p. 644.

occasion to secure definite promises that insured the turning of a very important page in American history. Thus on March 2nd, 1876, the last state was reached, the vote had been counted, and two days later Rutherford B. Hayes was President of the United States. In the process, from first to last, no one had borne a more prominent part than the Congressman from the Nineteenth Congressional District of Ohio.

During the first two years of Hayes's Administration the House was Democratic but, with a Republican Senate, partisan legislation was quite impossible. The chief legislative venture of those two years was the Bland-Allison Silver Purchase Act of 1878, a non-partisan measure of inflation providing for the coinage of a large number of silver dollars, which was passed against the views of Garfield and over a Presidential veto. In spite of strong opposition among most of the leaders of his party, Hayes, with great courage, applied a policy of pacification to the Southern States, promptly withdrawing the soldiers and refusing to prosecute individuals charged with violation of the election laws of 1870 and 1871. In this policy Hayes had the support of Garfield, who was regarded as the spokesman of the President in the House. For a time both men hoped that they had driven a wedge into the heart of the Democratic position and that they might even count on the aid of Southern Democrats in organizing the House of Representatives and in electing Garfield himself Speaker. Accordingly Hayes at the beginning of his term had persuaded Garfield to give up what seemed almost a certainty of election to the Senate and to continue to act as the representative of the Administration in Congress. But, though the Southern Congressmen were grateful, they were not grateful enough to become Republicans. As between Hayes and themselves there were few real differences of policy; but the decade of Reconstruction had drawn the lines of party very sharply and such boundaries had become increasingly difficult to cross.

Practical Republican politicians saw that the actual effect of Hayes's Southern policy, bold and full of imagination as it really was, would be at the outset to solidify the Southern opposition and to destroy completely the party in that region. For a time Hayes was assailed, especially by the leaders of his own party in the Senate, almost as bitterly and for precisely the same reasons that had led to the attempted impeachment of Andrew Johnson ten years before. The anger of these leaders was further increased when they found that Hayes had been quite sincere in his promises of Civil Service Reform and that he did not intend to make appointments contingent on services to the party. Even Garfield was greatly angered when the Secretary of the Interior, Carl Schurz, who more than any other man in America was completely devoted to the reform of the civil service, summarily removed one of his own friends, J. Q. Smith, against whose conduct of the Bureau of Indian Affairs serious complaints had been made. When the Democrats carried Ohio in the election of 1877, Garfield went to the President and told him frankly that the party was discouraged and divided and that he would have to consult Congressmen more freely in matters of appointments and change some of his ideas of the nature of public appointments. But with the steady obstinacy which characterized Hayes when his mind was made up, the President continued his two policies essentially unmodified, and Garfield wrote that he seemed to be entirely blind to the dangers and the criticisms that surrounded him. In the meantime Garfield barely prevented an open break with the President by refusing for six months to call a caucus where the rage of disappointed Congressmen would have made all their criticisms public.

It was soon evident that the President was doing for the first time since the end of the war precisely what the Democrats had been saying for ten years ought to be done and was continuing in these policies against the most bitter opposition of the leaders of his own party. It was a great Democratic opportunity; but, with almost incredible stupidity, instead of giving to the President the generous support which he so clearly deserved, and misled by their own apparent strength as revealed in the recent elections, the Democratic leaders of the House met the advances of the Administration by appointing a special committee under the chairmanship of Clarkson N. Potter which proceeded to take voluminous testimony on the disputed election of 1876 and especially as to the conduct of the returning boards in Florida and Louisiana. Such a step, seeming to challenge a title to the validity of which all the Republicans were so completely committed, not only caused a vague feeling of uneasiness among conservative men everywhere, but created an obvious basis of union for the shattered and discordant fragments of the party that had elected Hayes to the Presidency.

The Potter Committee discovered only what every one knew quite well already, that the members of the returning boards had been as graceless a set of scamps as had ever manipulated the politics of the smallest and most turbulent of South American republics; that these boards had been encouraged in their nefarious schemes by the presence of powerful Republican statesmen including James A. Garfield and John Sherman; and that without a single exception they had been rewarded by the gift of public office largely in the Treasury Department. On these points they wrote a rambling and very lengthy report which proved even as a campaign document to be entirely ineffective.[1] The investigation was not only a tactical blunder but a boomerang, for the points which the majority of the committee had discovered, while amply proved, were entirely

[1] *Potter Committee Report:* House Exec. Docs., 45th Cong., 3rd Sess., No. 140.

familiar to the public, while the Republican members had the good fortune to find something entirely new and unsuspected— a series of cipher telegrams from persons very close to the Democratic candidate which seemed to show that some of the Democratic leaders had been engaged in fighting fire with fire and had been quite as willing to use bribery as the Republicans were ready to use influence. The discovery of the cipher telegrams from Gramercy Park, New York, offering money to various politicians in the contested states almost at once destroyed the usefulness of the election of 1876 as a campaign issue. For the first time since the inauguration of Hayes, the two wings of the Republican party had found a common topic of conversation.[1]

Again as in 1874 and 1876, the Democrats carried the congressional elections of 1878, though by reduced majorities, and after the 4th of March, 1879, would be for the first time in many years in control of both the House of Representatives and also of the Senate. For a long time the Democrats had been making ineffective efforts to secure the repeal of the election laws that had been a leading part of the reconstruction program of the Republicans. For the first time these laws were no longer of great practical importance, for Hayes had in fact withdrawn the soldiers on whom their enforcement depended. It seems, accordingly, that the Democrats might now have left well enough alone. But the political opportunity could not be overlooked, for if these laws were repealed and Hayes signed the bills, the breach in the Republican party would be made irreparable, while if he vetoed laws that were calculated to put his own policy on the statute books, the Democrats would have a campaign topic that might well replace the lost issue of the disputed election. In the absence of serious legislative efforts

[1] For the use made of the cipher despatches, see Cortissoz, *Life of Whitelaw Reid,* Vol. I, pp. 392–424.

to deal with living problems, the work of Congress had become a game in which each of the two parties was seeking to place the other in a hole for the next election; and it was in his contest with the Democrats as to the election laws that Garfield was to display his capacity as a parliamentary leader.[1]

When Congress met for the short session at the close of the Forty-fifth Congress in December, 1878, the Democrats opened their attack on three provisions of the election laws to which they especially objected. By the first, passed in 1865, the President was authorized to use the army to keep the peace at the polls; by the second, all jurors in federal courts were required to take a test oath to the effect that they had not aided the rebellion, thus excluding the great majority of Southern white men from service on such juries; and by the third, and by far the most important, the federal marshals, in late years, of course always Republican politicians, were empowered to appoint as many deputies as they desired to prevent bribery, intimidation, and other offences against the laws. The Democratic speakers maintained with much force that in close and doubtful districts these laws placed the elections within the control of the party in power, and that the elastic provisions of the laws as to the marshals, especially, created just at election time an indefinite number of jobs within the gift of the leading Republican officer of every district. They were able to show conclusively that the chief importance of these laws was not their service in protecting negro suffrage in the South as the people imagined, but their use in the large cities where the number of deputies required seemed to vary directly with the closeness of the district. From the Democratic point of view, elections even for Congress should be left, as they had been for

[1] Garfield's position on these questions has been followed in his *Journal*, 1877–1879. For Garfield's virtual authorship of Hayes's veto messages, see especially, *Journal*, March 6, 1879.

the most part before the war, to the control and jurisdiction of
the individual States. On these points the Democrats North
and South were not only entirely agreed, but the Republicans
were hopelessly divided, with many determined not to yield
laws on which they still counted for appointments for faithful
workers, and others, including Garfield and the President, who
were certain to sympathise fundamentally with the Democratic
position. If politics is a game, the Democrats had come honestly
enough on a card that seemed to be an ace. No one saw more
clearly than Garfield that the President must veto such repeals to save his party, but must base his veto on considerations
that would not play into Democratic hands.

Right here, in their eagerness, the Democrats gave him substantial aid. Unwilling to wait until the next year, when they
would have control of both houses of Congress, after a caucus
that committed the members of the party to unity, they added
the three repeals to the leading appropriation bills of the year,
and when the Republican Senate refused to concur, risked the
unpopular necessity of a special session of Congress. Left without the money essential for the conduct of the government,
President Hayes called the new Congress in the exciting and
long remembered special session of 1879. In the events that
followed, more than any other member of Congress in either
house, James A. Garfield played a leading rôle.

The first thing was to make sure of the President, for rumors were current that when the Democrats passed their repeals through both houses, as they were now in a position to do,
the President would sign the bills, thus leaving the Republicans in a ridiculous position. On March 6th, Garfield called
on the President and urged him to support the party position.
When Congress met on March 18th, Secretary Evarts was
known to be opposed to the election laws and wanted to give
them up. This increased Garfield's anxiety and he laid his plans

with care. Before summoning a caucus, he called again on the President, had a confidential conversation with him, received definite assurances that he would veto the repeal, and then called a caucus, which agreed on a program that he outlined. The line of strategy was thus definitely established with the greatest care, even as to the details of the veto measure, before the first gun was fired. On March 28th, 1879, President Hayes called on Garfield when he was at breakfast, and read to him the proposed veto measure on laws that had not yet been passed or even debated and made sure that the lines of his veto were in harmony with the speech that Garfield intended to deliver the next day. On March 29th Garfield set the tone of the debate in a speech entitled, "The Attempted Revolution in Congress." [1]

On the merits of the proposals the Democrats were in a strong position, for the laws as to jurors, as to the army at the polls, and to a smaller extent as to the remarkable powers of marshals were now generally acknowledged by all but the strictest sect of Republicans to be anachronisms at best and dangerous anachronisms at that. But Garfield was able to show that under the Presidential system of Government a law must pass each of the two houses of Congress and receive the signature of the President. To attach such laws as riders to the essential appropriations tended to deprive the President of the element of free consent that is necessary to the maintenance of the central feature of the American as distinguished from parliamentary forms of government. Garfield was thus appealing to the traditional constitutional conservatism of the American people: "It makes no difference, Mr. Chairman, what the issue is. If it were the simplest and most inoffensive proposition in the world, yet if you demand, as a measure of coercion, that it shall be adopted against the free consent prescribed in the Con-

[1] Garfield *Journal*, March 28, March 29, 1879.

stitution, every fair-minded man in America is bound to resist you as much as though his own life depended on his resistance. Let it be understood that I am not arguing the merits of any one of the three amendments. I am discussing the proposed method of legislation; and I declare that it is against the Constitution of our country. It is revolutionary to the core and is destructive of the fundamental principle of American liberty, the free consent of all the powers that unite to make laws. In opening this debate, I challenge all comers to show a single instance in our history where this consent has been thus coerced. This is the great, the paramount issue, which dwarfs all others into insignificance." [1]

This passage, as a mere example of the development of Garfield's debating style, is noteworthy; but his speech was more than clever debating, for it raised details to the dignity of a principle. At the same time it gave all elements of the party, from Blaine and Conkling who believed fiercely in the election laws as essential devices of practical politics, to the President who no longer desired to invoke their aid for party purposes at least in the South, common ground on which they might all stand together. But Garfield's insistence on the revolutionary character of legislative riders on appropriation bills had all the merits of an original discovery. For his challenge was immediately accepted by the Democrats, who were soon able to fill pages of the *Congresssional Record* with numerous examples of similar riders attached to such bills in recent years and all apparently for the same purpose, to compel a reluctant President to sign measures which standing alone he would have promptly vetoed. Thus in 1865, Garfield himself and Henry Winter Davis had used a rider just as the Democrats were doing now. At first sight such examples were damaging to the case that Garfield had stated in his speech of March 29th. President

[1] Hinsdale, Vol. II, pp. 655–678.

Hinsdale, who knew a great deal of American history, wrote with his usual frankness to Garfield criticising him for using the word "revolution" which seemed to him to be employed in a loose, stump-speaking sense, when in the light of recent examples no revolution was really implied. Garfield was hard put to it to reply to his friend's criticisms.[1] But the whole debate played still further into the hands of Garfield, for though he was compelled in later speeches to recede from a part of his position, the Republican newspapers and the public had come to see that what had been a vicious practice when Congress and the President were of the same party was far more dangerous in a Constitutional sense when Congress was of one party and the President of another. Further, the very list of examples of numerous riders in the heydey of Republican supremacy, when published by the Democrats, showed conclusively how often the President had been right and how often Congress had been wrong. The rider was neither revolutionary nor even unusual, but it was absolutely indefensible, and Garfield would have been in a stronger logical though not partisan position if he had said so frankly at the beginning.

Garfield had accomplished his chief purpose, for when the bills accompanied by riders were passed by both houses, on May 29th, in fulfilment of his promise to Garfield two months before and in precisely the terms that had then been agreed upon, they were promptly vetoed by the President. No incident in American history proves more conclusively the legislative power of the President nor the attachment of the people to the right of veto; for, unable to pass the appropriation bills over the veto and faced with a hopeless impasse in which they were generally blamed for holding up the business of government

[1] Garfield to Hinsdale, May 20, 1879. Garfield Papers. It is worth noting, in passing, that this letter seems to be the first in which Garfield used a typewriter. The next year he saw his first electric light.

for partisan purposes, the Democrats receded from their position, allowing the general appropriation bill to go through without any repeal of the hated election laws and to receive the signature of President Hayes on June 19th, 1879. Thurman's pleas for redress of grievances before supplies were granted proved to be based on English rather than American precedents. Congress, however, as was clearly its right, failed to appropriate any money for the transportation of troops to the polls or for the payment of deputies in the next fiscal year. A separate bill relieving jurors from the necessity of the test oath was carried through both houses with the aid of Garfield, and with these small gains the Democrats were compelled to rest content. The result had not been a clean-cut victory for either side; for the election laws, as Blaine pointed out, had been weakened almost beyond repair. But the Democratic hopes of repeal, largely through the political strategy of the Republican leader in the House, had been at least for the moment defeated, and, above all, a party that had seemed hopelessly divided had now regained much of its fighting solidarity. Garfield little realised that he himself was to be the chief personal beneficiary of this outcome.

The results of the new situation, with prosperity returning, with resumption of specie payments easily inaugurated, and with absence of open divisions in the party, were at once apparent, for in the elections of 1879 the Republicans were generally successful and in Ohio elected their candidate for governor and won the control of both houses of the legislature that they had lost two years before. Garfield was now a candidate for the Senate and the next session of Congress was destined to be his last. The Democrats again attacked the election laws, and under the able leadership of Senator Allen G. Thurman whose term was now coming to an end, concentrated their fire upon the partisan methods used for appointing marshals and their deputies. Thus to a very large extent, the central figures in the debate were James A. Garfield in the House and Allen G. Thurman in the Senate, close personal friends, for Garfield had never forgotten that Thurman had refused to join in the hue and cry against him in 1874. In that year they had been before the legislature of Ohio for the Senatorial position occupied by the "old Roman," as his friends described Thurman, and both were, as it happened, at the close of their congressional careers.

Thurman's attack was devastating, for the election laws of 1870 and 1871 had been defended on a thousand hustings as the essential means for the protection of the negro. How hollow this pretence had now become Thurman pointed out from the figures. Thus in 1876, the federal government had spent $285,-921.27 for the payment of five thousand supervisors and more than eleven thousand marshals and deputy marshals, whose chief duty was to prevent the intimidation of voters. Of this sum $48,719.86 was spent in the South, and the rest, with the great majority of the officers, was assigned to close northern states, notably New York. In 1878, of a total of $222,714.22 only $18,241.06 was spent in the South, more than half of the remainder being again assigned to the closest districts in New York alone. No Republican speaker attempted to deny that the appropriation of Congress for the enforcement of the election laws had become to all intents and purposes an addition to the Republican campaign chest.

Garfield could not fail to realise the weight of Thurman's objections to the election laws in their existing form; he considered the position of many of his party associates "unreasonable and dangerous," but he was the titular leader of the minority, and the right of marshals to appoint their deputies had become a test of party regularity, and the question was one on which the Republicans could not afford to divide. Fortunately for Garfield, the Supreme Court in a recent decision, *ex parte Siebold,* had declared the laws constitutional, upholding the right of the national government to protect congressional elections. This point was immediately seized by the Republican floor leader, who in an elaborate speech on March 17th, 1880, argued at great length the constitutional question involved.[1] All of this was evidently beside the point, for the question was not whether the presence of partisan marshals at the elections was constitutional, but whether it was fair and wise. Evidently believing that the objections of the Democrats to the election laws were so deep-seated that they would accept no substitute, however reasonable, Garfield offered to vote for a change by which the deputies in control of elections should be appointed by the courts in equal numbers from both parties.

Republicans who did not understand Garfield's strategy attacked him as unsound, but his subsequent conduct can only be explained on the theory that he never intended to have his offer accepted. The Democrats, however, were, for once, shrewd enough to see that to reject Garfield's offer would be to make themselves responsible for the most objectionable feature of the election laws and to deprive themselves of a most useful subject for discussion in the coming presidential campaign. Accordingly, although any form of federal control of elections was as obnoxious to extreme Democrats as it was essential to Stalwart Republicans, the Democrats promptly took Garfield at his word and in the form of a rider to an appropriation bill passed the very measure that he had proposed. Garfield voted against the proposal for bi-partisan control of elections not on its merits but because it came in the form of a rider; and so far, he was consistent. But the Democrats were not to be put off so easily, and Bayard of Delaware introduced in the Senate a

[1]For Garfield's speech and offer of March 17, see *Cong. Record,* 46th Congress, 2nd Sess., pp. 1638–1640.

bill which copied almost word for word the terms of Garfield's offer. The Bayard bill, as an independent measure, was passed on May 20th, when Garfield was absent; but whether he had now changed his mind or whether as is more probable the offer had only been intended to put the Democrats in a hole, he now went to President Hayes and urged the veto of his own bill! The reluctant veto of Hayes was suggested by Garfield himself, and thus both men put themselves on record against ideas of which there can be very little doubt that they really approved. So far did the needs of regularity carry the leaders of a great party in the eighties. The election laws were to remain on the statute books for many years.[1]

The incident of the election laws, so characteristic of the almost inevitable conflict between the personal views of Garfield and the necessities of his party position, and which also appeared more than once on larger questions of reconstruction, the tariff, and other problems of his times, brought to a close Garfield's long and important career as a leader of the House of Representatives during eighteen vital and eventful years in the history of the nation. The legislature of Ohio, now Republican again, had elected him to the Senate of the United States in succession to the venerable Allen G. Thurman.

For a time there had been signs of opposition from other Republican claimants, but through the influence of John Sherman, who was now a candidate for the Presidency, rival candidates had withdrawn and Garfield had been chosen by the unanimous vote of his party associates in the Ohio legislature.

---

[1] Hayes's veto, dated June 15th, 1880, follows almost exactly the lines of Garfield's speech of March 17th. For the influence of Garfield on Hayes, see Smith, *op. cit.,* Vol. II, p. 696. For the veto message, see Richardson, *Messages and Papers of the Presidents,* Vol. VII, pp. 592–598. Smith, in his discussion, assumes that there was a real difference between Garfield's offer and the Bayard bill as finally passed, but this view is not sustained by a comparison of the two documents.

Thus on Jan. 7th, 1880, the day after Garfield's selection, ex-Governor William Dennison, Garfield's old friend, who had been his most dangerous rival in the recent contest, wrote to Sherman that he had withdrawn and supported Garfield because such a step would be sure to strengthen Sherman's chances for the Presidential nomination. On the same day C. W. Moulton wrote to Sherman: "The unanimous nomination of Garfield was caused by a break in the Hamilton County delegation, and two of those who broke (out of three) declined to vote for Matthews or Taft because they thought doing so would look like opposing you." J. W. Tyler reported that just before the meeting of the legislature he had had an interview with Garfield, who had promised that if Sherman's friends supported him for the Senatorship, he would do what he could for Sherman: "This I was enabled to let some of your friends know in a prudent way, and it greatly increased his strength." [1]

After Garfield's election, Sherman's friends were greatly disturbed because Garfield failed to come out in an open letter endorsing the candidacy of John Sherman against his two rivals, Blaine and Grant. Some of them began to wonder whether back of Garfield's silence were concealed Presidential ambitions of his own. Accordingly on January 20th one of Sherman's managers, R. A. Horr, wrote a carefully considered letter to Garfield in which he asked him definitely to come out for Sherman or to indicate his preference. There can be no doubt that Garfield would greatly have preferred to take a less prominent position in Sherman's campaign, and there are many indications that, in spite of a lingering distrust for Blaine, Garfield's

[1] Sherman Papers, Library of Congress—especially Tyler to Sherman, Jan. 15, 1880. In sending friends to Columbus to watch his interests, Garfield wrote:— "My orders are no liquor—no promises of office or any other thing. . . . I want the Senatorship with absolute freedom or not at all." Then he quotes Canning: 'My road must be through character to power.' Garfield *Journal*, Jan. 5, 1880.

personal choice would have come from Maine and not from Ohio. But his promises before the Senatorial election had already carried him too far, and on January 26th, Garfield came out openly for Sherman. In February he consented to enter into the active contest for Sherman delegates; and, though still reluctant, he agreed in April to attend the national nominating convention as a delegate at large; in May he went a step further and promised to become the spokesman of the Sherman forces on the floor of the convention and to place the favorite son of Ohio in nomination for the Presidency of the United States. When on May 25th, 1880, Garfield left Washington on his way to Chicago, little as he probably suspected it, his days of legislative leadership were over and when he returned it would be in highly changed circumstances and in the occupancy of a higher position.[1]

Garfield's eighteen years in the House of Representatives had already become a part of history. On some questions of great importance he had certainly drifted with the tide rather than helped to control the destiny of the nation. The high points of his legislative career had been, first, the effective aid he had brought as a young man in 1864 to the creation of a real national army; second, his consistent and courageous stand for the principle of what he called honest money, a campaign that in its first stage had just come to a glorious conclusion. Somewhat less dramatic were his four years as Chairman of the Committee on Appropriations from 1871–1875, at a time when that committee controlled all the expenditures of the government. These expenditures were soon to be parcelled out among a whole group of committees inaugurating an era of wasteful

[1] For Garfield's relations to Sherman see Sherman Papers, Library of Congress, Horr to Garfield, Jan. 20th, 1880; Thorp to Sherman, March 20th, 1880; Dennison to Sherman, March 23, 1880; Smith, *Life and Letters of Garfield,* Vol. II, pp. 943–953; and Sherman, *Recollections,* Vol. II, p. 771.

expenditures without responsibility in the hands of any one. But three successive chairmen of the new committee, Thaddeus Stevens of Pennsylvania, James A. Garfield of Ohio, and W. S. Holman of Indiana, were in their way virtually the Chancellors of the American Exchequer and wielded power second to that of no man in the government. Thus Garfield had spent sums of three hundred millions a year without a breath of scandal, and except in the matter of the salaries of Congressmen, without either public criticism or for that matter recognition of the labors and anxieties of a chairman whose conduct of the appropriation bills, often in the closing days of a session chiefly devoted to other things, was essential to the continued working of the government itself.[1] Finally, after the Democrats came into majority control of the House in 1875, Garfield was first one of the leaders of his party and in a short time the recognized spokesman of a Republican President. In his position as a leader of the minority he laid the strategy in its chief lines which brought Hayes to the Presidency in 1876; and then without rising, it must be confessed, to any great heights of constructive statesmanship, for which perhaps the times were not ripe, he led his party with such success that divergent wings remained at least outwardly harmonious and capable of winning again and under his own candidacy still another of a long series of dramatic triumphs. Such a man, with all his mistakes, in other countries might even be compared to Thiers and Guizot, or to Peel, Palmerston, and Bright; but in America, where legislative leadership is obscured by the often deceptive brilliancy of the Presidency, James A. Garfield was to be remembered chiefly because for a few short months in the spring and

---

[1] Garfield was an early advocate of a national budget:—J. A. Garfield: "National Appropriations and Misappropriations," *N. Am. Review* (1879): Vol. 128, p. 572.

summer of the next year he was President of the United States. With the most significant period of his life really over, he now entered on the final and most dramatic of his astonishing adventures.

Two theories of the Chicago convention of 1880 that nominated James A. Garfield to the Presidency of the United States have been widely held. According to the first, the nomination came to Garfield as a complete surprise, the work of a convention weary with fruitless balloting; while, in the opinion of others, Garfield was from the beginning a secret candidate, and thus gained the nomination by treachery to John Sherman. In the light of contemporary documents, however, neither theory seems to be tenable, and, as so often, the truth lies half way between.

As early as 1875, the name of Garfield had been prominently mentioned as a Presidential possibility; but Garfield had not taken these suggestions seriously. He was only forty-four years old and had, as he wrote, too much good work in him to be willing to consider the ending of his active life by the Presidency; he had seen the unhappiness that unrealised Presidential ambitions had brought to other men, and he did not believe that any man would ever again become President through an avowed candidacy.

As Hayes's Administration came to a close, the first man to suggest the Presidency to Garfield seems to have been Hayes himself, who on various occasions in 1878 and 1879 talked to Garfield about the matter and told him that he might reach the White House, much as he had done himself, as a compromise candidate. There are no indications that Garfield allowed his peace of mind to be disturbed; but if such suggestions did not enter into his calculations, the case was different with the Secretary of the Treasury, John Sherman, also from Ohio, and an active and eager candidate, who saw at once that Garfield might become a dangerous rival, dividing the Ohio delegation and thus destroying any chances for either one. Accordingly, as early as May 19th, 1879, Sherman sent a confidential friend to Garfield to ask him definitely not to contest the Presidential support of Ohio with Sherman. Garfield's best chance, he said was as a compromise candidate, and if Sherman had a solid delegation, it could be swung to Garfield if necessary. Again Garfield refused to commit himself, and about this time wrote to an eager Ohio supporter that while he was not indifferent to the good opinion of men who thought him fit for a high place, he did not believe that anything would come of it other than some general talk. Later, as we have seen, Garfield accepted the aid of Sherman in the matter of the Senatorship, promising to "do what he could for him" in the contest for the Presidential nomination. But even after Garfield had announced his support of Sherman in his open letter in January, Sherman was still anxious and, on February 18th, 1880, told Garfield definitely that he preferred him to any other man, and that if he could not be nominated, he was willing to transfer his entire strength to Garfield. It was on this basis that Garfield became a delegate at large from Ohio and consented to go to Chicago, where, as we shall see, he gave earnest support to the interests of Sherman; and, when the time came, and his own nomination was clearly hopeless, Sherman turned his strength to Garfield just as he had promised. There is every indication that both men acted in absolute good faith, and from the beginning, Sherman at least was not blind to the possibilities of the situation.[1]

In the meantime other men beside Hayes and Sherman were thinking about Garfield. Thus on February 4th, Governor

[1] This account is based on Garfield's *Journal*, Library of Congress, especially, July 23, 1878; Feb. 5, 1879; May 26, 1879; Nov. 23, 1879; and Feb. 18, 1880; and on the Sherman Papers, Library of Congress. Sherman was informed as early as May 18, 1880, that Indiana preferred a compromise candidate: Williams to Sherman, Sherman Papers.

T. L. Pound of Wisconsin came to Garfield and told him that he did not believe that Grant, Blaine, or Sherman could be elected if nominated; that his State wanted Garfield; and strongly urged Garfield not to commit himself to Sherman in such a way as to make his nomination impossible. To these overtures Garfield replied, with evident caution, that he did not take the possibility of his own nomination seriously, and he would act in perfect good faith towards Sherman and do nothing that would interfere with his chances for success; but that "within the limitations mentioned," he would consider seriously such suggestions as Pound had made.

Similarly, on February 18th, Wharton Barker of Philadelphia had an interview with Garfield in which he told him that a strong group of Pennsylvania Republicans was opposed to the three leading candidates and that he was perfecting an organisation to nominate Garfield. Again Garfield replied with caution as he had to Pound; but Barker was not discouraged and went back to Philadelphia to work actively for the nomination of Garfield. On April 24th, accompanied by Wayne McVeagh, later Attorney General in Garfield's cabinet, Barker was back in Washington ready to report on the results of his activities. The two men called on President Hayes and on Garfield, and told Garfield that although Senator Don Cameron had promised the solid vote of Pennsylvania to Grant, Barker had found nineteen delegates who were committed to disregarding their instructions. At first they would probably vote for Blaine, but in the long run these votes would come at the proper time to Garfield.[1]

According to Barker, Garfield made no objection to his plans, and after a long interview the two men parted, Barker, at least, feeling that they had come to a satisfactory understanding. But early the next morning, before Barker had had breakfast, Gar-

[1] Garfield *Journal*, Feb. 4, 1880; Feb. 18, 1880.

field appeared again at his hotel, and to Barker's consternation, announced: "You must get another candidate for President. John Sherman has been here this morning. He called on the way from the railroad station to his home. He wanted me to go to the convention as a delegate from Ohio and place him in nomination for the Presidency. I have yielded to his earnest request." Barker at once suspected that Sherman had learned in Philadelphia of his own activities and that he had come to Garfield to get him out of the way. But Garfield's journey to Chicago fitted in with his plans as they did with Sherman's. Accordingly he replied: "I shall go ahead as if nothing had happened. So far as you are concerned, do as you have promised to do. Be loyal to Sherman before and in the convention, and your friends will do far more for you than you could do for yourself." [1]

Even now, Garfield did not regard his own nomination as probable, but he encouraged Barker for much the same reason that he supported Sherman, whom he never expected to win in the convention, because such movements would make the task of Conkling in securing a third nomination for Grant increasingly difficult. Thus on May 9th, Garfield wrote to Barker: "If the independent delegates to Chicago from Pennsylvania and New York hold on, it is the end of the third term movement." In Garfield's judgment, the great danger to the Republican party was the nomination of Grant who was almost certain to be defeated.

One week before the opening of the convention, Barker, in

[1] Wharton Barker, "The Secret History of Garfield's Nomination," *Pearson's Magazine,* May, 1916. These reminiscences, written in 1912, must be accepted with caution. Barker undoubtedly overemphasized the importance of his own activities, for others, especially Pound of Wisconsin, Streight of Indiana, and Sheldon of Ohio, were working quite openly for Garfield's nomination. But the account of the three interviews in Garfield's contemporary *Journal* is similar to that given above: see entries of Feb. 18, 1880; April 24, 1880; April 25, 1880.

charge of the Garfield movement, reached Chicago. He had laid his plans with care. In the circumstances, it would never do to place Garfield in formal nomination which would compel him as the leader of the Sherman forces to forbid the use of his name, but Barker arranged with a single delegate, W. A. M. Grier of Pennsylvania, to vote for Garfield on the first or second ballot and to keep his name before the convention by continuing to vote for him.[1] At the decisive moment, Governor Pound had promised to transfer the vote of Wisconsin from Blaine to Garfield. Since Wisconsin came at the end of the list of States, the change would be peculiarly emphatic. On the next ballot Indiana was to change to Garfield also, and Barker hoped that with these two changes the necessary stampede would follow. If Sherman could be persuaded to withdraw in favor of Garfield, the result would be almost certain.

Barker also planned to secure an emphatic and regular recognition of Garfield by the vast audience and, as soon as possible, by the delegates. At strategic points in the gallery and on the floor Barker placed reliable groups of men whose business it was to cheer when Garfield entered the hall or when he rose to speak. Barker himself took a prominent place on the platform where he could direct these activities. It is not probable that Garfield was told of these detailed arrangements, but there is no question that they worked admirably and helped to add to the prestige which Garfield soon won by his own shrewd tactics. Thus on the second day of the convention, while Conkling was speaking, Garfield entered late, and the leader from New York was interrupted by loud and continued applause for his rival from Ohio. Such seemingly spontaneous demonstrations occurred more than once, and even Garfield's official biographer, who tends to discount the evidence of a

[1] Barker's account is corroborated at this point by Garfield's *Journal*, April 7, 1881, giving an account of a lunch with Grier.

GARFIELD AS A PRESIDENTIAL CANDIDATE
(*A Portrait by Sarony, New York, 1880*)

pre-arranged Garfield movement in the convention, acknowl-
edges that there were clear indications of a well-organised
claque in the galleries. Such a device was, of course, not an
invention of Barker's, for organised cheering, though not yet
carried to the point of rivalry and perfection that it was to reach
in later years, was already among the most familiar and effective schemes for arousing enthusiasm in American nominating
conventions.

The convention was to be called to order at noon on June
2nd, but much work was still to be done, and Garfield reached
Chicago on May 29th, where in the absence of a Blaine leader
with similar personal qualities, he at once took command of the
discordant forces that were opposed to Grant.[1]

The issues at stake far transcended the interests of any individual. Grant had returned in 1879 from his trip around the
world after an absence of more than two years and had been received everywhere as a great national hero. At first he seems
not to have been very eager for a third term, but powerful State
leaders, of whom the most important were Conkling in New
York, Logan in Illinois and Cameron in Pennsylvania, saw in
the immense popularity of Grant an opportunity to make the
simple-minded soldier President and to control for their own
purposes the next Administration. Whatever hesitation Grant
may have had were soon overcome by the desires of Mrs. Grant
who was frankly eager to become again the mistress of the White
House.[2]

Powerful journals like *Harper's Weekly* and the New York
Tribune, on the other hand, remembered the scandals of the
Grant regime and saw in the sinister forces that were now so
eagerly supporting him a grave danger to the welfare of the na-

[1] Garfield's *Journal,* Library of Congress, May 29th, 1880. Garfield had written the day before: "I go with much reluctance—for I dislike the antagonisms
and controversies which are likely to blaze out in the convention."

[2] Badeau, *Grant in peace,* pp. 315-323.

tion. For the next four years, at least, these great bosses would become the real power behind the throne. Fortunately, the opponents of Grant were able to capitalize the traditional opposition to the third term and vitalized this feeling in editorials and cartoons. In taking control of the forces against Grant, accordingly, Garfield was justified in his belief that he was rendering a great service alike to the party and to the nation. It was this more than anything else that had brought him to Chicago. He was now firing the opening gun in a battle against boss rule in the country—a contest in which events soon made him a central figure and through which he was to win one of his chief claims to a position of genuine historical importance.

Grant had a clear plurality of the votes; the State conventions in New York, Pennsylvania and Illinois had instructed their delegates in favor of the hero of Appomattox; and if the unit rule could be applied, as his managers were anxious to do, the independent delegates would be smothered, the whole vote of each of these States would be counted for Grant, giving him an additional sixty votes taken from the lists of his opponents, and Grant would certainly be nominated on the first or the second ballot. The only hope lay in uniting all the rivals of Grant in common action against the threatened rule. To this task Garfield devoted himself with great energy, with the result that when the convention met, the real battle had already been won and Conkling was compelled to accept without an open contest the nomination of Senator G. F. Hoar, suggested by Garfield as chairman.[1] Hoar was in a position to recognise the friends of the individual ballot, and from that time there was no serious likelihood that Grant could win necessary delegates by any merely technical process. The enemies of Conkling and of Grant were also enabled to organise the two important

[1] Garfield *Journal*, June 1, 1880.

committees, that on credentials and the one on rules, with Garfield himself as the chairman of the latter. When Garfield's name came before the convention in this connection, it received the first of those demonstrations of popularity which Barker had foreseen and so carefully prepared.

The reports of the two committees, received on the second day of the convention, had already been foreshadowed, and were accepted by the combined vote of all the anti-Grant forces. On the next morning, the disappointed Conkling decided to place his principle of solidarity to the test in a new form. Accordingly, he moved that every member of the convention should be honor bound to support the nominee whoever he might be. The result was a temporary victory, for Conkling's motion was carried with only three votes in dissent. The opposition of the three delegates from West Virginia, however, roused Conkling to fury, and he rose at once to move that they had forfeited their rights in the convention and should be expelled. Garfield hesitated, then came slowly to his feet, was at once recognised by the friendly chairman, and answered Conkling in a speech which was probably the greatest oratorical triumph of his career. He pleaded for the right of every member of the convention to vote "aye" or "no" in safety on every motion, and ended by a tribute to the long public services of one of the endangered delegates. Garfield had appealed to the sense of fair play and to the deep-seated individualism of his audience, and the wild storm of applause that now broke out was for the first time genuine and spontaneous and required no Barker to support it. It was at once evident that Conkling had gone too far, for Garfield had won votes even among the "Stalwarts." The motion was accordingly overwhelmingly defeated. Conkling himself was among the first to recognise the implications of the incident, for while Garfield was speaking he wrote across the top of a newspaper, "I congratulate you on being the dark horse," and when Garfield was seated tore off his note and wrote across it, "Please hand this to Mr. Garfield." [1]

The situation was peculiar. The Grant managers, Conkling, Logan and Cameron, had something more than three hundred votes on which they could certainly count through thick and thin. Blaine had almost as many, while the Sherman contingent numbered almost one hundred, the remaining votes being scattered among three minor candidates, Windom of Minnesota, Washburne of Illinois, and Edmunds of Vermont, none of whom were at all likely to secure the nomination. At first sight, between his two chief rivals, Garfield's candidate, John Sherman, seemed to be in a strategic position. But there were elements of weakness, for he did not have the united support of his own state in which some delegates had been captured for Blaine, an invasion that Sherman never forgave. Men said that he was not magnetic, but back of this vague charge were other more tangible objections. For independents had not forgotten how Sherman had rewarded the members of the Southern returning boards by positions in the Treasury department. Politicians, on the other hand, remembered that Hayes by the advice of Sherman had removed Chester A. Arthur from the important post of collector of customs at New York and had placed a reform candidate, E. A. Merritt, in power against the bitter opposition of Conkling. Anxious as they were to capitalise the excellent record of the Hayes Administration, politicians were determined that the next Republican President should turn his back definitely on what they regarded as the impractical idealism of Hayes and of Schurz.

One of his lieutenants wrote to Sherman that he found a general fear that if Sherman were elected, there would be a continuance and rigid enforcement of civil service rules. If that

[1] A. R. Conkling, *Life of Roscoe Conkling,* p. 592.

were to be the case, what was the use of a political career? Sherman's friend tried hard to quiet these fears: "I take occasion," he wrote, "to say quietly that you are a republican among republicans, a stalwart among stalwarts. . . . In fact I have said that if you had the power you would let down the bars in the New York custom house at this time." [1] But he had to acknowledge sadly that the politicians turned away unsatisfied, and in spite of Sherman's fame as the father of resumption, by the time the convention met it was generally apparent that Sherman could not command the necessary support, and that it would take even more than the eloquence of James A. Garfield to secure for him the eagerly desired nomination.

Now for the first time, Garfield was in a position to judge the importance of the movement in his own favor. Thus he wrote on May 31st to his wife: "You can hardly imagine the embarrassment I have been in from the moment of my arrival here, by the number of delegates from all quarters who are openly expressing the wish that I was the Ohio candidate." Again on June 4th, Garfield wrote: "The signs are multiplying that the convention is strongly turning its attention to me. Large numbers of men are confident that will be the result." And though Garfield refused to allow the use of his name and continued to work faithfully for John Sherman to the end, these letters are sufficient to show that the result foreshadowed so early would not come as a dramatic surprise to any experienced politician. [2]

That night, in the evening session, the various candidates were placed in formal nomination. The speech for Blaine by James F. Joy of Michigan was not equal to the remarkable performance of "Bob" Ingersoll, four years before, which, con-

[1] L. G. Martin to Sherman, Jan. 16, 1880, Sherman Papers. Several other letters are to the same effect.
[2] T. C. Smith, op. cit., Vol. II, pp. 965, 967.

sidering Ingersoll's reputation as the greatest orator of his day, is not to be wondered at. When time was up, the old gentleman from Detroit was only getting started. The chairman's hammer fell; but Garfield, with ready tact, was on his feet in an instant to ask for an extension of the orator's time. The Sherman leader was missing few tricks that day! When Joy finally produced it, the name of Blaine was received by a wild outburst of cheering that took small account of the relative merits of orations. General Grant was, of course, nominated by Roscoe Conkling, who pictured Grant as the one man who could carry New York and as the hero and symbol of a reunited nation. Conkling made no effort to conciliate opponents and struck hard blows right and left as he proceeded; and though the friends of Grant, who loved him with a zeal bordering on fanaticism, regarded the oration as superb, there were those who wondered whether a more tactful speaker might not have done more that night for the cause he represented. But that was not Conkling's way.

Garfield came next, and his position was difficult, for he could not hope to appeal to the same emotions that had been aroused by the supporters of the two leading candidates. But the quiet manner with which he managed the necessary transition was admirably dramatic, and the speech itself, tactful, conciliatory, and prudent, was well calculated to win Sherman votes. When Garfield had almost reached the end and was about to place his candidate before the assembly, the rhetorical question usual on such occasions was interrupted by a shout for "Garfield," received by laughter and applause that showed conclusively the one thing that many delegates already had chiefly in mind.[1] It was Saturday night; Garfield "had done his best for Sherman," as he had promised; and when the conven-

[1] *Proceedings,* Republican Convention, 1880, p. 175.

tion reassembled on Monday morning it would be to put to the test of actual ballots all the various intrigues and rumors which had filled the last days and weeks and months.

In the meantime John Sherman in Washington, like the other candidates, had kept in close touch with proceedings at the front. Early on Sunday morning he began to receive disquieting telegrams regarding the strength of the Garfield movement. Thus, at 4 A. M., Murat Halstead telegraphed from Cincinnati, "There is nothing in one quarter in the Ohio delegation supposed to be friendly to you but ding dong about Garfield. This seems participated in by Foster." Again at noon, W. P. Nixon telegraphed from Chicago, "My information is that Foster is conspiring with others to bring Garfield out as a candidate and transfer your forces to him. I think Garfield has full knowledge of this fact." But during the day, Sherman's only act was to refuse to throw his strength to Blaine, a position in which he persisted to the end, thus removing the chief obstacle in the path of Garfield's supporters. A telegram from Garfield indicated continued loyalty and suggested that the chief danger was in a possible transfer of Pennsylvania votes to Blaine.[1]

As the balloting began, perhaps fortunately for the peace of mind of absent candidates, a great storm was raging and the wires throughout the North were down. The managers in Chicago were thus left to their own devices. The first ballot stood: Grant, 304; Blaine, 284; Sherman, 93; Edmunds, 34; Washburne, 30; Windom, 10; and throughout the day the lines thus established remained substantially unbroken. Beginning with the second ballot, Garfield's name was kept constantly before the convention by one and sometimes two votes from Pennsylvania. On one occasion Grant received five more votes and

[1] Sherman Papers, June 6th, 1880.

again Sherman's count rose to 97, but when after twenty-eight fruitless ballots the convention adjourned, it was seemingly no closer to a decision than it had been a week before.

Early on Tuesday morning Sherman was under great pressure to withdraw in favor of Blaine or Garfield. Again he refused to help Blaine, but at 8:30 he telegraphed Dennison that he would "abide by the action of the Ohio delegation in any matter personal to myself." This practically left Dennison free to transfer Ohio to Garfield whenever he saw fit, but Garfield again refused to allow his name to be presented to the convention. On the first ballot taken (the twenty-ninth), Massachusetts transferred 21 votes to Sherman, and on succeeding ballots his vote rose to 120. The Sherman managers were jubilant and thought that they were in reach of success. But Sherman's boom was short lived and by the 33rd ballot the deadlock of the previous day had been reëstablished. Without waiting for further evidence, Sherman telegraphed to Dennison at 1.48: "Whenever the vote of Ohio will be likely to assure the nomination of Garfield I appeal to every delegate to vote for him. Let Ohio be solid. Make the same appeal in my name to North Carolina and every delegate who has voted for me." This telegram was crossed by another from the convention dated at the same minute which showed that the break that the astute Sherman had evidently expected had at length come. Wisconsin had voted for Garfield with great enthusiasm, and had been followed on the next ballot by Indiana. Garfield had refused to allow the use of his name, but had been disregarded. This created a new situation and Bateman, one of Sherman's managers, telegraphed for instructions. But, as we have seen, these instructions were unnecessary, for they had already been sent.[1] These telegrams show conclusively that there had been

[1] Sherman to Dennison, 1:48 P.M.; Bateman to Sherman 2:48 P.M. (1:48 Washington time), Sherman Papers, June 8, 1880.

FORBIDDING THE BANNS

THE BRIDE (GARFIELD): "But it was such a little one"

(The child in the arms of W. H. Barnum represents the Credit Mobilier affair. By Keppler from *Puck*)

no treachery and no real element of surprise. Garfield had supported Sherman loyally, and when the time came, Sherman had
released his delegates to Garfield just as he had promised
months before. Instead of being a dark horse in the ordinary
meaning of the term, Garfield's candidacy had been arranged
with special care and with unusual astuteness.

Garfield's chief contribution to the result had been his own
skill in handling the difficult problems that arose and his evident
loyalty to the man he represented. When Wisconsin voted for
him at the close of the 34th ballot, Garfield was on his feet in
a moment: "I rise to a point of order. No man has a right without the consent of the person voted for, to announce that
person's name and vote for him in this convention. Such consent I have not given." At this point, Chairman Hoar, who
feared that Garfield might say something to make his own
nomination impossible, interrupted to refuse to recognise the
point of order: "The gentleman from Ohio will resume his
seat." [1] On the next ballot, Indiana voted for Garfield, just
as Barker and Streight had planned, and on the thirty-sixth
ballot James A. Garfield received 399 votes and the nomination.
Grant's "guard of 306" had remained faithful to the end, but
Roscoe Conkling now arose and offered the usual motion to
make the nomination unanimous. The different States now
seized their banners and gathered around Ohio, where Garfield
sat evidently trying to hide a deep emotion. Cannons were
being fired outside.

Sherman received bitter telegrams from disappointed lieutenants similar to those of the previous Sunday, but William
Dennison, whose loyalty to Sherman was beyond question, testified that Garfield's "conduct has been frank and manly throughout." And Sherman refused to lose his head and telegraphed

[1] *Proceedings of the Republican National Convention* (1880), p. 622; G. F.
Hoar, *Recollections*, Vol. II, p. 775.

his recent spokesman: "I congratulate you with all my heart on your nomination as President of the United States. You have saved the Republican party and the country from a great peril and assured the continued success of Republican principles."

In the late afternoon, and with the evident knowledge of Garfield, Dennison went on behalf of the Ohio delegation to the New York leaders and offered to support for the Vice-Presidency any candidate they might select. The first choice was Levi P. Morton, but when he declined, Chester A. Arthur was selected and against the advice of the embittered Conkling, accepted. In the evening at seven-thirty, the convention ratified this bargain on the first ballot, and five minutes later adjourned.[1]

Just after the nomination, Garfield received at Mentor a call from his boyhood friend, Corydon Fuller, who found the Presidential candidate surrounded by a wagon load of newspapers and unanswered letters. He gave some rapid directions to his secretaries, put on his hat and coat, led Fuller out to the carriage which he had hitched at the gate, jumped in himself, and bidding Fuller do so, took the lines and drove down the long lane. As they drove along, Garfield said that he had not desired the nomination he had received at the present time, but would have preferred to have spent a few years in the Senate. He said he did not deny he should have hoped at some future time to receive it, after he had become better prepared to execute its great duties; but as it had come unsought, he would accept it and if elected, do the best he could. And these were sentiments that Garfield repeated more than once in these days.[2]

[1] Dennison to Sherman, Sherman Papers, June 8. In the light of contemporary documents Sherman's *Recollections* seems to be colored by later disappointments.

[2] Corydon Fuller, *Reminiscences*, p. 430.

Conkling had commenced his celebrated speech nominating
Grant with the lines borrowed from Miles O'Reilly:

> "If asked what State he hails from,
> Our sole reply shall be—
> He comes from Appomattox
> And the famous apple tree!"

But when the gleeful Ohio delegation reached Fort Wayne,
through the open windows could be heard the answering chant,
composed for the occasion by Governor Foster:

> "If asked what State he hails from,
> Our sole reply shall be—
> He comes from old Ohio
> And his name is General G." [1]

The chief problem of the candidate, who had now reached
Mentor, was to heal the divisions in the party of which these
songs were the symbol and to present a united front against
the Democrats; and so much bitterness had been aroused by the
events at Chicago that it was at once apparent that the task which
he had set himself would not be easy.

In his letter of acceptance issued on July 10th, 1880, Garfield showed that he realised the full importance of this situation. The Republican platform, written by a delegate from
New York, had contained the usual innocuous platitudes that
might easily be interpreted by each man in his own way. But
through the insistence of the Massachusetts delegation, a plank
had been added as an amendment that praised the record of the
Hayes Administration in the matter of civil service reform and
promised that fitness, ascertained by proper practical tests,
should be the basis of admission to the public service. Such
standards, honestly enforced, would wreck every political

[1] Murat Halstead, Reminiscences, *McClure's Magazine*, Feb., 1896.

machine in the country as at that time organised, and especially after the dismissal of Arthur for undue interest in politics, the whole idea was especially obnoxious to the practical politicians who in New York were called "Stalwarts." Garfield's friends had warned him that he must do something to soften the fears aroused by the national platform. On June 29th, Garfield wrote to Reid, promising that "the Grant and the Blaine men will have no cause of complaint about my letter of acceptance if I can help it." Accordingly in the only important sentence in that letter, Garfield practically amended the platform by promising that in making appointments he would consult those "whose knowledge of the communities in which the duties are to be performed best qualifies them to aid in making the wisest choice." This statement proved as disappointing to reformers as it was satisfactory to the typical politicians.[1]

Garfield's next problem was that of the organisation of the national committee for the campaign. From a list of names suggested by the candidate the committee chose for the chairmanship a former member of Grant's cabinet, Marshall Jewell of Connecticut, who proved to be, as was doubtless intended, an entirely respectable figurehead. It was customary to select as Secretary a practical politician who would be in actual control of the details of the campaign. For obvious reasons, in view of the delicate situation in New York, Garfield would have preferred Tom C. Platt, who was later to win fame as "the easy boss" of that State. Perhaps the services of Platt were not available; in any case, at the suggestion of Logan of Illinois the committee selected ex-Senator S. W. Dorsey of Arkansas, whom *The Nation* called "one of the most disreputable of the carpet-bag Senators," and whose letters to Garfield during the campaign reveal him as entirely devoid of any pretence to idealism.

---

[1] *The Nation*, July 15, 1880, though supporting Garfield, called the sentence "a cruel disappointment." Garfield to Reid, June 29, 1880. Garfield Papers.

The vital question of a Chairman of the Finance Committee was left open for Garfield's personal solution later on. Indeed from the beginning and increasingly as the campaign developed, perhaps to a larger extent than any American President since Jefferson, Garfield proved to be his own efficient campaign manager. The candidate, of course, received advice from many persons; but this advice was frequently disregarded, and even in matters of the most minute detail, as Garfield's papers abundantly prove, the little farm at Mentor became the actual headquarters of one of the most shrewdly conducted political campaigns in American history.[1]

An eminent American historian has written: "Garfield was a wonderful campaigner, and despite the warnings by friends of the fate of Scott, Douglas and Greeley discussed freely in public passing events and current issues." [2] Now, it was true that Garfield was an excellent campaigner and that he made many speeches, but the impression given is nevertheless misleading. For never once did Garfield refer in public to any political question that might be supposed to be before the American people for solution. Thus, in one of his early speeches he appeared at the neighboring town of Painesville, where he found a theme in the monument to the soldiers of the war: "What does the monument mean?", he asked the vast audience that was hanging on his words: "Oh, the monument means a world of memories, a world of deeds, a world of tears, and a world of glories." And with this outline, so reminiscent of his evangelistic days, the rest of the forty-five minutes was an easy task. Again, he spoke at Chautauqua, New York, to an audience of five thousand people on "The significance of the Chautauqua

---

[1] For example, we find Garfield at one time writing personally to the chairman of every county committee in Ohio and Indiana, and, again, planning the complete itinerary for Blaine's trip to the West. Many other illustrations might be selected in the same period. Garfield, *Journal*, Sept. 7, 1880; Oct. 6, 1880.

[2] J. F. Rhodes, *History of the U. S.*, VIII, p. 137.

educational ideal," scarcely a subject with which he might be expected to deal in Washington, and was greatly impressed when he had the novel experience of the Chautauqua salute instead of the more usual cheers. Again and again, when he recorded a speech, he confided to his diary: "I think no harm has been done," and he was of course quite right. Only once in these busy months is there a reference in his diary to any political question, and that came when in October he wrote that Hancock, his Democratic opponent, had made an almost fatal mistake in giving out an interview on the delicate subject of the tariff.[1] If Garfield was not the inventor, he was at least one of the first Presidential candidates to use the method of voluble silence which has proved so effective in many later campaigns.

For all of this Garfield was of course, personally, not in the least to blame, for he was merely judging accurately and obeying consciously a persistent prejudice of the people to whom he was appealing for support. The advice that he received was varied, and as usual he had to decide the question for himself. Thus, on June 12, his good friend Whitelaw Reid wrote to him with remarkable frankness: "Please don't make any journeys or any speeches. . . . There is no place where you can do so much for your supporters and be so comfortable yourself, from now until November, as on your farm." But as the campaign developed and the Democrats made the old charges of the Credit Mobilier affair and the De Golyer pavement the basis of their attack on the Republicans, his chairman, Jewell, became seriously disturbed and urged Garfield to take the stump in his own defence. Now, Garfield knew well enough that he was an excellent campaign orator and that he was quite capable of dealing shrewd blows to his opponents. Accordingly, he took the suggestion seriously: "The newspapers," he wrote, "now begin to urge me to take the stump. I will pause awhile

[1] Garfield *Journal,* Oct. 19, 1880.

before I consent. Yet on many accounts I would be glad to do so." After careful thought, however, in which in characteristic fashion he reviewed the experience of other men, he decided reluctantly that it would not do to make any political speeches, although he said that "if it were the custom, it would insure better nominations." In announcing his decision to Jewell he advised other speakers to ignore the charges and to limit themselves "to the solid South and to the business interests of the country." [1]

That this advice was followed to the letter, any examination of the campaign speeches of the period amply proves. Occasionally an orator, who was regarded by the practical politicians as addicted to some special hobby, kicked over the traces and insisted on discussing some subject that was not down on the program. Thus on July 20, at Indianapolis, Carl Schurz, devoted a part of his time to an eloquent defence of the principle of civil service reform and expressed frank regret at the failure of the candidate to make a clear-cut declaration on the subject. Again, in the closing days of the campaign, Henry Ward Beecher defended the Republican party as the consistent friend of liberty, but like Schurz, expressed regret that it was not moving in the direction of freer commercial intercourse with other nations. But these were the mere heresies of the orthodox, and might, perhaps, be forgiven.

Other speakers followed closely the two themes that had been suggested. The old topic of the South as the home of rebellion soon proved to be outworn, but it was still possible to attack the Democratic party, of which the core was the solid South, as representing "less than one tenth of the commercial, industrial and property interests of the country," and on this basis, Levi P. Morton appealed in New York on October 20th,

[1] Cortissoz, *Whitelaw Reid*, Vol. II, p. 35; Garfield *Journal*, Aug. 10, 1880, Aug. 30, 1880; Garfield to Sherman, Sept. 25, 1880, Sherman Papers.

for a Republican victory. One of the most popular of the campaign orators was still Robert G. Ingersoll, who four years before was yet using his eloquence to picture the atrocities of Andersonville. Now the conclusion was the same but the premise was different, and Ingersoll sought to win the favor of an intelligent constituency by the following course of reasoning: "I believe in a party that believes in good crops; that is glad when a fellow finds a gold mine; that rejoices when there are forty bushels of wheat to the acre. . . . The Democratic party is a party of famine; it is a good friend of an early frost; it believes in the Colorado beetle and the weevil." [1]

One reason for the change of issues that contrasted the campaign of 1880 so sharply with those that had preceded was the nature of the Democratic nominations. For meeting at Cincinnati in June, the Democrats had selected for the presidency General W. S. Hancock, whose services to the cause of the Union had been praised in the highest terms by no less a person than General Grant, and had given the Vice-Presidential nomination to Wm. H. English, who had served in Congress for four terms in the fifties, but whose record as a War-Democrat was difficult to assail. Hancock's personal and public record were beyond criticism, and though he could be challenged, and justly, for his comparative lack of experience in civil office, the dangers of the man on horseback was a delicate theme for the party which had come so close to the nomination of a great soldier for a third Presidential term. More could be made of the personality of English, who was a banker and reputed to be the wealthiest man in Indiana. His baldness, his full beard dyed black, and various eccentricities of dress were described in one of the campaign documents, which also listed the mortgages that he had foreclosed and announced solemnly that the Democratic candidate was the owner of a theater in Indianapolis. The

[1] N. Y. *Tribune,* Oct. 29, 1880.

WILLIAM H. ENGLISH

MAJOR-GENERAL W. S. HANCOCK

Democrats countered by describing their candidate as "tall, handsome, and dignified and gentlemanly in his manners." The list of mortgages was met by a similar list of public benefactions.[1]

More important even than the nominations of the Cincinnati convention, and far more significant than its platform, was the open break that took place with the Tammany delegation and that led to the exclusion of the powerful John Kelly and his followers from the list of delegates. Experienced Republican politicians like W. E. Chandler and Secretary Dorsey saw at once that the chances of winning New York, which had seemed none too good, were now excellent and urged Garfield in the strongest terms to come to New York and to win the definite support of Conkling and the New York Republican organisation. Both Chandler and Dorsey agreed that Conkling would not give energetic support unless he was sure that he would not be treated as he had been by President Hayes, who had made appointments against his will and even without consulting him as to the nominations. Chandler wrote: "The State of New York is important, probably vital, and it is worth while, perhaps, to stoop a little to conquer much." And Dorsey added, "I believe that a discussion of thirty minutes with the persons named will settle for all time the doubt that exists in their minds. What we want is the State of New York and we want to do whatever is necessary to secure it, so it does not imply dishonor or indignity."

Garfield had not been eager in May to go to Chicago, and he was now even more reluctant to go to New York in August. But if the election was to be won, there was clearly nothing else to do. So Garfield wrote, "It is an unreasonable demand that so much effort should be made to conciliate one man. But to

[1] Compare *Republican Campaign Documents*, No. 87, with *Democratic Handbook*, p. 227.

resist the opinion of the whole committee would be ungracious." Accordingly on August 3rd, 1880, the next President of the United States commenced his pilgrimage to the home of the chieftain who sought to rule the Empire State with almost feudal sway. Two days before, Roscoe Conkling had written to his friend Levi P. Morton that he had no intention of being in the city for the Republican candidate's visit. Accordingly, whatever his motives may have been, it was apparent that the negotiations were to be carried on through subordinates. The course of discipline to which he was evidently subjecting Garfield was made more pointed when Conkling announced to Morton that he would be back in the city on August ninth; in other words the day after Garfield had left.[1]

The trip to the seats of the mighty was apparently a huge success. At Buffalo Garfield was greeted by a large assembly which with pardonable exaggeration he estimated at 50,000 people. At twenty-five other stops, on the way to New York, the crowds were equally enthusiastic, but Garfield was not tempted from the rôle that he had chosen, and wrote in his faithful diary: "Say but little, beyond thanks and an occasional remark on the localities through which we pass." Between stations, the Presidential candidate conducted a series of informal receptions with local politicians who appeared and rode with him for a few miles. At Albany Governor Cornell and General Arthur boarded the train, which was later joined by Hamilton Fish, Chauncey Depew and other celebrities. Reaching New York, Garfield rode through great crowds to the Fifth Avenue Hotel, and was able as usual to record, "I think no harm has been done."[2]

[1] W. E. Chandler to Garfield, July 24; Dorsey to Garfield, July 26; Garfield *Journal,* July 28 and Aug. 3 (Garfield Papers, Library of Congress) ; and Roscoe Conkling to Levi P. Morton, Aug. 1, 1880 (Morton Papers, New York Public Library).

[2] Garfield *Journal,* Aug. 3, 1880; Aug. 4, 1880.

The meeting of the Republican National Committee, the ostensible object of the journey, was scheduled for August fifth. The day began with breakfast at 8:30, and then came a stream of callers. At noon the meeting was held in the hotel parlors, and speeches were made by Blaine, Logan, Sherman and many others. The absence of Senator Conkling, however, gave rise to unpleasant surmises as to his attitude, and his friends seemed to Garfield embarrassed and somewhat indignant. But Garfield comforted himself that Conkling probably wanted to avoid the appearance of some bargain that would limit the freedom of the candidate. Deprived of Conkling's company, the Republican candidate had a long talk with Blaine. Only one year before he had written: "There is an element in him that I distrust." At that time he had estimated him as "a brilliant, aggressive, calculating man." But now for the first time Garfield yielded, as so many others had done, to the charm of his personality, and wrote, "Blaine is the prince of good fellows." Before night he had a conference with Levi P. Morton, who agreed to take the chairmanship of the finance committee. So one bridge had been crossed, and there would be no lack of the necessary sinews of war.

The next day at the home of Whitelaw Reid the candidate had a quiet opportunity to meet powerful figures in the life of business and of politics, among others Jay Gould, of "Black Friday" fame. But if either man remembered that Garfield had once called him "the guilty plotter of all these criminal proceedings," it may be safely presumed that no reference was made to so embarrassing a subject. "We had a conversation on the campaign," wrote Garfield. "I think he will help." In the evening came a serenade by the "Boys in Blue," to whom Garfield made one of his usual non-political speeches. But the most important incident of the day in the light of later events had been almost overlooked. For the diary for the day ends: "Did

not sleep well. Had in the afternoon a long interview with
Morton, Crowley, Arthur and Platt." This was the meeting
with Conkling's lieutenants which had been the real object of
the whole journey and which in later years the various partic-
ipants were to remember so differently. Unfortunately, the
two sentences in Garfield's diary are the only strictly contemporary reference to the conference that has as yet come to light,
and there is no means of showing conclusively just what was
said, or whether by chance there was any connection between
the two sentences that closed the account of a busy day.[1]

The trip home, by a different route, was a repetition of the
one to New York. Garfield noticed with evident pleasure that
Platt was among those who came to the station in Jersey City
to see him off. Again Garfield spoke at the various stations
along the way, where the train was greeted by torchlight pro-
cessions and bonfires. Once more, the candidate felt as if he
were walking on a tight rope, and in the evening records: "A
day of peril safely passed!" Sunday was spent at Chautauqua,
where the longest address of the journey was delivered, and
on the evening of Monday, August 9th, Garfield reached home
"very weary but feeling that no serious mistake had been made
and probably much good had been done—no trades—no shackles
—and as well fitted for defeat or victory as ever." The next day
he was still very tired and his right hand was badly swollen;
but the trip seemed to have justified itself, for he received "a
good and cordial letter from General Grant." Whether or not
the conference on August 6th was confined strictly to the tariff,
there can be no question that from that time Conkling and his
friends took off their coats and began to work as they had not
done before for the success of the national Republican ticket.[2]

---

[1] Garfield *Journal*, Aug. 6, 1880. T. C. Platt, *Autobiography*, p. 130, must
be read with caution, for it was written many years later.

[2] Garfield *Journal*, Aug. 7 to Aug. 10, 1880.

But though Garfield was as "well fitted for defeat as victory" it was his clear duty to see that the result should be victory in November if possible. And as he surveyed the situation with practiced eye, Garfield saw at once that the key to the problem was Indiana. Maine held an election in September, but Maine, with undue confidence as the event was to show, was considered entirely safe. Indiana followed in October, and as Indiana went so would go the nation, for it was as true in the eighties as it is today that the American people love a winner and do not vote readily for the losing side. Unfortunately, New York had the money, and in spite of Garfield's pleas, there was at first a tendency not to send it outside the State. Again and again Garfield returned to the same theme, writing: "The capture of Indiana in October ensures New York in November," and strongly urging Dorsey to open a national headquarters in Indianapolis. But the results were discouraging, and, in despair, Garfield turned to another source of revenue, writing on August 22nd a note to Hubbell of Michigan which was later to be used against him: "My dear Hubbell," ran the letter, "Please say to Brady that I hope he will give us all the assistance he can. Please tell me how the Depts. generally are doing." In spite of later explanations, the correspondence shows that this referred to the common practice of levying campaign tribute on the clerks in government employ.[1]

Such minor contributions, however, were scarcely necessary, for contrary to the optimistic assurances of Blaine, the Republicans in September lost Maine to a combination of Democrats and Greenbackers and were at once sobered by the imminence of the dangers of a general defeat. Money was now abundant for use in doubtful districts in Indiana, and an organisation perfected which covered every county and numbered every voter.

[1] Garfield to Hubbell, Aug. 22, 1880; Garfield to Dorsey, Aug. 31, 1880 (Garfield Papers).

Special efforts were made to enlist the influence of various owners of factories and other industrial leaders. Thus, early in September, Garfield wrote to Amos Townsend of Cleveland: "The situation in Indiana is such that Mr. Rockafeller (*sic*) can do us immense service there if he will. . . . Do not think that this relates to the raising of means. Mr. Rockafeller can do what is even more important than that." Having made his inquiries, Townsend reported that Mr. Rockefeller was "all right": "It is *risky writing* and you will be wise to keep your hand off paper and keep out of all complications." But in spite of this warning, Garfield wrote to explain that the particular service desired was that Rockefeller should back up his superintendent: "He is a live Republican and would like to bring his men into line if Mr. Rockefeller would stand by him at home and he could use 500 more of the right sort if sent." Other letters show that similar pressure was brought to bear on workers in lumber mills and other industries.[1]

On October 9th Garfield made an entry in his diary that showed how closely he was watching the details of the campaign: "A busy day," he wrote, "sending final messages and directions to various parts of the field, preparatory to the battle of Tuesday next. Received from Indiana the final report which will test the thoroughness and efficiency of our organisation." This report indicated in great detail a Republican plurality of 5350 and proved to be marvelously accurate. But at the time, mindful of the hopes that had withered in Maine the month before, Garfield merely added, "We shall see." Nothing had been left to chance, and when the Republicans won their anticipated victory in Indiana, Garfield had no doubts concerning the ultimate victory which was now almost sure to come.[2]

[1] Garfield to Townsend, Sept. 2, 1880; Sept. 7, 1880. Garfield Papers.
[2] After the campaign, a group of New York politicians gave a testimonial dinner presided over by ex-President Grant, which gave full credit for the result in Indiana to Dorsey. Vice-President-Elect Arthur made the following

IN LINE AT LAST

Jewell   Conkling   Cameron   Logan   Beecher   Carpenter

(By J. A. Wales from *Puck*)

As a symbol of the outwardly reëstablished harmony of the once divided party Senator Roscoe Conkling consented to make a speaking trip into the West, of which the most dramatic occasion was to be a meeting at Warren, Ohio, in Garfield's own district. The presiding officer was to be no less a person than ex-President Grant, and the Republican committee at Warren thought that Garfield ought to be present to welcome their distinguished guests. But Garfield could not go to Warren without making a political speech, which he still felt to be unwise, and accordingly refused to be present. "If I could take the stump and bear a fighting share in the campaign," Garfield wrote, "I should feel far happier." He felt bound by a curious custom that would not allow a candidate to speak on the issues of the day, but which apparently did not object to his most minute supervision of the details, sometimes sordid, of his own campaign.

The meeting at Warren took place as scheduled on September 28th, and though the newspapers noticed that neither Grant nor Conkling had much to say about their candidate for the Presidency, it was generally regarded as a great success. After the meeting the party, including Grant and Conkling, stopped for a call at Mentor, where Conkling and Garfield met for the first time since the memorable days when they had been the two leading orators at the convention in Chicgo. But though Democratic newspapers tried to make much of the so-called treaty of Mentor, the testimony of both men showed that the meeting was purely formal and that there was no private conference between them. Garfield wrote: "Crete gave them a

remarks: "Indiana was really, I suppose, a Democratic State that might be carried by close and perfect organisation and a great deal of—(laughter). I see that the reporters are present; therefore I will simply say that everybody showed a great deal of interest in the occasion and distributed tracts and political documents all through the State." *The Nation*, Feb. 24, 1881. Garfield's comment in his journal shows that he saw in the dinner an attempt to discredit his own exertions. Garfield *Journal*, Feb. 17, 1881.

lunch and coffee in the dining room. After remaining an hour, the party were driven again to the station. . . . I had no private conversation with the party, but the call was a pleasant and cordial one all round." [1]

As the campaign developed, Republican speakers began to make much of a plank in the Democratic platform which called for "a tariff for revenue only." Hancock gave out an interview in which he sought to amend his platform, as the Republican candidate had done earlier in the matter of civil service reform, by saying that he regarded the tariff as a local issue, with which the national government was not likely to deal, and that accordingly the business interests of the country had nothing to fear from a Democratic victory. Though the sentiments expressed by Hancock were almost word for word the same as those with which Garfield himself had once met the contentions of the iron men of the Mahoning Valley in the now forgotten days of his own low tariff leanings, Garfield was among the first to realise that Hancock had made a serious mistake in thus evading what might well have been a clear-cut issue between the two parties. [2] But it was now October, Indiana had been carried, and it is unlikely that Hancock's interview had anything like the significance that has often been attributed to it. Where it alienated some by its evasions, it is at least possible that it reassured others as Hancock undoubtedly intended. But one thing is perfectly clear; the campaign of 1880 was neither to be won nor lost through the frank discussion of any question of political policy.

More significant than Hancock's Paterson interview of October 7th, was the publication of the so-called Morey Letter two weeks later, although few incidents in American political history have been more generally misunderstood. According to his sworn testimony at the later investigation, on the morning of October

[1] Garfield *Journal*, Sept 28, 1880.
[2] Garfield *Journal*, Oct. 19, 1880.

Personal and Confidential.

House of Representatives,

Washington D.C., *May 23*, 1880

Dear Sir;

    Yours in relation to the Chinese problem came duly to hand.

    I take it that the question of employes is only a question of private and corporate economy, and individuals or companys have the right to buy labor where they can get it cheapest.

    We have a treaty with the Chinese Government, which should be religiously kept until its provisions are abrogated by the action of the general Government, and I am not prepared to say that it should be abrogated, until our great manufacturing and corporate interests are conserved in the matter of labor.

Very truly yours
J A Garfield

H. L. Morey,
Employers Union
Lynn Mass.

A GENUINE LETTER

FROM

GENERAL JAMES A. GARFIELD.

Telegram

MENTOR, OHIO. Oct 23. 1880.

Hon Marshall Jewell
241 Fifth Avenue N.Y.
            Your telegram of this
afternoon is received. Publish my
dispatch of last evening if you think
best. Within the last hour, the mail
has brought me the lithographic
copy of the forged letter. It is the
work of some clumsy villain, who
cannot spell, — nor write English.
nor imitate my hand-writing.
    Every honest and manly demo-
crat in America who is familiar
with my hand-writing, will denounce
the forgery at sight — Put the case
in the hands of able detectives at
once, and hunt the rascals down
                    J. A. Garfield

18th, Joseph Hart, the publisher of an obscure penny paper, the New York *Truth*, found on his desk a letter, dated Jan. 23, 1880, purporting to be written at that time by no less a person than James A. Garfield to one H. L. Morey of Lynn, Massachusetts. The essential sentence of the letter was as follows: "Yours in relation to the Chinese problem came duly to hand. I take it that the question of employes (*sic*) is only a question of private and corporate economy, and individuals or companys (*sic*) have the right to buy labor where they can buy it cheapest." The letter was plausible, because Garfield in 1879 had opposed a Chinese exclusion law that violated existing treaties. Hart showed the letter to a number of persons, including Abram S. Hewitt, who pronounced the signature, in their opinion, genuine, and accordingly announced on the next day that *Truth* would publish a sensational letter from the Republican candidate for the Presidency. The letter appeared on October 20th and a facsimile of the letter and the envelope two days later. The letter was given a wide circulation by Wm. H. Barnum, the chairman of the Democratic Campaign Committee, and was used in speeches by Abram S. Hewitt and Samuel J. Randall, who later apologised personally to Garfield for the part he had taken in the matter.

It was soon apparent that the letter was only a fairly clever forgery. Indeed, the two misspelled words in the facsimile should at once have placed the Democratic leaders on their guard, for whatever else his enemies might say about James A. Garfield, he was undoubtedly a good speller. But there can be no question that Hewitt and Randall, both of whom were high-minded gentlemen, were sincerely taken in. Garfield, for his part, was not greatly disturbed and sent a confidential emissary to Washington to find whether any letter of similar purport had by any chance been placed in his files, and when he was reassured on this point, issued a sweeping denial of the authenticity of the letter. The Republican National Committee placed John I. Davenport in charge of the investigation; large rewards were offered for the arrest of the forger; and on October 28, Hayward Philp, a reporter on *Truth*, was arrested. But though the testimony of handwriting experts at the hearing proved the letter to be a forgery, the only evidence against Philp was the fact that he had sometimes amused himself by imitating manuscripts. At the request of Davenport, the case against Philp was dropped, and though later investigations pointed to an obscure New York lawyer as the probable writer, even on Davenport's own showing, when all efforts to connect the forgery directly with the Democratic Committee had failed, the matter ceased to be of any further political interest and the case was dropped.[1]

Today it is entirely unlikely that we shall ever know precisely who wrote the Morey letter. It may have been a discontented labor leader or, as seems more probable, some crank or practical joker of the type of Guiteau. Possibly Joseph Hart knew more about the matter than he ever revealed. But though it is entirely improbable that any responsible Democratic leader had had any connection whatever with the forgery itself, there was justice in Garfield's remark that, "whoever the actual scribe may be, Barnum is the chief criminal by his conduct in peddling the forgery." Indeed, the appointment of the Potter Committee in 1878, with the unfortunate aftermath of the Cipher Despatches, and the circulation of the Morey letter in October of 1880 may well be regarded as the two great political blunders of the decade, sufficient by themselves to account for the outcome of the extremely close Presidential election of the latter year.

According to the traditional view, the circulation of the Morey letter caused Garfield to lose the electoral votes of California and Nevada. But the evidence in the Garfield papers and an examination of the newspapers of the period leads to a wholly dif-

---

[1] J. I. Davenport, *History of the Forged Morey Letter*, N. Y., 1884. This account has a strong partisan flavor.

ferent conclusion. For Garfield's position on Chinese exclusion
had been made public in 1879, and during the summer the candidate had been warned more than once that the two Pacific States
were very doubtful. Garfield, always well informed, had already discounted these two States in his list of Republican electoral votes. When the matter first came to his attention, Garfield
wrote: "I can hardly believe that a rational and just minded
public will be influenced by such a wicked device." Again, on the
day after the sensational arrest of Philp, Garfield recorded his
judgment: "I may be in error, but I confidently believe this
forgery will injure the party in whose interest it has been con-
cocted and circulated." And this opinion was fully justified, for
on October 30th, Dana, who had long been the most bitter of
the critics of Garfield's public career, wrote in the New York
Sun: "If a party requires such infamous aids, that party, by whatsoever name it may be called, deserves to perish." Similar sentiments were echoed by many rockbound Democratic papers, including the Atlanta *Constitution.* The center of the Democratic
position had been the evidence furnished by the Credit Mobilier
Affair and the De Golyer matter as to the personal fitness of
James A. Garfield for the high position of President of the United
States. But even these charges which had once been so widely
echoed by Republican newspapers were now partially obscured.
The American sense of fair play had been called into life, and
Republican speakers at once took up the refrain. Thus the eloquent Ingersoll found for the first time a real subject for an address, and speaking on October 28th in front of the Sub-Treasury
in New York, used the Morey Letter as the basis of his appeal
for the vindication of James A. Garfield: "That letter," he said,
"makes doubly sure the election of James A. Garfield." [1]

[1] This paragraph is based on: Garfield *Journal,* Oct. 21, 1880; Oct. 26, 1880;
Oct. 28, 1880; New York *Sun,* Oct. 30, 1880; *Republican Campaign Speeches,*
1880, Ford Collection, N. Y. Public Library; Atlanta *Constitution,* Nov. 1, 1880.

From the point of view of the admirable gentleman who
headed the Democratic ticket, remembering that Garfield's
plurality over Hancock was less than ten thousand and that a
small change in the votes of pivotal States would have secured
Democratic victory, the publication of the Morey Letter and the
knowledge generally circulated in papers of both parties a week
before the election that the letter was a forgery, may well seem
a calamity of the first order.

Garfield's good sense, his immense capacity for hard work, his
ability to keep his head when others were over-anxious, above
all the human, lovable qualities of the man, his generous hospitality and the unspoiled simplicity of his manners, never stood
out in such bold relief as they did in those busy weeks on the farm
at Mentor. The place was thronged with visitors, but there is almost no note of irritation, which in the circumstances might have
been pardonable. Thus, on August 13th, "Cam and Nell and
their two children were here when I returned from New York,
and they are making us a pleasant visit." Again, about the same
time, "Mr. S. S. Coffin of Iowa came today. He is anxious
about my smoking and labors with me like a missionary. We had
a pleasant visit with him." Many entries in the diary refer to the
crops on the beloved farm, to games of croquet with the children, and to the sermon at the neighboring meeting house. The
immense mail was handled with marvellous promptness and efficiency. Many letters already applied for positions or asked for
gifts. But once in awhile, Garfield received a letter from a generous friend, with no political ambitions, like one from Charles
P. Eels of Cleveland: "If you have room in your 'barl' for the
enclosed check for $1000 please put it in." [1] And such a contribu-
tion to his ruinous personal expenses, Garfield accepted in the
spirit in which it was sent.

Election day, November 2, 1880, "opened clear and bright.

[1] Eels to Garfield, June 30, 1880. Garfield Papers.

. . . Arranged for plowing and seeding garden east of the house. . . . At 2 P. M. went to Town Hall and voted for Republican electors. . . . At six returns began to come in. . . . By 11 P. M. it became evident that we had carried New York. At midnight we gave supper to about twenty-five friends. At 3 A. M. we closed the office. Secure in all the Northern States except N. J. and the Pacific States which are yet in doubt." The Republican ticket had been elected by a vote of 214 to 155, and when James A. Garfield went to bed in the early morning he knew that he was to be the next President of the United States.[1]

---

[1] Garfield *Journal,* Nov. 2, 1880. Garfield wrote to a friend just before the election: "The campaign has been fruitful to me in the discipline that comes from endurance and patience. I hope defeat will not sour me, nor success disturb the poise which I have sought to gain by the experiences of life." Garfield to Rockwell, Nov. 1, 1880.

THE presidential term of James A. Garfield practically began the day after his election. For the inauguration in March proved to be a mere episode, interrupting for the moment activities which had been continuous from November and that did not change appreciably in character. Others might have time to consider large questions of policy, but the chief task of the President as of the President-elect was to see that the offices were filled in such a way as to promote the harmony of the party and the consequent success of the new Administration. Until the July morning when he was shot down in the station in Washington, this was now to be the chief theme of Garfield's life.

The King was dead, and no one recognised the fact more clearly than Hayes who had now become the loneliest figure in American political life, an outgoing President in the period between the election and the inauguration. There was a wistful quality in the interview, for Hayes was in Ohio and came at once to Mentor to pay a visit to his successor. Hayes was undoubtedly "very happy over the result of the election"; and Garfield, for his part, gave him generous credit for the outcome: "Whether his critics may say he has given the country a very clean Administration and his party has not been handicapped in the late contest by any scandals caused by him." [1] Neither man had as yet any hint that Postmaster General Key, Hayes's single Democratic experiment in his cabinet, had been sound asleep while Brady and other subordinates had been defrauding the country through the Star Route frauds. Strangely enough, when these were revealed, they were to be vaguely con-

[1] Garfield *Journal,* Nov. 4, 1880.

nected in the popular mind with Garfield's presidency, rather than with that of Hayes, to which they really belonged. But in spite of these later revelations, Garfield had done no more than justice to the fine record of an Administration that had been like a breath of fresh air across the noisome places of American politics.

The two places of greatest prestige in the Cabinet were, of course, the State Department and that of Secretary of the Treasury. For the first position Garfield seems to have considered no other name except that of James G. Blaine. He had no serious doubts that Blaine would accept, for Blaine's term in the Senate would come to a close in 1883 and the recent election in Maine had shown signs of revolt against his leadership that seemed to make at least temporary retirement personally desirable. For the nomination at Chicago, although at the last moment, Garfield was partially indebted to the lack of opposition from Blaine, and during the campaign the assistance of the Maine Senator had been cordial and generous. Blaine had ability and would make a brilliant Secretary. One thing only troubled Garfield. Blaine was ambitious and had in two conventions been a leading candidate for the presidency. Would he make his place in the Cabinet a vantage ground for his future plans?

Soon after the election, Garfield had occasion to return to Washington to supervise the dismantling of the house that had so long been his home, and the personal relations between the two men were so good that Garfield felt that he could put his problem squarely to Blaine himself. The interview took place on November 27th: "If I should ask you to take a place in the Cabinet," Garfield inquired frankly, "what would be your probable response, and before you answer, please tell me whether you are or will be a candidate for the presidency in 1884. I ask this because I do not purpose to allow myself nor any one else to use the next four years as the camping-ground for fighting the next presidential battle." Blaine answered that he would not again seek the nomination, and on December 20, after Garfield had returned to Mentor, accepted the post with evident gratitude, extending and amplifying his previous pledge in the following words: "In accepting this important post I shall give all that I am and all that I can hope to be freely and joy-fully to your service. . . . Your Administration must be made brilliantly successful and strong in the confidence and pride of the people; not obviously directing its energies to reëlection, but compelling that result by the logic of events and by the imperious necessities of the situation." From that time the loyalty of Blaine was beyond question and during his brief presidency the record shows that Garfield had no personal reason to re-gret the choice that he had made.[1]

An attempt was made to keep the appointment secret, but Blaine told Reid, and Reid wrote to Phelps, and everybody told his wife, all under the pledge of the most profound secrecy, and whether through one of these channels or some other, a secret which it did not require any unusual political astuteness to guess was soon common knowledge.[2] Nor did this knowledge make any easier the most difficult of Garfield's problems, that of filling the post of Secretary of the Treasury, for if Conkling had been likely to demand at least the second place in the Cabinet, he was now sure to do so when the first had fallen to the lot of his hated rival. Indeed, in some re-spects the Treasury was more desirable than the Department of State; for the head of that Department had at the time many functions that are today distributed among newer departments, and was accordingly in control of a vast amount of patronage,

---

[1] Garfield *Journal,* Nov. 27, 1880; Blaine to Garfield, Dec. 20, 1880, Gail Hamilton, *Life of Blaine,* p. 495.
[2] Reid to W. W. Phelps, Dec. 31, 1880; Cortissoz, *op. cit.,* Vol. II, p. 40.

"FROM THE TOW-PATH TO THE WHITE HOUSE"
A cartoon-portrait of President Garfield by J. Keppler appearing in *Puck*

including the appointment of a veritable army of officials and clerks. Such appointments were, of course, the very breath of life to an efficient organisation, and New York politicians were therefore quite willing to sacrifice the traditional dignity and prestige which went with the Department of State to the more solid advantages that were connected with the Secretaryship of the Treasury. Further, the bonds of the government to the amount of more than seven hundred millions were about to come due, necessitating vast refunding operations of great interest to the various banks which desired to become the agents of the government for the purpose. The selection of these agencies would undoubtedly fall to the lot of the new Secretary of the Treasury, whose advice would also be of great importance in either retaining the existing volume of greenbacks, as the West desired, or in cancelling them and thus contracting the currency as was advocated by certain financial interests in East. Accordingly, a contest for this particular post in the Cabinet of Garfield now began and was soon almost unmatched in obstinacy or virulence. Until this question was finally settled, all other arrangements for the Cabinet must be regarded as tentative and doubtful.

The two most obvious names to be considered in this connection were those of the experienced Secretary of the Treasury in the cabinet of Hayes, John Sherman, of Ohio, to whom, perhaps even more than to Blaine, Garfield was under heavy personal obligations, and Levi P. Morton of New York, a personal and business friend of Conkling, and the head of an important bank. Quite apart from the rivalries of New York politics, Western leaders, representing to some extent the point of view of the farmers and more especially the interests of the rival city of Chicago, were opposed both to Sherman, who was suspected of a special friendship for the First National Bank, and to Morton, whose connection with Morton, Bliss, and Com-

pany made him even more obviously a representative of those
influences in national life which the West had learned to lump
together under the general name of Wall Street.[1]

Thus, on November 16th, Joseph Medill, the editor of the
influential Chicago *Tribune*, called on Garfield to advise him
about the composition of his Cabinet. Medill, who was on
friendly terms with Logan, one of the leaders of the famous
group of 306 who at Chicago had voted to the end for General
Grant, told Garfield that Logan did not desire any position
in the Cabinet, but advised Garfield to recognise some conspicuous member of the group. Garfield replied to these overtures that he wanted "all Republicans, including the 306, to
consider themselves in full fellowship," and later fulfilled his
pledge by making Robert T. Lincoln of Illinois, the son of
the great war President, Secretary of War in his Cabinet. Medill
also explained to Garfield that the West was unalterably opposed to the retirement of the existing volume of greenbacks as
to all similar measures of deflation, and that for that reason,
"neither Sherman nor any other Eastern man would do for
Secretary of the Treasury."[2] This was obviously an ultimatum
from the West, and though Garfield wrote that he was only a
listener, there can be little doubt that he took the advice seriously and made it the basis of his conduct.

The difficulties of Garfield in making up a satisfactory Cabinet were chiefly due to the development of the boss system in
some of the most important States, notably New York. Under
an earlier system the political control of the party in cities,
counties and other local subdivisions had been left to some
petty chieftain who was expected to keep up an active organisa-

[1] Morton to Bliss, March 29th, 1881, March 30, 1881 (Morton Papers), show
that Morton's interest in the refunding operations continued to overshadow his
merely political activities.
[2] Garfield *Journal,* November 16, 1880.

tion and to "get out the vote," often a laborious and even a costly task, in return for which he expected to have control of the patronage and to exercise substantial influence in the awarding of contracts. With comparatively small campaign funds, and in view of the bitter contests that marked the political history of the sixties and the seventies, individual leadership had proved singularly effective, and had been extended to the States. Perhaps because the two States were often doubtful and closely contested, or on account of the personal qualities of the leaders themselves, Indiana under Oliver P. Morton and New York controlled by Roscoe Conkling had become the most perfect illustrations of a tendency that under existing political conditions was almost inevitable. Michigan and New Hampshire under the Chandlers and Pennsylvania under the Camerons, father and son, were managed with almost equal efficiency, but on account of the doubtful character of their States and the unusual exertions that were often required to carry them in a presidential year, Indiana and New York had carried the powers of the boss to a high degree of perfection. During the long years of the Grant régime the leaders in these States had become accustomed not only to control the minor offices and to select the slates that were later approved by so-called nominating conventions for elective positions within the States, but also to be consulted and to have the virtual appointment of officers who were in theory nominated by the President and had their appointments ratified by the Senate of the United States. Indeed, the amount of authority had become so great that these chieftains had come to feel that they had a right to dictate even the policy of delegates to national nominating conventions just as they did in State conventions for the office of governor.

The boss system did not necessarily imply either bribery or corruption, and though leaders of the dominant type of Morton and Conkling at the height of their powers undoubtedly took carefully into account the desires of railroad presidents and other financial magnates to whom they were compelled to apply for campaign funds, they also gave serious consideration to the abilities of various candidates for public office. Thus Roscoe Conkling prided himself in scrupulous fidelity to his political engagements and consulted many persons in what was undoubtedly a sincere effort "to fit the office to the man." [1]

In Ohio, where Garfield had of course received his political training, the boss system had not taken root. The most probable explanation lies in the distribution of the centers of Republican strength, for where to some extent in Indiana and notably in New York, Republican counties were divided from those under Democratic control by boundaries almost as definite as those of the State itself, in Ohio the power of the two parties was scattered over the State like pepper and salt and there was not the same necessity for a unified leadership which would insure victory in a perennial contest which was at once political and also sectional. Thus Roscoe Conkling and his successors were quite as much the leaders of the up-state counties in a contest with the city of New York as they were the managers of an efficient political machine. In Ohio, on the other hand, many leading politicians and Congressmen were equally influential in different places, and in spite of the remarkable series of Ohio Presidents, no single individual, not even Mark Hanna at the height of his powers, ever attained the masterful position that had become the axiom of organisation in New York. Accordingly, as Garfield later pointed out, President Grant, who had never rejected the advice of Morton or of Conkling, felt entirely free to make nominations for office in Ohio, and on one occasion in Garfield's own district, against the will and without

[1] G. C. Gorham, *Roscoe Conkling Vindicated* (1888).

any attempt to consult the desires of the Congressman whose political interests were at stake.[1]

The very power of the political boss entailed huge responsibilities, created rivalries, and brought criticism both from those who were opposed to the whole system and from others who had no objections to the machine as such but who became dissatisfied with the use that the leader made of authority to which in principle they did not object. Absolute powers are always precarious in proportion to their size, and in 1880 there was more than one indication that Roscoe Conkling was fighting the battle of his life for a position which he valued far more highly than he did the outward symbol of his Senatorship. When at Chicago the leader from Utica had entered the field of national politics and had tried to carry New York as a unit in favor of the nomination of Grant, he had strained even his great authority to the breaking point. The open revolt of nineteen delegates under the leadership of W. H. Robertson, who had refused to vote for Grant as they had been instructed to do by Conkling and the State convention, had been followed by the complete miscarriage of all of Conkling's plans and had greatly reduced his prestige. This defeat was doubly bitter, because it had been made the occasion for open opposition on the part of a group of younger men with great ambitions, of whom the leader was the "tall blond young man," as Conkling called the new editor of the New York *Tribune*. Whitelaw Reid made no secret of his desire to displace Conkling in the control of New York politics, and for this purpose he had in his hands the weapon of the powerful journal to which the genius of Horace Greeley had given so great influence and prestige. In addition Reid had the support of Jay Gould, Chauncey M.

[1] Garfield to Foster, Dec. 15, 1880, and Garfield to Grant, May 15, 1881, point out the contrast between the systems in Ohio and New York. Garfield Papers.

Depew, and other financial chieftains who were dissatisfied with the treatment that they had received from Roscoe Conkling.

Recognising fully the nature of the battle in which he was engaged and the dangers of a defeat, it was no wonder that Conkling tried to strengthen his position by some understanding with Garfield before he consented to use his influence in the campaign. When the campaign was safely over it was clearly important to him to show his power by appointing a man of his choice to the Department of the Treasury, as it was from his point of view a matter of life and death to continue to control the chief appointments to Federal offices within the State as he had done in the golden days under Grant. Conkling believed sincerely that he had earned his position by hard work and by great services to the party, and if his scepter passed to some younger man he was at once too proud and too sensitive to be willing to remain in a career of politics. All this, no one understood better than Conkling's young antagonist Whitelaw Reid, who wrote soon after the election to his friend John Hay: "What we now look to is a broadening of the machine, with our fellows in and a united party, minus Conkling, who won't last forever!" [1]

The opposition of Whitelaw Reid to Conkling and all his friends was thus from the beginning much more thorough than that of Blaine, who saw that the Conkling element within the party would have to be recognised by some Cabinet appointment and at one time would have been reconciled even to Conkling himself as Secretary of the Treasury. Reid, on the contrary, wrote a little later that he hoped that Garfield "would make an end of Conkling." But in spite of the ruthlessness of the political differences that divided the old leader from his young rival, there was one point on which Reid and Conkling were entirely agreed, and that was the necessity for a machine, of one kind or the other, and the danger of relying on the reform

[1] Cortissoz, *Whitelaw Reid*, Vol. II, p. 51.

element within the party of which Schurz was the most eminent representative. Both Reid and Blaine wrote to Garfield warning him against any such alliance, and Garfield replied to Reid assuring him that it was his purpose to construct a Cabinet that would satisfy the prevailing wishes of the party and that he need have no fears of any undue influence from reformers such as had marked the previous administration.[1]

A few days after the interview in which Joseph Medill had told him that the West was opposed to Sherman or "any Eastern man" in the Treasury, Garfield's difficulties were partially relieved for he had a satisfactory talk with the outgoing Secretary, in which Garfield asked him directly "if he would feel wholly cordial if he were not retained." Sherman responded "affirmatively and I think earnestly." Garfield's troubles, however, were not entirely at an end, for Sherman wanted to go back to the Senate, an ambition that was shared by one of Garfield's closest friends and supporters, Governor Foster, whom Sherman blamed with some justice for the failure of his own efforts at Chicago. Reluctant as Garfield was to intervene in the Senatorial contest and though anxious to avoid all appearance of becoming the first State boss in Ohio, he saw at once that Sherman was too powerful a figure to be left quite in the cold. Therefore he appealed at once to Foster's friendship and to his loyalty to the party, telling him that it would be very much better for the politics of Ohio and for the Administration if Sherman were reëlected to the Senate. Accordingly, a few days later, Foster withdrew from the contest, thus insuring the election of Sherman and securing for the President-elect a powerful and experienced leader in the Senate.[2]

An interview with the other possible claimant was less reassur-

[1] Garfield to Reid, Oct. 7, 1880; Gail Hamilton, *op. cit.*, p. 490; Cortissoz, *op. cit.*, Vol. II, pp. 40, 41.
[2] Garfield to Foster, Dec. 15, 1880. Garfield Papers.

ing, for Levi P. Morton had understood from the interviews of the previous August that the Treasury Department was to go to New York and that he personally was to have the choice of the Treasury, of a foreign mission, or of becoming the chief fiscal agent of the government in the refunding operations that were soon to commence. Garfield told Morton that that was not his understanding of the interview of August 6th, and that the solution which the New York banker desired was wholly inadmissible because it would mean "a congestion of financial power at the money center and would create great jealousy at the West." [1]

It is entirely probable that Morton might have been willing to let the matter rest, for looking on the whole problem from the point of view of a business man there were a number of positions in the gift of the President that might satisfy his ambitions, and his correspondence shows that he never allowed any disappointment over the Secretaryship of the Treasury to interfere with his friendly relations with the President. But the matter was different with Roscoe Conkling, with whom in view of the bitter State contest in which he was engaged, the appointment of the second officer in the Cabinet was essential to the strengthening of a position that was being seriously assailed. The very suggestion that an Eastern man would not do for the Treasury was in itself a challenge to the leadership of Conkling that could scarcely be overlooked.

How seriously Conkling was prepared to fight for his place in the sun at once became apparent, for just two weeks after Garfield had explained his difficulties to Morton, Governor

---

[1] It seems probable that Garfield had made some promise in August, suggesting various possible positions for Morton, but intending to keep his choice in his own hands, while Platt and Morton understood Garfield to leave the final choice to Morton himself. Garfield's account is in his *Journal* for Nov. 27, 1880. For Platt's account, see, T. C. Platt, *Autobiography*, p. 130. G. C. Gorham, *op. cit.*, p. 16, discusses the incident from the point of view of conversations with Conkling.

PRESIDENT GARFIELD AND HIS CABINET

James G. Blaine   James A. Garfield   Samuel J. Kirkwood   Robert T. Lincoln   Thomas L. James
Secretary of State   President   Secretary of the Interior   Secretary of War   Postmaster-General

William H. Hunt

William Windom   Secretary of the Navy   Wayne MacVeagh
Secretary of the Treasury   Attorney-General

By J. Keppler, from *Puck*, March 16, 1881

Cornell, Richard Crowley, and L. F. Payn of New York arrived in Mentor as the emissaries of Conkling and Morton. They said that in August Garfield had promised Morton the Treasury if he wanted it. "I answered," wrote Garfield, "that I did not give him the option and by no implication tendered him the Treasury . . . that it would be most unwise in a party sense to give the place to N. Y. city." "They left at 10 P. M.," adds Garfield, "evidently disappointed. Crowley said Conkling hoped to sustain my administration." This was evidently at once a promise and a threat and Garfield answered with some heat in almost the same words that he had used to Blaine, that he "would not permit this four years to be used to secure the next for anybody." [1] A serious issue of veracity had thus been raised and from that time the contest between Conkling and his rivals in New York was accepted by Garfield as his own.

Many newspapers, slightly informed as to the way the current was running, now began to prophesy with confidence that Levi P. Morton of New York would be the next Secretary of Treasury, and the unfavorable tone of many of these comments strengthened the position of Whitelaw Reid, who was moving heaven and earth to prevent any possibility that Garfield might be induced to change his mind. And though Garfield merely wanted a free hand in the organisation of his Administration and had none of the rancor that made Reid anxious to use the occasion to crush the proud leader of the New York Republican machine, the course of events had brought the President-elect into a virtual alliance with the enemies of Conkling.

The legislature of New York was about to meet to elect a Senator. Among the "Stalwarts" there were three prominent candidates, Crowley, Morton, and Platt. Conkling was evidently embarrassed, for if he selected any one he would not be in a

[1] Garfield *Journal,* Dec. 13, 1880.

certain position to satisfy the two disappointed claimants, as he might once have done, with suitable Federal positions. Reid saw at once an opportunity to divide and conquer and selected Chauncey M. Depew as the candidate of the faction which was known by Conkling and his friends by the derisive nickname of "Featherheads."

In view of the prestige of Conkling there was evident danger that no member of the legislature would have the courage to vote against his wishes. This situation Reid described in a letter on the last day of the year: "There seems a chance of Depew for the Senatorship," he told his friend Phelps. "Platt and Morton are both keen, but Conkling doesn't decide. I'm to go to Albany Sunday night to tell our friends that they'll be defended if they defy Conkling and that they won't lose the good graces of Garfield. Over this we've had a dinner here tonight, Blaine, Depew, Robertson and some others and they've only just left me." So Reid went to Albany accompanied by Jay Gould, who was taking an active interest in the politics of New York, and Blaine prepared an editorial for the New York *Tribune* which assured the malcontents of protection in case of the threatened revolt. But the power of Conkling was still great and in spite of all the pressure that was used it proved to be impossible to elect Depew as Reid had hoped. "Tom" Platt was chosen instead; but in order to win the coveted honor he was compelled, according to Reid, to carry water on both shoulders, a task which he could perform with greater skill than any man in America. For while Platt continued to pose as a "Stalwart," he promised that if he entered the Senate he would not oppose the confirmation of any appointments, not even that of the arch-traitor, W. H. Robertson, which Garfield might make for Federal positions. On the whole Reid was satisfied with his first essay in political management, and wrote to John Hay: "Platt has been in to renew allegiance. He means it. . . . Platt's last words to me were, I am yours to command; draw on me at sight." [1]

Garfield in Mentor had no direct connection with the intrigues in Albany, but his friends through a public editorial written by his future Secretary of State had committed him to a position from which even if he wanted to do so it would be next to impossible to withdraw. After an interview with Sherman, who was generous and friendly, Garfield practically decided to give the Treasury either to Allison of Iowa or to Windom of Minnesota. Dorsey, who called about this time, evidently saw how the wind was blowing and assured Garfield that the New York proposition was "wholly inadmissible." Garfield found him "a man of great abilities and with strong and decisive views of the merits of men." There were even some indications of increasing weakness close to Conkling. Thus on January 24th, Edwards Pierrepont of New York, a close friend of Conkling and the author of the Republican platform of 1880, came to Mentor, and though he said that the New York leader "wanted Morton in the Treasury as New York's reply to Blaine in the State Department," he made no threats as Crowley had done, and suggested that some other position in the Cabinet might satisfy the just demands of the State. He told Garfield frankly that what Conkling feared more than any other thing was the possibility of the appointment of W. H. Robertson, who was the outward symbol of the revolt against Conkling.[2]

Garfield was essentially generous and forgiving, and accepted Pierrepont's visit as a peace offering. If he could satisfy both Reid and Conkling he would have been glad to do so. Accordingly he even considered doing more than he had at first thought desirable and began to give serious attention to the name of

[1] Cortissoz, *op. cit.,* Vol. II, p. 51. The credibility of Reid's story was later challenged by Platt, but seems to fit in with events as they developed. If true, it is clear proof of Conkling's precarious hold on power.

[2] Garfield *Journal,* Jan. 24, 1881.

Judge Folger of New York for the coveted post. But Pierrepont had undoubtedly underestimated the tenacity of Conkling's will, for Garfield was soon visited by Platt and Cornell, who again urged the appointment of Morton and refused to suggest any alternative. Even Grant came to the aid of Conkling with a strong letter urging the appointment of Morton.

Garfield was clearly right, for the appointment of a New York banker in all the circumstances would have been subject to much just criticism; and yet his desire to satisfy the conflicting elements in the party in New York was so sincere, that he decided to take a step of unusual boldness and to invite no less a person than Conkling himself for a personal interview such as had cleared away his difficulties with Sherman and with Blaine. The time was getting perilously short, the composition of the Cabinet was still in the melting pot, and in the midst of his worries, Garfield had had no time to give to the state paper which he must read in front of the Capitol on the fourth of March. So far, Garfield's dealings with Conkling had been entirely through subordinates and the two men had never met for a personal interview. But, somewhat to Garfield's surprise, Conkling accepted his invitation and reached Mentor in the afternoon of February 16th.

The interview was dangerous for both men, for such a meeting was sure to be heralded and misunderstood by unfriendly newspapers, and Garfield's disappointments at the results was correspondingly great: "We had a full conversation," wrote Garfield when Conkling had left, "on the Cabinet and kindred subjects. His knowledge of men was fuller and more intimate than I had expected, and in the main his judgment was sound." But on the chief issue there was no yielding, for Conkling again proposed Morton just as his lieutenants had done, and even though Folger was a member of his own group, made objections to the promotion of the Chief Justice of New York. "I told him I wanted his friendship," wrote Garfield, "and believed we could work together with independent and mutual respect—but I could not give Morton more than the War or the Navy. He went at 11.30." [1] Whom the Gods would destroy they first make mad, and when on that February evening Roscoe Conkling refused the generous compromise that was offered to him by the next President, even an understanding of Conkling's difficulties still leaves the impression that he deserved as he had made inevitable the measureless calamity that his enemies were preparing for him.

In spite of Conkling's virtual veto Garfield telegraphed at once for Folger. When he came Garfield liked him, and offered him the Treasury. But evidently Folger had been well coached, for he demurred, suggesting objections to his appointment. Garfield then offered him the position of Attorney General, to which the same objections did not apply, a tender that Folger consented to take under advisement. But when he reached New York, Garfield was disappointed to receive a letter in which Folger declined this position as he had the other.[2]

Garfield still felt that an appointment to the Cabinet from the regular wing in New York was essential to the harmony of the party. Accordingly, he wrote: "The delay of the New York appointment is crowding me into a close corner and may be embarrassing." For the moment he left the unsettled problem of the Treasury on one side, and telegraphed to Morton, offering him the Navy. This time he had better luck, for Morton was evidently pleased with a minor post in a cabinet where his friends had hoped to have him play a leading rôle. Just as Garfield was leaving Hiram for the last time on the journey which

---

[1] Garfield *Journal,* Feb. 16th, 1881.

[2] The political character of Folger's refusal was made evident when he accepted from President Arthur the position of Secretary of the Treasury which he had so recently refused from Garfield. For Garfield's overtures, see the *Journal,* Feb. 19, 1881; Feb. 23, 1881.

was sure to prove so momentous in his career, he received the acceptance of Morton, and his chief difficulty seemed to have been settled.

The Garfield family left Mentor on the last day of February. Several hundred people were at the depot and Garfield made a short address of farewell to his neighbors, and after speeches that evening at Warren, Ashtabula and Youngstown, reached Washington on the following day. The last weeks had been given exclusively to the problem of the Cabinet. Each successive arrangement had been like a house of cards, and everything had to wait until all the doubtful places were filled. It is curious to notice that in Garfield's various memoranda of possible Cabinets, all positions except the Department of State were considered in the light of geography and that the special fitness of a given man for the duties of his office was never allowed to complicate still further the political considerations that required recognition of each section of the party and the nation. Thus one list read: "State Department, Blaine; Treasury, Knox or Allison; New York, James or Morton; Pennsylvania, McVeagh; Indiana, Harrison; Illinois, Lincoln; South, Phillips or Morgan." Garfield's methods were probably not essentially different from those of other Presidents, and it is accordingly not to be wondered at that America has had Secretaries of the Navy who never saw a ship and other high officers who have learned the chief duties of their departments from some old clerk.

When Garfield reached Washington, in spite of the anxious study he had given to his chief problem, only three positions could be regarded as finally settled: Blaine for Secretary of State, Robert T. Lincoln for Secretary of War, and Wayne McVeagh of Pennsylvania for Attorney General. For though Morton was pleased with the post that he had accepted, his friends were not, and without apparent disloyalty he could not enter the Cabinet. Accordingly he declined, to be satisfied a little later with an appointment as minister to the republic of France. This left the two major problems, the Treasury and New York, exactly where they had been from the beginning. Having failed with Morton, Garfield asked Whitelaw Reid to telegraph for T. L. James, who was regarded as a regular, but whose conduct of the New York post office had proved him to have administrative abilities of a high order. To select a follower of Conkling without consulting him was even more contrary to the rules of the game than to appoint one of his enemies. Accordingly, James was virtually smuggled into Washington and to the hotel where Garfield was staying. "I asked him," wrote Garfield, "whether he was so connected with any person that he would be embarrassed in giving his full and just support to me about matters of administration and policy. He seemed free and earnest." Accordingly, Garfield appointed him on the spot to the position of Postmaster General, a place which as we shall see James filled with great distinction. The precautions that had been taken were apparently necessary, for later in the day, Conkling, Arthur and Platt came to protest, and though the last two said little, Conkling "was full of apprehension that he had been or was to be cheated." Thus with evident satisfaction Garfield records what seems to have been a stormy interview, for he had stolen a march on his adversary and won away from him one of his own followers. Conkling was in no position to protest the appointment of James, whom he now regarded as a traitor, but he was not yet at the end of his rope. In the evening, only a few hours before the inauguration, Garfield offered the Treasury to Allison of Iowa, who accepted at once.[1]

[1] Garfield *Journal,* March 3, 1881; Cortissoz, *op. cit.,* Vol. II, p. 55. Reid wrote to Miss Mills, March 2, 1881: "The policy is to detach James from Conkling and make him feel that he owes his appointment to that."

Garfield spent a busy night. After dinner at the White House, where he met the Cabinet of the outgoing President, he went to Wormley's, where he found sixteen of his classmates of college days at Williams and made them a speech. "Hotel at 11," wrote Garfield. "Worked on inaugural two and a half hours and wrote the last sentence at two thirty A. M., March 4." It was no wonder that those who listened to the inaugural address at noon that day found it the speech of a tired man, entirely unworthy of the high reputation that Garfield had justly earned as one of the most effective of American orators.

The next day should have been a red-letter day in the career of James A. Garfield, but his immediate anxieties quite overmatched the dramatic possibilities of a great occasion. Thus the diary commences: "At 8:30 A. M., Allison broke down on my hands, and absolutely declined the Treasury, partly for family reasons but mainly from unwillingness to face the opposition of certain forces. Though this disconcerts me, the break had better come now than later." Garfield's suspicion that Allison had declined for fear of Conkling was later partially justified when the Senator from Iowa supported Conkling against the President in the matter of the nomination of Robertson. After the inaugural ceremonies, the President of the United States took up again the question of his Cabinet, and late that night offered the Treasury to William Windom of Minnesota. At midnight, he went to bed "very weary." The next day Windom accepted and with the selection of Kirkwood of Iowa for the Department of the Interior and W. H. Hunt for the Navy, the slate was finally complete. Garfield wrote: "The result is better than I expected. Though not an ideal cabinet it is a good combination of esse et videri." The newspapers seemed to think, however, that the second element was predominant, although even *The Nation*, usually critical, was especially pleased

with the selections of James and McVeagh. But apart from
the qualities of individual members, Garfield had fought and
won a battle of genuine constitutional importance and no one
could say that his Cabinet had been imposed on him by any
leader however powerful. It is for that reason only that the
story is worth telling today.[1]

Brief as Garfield's presidency was to be, administrative policies of great moment to the welfare of the nation were undertaken and carried out. Thus, the new Secretary of the Treasury, William Windom, to whom advisers ordinarily as far
apart as Conkling, Blaine and Godkin had been equally opposed, and whom Garfield had chosen only at the last moment
and when his back was to the wall, proved to be remarkably
well fitted for the delicate and responsible duties of his position. A period of prosperity had set in after the long depression
of the seventies and, taking advantage of the abundance of
capital, by a bold use of executive authority, Windom paid about
fifty millions of the bonds that were now due and refunded
the rest, to the amount of more than six hundred millions, at
a rate of three and a half percent instead of five and six percent which had previously been paid. Best of all, these important transactions took place without arousing any of those
charges of favoritism to special banking interests to which any
Eastern banker would undoubtedly have been subject. The
decision to give Windom a free hand and not to call Congress
into an extra session was, as Garfield's journal shows, made by
the President in advance of any meeting of the Cabinet and
after consulting no one but Windom himself, an incident that
goes far to show the falsity of the tradition that during Garfield's term Blaine was the real President, a tradition against
which Blaine himself was one of the first to protest.

The incident of the refunding operations is apparently quite

[1] Garfield *Journal*, March 4, 1881; March 5, 1881; *The Nation*, March 17, 1881.

typical of the relations of Garfield to his Cabinet members, with whose activities he kept in general contact and to whom he gave adequate support. But Sherman is authority for the statement that both the general plan of the refunding and the details belonged to Windom, testimony to which the few brief references to the matter of Garfield in an unusually detailed account of his daily activities tend to give complete support. The lack of interference on the part of the President is the more striking because financial problems were the very ones on which Garfield had specialised for many years and in which he was justly regarded as one of the most competent men in the country.[1]

Similarly, Blaine in the Department of State was working out a policy that for better or for worse undoubtedly turned the foreign relations of the country in a new direction and that without anything more than a general approval and consent on the part of the President. A French company under the leadership of De Lesseps was attempting to build a canal across the narrow isthmus of Panama. The new importance of the canal problem gave Blaine an opportunity to announce that the United States would be the sole protector of the neutrality of the canal zone and that if a second canal by the Nicaragua route should become feasible, in spite of the hampering provi-

---

[1] That Garfield gave complete support to the policy of his Secretary but at the same time referred all details to Windom appears in a number of letters in the Morton Papers. Thus Levi P. Morton wrote, March 29, 1881, to his partner Bliss: "I had a conversation with the President on Sunday, with reference to the sale of Bonds, and had one today with Secretary Windom. . . . The President's idea was that it would be necessary to advertise for public proposals, and I therefore suggest that you should confer with friends with the view of making up a syndicate to bid for the 104 millions of 4s." After a second interview with Garfield, Morton was again referred to Windom and telegraphed at once to Bliss advising him to come to Washington to make the personal acquaintance of the new members of the Cabinet. (Morton Papers, N. Y. Public Library.) Garfield's decision on the fundamental question of an extra session of Congress appears in the following entry in his journal for March 24: "Wrote a summary of the arguments for and against the extra session. At Cabinet tomorrow will decide against it."

sions of the Clayton-Bulwer treaty America would build it. While this new proclamation of the Monroe Doctrine was characteristic of the policy of Blaine, it was Garfield who saw first the new importance of the Hawaiian Islands, who raised the question in a Cabinet meeting and, in offering the seemingly unimportant post of American minister to Hawaii to his friend Hinsdale, suggested that with the building of the canal these islands would become an American sphere of influence and a virtual extension of the American coast line. Later, the attempted intervention in the bitter war between Chile and Peru and the dramatic extension of the Monroe doctrine into a policy of Pan-Americanism to culminate in a great conference of the various American Republics, a plan for which, as the event proved, public opinion in the various countries was not as yet ready, were ideas originally suggested by Blaine. The details were also worked out by the Secretary of State, and though the plans were approved by the President and if he had lived the responsibility of these momentous decisions would necessarily have fallen on the Chief Executive, there can be no doubt that the story of our foreign relations in that busy spring and summer of 1881 belong to the career of the brilliant Secretary and not to the biography of James A. Garfield.

Thus at every point, the relations of Garfield to his Cabinet had a substantial similarity to those in the days of Washington. For having taken great precautions as we have seen to make sure of the necessary loyalty of his various ministers, Garfield preserved his constitutional right to be consulted, but gave to each minister within the limits of his own department the greatest possible freedom. Thus, as in the cases of Hamilton and Jefferson, there are no references to important decisions on questions of policy by President Garfield alone or even by the whole Cabinet in joint council, but many to ideas that were worked out by Blaine, or Windom, or James after consultation

with the President. To each plan Garfield made some important contribution which proved an unexpected capacity for
prompt executive decision.

The Cabinet appointments that met with the most general
approval of the reform elements within the party were those
of Wayne McVeagh of Pennsylvania for Attorney General and
especially of T. L. James of New York to become Postmaster-
General. But the very approval with which these names were
generally received was in itself sufficient to arouse the forebodings of typical machine politicians. The most powerful individual in the Post Office Department was T. W. Brady of Indiana, a former lieutenant of Senator O. P. Morton, who after
winning his spurs in the bitter political contests that marked
the career of his powerful chieftain, had been promoted by
President Grant to his present position. Here for many years
he had been in control of a large amount of patronage, including the awarding of contracts, in return for which he was apparently expected to levy campaign assessments on clerks in his
department and thus to contribute to the certainty of Republican
victories.

Brady had entrenched himself in a position already strong
by becoming the owner of a newspaper, the *National Republican* of Washington, of which the editor was a well known politician, George C. Gorham. Gorham was a close friend of Senator Conkling, a fact which gave special pungency to an editorial
that appeared in the *National Republican* soon after the appointment of James, in which that official received the significant warning "not to play the reformer."

For the past two years the postal service had been faced by
huge deficits of more than a million dollars a year which had
been met by special appropriations by Congress. It appeared
that these deficits were due to the unexpected cost of delivering
mails in certain thinly populated regions of the West. But the

matter seems to have aroused little public attention until it was taken up by the New York *Times,* which had already earned a reputation by its revelation of the activities of the Tweed ring in New York, and which now pointed out that some of these routes served by stage coaches rendered almost negligible services, one for example having a record of delivering three letters in a year for which it was paid by a grant of thousands of dollars from the public Treasury. When James became Postmaster General in the new Administration, the *Times* was already insistent on the investigation of what came to be called the "Star Route Frauds." In spite of the warning that he had received, James determined to get to the bottom of the matter and on March 7, 1881, received from President Garfield the necessary authority to let the chips fall where they would. Throughout what proved to be an unusually trying enterprise, the record shows that James had the support of the President and the hearty assistance of Attorney General McVeagh. In the circumstances, even before the results could be fully suspected, the decision to make the whole matter public was highly creditable to each of the three men.[1]

Brady and his associates appear to have been so certain that no investigation would ever be undertaken that incriminating documents of the most serious nature had been left in the easily available records of the department. The methods used had been astonishingly simple. Brady merely selected 93 mail routes, to which contracts had been awarded carrying an annual expenditure of $727,119, and in answer to petitions sponsored by interested Congressmen of both parties and under the pretence of "expediting the service" raised the public appropriations to $2,802,214 a year. The evidence secured by James and McVeagh made it perfectly clear that there was not the

[1] The report on the Star Route Frauds is in House Misc. Doc. No. 38, 48th Cong., 1st Sess.; the testimony of James as to the inception of the inquiry is in Pt. 2, p. 2.

slightest color of connection between the virtual gift of two millions of the public money and either the needs of the service or any increase of expenses actually incurred by contractors. As may easily be surmised, the favored routes had not been selected by accident. The family of S. W. Dorsey, the Secretary of the Republican National Committee, had been especially fortunate. Thus J. W. Dorsey, a brother, with eight contracts carrying an annual expenditure of $14,479, had his compensation increased to $147,273; J. M. Peck, a brother-in-law, was assigned $218,141 instead of $30,396 for which his contract called; and J. R. Miner, a partner of Dorsey, had received a similar increase which raised his revenues from $10,-371 to $135,678. The rest of the two millions had been spent in similar ingenious ways, and it was soon apparent that the country had seldom suffered from such barefaced rascality. When the matter became public the newspapers naturally began to ask who had really paid the expenses of the recent Dorsey testimonial dinner at which ex-President Grant and Vice-President Arthur had been honored guests.[1]

The first entry in Garfield's journal refers to the matter on April 9th: "In the evening," he wrote, "the P. M. Gen. and special agent, Lockwood, came and reported what they had discovered concerning the star contract service. Great frauds have been practiced and I will clear out the contract office." A few days later the President consulted Blaine, McVeagh, Windom and James. The situation evidently required the removal of prominent officers. "The corruption and wrongdoing," Garfield wrote, "has been of a very gross and extensive kind. I am surprised that it could so long have escaped the attention of the Hayes Administration." Garfield would have preferred to have removed Brady summarily, but by the advice of his Cabinet officers, on April 20 he "demanded and received his resig-

[1] *N. Y. Times,* May 19, 1881; *The Nation,* May 12, 1881.

nation." A few days later Brady published Garfield's letter to Hubbell, written during the campaign, in which Garfield asked Brady for assistance and inquired how the departments generally were doing.

Garfield had known that Brady had this very embarrassing letter in his possession, and acted with his eyes open to the very serious personal and political implications of the investigation. Thus at the very beginning of the inquiry, the Attorney General and the Postmaster General had waited on the President and McVeagh had said to Garfield: "Before a final decision, remember that these proceedings may strike men in high places; that they may result in changing a Republican majority in the United States Senate into a Democratic majority: that it may affect persons who claim that you are under personal obligations to them for services rendered during the campaign—and one person in particular who asserts that without his management you could not have been elected. Look these facts squarely in the face before taking a final stand, for neither the Postmaster General nor myself will know friend or foe in this matter." The President thought for a moment, walking up and down the room, and then replied, "No, I have sworn to execute the laws. Go ahead regardless of where or whom you hit. I direct you not only to probe this ulcer to the bottom, but to cut it out." [1]

Though most of the perpetrators of these frauds got off without punishment and certainly without refunding the sums that they had received, the immediate effect of the revelations was to save a sum that reached each year into the millions and to introduce a new tone into the conduct of the public business. Men like Schurz, Curtis and Godkin had long been saying that the common practice of asking officials of the government for financial assistance in campaigns was both improper and dangerous. But they had been called "professional reformers" and no one

[1] House Misc. Doc. No. 38, 48th Cong., 1st Sess., Pt. 2, p. 4.

had really believed them. Now the dismissal of Brady and the unwelcome publication of the Hubbell letter had furnished an object lesson of the essential soundness of their contention which was to prove more valuable than pages of argument.

Naturally enough, Garfield was especially troubled by the connection of Dorsey's name with the Star Route frauds. Thus on May 14, he wrote in his diary: "I was kept up until midnight by business connected with Dorsey's trouble. I have great sympathy for him and some doubts." And again, "McVeagh and James came to talk of Star Route frauds and Dorsey's connection with them. Windom to counsel caution in listening to accusations. I gave orders that no prosecutions should be begun without my orders." But one of the last entries in the diary records Garfield's insistence on vigorous prosecutions and corroborates the testimony of both James and McVeagh that the President gave them to the end the complete authority that they needed.[1]

The apparent necessity of conciliating politicians who were dissatisfied by the policy of civil service reform as it had been enforced by President Hayes and his Cabinet had, as we have seen, led Garfield during the campaign to make important concessions. His letter of acceptance with its promise to make appointments on the advice of members of Congress was undoubtedly a backward step. Although in his inaugural address he made a vague recommendation for a law on the subject by Congress, until such a law was passed, it was at once apparent that as far as executive action was concerned, the President would be guided by the principles of the spoils system as they had been made familiar to Americans in the last half century of their politics. The tide of office seekers had been partially dammed up for four years, and even Garfield with his wide experience

[1] Garfield *Journal*, May 14, June 1, June 29, 1881. House Misc. Doc. No. 38, 48th Cong., 1st Sess., Pt. 2, p. 29.

THE NATIONAL BARBER SHOP. "NEXT!"

(By J. Keppler, from *Puck*, 1880)

of Washington could not have foreseen the flood that was now to burst upon him. The campaign had been close and bitter and now apparently every one who had done any work, however insignificant, for the success of the ticket expected to be rewarded by a suitable position in the government service. Experienced politicians remarked that nothing like it had been seen since Lincoln laid the political foundations of a new party in that eventful spring twenty years before. John Hay, who had declined Garfield's offer of the position of private secretary to the President, now congratulated himself on his foresight. He wrote that the clamor for jobs was like the sound of beasts at feeding time, and he described the President as "living in a whirlwind, fighting like a baited bull against the mob, hounded down by politicians from morning till midnight." [1]

Garfield must have wished more than once that he had taken a firmer tone from the outset on the subject of the relation of experience and merit to appointments. Beginning on the day after the inauguration the entries in the diary refer for the most part to the insistent problem of the offices: "Four hours sleep only. The crowd of callers commenced early and continued in great force." Again two days later: "The core of these crowds is the indurated office seeker who pursues his prey with the grip of death." On March 8th, Garfield wrote: "The fountains of the population seem to have overflowed and Washington is inundated . . . I received several thousand in the East room. This was the easiest part of the day's work—for these callers were earnest kind people who wished to see me and shake hands before going home. But the Spartan band of disciplined office hunters, who drew papers on me as highwaymen

[1] Cortissoz, *op. cit.*, Vol. II, p. 58. Morton wrote to a constituent: "It is a vastly more difficult matter to secure a consulship than you seem to imagine. There are, I think, only 163 consulships in the whole world that pay a salary of $1000 or more, and there are, I fancy, several thousand urgent applications for such appointments." Morton Papers.

draw pistols, were men with whom I had to wrestle like a Greek—and the night brings me great weariness."

Garfield had none of that quality of melancholy that characterised Lincoln, but even he had to resist a strong tendency to be dejected and unhappy at the prospect that was offered by the work before him. "I love to deal with doctrines and events," he wrote. "The contests of men about men I greatly dislike." Though Garfield kept old friends in mind and found a surprising number of positions for some of them, others were necessarily disappointed and the President, with his warm heart and his craving for affection, was always deeply distressed. Thus G. U. Rose, who had been for many years a confidential secretary and almost a member of his family, was displaced by Joseph Stanley Brown, who without the title became the Secretary to the President. Rose wrote to Garfield, "My children bear the name of those you love. . . . Do you believe I named them because you were Congressman or President?" And, recognising his friend's deep loyalty, Garfield was grieved that through no fault of either the place had grown beyond his powers.[1]

There can be little doubt that if Garfield had lived he would now have taken a lead in the movement for a new method of appointment to office which the mere growth of the country had made so obviously necessary. Thus in one of the later entries in his diary he wrote: "I am feeling greatly dissatisfied with my lack of opportunity for study. My day is frittered away with the personal seeking of people when it ought to be given to the great problems which concern the whole country. . . . What ought not a vigorous thinker to do, if he could be allowed to use the opportunities of a Presidential term in vital useful activity? Some civil service reform will come by neces-

[1] Garfield *Journal*, March 5–March 15, 1881. Rose to Garfield, March 15. Garfield Papers.

sity, after the wearisome years of wasted Presidents have paved the way for it." [1]

In the meantime the old controversy with Conkling was entering a new phase, for Garfield, even if he had wished otherwise, had been thoroughly committed by Blaine's editorial in the *Tribune* to the recognition of W. H. Robertson and others of the revolting faction in New York, and Conkling was, of course, equally insistent that they should not be appointed to important positions within the State. On March 20th, while Garfield was considering New York offices, Senator Conkling called and made several suggestions for appointments which the President accepted. When Garfield remarked that he must recognise some of the men who had supported him at Chicago, Conkling urged him to give them foreign appointments. But the President replied that they did not deserve exile but rather a place in the affairs of their own State. "I will go as far as I can to keep the peace," Garfield remarked in his diary that night, "but I will not abandon the New York protestants."

Garfield's account, the only one that can be regarded as strictly contemporary, ends at that point. But Conkling later told his friends that as he was leaving he raised the question of the New York custom house, in which he was especially interested. It will be remembered that President Hayes had removed Arthur from the collectorship on the ground of his use of the position for political purposes and had appointed a friend of Sherman, E. A. Merritt. Merritt's term had still two years to run and he had apparently performed the duties of his post in such a way as to give satisfaction even to the most critical of reformers. Now, Conkling had no love for Merritt, but the position, on account of the nature of its duties and the large number of clerks, carried with it very great political powers. If a change were made and an outspoken enemy of Conkling's ap-

[1] Garfield *Journal,* June 13, 1881.

pointed, the absolute authority so long enjoyed by the Senator from New York as the dispenser of patronage within the State would be at an end. But Conkling was partially reassured, for when he asked: "Mr. President, what do you propose about the collectorship of New York?" Garfield replied, according to one account, that he might make no change until the end of Merritt's term, and according to another, merely said, "We will leave that for another time."[1]

On the day after his interview with Conkling, Garfield sent to the Senate a large group of nominations, including the names of five friends of the Senator from New York for high positions within the State. The newspapers generally at once interpreted the list as a surrender by the Administration to the demands of the New York machine. Whitelaw Reid and other friends of Blaine were of course greatly disturbed and in the evening the Secretary of State came in person to enter his formal protest. It does not seem probable that Garfield had as yet fully determined the next move in his program. But if he had been doubtful before, it was now entirely apparent that he must take some decisive steps to redeem his pledges to the Independent group in New York, as he had already in his judgment satisfied the just demands of Conkling. Accordingly on March 23, 1881, apparently without announcing his plans to any one, Garfield removed Merritt from the coveted position in the custom house, transferring him to the consulate in London, and sent to the Senate the name of W. H. Robertson, whom Conkling regarded as his most dangerous rival, for the

[1] Garfield *Journal,* March 20, 1881; G. C. Gorham, *op. cit.,* p. 10; G. S. Boutwell, *Reminiscences of Sixty Years,* Vol. II, p. 273. It will be noticed that the three accounts of the interview of March 20 have no necessary inconsistency and merely supplement one another, and that they give no support to the charges first made in the New York *Herald* for May 11 and later repeated by T. C. Platt, *Autobiography,* p. 154, that Garfield made a promise that he later violated.

vacancy which had been thus created. Garfield wrote in his journal: "This brings the contest to an early close and fully recognises the minority element. . . . The sensation produced by the above nominations was very great but I think the Senate will approve." More than once in previous years Garfield had protested against the encroachment of powerful Senators on the President's constitutional powers of nomination, and there is every indication that he welcomed and enjoyed the contest which was now sure to come for the establishment of a principle to which he was deeply committed.[1]

Conkling, for his part, saw at once that the appointment of Robertson was the beginning of the end. Thus, when his friend G. C. Gorham asked him what the news meant, Conkling answered quietly: "I don't know. All we ask is to be allowed to win in New York, and it is hard enough to do at best." [2] There was from his point of view only one hope, and that was to compel the withdrawal of Robertson's hated name or to prevent the confirmation which the President expected from the Senate, and to these ends his energies were now directed. He too could place his position in a high constitutional light and claim to be fighting for the independence of the Senate as the President was for that of the executive. But the American people generally saw that the real issue was not between these two departments of a recognised government, but rather between the

[1] Some of Garfield's best friends, including B. A. Hinsdale, and James and McVeagh in his Cabinet, believed that Garfield had made a serious mistake, not so much in appointing Robertson, as in removing the perfectly satisfactory Merritt for the purpose. *The Nation*, April 7, 1881, took a similar view: "The plan of satisfying everybody with something—or, in other words, of treating the administration of the government as a sort of Christmas tree, with bon-bons for all his little friends hanging on the branches—is not succeeding." On the other hand, the position now taken by Garfield, as shown by many letters received in these days, was undoubtedly popular and entirely consistent with principles expressed long before. See, Garfield, *Works*, Vol. I, p. 698.

[2] Gorham, *op. cit.*, p. 10.

President as an elective official and the system of boss rule as it had been established in some of the larger and more doubtful States. It was for this reason that the ultimate victory was almost sure to come to Garfield in the White House rather than to Conkling in the Senate.

The contest between the President and Conkling was unusually prolonged because the Senate for two months was deadlocked and unable to proceed to the consideration of executive business for which it had been summoned to Washington. The situation was in itself typical of the petty greed for offices that characterised the period. The division between the parties was very close, and at first it was supposed that the Democrats might be able to organise the Senate with a narrow majority. Since the business to be done was purely executive, the appointment of committees might well have waited until the regular meeting of Congress in December. But the various petty offices, of which the most important were the Secretaryship and the position of Sergeant at Arms and which included a number of ushers, pages, and the like, were now held by Democrats appointed when their party gained control two years before. The Republicans were anxious to replace these appointees with candidates of their own. Now finding that Senator Mahone of Virginia, who had been elected on an independent ticket as a so-called "Readjuster," occupied a strategic position, they arranged a bargain by which Mahone was promised the position of Sergeant at Arms for one of his supporters, Henry Riddleberger, provided Mahone would vote for Brady's editorial friend, George C. Gorham, as Secretary and for the other candidates on the Republican ticket. The result was to make the number of Senators on each side exactly equal, and since the Democrats were just as stubborn in demanding that no changes should be made as the Republicans were in their support of the

claims of Gorham and Riddleberger, everything was at a stand-
still until the feud was settled. It is probable that the controversy was prolonged by timid Senators who did not desire
to have to meet the problem of the Robertson appointment if
they could avoid it. Senator Dawes, the leader of the Republican caucus, had insisted that there was a great principle at
stake; but the growing tone of irritation in the newspapers
showed that the public had been unable to discover the principle
to which the Senator referred. Then had come the revelation
of the Star Route frauds, which made a contest for a friend of
Brady a definite political liability. Accordingly, on May 4th,
Dawes announced that the Republicans were ready to abandon
Gorham and Riddleberger and to proceed to the consideration
of the nominations submitted by the President of the United
States.

While this absurd controversy was occupying the attention
of the Senate, Garfield was under very heavy pressure to withdraw the obnoxious nomination. For Conkling had appealed to
the Republican caucus, where the burden of his complaint was
that Garfield had not consulted him about the appointment of
Robertson and had thus violated an unwritten rule which was
called "the courtesy of the Senate." In this position the Senator
from New York found substantial approval from men ordinarily so far apart as Dawes, Fry, Edmunds, Allison and Platt, all
of whom wanted the President to withdraw the nomination.
Whitelaw Reid was evidently fearful that the President might
yield to arguments of party advantage. Thus, on March 27, he
sent to John Hay a telegram to be shown to Garfield: "I wish
to say to the President that in my judgment this is the turning
point of his whole administration—the crisis of his fate. If he
surrenders now Conkling is President for the rest of his term
and Garfield becomes a laughing stock. . . . If necessary, we

can surely get enough Democratic votes to offset anything Conkling can do." [1]

But Reid had no need for anxiety, for every entry in Garfield's diary shows that he knew that he was right and that he was determined to see the matter through. As he remarked at the time, "They might take Robertson out head first or feet first, but he would not withdraw him." The day before he read the telegram from Reid he had already written, "If I am right in my plan of adjusting N. Y. affairs, I may conquer a peace." The next day when Allison came to present the complaint of Conkling that he had not been consulted, Garfield answered, "I stand joyfully on that issue. Let who will fight me." He now wrote in his diary for April 2, "I have taken occasion during the day to let several Senators know that the vote on R's confirmation was a test of friendship or hostility to the administration. . . . If Conkling assails me he will find it no rose water war." And on April 27th, he helped to break the deadlock of the Senate by telling Dawes that he wanted to know soon whether he was the registering clerk of the Senate or the Chief Executive of the United States.[2]

In the meantime, as the country became familiar with the important principles that were at stake, the tide that at first seemed to be running strong in favor of the position of Conkling began to turn. John Sherman, again in his old place as a Senator from Ohio, consented to become the spokesman of the Administration, thus relieving Garfield from the embarrassing necessity of relying in the emergency on Democratic leadership. Even the legislature of New York passed resolutions favoring the confirmation of Robertson. On May 4th, when the long

---

[1] In some mysterious way this telegram fell into the hands of Conkling and was later published in the New York *Herald*. See, N. Y. *Herald*, Jan. 6, 1882; Gorham, *op. cit.*, p. 11.

[2] Garfield *Journal*, March 26, March 27, April 2, April 27, 1881.

A HUMILIATING SPECTACLE

(See—Gospel according to St. Matthew, XXVII—35.—Revised Edition)

At the time of Garfield's death. A savage attack on Dorsey, Grant, Platt, Conkling and Arthur by Keppler
in *Puck*

deadlock was at last broken, and the Senate was ready to consider the nominations, it was generally conceded even by newspapers close to Conkling that the name of Robertson would not be rejected. From Conkling's point of view, there was only one way to save a desperate situation and that was to confirm promptly the uncontested nominations of Conkling's friends and then to adjourn without any action in the case of Robertson.

The President, however, was in no mood to be finessed out of a test. As soon as he heard that the Republican caucus had approved the plan of adjournment, and that one of the names from New York had already been approved, Garfield on May 5th promptly withdrew five of the New York appointments, thus leaving the name of W. H. Robertson standing alone, and, in the afternoon when five Senators came in a body to enter their protest, they were told by the President that he insisted on a showdown.

Garfield's coup d'état of May 5, 1881, has seldom been surpassed in decisive boldness or in brilliance even in the long story of contests between the American President and the Senate. For it was now obviously impossible to adjourn, as had been planned, without sacrificing five lucrative posts in New York. Conkling had made a sturdy fight, but he knew that he was beaten and that his political career, as Reid had foreseen, was almost at an end. Accordingly, on May 16th, in a long letter to the Governor of New York, Roscoe Conkling and Tom Platt, the two Senators from New York, presented their resignations from the Senate and appealed to the legislature of their home State for vindication. As so good a politician as Roscoe Conkling must have known, the dramatic gesture was from the beginning almost hopeless. In July, after a bitter contest in Albany and when the President was lying under an assassin's bullet in distant Washington, the names of the two Senators

were withdrawn and they were replaced by Warner Miller and
E. G. Lapham, two individuals who had previously been almost
unknown.[1]

Two days after the dramatic resignation of Conkling and
Platt, William H. Robertson was confirmed without a roll call
for the position of collector of customs at the port of New York,
and when on May 20th, 1881, the Senate adjourned, Garfield
wrote in his diary with even more than the Presidential fervor
usual on such occasions: "This is a great relief."

[1] The reasons for Conkling's resignation are easily understood, for he was too
proud a man to play a second rôle in a State where he had so long been in chief
command. But the real reasons for Platt's resignation still remain something of a
mystery. See on this point, H. F. Gosnell, *Tom Platt,* pp. 26–29. When Garfield
was shot, Conkling is reported to have said, "I cannot speak into an open grave,
I cannot battle with a shroud." But the contest for vindication was apparently
already hopeless. See, on this point, Cortissoz, *op. cit.,* Vol. II, p. 66, and H. L.
Stoddard, "As I Knew Them," p. 113. As to the contest in Albany, Garfield wrote
(*Journal,* May 25, 1881) : "Blaine has gone to New York. . . . I have fought the
assumption of Mr. C. against my authority, but do not think it best to carry the
war into N. Y." This was not the only time that Garfield differed from Blaine.

To Garfield in these busy weeks, while the White House was thronged with office seekers, the quiet strength of his wife had been as the shadow of a great rock in a weary land. Thus after a reception to the diplomatic corps, he wrote in his diary: "Crete grows up to every new emergency with fine tact and faultless taste." When she was away on a short visit the great house seemed very empty, and Garfield stole enough time from the place hunters to read "Ben Hur," which he admired as extravagantly as other Americans of his period. After sitting up one night until two to finish the fascinating pages, he determined to send Lew Wallace, the author, as minister to Constantinople to give him an opportunity to gather materials for another novel. When his wife returned, and especially after the beginning of the contest with Conkling, the depression of the early days of the Presidency seems to disappear. Garfield noted one morning in April, as if his eyes had been closed for a month, the long shadows on the grass and the beauties of the spring.

Then came his wife's serious illness, when, in May, for days at a time, Mrs. Garfield's life seemed to hang upon a thread, and the President moved as in a dream, scarcely willing to leave her bedside even to attend a very important meeting of the Cabinet. At this time, at the very climax of the contest with Conkling, Garfield wrote: "My anxiety for her dominates all my thoughts and makes me feel I am fit for nothing." At the end of the month, the fever suddenly abated and the load of anxiety was lifted. In June she was strong enough to go to Elberon on the coast, where the President spent a few days rejoicing in the growing strength of his wife. There he wrote: "The worry and work of Washington seem very far away and I rest in the large silence of the sea. . . . I have always felt that the ocean is my friend and the sight of it brings rest and peace." In a few short weeks he was to return to seek in vain the healing of the same friendly presence.[1]

The only unpleasant incident of the visit to Elberon was the coldness of Grant, who was visiting in the same place, and who managed to show plainly enough that he had not forgiven what he regarded as injustice to his friend Conkling. But the President was soon back in Washington, where the stream of callers, dammed up by his absence again swept away the brief remaining hours of his active life. On July 1, 1881, the diary which reveals so completely a personality, not faultless, for Garfield was essentially human, but warm, compelling, culti- vated, to the end almost boyish in the candor of its self- revelation, always lovable, suddenly ends with a last brief entry. For the next morning Garfield was to start to New England, where he hoped to give to his two boys, now ready to enter col- lege, a personal introduction to the institution where he himself had gone so long ago and from so different an environment.

The murderer, Charles J. Guiteau, apparently half crazed, certainly ill balanced, a disappointed office seeker, whose worth- less life had been a series of sordid failures, now feeling in some strange way that he had a great political mission to per- form, had for days been stalking the path of his unsuspecting victim. An evening or two before, when Garfield had taken a walk with his friend Blaine, Guiteau had had his opportunity but had apparently lost his nerve. But now, as Garfield, again accompanied by Blaine, entered the waiting room of the station, Guiteau stepped behind him, and shouting, "I am a Stalwart and now Arthur is President!" fired two shots. One merely grazed the President's arm but the other, after striking one

---

[1] Garfield *Journal*, May 6; May 30; June 18, 1881.

of the vertebrae of the spinal column, became deeply embedded in the muscles of the back. While an attendant seized the murderer before he could escape, the President fell in a faint from the shock, but recovered consciousness almost at once. Physicians were hastily summoned, and after a superficial examination, removed Garfield first to an office on the second floor of the station and from there to the White House.[1]

Mrs. Garfield was still at Elberon, when a tactfully worded telegram summoned her to the long vigil, in which a nation without regard now to party or to section watched with her in anxious sympathy at the bedside of her husband. In the first days, when the life of Garfield was regarded as in the

---

[1] During the long illness of Garfield, Guiteau was of course kept in prison, guarded by soldiers, where one of his guards attempted to kill him by shooting through an open window. On November 14, 1881, he was placed on trial for his life; more than two months later, on January 25, 1882, the jury brought in their verdict of guilty, and after the usual appeals, which were denied, Guiteau was executed on the day originally set by the court, June 30, 1882. The trial was generally regarded as a disgrace to American jurisprudence. For the only question at issue was whether Guiteau was in the legal sense insane. Yet the district attorney, Corkhill, who was apparently not averse to publicity, insisted on wasting days in proving the notorious fact that Garfield had been murdered, even going to the length of exhibiting in the court-room the injured vertebra from the body of the dead President. Guiteau himself commenced the proceedings every morning by a wild harangue and interrupted lawyers and witnesses constantly. Either because these outbursts might throw light on the disputed question of sanity, or because he did not know how to prevent them, the judge allowed not only these interruptions but even more scandalous outbursts of laughter and applause from the crowds of society people who attended the trial. The chief burden of the defence fell to the brother-in-law of Guiteau, George Scoville, whose lack of familiarity with criminal law was apparent at every stage. At the end, to make a bad matter worse, ten days were used in harangues to the jury, one by an assistant to the prosecutor named Porter appearing today peculiarly indecent. As usual in such cases, the experts differed widely on the question of Guiteau's sanity, proving conclusively that no one knew precisely what was meant by the legal term "insane." But the weight of testimony favored the conclusion which the jury reached after a brief deliberation of less than thirty minutes.

The records of the case fill three large volumes, one of the most curious documents in the history of jurisprudence: *Report of the Proceedings in the Case of the U. S. vs. Charles J. Guiteau* (Washington, 1882).

gravest danger, a popular subscription for the family of the President was sponsored by Cyrus Field of New York. This was later completed and brought to Mrs. Garfield a sum of more than three hundred thousand dollars, which placed her beyond the necessity of those pitiful appeals to the charity of Congress that had characterised the case of Mrs. Lincoln.

Through long weeks and months of alternate despair and hope, though Garfield himself once remarked, "People must be tired of hearing of my symptoms," the public never wearied of reading the detailed bulletins that came from the sick room and insisted on every scrap of gossip that might throw light on the chances of recovery. And this was not mere idle curiosity, since there was every indication that Garfield had now become far and away the most popular man in the country. For America saw in him as she was just beginning to see also in Lincoln, a symbol of her own unrivalled opportunities for the development of the individual. Had he lived, there can be little question that with his clear vision of what needed to be done, and now unhampered by any binding limitations of party or of faction to which the ordinary political leader is necessarily subject, Garfield at the age of fifty, mature and ennobled by a nation's sympathy, would have had an unequalled opportunity for public service. In that sense, the tragedy of Garfield was a greater and more pitiable, even, than that of Lincoln.

Those months showed also how well, in a great emergency, America might get along for a time without a President. For Garfield signed only one state paper and that unimportant, and the interviews with the members of his Cabinet were few and brief. And though the newspapers discussed the meanings of the word "disability" in the Constitution and speculated on the circumstances in which the Vice-President might assume the duties of the Presidency, as long as Garfield lived there was no real demand that the problem should be settled in any practical way. Nor did Arthur himself, of course, press for any such solution.

The finer qualities of Garfield which his friends had long experienced, his courage, his unfailing kindness, his generosity, above all his essential sanity, were now emphasised by the poignancy of his tragic situation. Thus on the day of the attack, one of the first persons to reach the White House was General Sherman, who telegraphed at once to his brother: "Just came from the White House. Saw and talked with General Garfield. Mind and memory clear and he is personally hopeful. The doctors shake their heads." [1] From the beginning Garfield took the cool interest in the case which one might have expected from a detached observer. The surgeon in charge of the case was Dr. D. W. Bliss of Washington, who had been originally summoned by the Secretary of War, Robert T. Lincoln, but whom, partly because he had once been a neighbor in the Western Reserve, Garfield himself selected as his chief physician. On July 3, Garfield asked Bliss whether he had a chance, and the doctor answered: "Mr. President, your injury is formidable. In my judgment, you have a chance for recovery." [2]

Thus through seventy-nine long days, while the nation waited, alternate hope succeeded to despair. More than once Garfield himself with his calm judgment must have realized how slender were the chances. For on July 17th, lying on his back, he wrote on a card prophetic words that were afterwards

---

[1] R. S. Thorndyke, *The Sherman Letters*, p. 350.

[2] Other physicians connected with the case were Surgeon-General J. K. Barnes, Dr. J. J. Woodward, and Dr. Robert Reyburn. On July 3, Drs. D. H. Agnew of Philadelphia and F. H. Hamilton of New York were summoned and were after that time closely connected with the case (Interview, 1931, with Dr. J. H. Girdner, who as an assistant to Hamilton was frequently present).

The account of the illness of Garfield is based on D. W. Bliss, "The Illness of President Garfield," *Century Magazine,* Vol. XXIII, on the report of the surgeons in the *Medical Record,* October 8, 1881, and on their papers, including an account of the autopsy preserved in the N. Y. Public Library.

published in facsimile: "Strangulatus pro Republica," and signed it, "J. A. Garfield." But one month later he wrote to his aged mother in Ohio the one letter that came from his sick room during that long illness and which was widely reproduced: "Don't be disturbed by conflicting reports about my condition. It is true I am still weak and on my back, but I am gaining every day, and need only time and patience to bring me through." When he heard, late in July, that Roscoe Conkling was finally defeated for the Senate, the man who had refused to carry the war into Albany or to strike even an opponent when he was down, merely said: "I am glad it is over. I am sorry for Conkling. He has made a great mistake in my judgment. I will offer him any favor he may ask, or any appointment he may desire." And Conkling called in person at the White House to express his sympathy. Once only, Garfield asked about Guiteau, and then with characteristic detachment gave his judgment: "He must be insane. Why should he want to kill me?"

The pity of it all was that, in the judgment of modern surgeons, with the development of the X ray and with more careful use of antiseptic methods that even then were being advocated by Lister, the wound itself should not have proved dangerous or even serious. But at the time, in spite of the efforts of no less a person than Alexander Graham Bell to come to the aid of the doctors with a clever electrical device, the location of the bullet remained an unsolved mystery. Thus at the beginning it was supposed to be embedded in the liver and even at a late period to have passed quite through the body and to be located in the front of the abdomen, when as a matter of fact, it was only a few inches from the point of entry in the muscles of the back. As time went on, the bullet became encysted and caused no serious trouble. But in the meantime, the wound itself had become infected, and the probes of the surgeons followed and made still more dangerous the channel caused by the burrowing pus which they supposed to be that of the bullet. According to their lights, in view of the development of the science of medicine at the time, the surgeons did what might be done, and cared for Garfield with infinite anxiety and tenderness. But as the fever rose and fell the great form of the President was wasted until his strength was gone and even his relentless courage could see ahead no hope of victory.[1]

During July and August, Garfield had asked more than once when he would be strong enough to go to the old farm at Mentor. But even then he must have realised that so long a trip would not soon be possible. The heat of the summer was intense, and after many hesitations and almost as a counsel of despair, on September 6th, with infinite precautions, in which the perfection of the railroad arrangements aroused general admiration, Garfield was taken to what he hoped for the moment might be the healing presence of the sea. As he was carried out of the White House, those watching were shocked by the change that had come over the great, strong man who had been the President of the United States. But Garfield waved his hand cheerfully to the friends whom even now he recognised.

Garfield was comforted by the nearness of the sea, and for the first few days after his arrival at Elberon, he seemed to be improving. But he was now far too weak to have any real hope of recovery and he was not deceived. On September 18 Garfield asked A. F. Rockwell, who was one of his constant attendants: "Old boy, do you think my name will have a place in history?" His friend answered: "Yes, a grand one, but a grander one in human hearts. Old fellow, you mustn't talk in that way. You have a great work yet to perform." Garfield seemed to pause and think, and then answered with sad solemnity: "No, my work is done." The next evening, almost unex-

[1] This paragraph is based on conversations with surgeons of today.

pectedly in spite of the long vigil, there came a sudden spasm
of pain and the President was dead. It was the anniversary of
the great battle of Chickamauga in which he had borne so
large a part.

For two days the body lay in state in the rotunda of the
Capitol and was then taken to Cleveland, where the whole population of the Western Reserve seemed to have poured out to
pay their last tribute of homage to its favorite son. Literally,
thousands of sermons and addresses, with the life and death of
Garfield as a theme, were delivered and enough were published
to fill today a substantial place in the catalogue of any one of
America's greater libraries. Of these, in discriminating estimate of the character and career of the dead President, in the
fine eloquence of deep feeling, or in the music of its words,
none equalled the eulogy of James G. Blaine. The occasion was
dramatic, for on February 27, 1882, Blaine spoke in the hall
that had so long known Garfield's presence and to an audience
that included President Arthur and the assembled Senate and
House of Representatives of the United States. As Blaine
touched the career of Garfield he came to the late contest which
he described without evasion but, in the presence of many who
had so recently felt bitter, with faultless taste. As the speaker
finished that part of his address there was an audible sigh as
if of relief, and the peroration caught perfectly both the beauty
and the tragedy of Garfield's death: "Gently, silently, the love
of a great people bore the pale sufferer to the longed-for healing of the sea, to live or die, as God should will, within sight
of its heaving billows, within sound of its manifold voices. With
wan, fevered face tenderly lifted to the cooling breeze, he
looked out wistfully upon the ocean's changing wonders,—on
its far sails, whitening in the morning light; on its restless
waves, rolling shoreward to break and die beneath the noonday
sun; on the red clouds of evening, arching low to the horizon;

on the serene and shining pathway of the stars. Let us think that his dying eyes read a mystic meaning which only the rapt and parting soul may know. Let us believe that in the silence of the receding world he heard the great waves breaking on a farther shore, and felt already on his wasted brow the breath of the eternal morning."

To one who has not shirked the inevitable inconsistencies of a man who lived not in the cloister but in the thick of battle and of politics, this story must have shown that through the years James A. Garfield had grown in vision, in capacity, and in courage to the time that made his final hour a fitting climax to a great career. There lay at once the glory and the tragedy of his life.

The qualities which made Garfield an outstanding figure in the life of his times are now apparent; for few public men have left so complete and frank materials for historical judgments. In his innate capacity for hard work he was surpassed by no other congressional leader of his generation. Garfield gave to the study of a bill, to the preparation of a speech, to the infinite details of the Committee on Appropriations, to the exacting correspondence of a congressman and a candidate, the same painstaking care that in spite of an inferior training had made him the equal and the superior of his fellow-students at Williams. When he was an evangelist, his sermons were all written with meticulous care and are still preserved among his papers. Nothing reveals more completely this quality of industry than the diary which he began as a boy and in which, even when his days were full with the exacting duties of the Presidency, the entries continue to be long and almost unbroken. In contrast with Polk, who also kept a diary, Garfield is intimate and able to look on his own career with critical detachment; and, unlike John Quincy Adams, who is equally methodical and painstaking, Garfield is always scrupulously fair to his most bitter opponent.

More than most men of his day, he was a lover of books, with an eager curiosity and wide sympathy for many different types of ideas. In that respect he was very like Roosevelt, whose reading is a summary of most of the books which influenced the thought of his times. To the end the man's mind never lost its remarkable and inherently youthful elasticity. Garfield always went to school and never ceased to learn from men as well as books. So he came back from Williams with a much more generous attitude to other forms of religious expression than had seemed at all possible when he went away to New England; he was able from his preparation for the debate with Denton to acquire a real insight into the problems and the methods of modern science as it was beginning to develop, and in this contest he gained new interests which he never lost. Imagine Bryan learning as much from the Scopes' trial as young Garfield did from Denton! A little later, fresh from his evangelism, he could appreciate the point of view of an ardent Roman Catholic like Rosecrans and listened without prejudice to new ideas; and, in other years, he read with eager interest such books as Freeman Clarke's "Ten Great Religions" and could without disloyalty to his own convictions understand and accept as a friend even so severe a critic of the orthodox position as Robert Ingersoll. And all this without considering for a moment any outward change in his religious affiliations! Thus, throughout his life, he remained a faithful member of the church of his father and mother. Similarly, Garfield was always prominent in the ranks of the Masons.

Accordingly it often happened that problems, which to men of duller minds seemed simple because they were unable to grasp more than one point of view, were to Garfield very complex. His ancestry and training alike made him consider every question not merely from the point of view of immediate advantage but as a choice between immutable right and wrong.

More than once, with sensitive Puritan conscience, he worried about the implications of a decision that to another might seem easy and inevitable.

On the other hand, his personality was human, generous, sensitive to the point of weakness, eager for approval. Garfield instinctively shunned a quarrel, sometimes even when the cause was good; was always anxious to adjust his views to those of others; liked to be surrounded by friends who loved and admired him; disliked and was greatly worried over the slightest breath of criticism. One of his friends had this quality in mind when he said that Garfield liked an easy chair, a soft hat, and simple manners. To the end he remained entirely unspoiled, lacking any trace of personal vanity, astonishingly generous in gifts to family or church or school, friendly and hospitable to a fault. Thus, all too often, if Garfield was asked to do something, he did it first and then thought about it afterward. One of the best of many illustrations of this tendency was his acceptance of an invitation to address his classmates at Wormley's on the evening of March 3, 1881, when he knew that his inaugural address was still unwritten.

On this side of his nature, in which he was so much like McKinley, Garfield was certain to be a good party man and to play the game according to the rules. From such lovable qualities also came the chief mistakes of his life: his boyhood engagement with a young lady whom he scarcely intended to marry; his injustice to Lincoln and to Fitz-John Porter; the Credit Mobilier affair in which almost without directing will he allowed himself to be entangled; the De Golyer business where he took an easy path and, to accommodate a brother congressman, accepted a brief, without enough study of the motives of those who offered it to him; the promise to become a spokesman for Sherman which proved so incompatible with his own half-acknowledged ambitions; the letter of acceptance in which to avoid enmities he virtually knifed in the back the idea of Civil Service Reform; the unfortunate trip to New York in August, 1880, which solved an immediate problem at the risk of almost certain misunderstandings; and the easy good nature with which he endured the pest of office seekers. In each of these cases, as in others of less moment, Garfield's clear judgment led in one direction, his actions in the other.

Can such a man who so often drifted with the tide without even a look ahead be regarded as a great American? Never, if life were always a study in black and white—which, fortunately for most of us, it seldom is. The faults of will that arose from a sensitive, friendly nature were never mean. And more than once, on great occasions, Garfield's other quality came sharply into play. Behind his actions there was one of the keenest of brains, a cultivated intelligence. So when Garfield took time to study any question, when the clamor of friends and party associates was not too loud, his judgment was unusually sound. In such cases his mind rather than his loyalties dominated conduct. So here we have another story—in which, taken alone, we find a man clear in vision, marching with ready courage to ends definitely foreseen, rejoicing in the smoke of battle—every inch a statesman. The outstanding illustrations were the immediate and unhesitating decision to turn his back on the tenets of his youth and to come to the defence of an endangered Union; his shrewd analysis of the weakness of the volunteer system; his support against heavy odds of a national army; his stand against the views of his own section and in spite of such powerful leaders as Stevens, Butler and Logan for a sound financial system; his years of service as Chairman of the Committee on Appropriations when he weathered many a storm for economy in national expenditures; and above all the great fight that he made against Conkling and for the central constitutional principle of the Presidential form of government.

In this last case, Garfield's mind and heart, his grasp of principle and his friendship for Blaine and Reid, made the right path easy. So it was too, for the most part, as to the Star Route frauds, where Garfield's knowledge of the necessity for honest government ran in the same groove with the powerful influence of his great Secretaries, T. L. James and Wayne McVeagh. And, if for the moment he hesitated or seemed to hesitate when he found that his friend Dorsey was deeply involved, it was the more to his credit that he allowed the investigation to go on in spite of the certainty of a bitter back-fire from the endangered Brady. Surely, the man who in 1881 allowed the Hubbell letter to come out was a bigger and a more courageous person than the one who in September, 1872, out of considerations of party advantage, dictated his first and entirely misleading reply to the Credit Mobilier charges.

Face to face with a series of great intellectual and moral decisions, more critical than fall to the lot of most men in a short life of less than fifty years, Garfield's mind was always as clear as crystal. But the world—a world of partisan bitterness—was too much with him. So Garfield remained to the end essentially a party chieftain—loyal to his friends, magnanimous to his enemies, a good husband, a perfect father to his children, but only when his mind and his immediate loyalties pointed in the same direction able to rise above circumstances and to point the way to a better day.

On those occasions Garfield is a fighter—stern, uncompromising, courageous, but always generous. If he had followed more often his own best judgment, here would appear a statesman of the first rank. On the central problem of Reconstruction, he believed in impartial suffrage guarded by suitable educational qualifications; in his great plea in *ex parte Milligan* he pointed out more clearly than any other Republican of his day the dangers to American institutions that were inherent in military rule.

But when it came to voting he was praised as "one of the most trusty of the radical majority." He himself acknowledged some surprise, as well he might, when he introduced the bill which tied the hands of Hancock who was putting into effect the very principles which no one had stated with more force than Garfield. He did not believe in the election laws, but he was compelled by what seemed the necessities of his party position to block efforts to improve them. The tariff appeared to him a dangerous and at best a temporary experiment and, in time, he desired to have it lowered. But that time never came and after 1872 Garfield was found voting again and again for even higher rates. He believed in Civil Service Reform, but in a great crisis was compelled to yield to practical necessities which appeared too powerful.

These, from Garfield's point of view itself, must be regarded as his outstanding failures. But over against them were his great services to the endangered Union, his pleas for honest money when the skies were overcast, his contest for the rights of the Presidential office which he held in trust, and his contributions both in Congress and in the Presidency to the cause of honest and efficient administration. For these he still deserves as he once fully won the admiration of the country.

And if he had recovered, how free he would now have been from the petty demands of party and of faction! For he died just when, for the next eight years beyond a doubt, his clear mind could have been applied unhampered to the living questions of his times. Something of all this the dying man must have grasped when he asked whether his name would live in history. The answer came in the Pendleton Bill, of which the immediate sponsor was a Democratic rival from Ohio and which in the administration of Arthur first placed the principle of Civil Service Reform on a secure basis. History has many ironies, but surely none greater than the series of events, the Star Route frauds, the publication of the Hubbell letter, the dramatic resignations of Conkling and Platt, the shot in the old station in Washington, the wild cries of Guiteau, and the death of Garfield, which convinced even the most reluctant politician that some reform in methods of appointment was absolutely necessary. If Garfield lives in history, it will be partly on account of the charm of his personality—but also because in life and in death he struck the first shrewd blows against a dangerous system of boss rule which seemed for a time about to engulf the politics of the nation. Perhaps if he had not died he could have done no more.

THE END

Alexander, D. S. A political history of the state of New York. 3 Vols. New York. 1909.

Assassination of Garfield compiled from newspapers of the day. 3 Vols. New York. 1883.

Badeau, Adam. Grant in peace. From Appomattox to Mount McGregor. A personal memoir. Hartford. 1887. The relations of Grant and Garfield are discussed, pp. 324–333.

Balch, W. R. From the towpath to the White House. New York. 1882 (various other editions). The most popular of the early biographies.

Barker, Wharton. The nomination of Garfield. *Pearson's Magazine*. 1916. Important reminiscences by an active participant in the events he describes.

Beale, H. K. The critical year, 1866. New York. 1929.

Beale, Harriet S. Blaine (editor). Letters of Mrs. James G. Blaine. 2 Vols. New York. 1908. Contains numerous glimpses of Garfield.

Bigelow, John. The life of Samuel J. Tilden. 2 Vols. New York. 1895.

Black Papers (Library of Congress). The papers of Jeremiah S. Black, containing documents of importance, especially on the Milligan case, 1864–66, and on the Credit Mobilier affair, 1867–68.

Blaine, James G. Eulogy on James A. Garfield, February 27, 1882. Boston. 1882.

Blaine, James G. Political discussions, 1856–1886. Norwich. 1887. (Diplomatic correspondence, pp. 311–420; eulogy on Garfield, pp. 503–525.)

Blaine, James G. Twenty years of Congress. 2 Vols. Norwich, Conn. 1884.

Bliss, D. W. The story of Garfield's illness. *Century Magazine*, Vol. XXV, p. 299 ff. By Garfield's chief physician.

Boutwell, George S. Reminiscences of sixty years in public affairs. New York. 1902.

Bowers, Claude. The tragic era. New York. 1929.

Brigham, Johnson. Blaine, Conkling and Garfield; a reminiscence and a character study. New York. 1919.

Brisbin, J. S. Life of President Garfield. New York. 1881.

Brown, E. E. Life and public services of J. A. Garfield. New York. 1882.

Bundy, J. M. The life of James A. Garfield. New York. 1880, 1881. The authorized campaign biography by the editor of the New York *Evening Mail;* contains many important letters to Hinsdale. The account of Garfield's early life was obtained from his mother.

Chase, Salmon P. Diary, in *Amer. Hist. Ass'n Rep.,* 1903, Vol. I. Contains interesting references to Garfield.

Chase Papers (Library of Congress). Especially important in 1863 and 1864, when the relations between Garfield and Salmon P. Chase were very intimate.

Cleveland *Leader.* Friendly to Garfield and in close touch with affairs in his district. Especially important for Garfield's contest in 1874. (See issues of September 16, 1874; September 19, 1874; September 22, 1874; October 14, 1874.)

Congressional Globe, 1863–1873; *Congressional Record,* 1873–1881. There are frequent references in the footnotes to these debates, which are, of course, of the first importance.

Conkling, Alfred R. The life and letters of Roscoe Conkling. New York. 1889.

Connery, T. B. Secret history of the Garfield-Conkling tragedy. *Cosmopolitan Magazine,* 1897, Vol. XXIII, pp. 145 ff. By a friend of Conkling.

Conwell, Russell H. The life of James A. Garfield. Portland. 1881.

Cortissoz, Royal. The life of Whitelaw Reid. 2 Vols. New

York. 1921. Uncritical, but important on account of letters not otherwise available.

Cox, J. D. Military reminiscences of the Civil War. 2 Vols. Cincinnati. 1900. By one of Garfield's intimate friends.

Cox, S. S. Three decades of federal legislation. 1855–1885. Washington. 1885.

Credit Mobilier Report. House Reports, No. 77, 42nd Cong., 3rd Session. The chief source for an important incident in Garfield's life. As to Garfield see pp. 5, 6, 20, 21, 28, 40, 91, 92, 128–131, 136, 180, 181, 223, 228, 303, 353–361, 450, 451, 471.

Cullom, S. M. Fifty years of public service. Chicago. 1911.

Davenport, John I. History of the forged Morey letter. New York. 1884. An account by the official investigator appointed by the Republican national committee. Important but partisan in tone.

Dawes, H. L. Conkling and Garfield. *Century Magazine.* January, 1894. Dawes was a Republican leader in the Senate at the time of the controversy he describes.

Depew, Chauncey. My memories of eighty years. New York. 1922.

Documents Issued by the Union Republican Congressional Committee, 1880. 2 Vols. Washington. 1880. (Collected by Geo. C. Gorham) 83 documents.

Dunning, W. A. Reconstruction political and economic. New York. 1907.

Eckenrode, H. J. Rutherford B. Hayes: statesman of re-union. New York. 1930.

Fitz-John Porter Case. Official reports of investigations: 1862, in *House Reports*, 37th Cong., 3rd Sess., No. 71; and 1878, in *Senate Reports*, 46th Cong., 1st Sess., No. 37.

Fleming. W. L. Documentary history of reconstruction. 2 Vols. Cleveland. 1906–7.

Fuller, Corydon E. Reminiscences of James A. Garfield. Cincinnati. 1887. An important source for the early life of Garfield.

Garfield, J. A. A century of Congress. *Atlantic Monthly*. July, 1877.

Garfield, J. A. Letter to the Republican voters of the nineteenth district. Hiram, Ohio. 1873. Garfield's defence against various charges.

Garfield, J. A. National appropriations and misappropriations. *N. Am. Review*, 1879, Vol. 128, p. 586 ff. An early advocacy of a national budget system.

Garfield, J. A. and others. Symposium on negro suffrage. *N. Am. Rev.* (1879): Vol. 128, pp. 125 ff.

Garfield, J. A. Review of the transactions of the Credit Mobilier Company. Washington. 1873.

Garfield Papers (New York Public Library). A small collection dealing entirely with details of Garfield's last illness.

Garfield Papers (Library of Congress). An extensive collection containing: *1*. Manuscript Journal, 1872–1881. The journal is continuous except for a brief period in 1880 and is the chief source for the later chapters. 2. Letters sent, 1868–1881. *3*. Letters received (with index). 1852–1881. The early letters are especially useful to supplement printed accounts of Garfield's young manhood. *4*. Public utterances. 1852–1881. *5*. Notes and Miscellaneous Papers. 1859–1881. This collection is referred to frequently in the footnotes.

Gilmore, J. R. The life of James A. Garfield. New York. 1880.

Gilmore, J. R. Personal recollections of Abraham Lincoln and the Civil War. Boston. 1898.

Gladden, Washington. Recollections. Boston. 1909.

Goodrich, F. E. Life of W. S. Hancock. New York. 1886.

Gorham, George C. Roscoe Conkling vindicated; his controversy with Mr. Blaine, 1866; his resignation from the Senate and the causes that led to it, 1881. New York. 1888. By a personal friend of Conkling and based on conversations. Biassed but important for Conkling's side of the controversy with Garfield.

Gray, John P. Review of the Guiteau trial. *Am. Journal of Insanity*. 1882. A discussion by one of the alienists for the prosecution.

Halstead, Murat. The tragedy of Garfield's administration; personal reminiscences and records of conversations. *McClure's Magazine*, 1896, Vol. VI, pp. 269–279.

Hamilton, Gail (pseud.). Biography of James G. Blaine. Norwich, Conn. 1895. Contains important Garfield letters.

Hancock, Mrs. W. S. Reminiscences of Winfield Scott Hancock. New York. 1887.

Harmon, Joseph. Garfield, the lawyer. Yonkers, N. Y. 1929.

Harper's Weekly. Generally friendly to Garfield and especially important for its cartoons and illustrations.

Henry S. McComb vs. the Credit—Mobilier of America. Pa. Supreme Court, in Equity, Eastern District, January term, 1869, No. 19. The document on which the *Sun* based its startling revelations of September 4, 1872.

Hepburn, A. Barton. A history of currency in the United States. New York. 1915.

Hinsdale, B. A. (editor). The Works of James A. Garfield. 2 Vols. Boston. 1882. Each document is preceded by an able introduction by the editor. One of the chief sources for this biography.

Hinsdale, B. A. President Garfield and education. Boston. 1882.

Hoar, George F. Autobiography of seventy years. 2 Vols. New York. 1903.

Hoar, George F. James Abram Garfield. Boston. 1882. A eulogy delivered at Worcester, Mass., December 30, 1881.

Howells, William Dean. Life in letters of William Dean Howells, edited by Mildred Howells. 2 Vols. Garden City. 1928.

Howells, W. D. Years of my youth. New York. 1917. The father of Howells was one of Garfield's chief editorial supporters.

Hutchins, Stilson. Democratic political manual, 1880. Washington. 1880.

Ingersoll, Robert G. and others. Great Republican speeches, campaign of 1880. (New York Public Library, Ford Collection.)

Kerr, Winfield S. John Sherman. 2 Vols. Boston. 1908.

Mayes, E. Life of L. Q. C. Lamar. Useful for Garfield's reply to Lamar.

McCabe, James D. Our martyred president. Philadelphia. 1881.

McCulloch, Hugh. Men and measures of half a century. New York. 1888.

McElroy, Robert M. Levi Parsons Morton, banker, diplomat and statesman. New York. 1930.

Morton Papers (New York Public Library). A small collection, but containing important items for the period of Garfield's presidency.

Nation, The. 1865–1881. Defended Garfield in 1873 and supported him in 1880, but with frequent criticisms and reservations. The chief exponent of the growing demand for various reforms.

Nevins, Allan. The emergence of modern America, 1865–1878. New York. 1928.

New York Herald. Especially useful as the mouthpiece of Conkling in 1881. The issues for January 19, 1880, and March 8, 1880, contain important letters.

New York Sun. Especially important for the Credit Mobilier affair and later charges against Garfield. The issues which refer to Garfield are mentioned in footnotes.

New York Tribune (1861–1881). Generally friendly to Garfield except in 1873. Especially important in 1880 and 1881, when it was regarded as the chief exponent of Garfield's views.

New York World. Perhaps the leading Democratic newspaper and as such important for the campaign of 1880.

Oberholtzer, E. P. A. A history of the United States since the Civil War. 3 vols. New York. 1917–1926.

Official bulletin of the autopsy on the body of President Garfield. *Medical Record*, New York, 1881, Vol. XX, p. 364.

Official Records, War of the Rebellion. For Garfield's life, the most important volumes are, Series 1, Vols. 7, 10, 12, 23, 30, 31. These are referred to in more detail in footnotes.

Pedder, H. C. Garfield's place in history. New York. 1882.

Platt, Thomas Collier. The autobiography of Thomas Collier Platt. New York. 1910. Recollections which do not always stand the test of critical examination.

Potter Committee Report. 45th Cong., 3rd Sess. No. 140 (1879). The chief source for the disputed election of 1876.

Proceedings of the Electoral Commission. Cong. Record, Pt. 4, 44th Cong., 2nd Sess.

Proceedings of the Republican National Convention. Chicago. 1880.

Ramsdell, C. W. Reconstruction in Texas. New York. 1910.

Reid, Whitelaw. Ohio in the war; her statesmen, her generals and soldiers. 2 Vols. Cincinnati. 1868. Contains one of the earliest authorized sketches of Garfield's life. Useful for Garfield in the legislature of Ohio and in the war.

Report of the Allison-Wilson committee on the District of Columbia. Senate Reports, No. 453, 43rd Cong., 1st Sess. This is the chief source for the De Golyer charges.

Report of proceedings in the case of the U. S. vs. Charles J. Guiteau. 3 Vols. Washington. 1882.

Republican textbook for the campaign of 1880. New York. 1880. Contains a life of Garfield by B. A. Hinsdale.

Rhodes, James Ford. History of the United States. Vol. VIII. New York. 1909.

Riddle, A. G. The Life of James A. Garfield. Philadelphia. 1880. Early life based on Williams' "History of Lake and Geauga Counties." The author was a personal friend of the Garfield family.

Ridpath, John Clark. The life and work of James A. Garfield. New York. 1881.

Robinson, William A. Thomas B. Reed, parliamentarian. New York. 1930.

Rockwell, A. F. From Mentor to Elberon. *Century Magazine,* Vol. XXIII.

Scrap book relating to James A. Garfield (Columbia University Library).

Sheridan, P. H. Personal memoirs. 2 vols. New York. 1888. Unfriendly to Garfield.

Sherman Papers (Library of Congress). These papers have proved of great value for the relations of Garfield and Sherman in 1880.

Sherman, John. Recollections of forty years. 2 Vols. Chicago. 1895. Important, but as to Garfield, colored by later disappointments.

Sherman, Thomas H. Twenty years with James G. Blaine. New York. 1928. Mrs. Blaine's story of the assassination of Garfield, "July 2, 1881, a narrative of a day," pp. 80–90.

Shores, V. L. The Hayes-Conkling Controversy, 1877–1879. Northampton. 1919.

Smalley, E. V. Characteristics of President Garfield. *Century Magazine,* Vol. XXV, p. 168 ff. By a corerspondent who was intimately acquainted with Garfield.

Smith, Charles Emory. How Conkling missed nominating Blaine (*Sat. Eve. Post.* June 8, 1901).

Smith, Theodore Clark. Life and letters of James Abram Garfield. 2 Vols. New Haven. 1925. The authorized biography. Full and scholarly in its quotations of manuscripts and especially useful for Garfield's early years. Many of the conclusions on controversial topics require more critical examination.

Stanley, D. S. Personal memoirs. Cambridge. 1917. An unfriendly estimate of Garfield as chief of staff.

Stanwood, Edward. A history of the presidency. Boston. 1898.

Useful for party platforms and figures of returns in presidential elections.

Star Route frauds. Report in House Misc. Doc. No. 38, 48th Cong., 1st Sess., Pt. 2. The chief source for the Star Route frauds.

Stoddard, Henry Luther. As I knew them; presidents and politics from Grant to Coolidge. New York. 1927.

Taussig, F. W. The tariff history of the United States. New York. 1923 (and various other editions).

Thayer, W. M. From log-cabin to White House. Seventh Edition. London. 1882. A typical early biography.

Thorndyke, R. S. (editor). The Sherman Letters. London. 1894.

Upton, General Emory. The military policy of the United States. Washington. 1907.

Villard, Henry. Memoirs, 2 vols. Boston. 1904.

Watterson, Henry. "Marse Henry," an autobiography. New York. 1919.

Williams, C. R. The Life of Rutherford B. Hayes. 2 Vols. Boston. 1914.

Williams, C. R. Diary and letters of Rutherford B. Hayes. 5 Vols. Columbus. 1922–1926.

INDEX

Abolition sentiment in Ohio, 42
Academies in the West, 17, 18, 19, 20
Adams, John Quincy, 246, 357
Agnew, Dr. D. H., 353n
Allison, Senator W. B., 237, 325, 328-330, 345
Allison-Wilson committee, 237, 238
Ames, Oakes, 220, 221, 222, 223, 225, 227, 230-232
Amnesty bill, 248
Army bill of 1864, 144
Army of the Cumberland, 120
Arthur, Chester A., 286, 300, 302, 329, 336, 350
Ashtabula, Ohio, 328
Atlanta *Constitution,* 309
Atlantic Monthly, 182
Austin, Harmon, 42, 51, 88, 90, 239

Ballou, Eliza, see Garfield, Eliza Ballou
Ballou family, 3, 5
Ballou, Hosea, 4, 6
Ballou, James, 7
Ballou, Mathurin, 4, 5
Banks, N. P., 224
Barker, Wharton, 280-283
Barnard, Henry, Commissioner of Education, 186
Barnes, Surgeon-General J. K., 353n
Barnum, William H., 307, 308
Bateman, W. M., 290
Bayard, Senator T. F., 234, 272, 273
Beauregard, P. G. T., Confederate General, 84
Beecher, Henry Ward, 96, 297
Belknap, W. W., 249
Bell, Alexander Graham, 354
Ben Hur, 349
Bethany College, 9, 11
Big Sandy Valley, campaign of, 71-80
Black, Chauncey, 166
"Black Friday," 212, 245, 301
Black, Jeremiah S., 166, 167, 169, 176, 187, 188, 222, 229, 258

Blaine, James G., congressional career, 135, 137, 151, 181, 193, 211, 221, 224, 243, 246, 247, 248, 274, 280, 283, 286, 289, 290, 301, 303; in the cabinet of Garfield, 313, 314, 324, 326, 328, 331-333, 341, 350, 356, 361
Blair, Francis P., Jr., 132
Blair, Montgomery, 116, 149, 181
Bland-Allison silver act, 216, 261
Bliss, Dr. D. W., 353
Board of Public Works, 237, 241
Bond, Dr. Samuel, insurance case, 189
Booth, Almeda A., 4, 27, 30
Boss system, 283, 317-319, 329
Boutwell, G. S., 222, 342
Bowles, W. A., 168
Boynton, Amos, 8, 12
Boynton, Henry, cousin of J. A. G., 29
"Boys in Blue," 301
Bradley, J. P., 258, 259, 303
Brady, T. W., 312, 334-336, 344, 345, 361
Bragg, Braxton, Confederate General, 113, 117, 118-120
Brannan, Brigadier-General John M., 122
Bright, John, 210
Brooks, James, 135, 230, 231, 232
Brownlow, W. G., "Parson," 97
Bryan, Lewis R., 257
Bryan, William Jennings, 358
Buchanan, James, 166
Budget system, 276
Buell, Major-General Don C., 72, 74, 82, 83, 87, 89
Burchard incident, 252
Bureau of Education, 186
Bureau of Indian Affairs, 262
Butler, Benjamin F., 170, 204, 209, 211, 215, 232, 233, 360

Cabinet, formation of Garfield's, 313-331; relations of J. A. G. with his, 331-336

375

California, in election of 1880, 308
Cameron, Don, 280, 283, 286, 317
Cameron, Simon, 317
Camp Chase, 70
Campaign of 1872, 246
Campaign of 1880, 293-311
Campbell, Alexander, 4, 9, 11, 23, 29, 68, 187
Campbell, John A., 188
Carpenter, Senator Matt. H., 188, 234
Census, 186
Chadbourne, P. A., 185
Chandler, W. E., 252, 299, 317
Chandler, Zachariah, 317
Chase, Kate, 93
Chase, Salmon P., 52, 58, 81, 92, 96, 114-116, 129, 149, 150, 153, 162, 170
Chattanooga, 117
Chautauqua, New York, 302
Chautauqua salute, 295
Chicago, rivalry with New York, 315
Chicago Times, 243
Chicago Tribune, 238, 316
Chickamauga, battle of, 131
Chickamauga campaign, 117-131
Chile, war with Peru, 333
Chinese exclusion, 307-309
Chittenden, G. R., 237, 241, 242
Cincinnati Commercial, 223, 230
Cincinnati convention of 1880, 298
Cipher telegrams, 264, 308
Civil Rights Bill, 165
Civil service reform, 262, 286, 287, 293, 303, 337-348, 360, 362, 363
Clark, Brigadier-General W. T., 179
Clarke, James Freeman, 358
Clay, Henry, 246
Clayton-Bulwer treaty, 333
Cleveland, Ohio, 10, 356
Coffin, S. S., 310
Colfax, Schuyler, 132, 134, 155, 211, 222, 225
Collector of customs, port of New York, 341, 342
Committee on Appropriations, 214, 233, 238, 241, 246, 275, 357, 360
Committee on Banking and Currency, 195, 212
Committee on Ways and Means, 191, 199, 207, 212, 243
Confederate debt, 207

Conference of American Republics, proposed by Blaine, 333
Confiscation bill, 141
Congressional election of 1866, 165
Congressional Globe, 155
Congressional Record, 268
Conkling, Roscoe, congressional career, 135, 162, 256, 257; in campaign of 1880, 282, 283, 286, 288, 299-301, 305; controversy with Garfield, 314, 315, 317, 319, 320, 322, 324, 326, 327, 329, 341-343, 345, 347, 348, 354, 360, 363
Conscription, 144
Contraction of the currency, 207, 209
"Copperheads," 150
Corbin, A. R., 213
Corkhill, District-attorney in Guiteau case, 351
Cornell, A. B., 300, 323, 326
Cox, Jacob Dolson, 59, 65, 68, 127, 143, 161, 245
Cox, Samuel S., 134, 141, 148
Cranor, Colonel Jonathan, 75, 76
Credit Mobilier Company of America, 220, 221, 222, 224, 226, 229, 231, 296, 309, 359
Crittenden, Major-General T. L., 112, 113, 120
Crowley, Richard, 302, 323
Curtis, Benjamin R., 188
Curtis, G. W., 337

Dana, Charles A., 114, 123, 125, 128, 129, 222, 309
Davenport, John I., 307
Davis, David, 170, 246, 258
Davis, Henry Winter, 131, 134, 151, 152, 153, 168, 268
Davis, Jefferson, 125, 248, 249
Dawes, Henry L., 134, 193, 197, 204, 222, 225, 345, 346
Debates in Ohio, 45
Debtors, point of view as to paper money, 206, 210
DeGolyer-McClelland Company, 237
DeGolyer paving contract, 236, 238, 239, 296, 309, 359
DeLesseps, Ferdinand, 332
Democratic candidates of 1880, 298

Democratic National Committee, 307, 308

Democratic party, 147, 166, 180, 223, 224, 245, 263, 265, 266, 272, 298

Dennison, William, 52, 57-60, 64, 70, 274, 290, 291

Denton, John, 46-48, 358

Depew, Chauncey, 300, 320, 324

Disability of the President, 352

Disciples of Christ, 4, 11, 24, 40, 187, 358

Dorsey dinner, 304n, 305n, 336

Dorsey, J. W., 336

Dorsey, S. A., 257

Dorsey, Stephen W., 294, 299, 303, 325, 336, 338, 361

Douglas, Stephen A., 246, 295

Dunshee, Norman, 42, 43

Durant, T. C., 220, 221

Economic Geography, influence of in career of J. A. G., 9

Edmunds, Senator G. F., 286, 289, 345

Eels, Charles P., 310

Elberon, New Jersey, 349, 351, 355

Election laws, 265, 270, 271

Election of 1876, 247-256

Electoral Commission, 258, 259

Electoral count, 255, 256, 260

Emancipation Proclamation, 54

Emerson, Ralph Waldo, 5, 33

English, James E., 172

English, William H., 298

"Era of bloody shirt," 247

Erie Canal, 8, 10

Eulogies of J. A. G., 356

Evarts, William M., 266

"Evening Star," 15, 25

Faneuil Hall, speech of Garfield in, 217

"Featherheads," 324

Federalist, The, 164

Ferry, O. E., 256

Field, Cyrus, 352

Field, David D., 166

Fifth Avenue Hotel, New York, 300

Fifth Military District, 175-177

First National Bank, of New York, 315

Fish, Hamilton, 300

Fisk, James, 212, 213

Five-twenty bonds, 205

Folger, C. J., 326, 327

Forty-second Ohio Infantry, 70

Foster, Charles, 289, 293, 321

Fourteenth Amendment, 165, 247

Freedmen's Bureau bill, 165

Freemasons, membership of J. A. G. in order of, 358

Free Will Baptists, 24

Frémont, John C., 150

Fry, W. P., 345

Fuller, Corydon E., 27, 251, 252, 292

Fuller, Margaret, 4

Garfield, Abram, father of J. A. G., 6, 8, 12

Garfield, Abram, son of J. A. G., 183

Garfield, Edward, 4

Garfield, Eliza Ballou, mother of J. A. G., 3, 6, 7, 10-12, 16, 17, 52, 53, 354

Garfield family, 3, 5

Garfield, Harry Augustus, son of J. A. G., 132

Garfield, Hitty, 8, 12

Garfield, Irvin McDowell, 183

Garfield, James Abram

Early lives of, 1; ancestry, 5; early education, 13, 14; on the Ohio canal, 14, 15; at Geauga Academy, 17, 18; teaching a district school, 21; religious backgrounds, 11, 23-26; at Western Reserve Eclectic Institute, 26, 27; classical studies, 27; an early love affair, 28, 29; choice of a college, 31; at Williams College, 33-38; as a college teacher, 39; as an evangelist, 40, 49; in the campaign of 1856, 42; a college president, 42; marriage, 44; debate with Denton, 46, 47, 48; relations to college students, 48, 49; personal appearance, 50; transition to politics, 51-53; enters Ohio Senate, 57; speech at Louisville, 60; in campaign of 1860, 61; secession, 62; attitude to Lincoln, 63; enters the army, 69; colonel of forty-second Ohio infantry, 71, 72; in Big Sandy campaign, 72-75; growing bitterness towards the South, 80; becomes a Brigadier-General, 81; attitude to West Point men, 82; in Buell's army, 82-86; the Turchin court-martial, 87; candidate for Congress, 91; the guest of Chase, 92-94; criticisms of Lincoln, 92, 93; election to Congress, 96; the Fitz-John Porter court-martial, 99; later attitude to Porter, 102; returns to the army, 104, 105; at headquarters of Rosecrans, 106-108; Chief of Staff, 108, 109; early admiration for Rosecrans, 111; influence on strategy, 112, 113; advice rejected, 113; in Tullahoma campaign, 113, 114; criticisms of Rosecrans, 116; in Chickamauga campaign, 117-127; the ride to Thomas, 123, 124; resignation as chief of staff, 126; the Quarrel with Rosecrans, 128-130; enters the Thirty-eighth Congress, 131; qualities as a Congressman, 137; changing estimates of Lincoln, 138-156; views of confiscation, 142, 143; on the Military Committee, 144-146; attack on Long, 148, 149; at Warren convention, 153; views on Reconstruction, 158-180; negro suffrage, 161, 181, 182; *ex-parte Milligan,* 166, 167, 168; attitude to military arrests, 167; contest with Hancock in 1867, 174, 175; family life at Hiram, 183-184; educational interests, 185, 186; the census, 186; law practice, 187-191; attitude on protection, 191-201; Chairman of Committee on Appropriations, 190; position on financial measures, 202-218; arguments against inflation, 207-209, 210; elected to Cobden Club, 210; clash with Logan and Butler, 211; Gold panic investigation, 212, 213; attitude to free silver, 216; advocates "honest money," 217; mentioned in Credit Mobilier scandals, 222; denials and explanations, 222; testimony before Poland Committee, 225, 226; report of committee, 228; publishes a defence, 229; newspaper attacks, 232; "salary grab" incident, 233-236; the DeGolyer scandal, 236-240; reelection to Congress, 239, 240; refusal to accept a Democratic nomination, 245; minority leader in the House, 246; replies to Hill and to Lamar, 247-250; the "visiting statesman," 252-254; the Electoral Commission, 255-261; spokesman for Hayes, 261, 262; contest over election law, 265-273; election to Senate, 273-274; supports Sherman, 274-275; summary of eighteen years in the House, 275-277; suggested for the Presidency, 278-281; relations to Sherman, 281; evidence of an organized movement for, 282, 283; leadership of anti-Grant forces, 281-285; speech for Sherman, 288; nomination for the Presidency, 289-292; campaign songs, 293; letter of acceptance, 293; organization of a national committee, 294, 295; policy of silence, 295-297; trip to New York, 299-302; letter to Hubbell, 303; enlists aid of John D. Rockefeller, 304; attitude to Morey letter, 309; received news of victory, 310, 311; selection of a cabinet, 312-330; inauguration, 330; relations to cabinet members, 331-334; the Star Route frauds, 334-338; office seekers, 339, 340; controversy with Conkling, 341, 348; his wife's illness, 350, 351; shot by Guiteau, 350; hopes for recovery, 351-353; nature of the wound, 354; transfer to Elberon, 355; death, 356; funeral obsequies, 356; personal qualities, 357-362; his place in history, 362, 363

Garfield, James Rudolph, 183

Garfield, Lucretia Rudolph, 30, 36, 37, 44, 45, 183, 184, 305, 349-352

Garfield, Mary (Mrs. Stanley-Brown), daughter of J. A. G., 8, 183

Garfield, Solomon, 6

Garfield, Thomas, grandfather of J. A. G., 6

Garfield, Thomas, brother of J. A. G., 8, 12, 13

Geauga Academy, 18

General orders, No. 40, 176
Giddings, Joshua R., 90, 137, 138
Gilmore, J. A., suggests Rosecrans for the Presidency, 111
Girdner, Dr. J. H., 353n
Gladden, Washington, 50
Glover committee, 241, 242
Glover, J. M., 241, 242
Godkin, E. L., 331, 337
Gold Act of 1900, 204
Gold panic investigation, 212-214
Gorham, George C., 334, 342-345
Gould, Jay, 212-214, 301, 319, 324
Gramercy Park, New York, 264
Granger, Major-General Gordon, 113, 123, 126
Grant, General Ulysses S., 84, 180, 198, 212, 213, 215, 245-247, 280, 283, 288, 289, 298, 302, 305, 316, 326, 334, 336, 350
Grant, Mrs. U. S., 283
Greeley, Horace, 18, 96, 179, 180, 193, 223, 295, 319
Greenbacks, 205
Greenback party, 217, 303
Grier, W. A. M., 282
Guiteau, Charles J., 2, 308, 350, 351, 354, 363

Halleck, Major-General H. W., 72, 84, 93, 97, 131
Halstead, Murat, 289
Hamilton, Alexander, 333
Hamilton, Dr. F. H., 353
Hampton, Wade, 172, 181, 182
Hancock bill, 362
Hancock, Major-General W. S., 174, 175, 196, 306, 310
Harker, Colonel C. G., 82, 83
Harper's Weekly, 283
Harrison, Benjamin, 328
Hart, Joseph, 307, 308
Hawaii, 333
Hay, John, 320, 324, 339, 345
Hayden, A. Sutton, 41
Hayes, John L., 192, 196
Hayes, Rutherford B., 9, 103, 162, 215, 218, 251-253, 257, 258, 260-262, 264, 267, 273, 278, 279, 286, 293, 296, 298, 299, 312, 315, 336
Hendricks, Thomas A., 181

Hewitt, Abram S., 307
Hibbard, E. A., 234n
Hill, B. H., 248, 250
Hinsdale, Burke A., 27, 63, 97, 163, 165, 177, 183, 184, 189, 215, 223, 229, 245, 333, 343
Hiram College, 39, 42, 183, 184
Hitchcock, H. L., President of Western Reserve University, 45
Hoar, George F., 284, 291
Holman, W. S., 134, 246, 276
Holmes County, Ohio, 151
Holt, Joseph, 101
Hooker, Major-General Joseph, 93
Hopkins, Mark, 31, 32, 38, 184, 185
Horr, R. A., 274
Horsey, Stephen, 168
Howells, W. C., Editorial supporter of J. A. G., 184
Howells, William Dean, 78, 184
Hubbell, Jay A., 303
Hubbell letter, 361, 363, 377
Hunt, W. H., of Louisiana, 330
Hunter, Major-General David, 99, 101
Hutchins, John, 90, 91

Independent group, in New York, 342
Independent Republicans, in 1872, 245
Indiana, boss system in, 317
Indiana delegation in Chicago, 290, 291
Indiana, election of 1880 in, 303, 304
Inflation, 205
Inflation bill, 215
Ingersoll, Robert G., 287, 309
Insurance cases, 189
Iron and Steel Bulletin, quoted, 200

Jackson, T. J., "Stonewall," 99
James, T. L., 328, 329, 331, 333-338, 343, 361
Jefferson, Thomas, 333
Jenkins, C. E., 242
Jewell, Marshall, 294, 296, 297
Johnson, Andrew, 9, 134, 150, 155, 158, 160, 162, 172, 177, 204
Johnson, Reverdy, 101, 204
Johnston, Albert Sidney, Confederate General, 84
Joy, James F., 287, 288
Julian, George W., 158

Kelley, W. D., known as "Pig-iron," 135, 193, 196, 208, 222
Kellogg, W. P., 252
Kelly, John, 299
Kentucky, attitude of eastern section in Civil War, 76
Kenyon College, 9, 257
Key, David M., 312
Kirkwood, S. J., 330
Knox, John J., 328
Ku Klux Klan, 179

Lamar, L. Q. C., 172, 181, 182, 247, 249, 250
Land grants to railroads, 219
Lapham, E. G., 348
Learned, Mrs. Maria, 37
Lee, Robert E., Confederate General, 99
Letcher, Amos, 15
Lincoln, Abraham, compared with Garfield, 1, 2, 3, 23; relations to Garfield, 63, 81, 92, 94, 95, 99, 131, 132-134, 139-141, 146, 150, 168, 172, 352
Lincoln, Mrs. Abraham, 352
Lincoln, Robert T., 316, 328, 339, 353
Lincoln, Thomas, 2
Lockwood, agent in investigation of frauds, 336
Logan, John A, 209, 211, 283, 286, 294, 304, 316, 360
Long, Alexander, 148, 149
Longstreet, James, Confederate General, 99, 101, 102
Lookout Mountain, 117, 125
Louisiana in 1876, 252-254

Mahone, William, 344, 345
Mahoning County, Ohio, 195
Maine, election of 1880 in, 303
Marshall, Humphrey, Confederate General, 72, 75-81
Marshall, John, 163
Maryland, emancipation in, 131
Masons, see Freemasons
Matthews, Stanley, 253, 260
McClellan, Major-General George B., 66, 72, 81, 92, 94, 99, 100, 107, 153
McComb, Henry S., 220-222

McCook, Major-General A. M., 113, 120
McCrary, George W., 224
McCulloch, Hugh, 207, 209
McDonald, J. P., 168
McDowell, Major-General Irvin, 66, 102
McGarrahan claim, 245
McKinley, William, 196, 204, 359
McVeagh, Wayne, 280, 328, 331, 334-338, 343
Meddill, Joseph, 316, 321
Mentor, Ohio, 183, 310, 314, 323, 325, 328, 355
Merrick, W. M., 224
Merritt, E. A., 286, 341, 342
Middle Creek, battle of, 77-79
Military Committee, 190
Militia System, 66
Miller, Warner, 348
Milligan, ex parte, 166, 173, 176, 187, 361
Milligan, L. P., 168
Miner, J. M., 336
Missionary Ridge, 117
Mitchell, Major-General O. M., 87
Monroe Doctrine, 333
Monroe, James, associated with Garfield in Columbus, 59
Morey, H. L., 307
Morey letter, 306-310
Morgan, G. W., 328
Morrill, J. S., 134, 234
Morton, Bliss, and Company, 315
Morton, Levi P., 292, 297, 299, 300-302, 315, 322, 323, 326-329, 332, 339
Morton, Oliver P., 317, 334

Napoleonic Axioms, 99
Nation, The, 294, 330, 343
National Association of School Superintendents, 186
National Republican, 334
Navy Department, 327
Negley, Brigadier-General J. S., 119
Negro in Congressional apportionment, 159
Negro Suffrage, 161, 172, 181, 182
Nevada, in election of 1880, 308
New Orleans, 252
New York, boss system in, 317

New York *Independent,* 243
New York *Sun,* 114, 128, 222, 309
New York *Times,* 150, 231, 334, 335
New York *Tribune,* 17, 18, 126, 151, 179, 180, 231, 283, 319, 324, 341
New York *Truth,* 307
New York *World,* 154
Niblack, W. E., 224, 234
Nicaragua route, 332
Nineteenth Congressional District, 90, 240, 243
Nixon, W. P., 289
North American Review, 181, 182

Office seekers, 339, 340
Ohio Canal, 14, 15
Ohio, political divisions, 54
Opdyke, Brigadier-General Emerson, 125
O'Reilly, Miles, song of, 293

Pan-Americanism, 333
Panama canal, 332
Paper money, 205
Parsons, Richard C., 237, 238, 241, 242
Party regularity, 245, 246
Paterson, N. J., 306
Payn, L. F., 323
Pease, Governor of Texas, 178
Peck, J. M., 336
Pendleton bill, 362
Pendleton, George H., 134
Peonage laws in the South, 159
Peru, war with Chile, 333
Phelps, W. W., 314
Phillips, F. W., 328
Phillips, Wendell, 181, 182
Philp, Hayward, 308, 309
Pierrepont, Edwards, 325, 326
Platt, Thomas Collier, 294, 302, 322-324, 326, 329, 342, 345, 347, 348, 363
Poland Committee, 224, 228, 231
Poland, Luke P., 224, 226, 228, 231
Polk's diary, compared with that of J. A. G., 357
Pomeroy circular, 150
Pope, Major-General John, 90, 101
Porter, Major-General Fitz-John, 98-105, 359
Porter, assistant prosecutor in Guiteau case, 351

Portland *Advertiser,* 232
Post-office Department, 334, 335
Potter, Clarkson N., 262, 263
Potter committee, 263, 308
Pound Gap, battle of, 81
Pound, T. L., 280, 281
Poverty of the frontier, 2
Prosperity and inflation, 210

Randall, Samuel J., 135, 233, 260, 307
Raymond, Henry J., 150, 172
"Readjuster" movement, in Virginia, 344
Reconstruction, 140, 157-182, 250
Refunding operations, 315, 332
Reid, Whitelaw, 78, 112, 166, 297, 301, 314, 319, 320, 323, 324, 329, 345, 346, 361
Republican convention of 1880, 278, 282, 286-292
Republican National Committee, 252, 301, 307, 336
Republican party, 150, 180, 223, 246, 252, 261, 262, 272
Republican platform, 1880, 325
Resumption of specie payments, 215
Returning Boards, 252, 256
Returning Board of Louisiana, 253, 254
Reyburn, Dr. Robert, 353n
Rhodes, James Ford, 239, 295
Rhodes, J. Harrison, 43, 53, 90, 97
Riddleberger, Henry, 344, 345
Riders on appropriation bills, 266, 267
Robertson, W. H., 319, 324, 325, 341-343, 346-348
Robison, J. P., 228
Rockefeller, John D., 304
Rockwell, A. F., 355
Roosevelt, Theodore, 358
Rose, G. U., 340
Rosecrans, Major-General W. S., 106-108, 111, 113, 115-130
Rossville, Tennessee, 120, 123, 124
Rousseau, Brigadier-General, 115, 116
Rudolph, Lucretia, see Garfield, Lucretia Rudolph

Safe districts, importance of, 136
Salaries of Congressmen, 234-236
"Salary Grab of 1873," 233

Schenck, Robert C., 132, 134, 143
Schofield Board, exonerates Fitz-John Porter, 103
Schofield, Major-General John M., 103
Schurz, Carl, 132, 210, 246, 262, 297, 321, 337
Science, relation to religion, 45; introduction into the colleges, 48
Scofield, J. F., 222
Scopes trial, 358
Scott, Winfield, 295
Scoville, George, 351
Secretary to the President, 340
Sectionalism, 9
Sellick, Rebecca, 37
Senatorial courtesy, 342, 343, 345, 346
Sheldon, L. A., 281
Shepherd, Alexander R., 236, 237
Sheridan, Brigadier-General P. H., 112, 174
Sherman, John, 64, 216, 218, 263, 273, 274, 278-282, 286-290, 301, 315, 321, 325, 326
Sherman, Major-General W. T., 82, 353
Siebold, ex parte, 272
Sigal, Brigadier-General Franz, 93
Smith, J. Q., 262
Smithsonian Institution, 187
Speed, James, 170
Springfield Republican, 38
"Stalwarts," 262, 272, 285, 294, 323, 324
Stanbery, Henry, 170
Stanley-Brown, Joseph, 340
Stanley, Major-General D. S., 88, 112, 115, 175
Stanton, Edwin M., 94, 96, 114, 126, 127, 131
Star Route frauds, 312, 334-339, 361
Starling, Colonel Lyne, 122
State Department, 313, 314
States' rights, 259
Stephens, Alexander H., 181, 204, 236
Stevens, Thaddeus, 133, 135, 163, 175, 208, 209, 211, 276, 360
Stockton, Senator John P., 165
Streight, Colonel A. D., 110, 281, 291
Streight expedition, 110
Sumner, Charles, 163, 204, 250

Surgery in 1881, 354
Swan, Chief Justice, 57

Tammany in 1880, 299
Tariff measures, 191-201
Tariff system, 306
Taussig, F. W., quoted, 194
Thayer, Eli, 96
Third term, opposition to, 284
Thirteenth amendment, 158
Thirty-eighth Congress, 132
Thomas, Major-General George H., 72, 73, 113, 120, 123, 125, 127, 128
Thurman, Allen G., 204, 270, 271, 273
Tilden, Samuel J., 251-253, 260, 264
Townsend, Amos, 304
Train, George Francis, 223
Treasury Department, 263, 286, 314, 320, 323, 325, 329, 332
"Treaty of Mentor," 305
Tullahoma campaign, 113, 114
Turchin, Colonel J. B., 87-89, 112
Twenty-second joint rule, 255
Tyler, Erastus B., 66
Tyler, T. W., 274
Typewriter, first used by J. A. G. in 1879, 269

Union Pacific Railroad, 219, 220, 224, 229
Utica Herald, 232

Veto power, 266-269, 273
Villard, Henry, 126
"Visiting Statesmen," 252
Volunteers in the Civil War, 67, 68
Voorhees, D. W., 134

Wade, Benjamin F., 138, 152, 153, 158, 195
Wade-Davis manifesto, 152
Walker, Robert J., 166
Wall Street, 212, 316
Wallace, Lew, 349
War debts, 1865 and 1918 compared, 207
Warren, Ohio, 305, 328
Washburne, C. C., 221, 229n
Washburne, Elihu, of Illinois, 286, 289
Washington, scandals in government of, 236-240

Watertown, Massachusetts, 4
Watterson, Henry, 260
Webster, Daniel, 163
Wells, David A., 191, 194, 196, 198, 210
West Feliciana, parish of, 254
Western Reserve of Ohio, 3, 4, 7, 9, 10, 356
Western Reserve Eclectic Institute, 11, 26, 27
West Point Men in Civil War, 67, 68, 82
Whittlesey, Elisha, 137
Widow Glenn's house, headquarters of Rosecrans, 120
Wilber, Charles D., 27
Williams College, 31, 32, 132, 185, 330, 359
"Williams Quarterly," 33

Wilson, Henry, 222
Wilson, J. F., 141
Windom, William, 286, 289, 325, 330, 331-333, 336, 338
Wisconsin delegation in Chicago, 290, 291
Wood, Fernando, 135, 200
Wood, Major-General T. J., 83, 112, 115, 122, 125
Woodward, Dr. J. J., 353
Wool Manufacturers Association, 192
Worcester, New York, 6, 7
"Wormley Conference," 260
Wormley's restaurant, 330

Youngstown, Ohio, 328

Zanesville, Ohio, 7